INDIAN POLITICAL THOUGHT

Readings and Reflections

INDIAN POLITICAL THOUGHT
Readings and Reflections

Prof. B.N. Ray
Ramjas College, Delhi University

Prof. R.K. Misra
Department of Political Science
Lucknow University

Kaveri Books
New Delhi - 110 002

Edition 2015
ISBN: 978-81-7479-127-6 (Library Edition)
ISBN: 978-81-7479-128-3 (Student Edition)

Published by
Kaveri Books
4832/24, Ansari Road
New Delhi - 110 002 (India)
Ph.: 011-2328 8140, 2324 5799
E-mail: info@kaveribooks.com
E-mail: kaveribooks@gmail.com
website: www.kaveribooks.com

Laser Typesetting by
Aarati Computers, Delhi - 110 009

PRINTED IN INDIA

Acknowledgement

Completion of this book would not have been possible without the generous support, encouragement and advice of our colleagues. The staff of the libraries of the Delhi University, Lucknow University and Teen Murti Library have been very helpful in the location of material. Many thanks also to Mr. Rakesh Goel of Kaveri Books for his encouragement and support of this project from its inception.

Grateful acknowledgement is made to publishers for permission to reproduce copyright material from books. Every effort has been made to contact all the copyright-holders, but if any have been inadvertently omitted, the authors will be pleased to make the necessary arrangement at the earliest opportunity.

Preface

The tradition of political thought in India is very long and rich. Since time immemorial, sages and seers have not only grappled with abstruse metaphysical issues, they have been equally concerned about the temporal matters. Elaborate treatises have been written on theoretical and organisational aspects of socio-political life, and a galaxy of thinkers like Manu, Sukra, Bhisma, Kautilya, Kamandaka have pondered over the intricate issues relating to the political order, This tradition of political thought continued right upto 18th century, and thinkers and scholars kept it alive either by way of writing independent treatise or by writing commentaries on the old classics. Among the outstanding political thinkers and commentators of the 17th and 18th centuries, the names of Laxmidhar, Mitra Misra, Neelkanth, Anant Dev, Shambhaji, Keshav Pandit are worthy of mention.

But political thought in India represents both continuity and discontinuity. The political thought of the 19th century is representative more of discontinuity as we find a long and living tradition suddenly growing thin and new and alien winds blowing the Indian firmament. Prof. Appadorai is quite perceptive when he says that "the political theory in India during the last one hundred years is a blend of Indian tradition, Indian experience under the British rule and Western (i.e. French, American and British) political experience and thought." The English classical liberalism sets the agenda for the mainstream political thought in India. Ram Mohan Roy, Ranade, R.C. Dutt, Gokhale - all proceed along rationalistic and secular lines and liberalism in all its splendour and forms - religious, political, social, economic - comes to dominate the scene. However, there is re-assertion of the ancient ideals as well. The thought and spirit, turn and tinge of Bankim's novels and poems are characteristically Indian. Tilak and Aurobindo give superb exposition of Indian theory of politics. Vivekananda is a leading example and most powerful exponent of 'preservation by reconstruction'. And Mahatma Gandhi, in his short but illuminating work *Hind Swaraj* makes a fervent appeal to countrymen not to be carried away by the ideas and institutions of modern western civilization which is but 'a nine-day wonder'.

If the 19the century was the century of overwhelming of India by the English liberal ideals, the 20th century found Indian thinkers negotiating strong winds of socialism. Thinkers like Narendra Dev, Ram Manohar Lohia, Jaya Prakash Narayan were busy fashioning an Indian brand of socialism. Besides, thinkers like Jyotiba Phule, B. R. Ambedkar, Ramaswamy Naicker raised issues regarding the Indian social system and vehemently attacked the Varna system. Thus, political thought in modern India exhibits an amazing range of ideas and ideologies, sometime old pushing back new and other times new overshadowing the old. The traditional ideals and modern ideologies are in continuous interaction.

However the richness of Indian political thought will elude us if we do not go to the original texts. The general trend in the Indian universities is to go by the secondary sources and the students are particularly tempted to this approach. This trend is not just unfortunate but scandalous. We can not understand a thinker unless we enter into direct communion with him. Secondary sources, no doubt, make our path easy, and mediators do make things negotiable, yet mediators are as much a source of illumination as confusion. While some authors are honest to their job, others are biased and uncritical while still others are downright superficial. In order to have a correct understanding of a thinker, secondary sources must never be allowed to substitute the study of original writings of thinkers and philosophers. Moreover, when one goes through the texts, one gets acquainted not only with the idea and the argument but the literary gifts and oral endowments of a thinker. Texts take us to the intellectual mansion of a philosopher, making visible and intelligible every nook and corner, and we come to understand how the various parts of the edifice are structured and related, and what they are intended to serve.

The present book is an exercise in that direction. It takes up some important texts of a thinker and provides a backdrop to his thinking. The purpose is to encourage the readers not to be just fence-sitters and spectators but participants in the discourse. It is hoped that this exercise will help promote the pursuit of wisdom and knowledge which has been dislodged by the craving for information. We are of the firm view that the triumph of the banal in the field of political science is a fallout of neglect of the study of texts and treatises in the original. The present book is a humble effort to check the trend and restore the dignity and prestige of the master science.

Prof. B.N. Ray
Prof. R.K. Misra

Contents

1

Manu

Life and Times

Sanatan Dharma takes a comprehensive view of man's telos, and therefore dwells upon the physical and metaphysical, material and spiritual aspects of our life. The Vedas based on the timeless wisdom are the source of knowledge guiding man in temporal as well as transcendental realms. In Vedas are contained the first principles of all the sciences (Vidyas) that are instrumental to human good. In Indian tradition, these sciences are divided into four Logic or 'Anvikhaki', 'Trayi' or Three Vedas, 'Varta' or science of economic prosperity and *Dandaniti* or the science of politics. Logic is the science which trains and disciplines the mental capacities and inculcates right attitude towards man and things, the three Vedas train the character by laying down duties to various orders of existence, economics expounds the principle of sound economic organisation, and science of politics deals with right ordering of the state. All the four sciences are inter-related as the natural and supernatural ends of man are attainable only with the proper harmonization of the four. However it has also been declared that without *Dandaniti* all the three sciences or Vidyas are lost. Now, what this maxim emphasizes is that only in a well-governed state mundane and supra-mundane pursuits are possible. In this context, the science of politics is regarded as the supreme science.

Besides *Dandaniti* many other terms have been used for science of politics i.e. Arthashastra, RajVidhya, Nitishastra etc. The pre-eminent position enjoyed by the science of politics in ancient Indian thought is evident from the fact that independent and exhaustive treatises have been written on it since time immemorial. Like all other sciences or vidyas, the science of politics is considered to have had divine origin. According to *Mahabharata*, Lord Brahma, in order to ensure human welfare and happiness, composed a vast treatise of one lakh verses dealing with the four ends of man's existence- Dharma, Artha, Kama and Moksha. Lord Shiva whose other name is Vishalaksh abridged it into ten thousand chapters and after his name the treatise is khown as 'Vaishalaksh', later on Indra, Vrihaspati and Shukra further abridged it in five, three and one thousand chapters respectively. Thus science of politics is co-eval with creation, a gift of God to conduct the affairs of men righteously and smoothly. Manu carries forward this tradition through his treatise.

In tradition, Manu is regarded as the son or *Manasputra* of Lord Brahma, and his preaching to seven sages or rishis is contained in the *Manusmriti*. It occupies a high position among ancient Indian texts and is praised for its superior wisdom, its completeness, orderly arrangement and intelligibility. Theauthority and respect bestowed on Manusmriti by scriptures is evident from such comments as 'whatever Manu said is curative' or 'a smriti opposed to Manu is not approved'. Vrihaspati says that Manu holds the first rank among legislators because he had expressed in his code the whole sense of Veda, that no code is approved which contradicts Manu, that other shastras retain splendor so long as Manu is not seen in competition with them. Sage Vyasa ranks Manusmriti among the four books of supreme authority which ought never to be shaken by arguments, merely human. In modern time, among other scholars and thinkers, Neitzsche has spoken about it in an eloquent manner-'The law-book of Manu is an incomparably greater intellectual work than the Bible'. Sir William Jones who translated *Manusmriti* into English had great praise for it -'A spirit of sublime devotion of benevolence to mankind, and amiable tenderness to all sentient creatures pervades the whole work, the style of it has a certain austere majesty that sounds like the language of legislation and extorts a respectful awe and admonitions even to kings are truly noble.'

Manusmriti divided in 12 chapters is a comprehensive work, covering all aspects and dimensions of human life and elaborating the ideals to be followed by the various sections of society and by king himself. The book is an exposition of the temporal in the light of transcendental. Beginning with an account of genesis of the universe, it goes on to deal with ideal social order the system of Varnas and Ashramas, position and duties of woman, duties of king, civil and criminal law, penance and expiation, and attainment of final liberation or Moksha. Its philosophical depths attracted a number of scholars to write exhaustive commentaries, and chief among them are Medhatithi, Kullukbhatt, Govindraj, Madhav-Sayan and Narayan.

Brahma, the causeless cause of the universe, the self-existent Lord becomes manifest and produces from his body innumerable worlds and within them countless forms of animate and inanimate life. The universe is governed by a cosmic law or Rta which is the source of order and evolution. The human society is a reflection and replica of the Brahma in which various individuals, groups and communities are held together by the principle of Dharma. Dharma is the bedrock of personal and social life, the source of order and fulfillment and its transgression imperils the very existence of society. According to Manu, state is a community of communities, comprising four Varnas -Brahmin, Kshatriya, Vaishya and Shudra which constitute the pillars of the commonwealth, and four Ashramas - Brahmacharya, Grihastha, Vanprastha, Sanyas which form the four stages in the life of the individuals. Since the two institutions are germaine to social stability, the king's foremost duty is to ensure that members of body politic perform duties enjoined by their Varna and Ashrama.

As fundamental principles of politics are divine in origin, there is a marked unanimity regarding them in so far the ancient Indian political thought is concerned. Manu subscribes to the view that state is divine in origin, which in other words means that state is natural and necessary and it is inconceivable to think of man in a condition of statelessness. He, like other exponents of Rajvidya holds that there are seven organs (Saptang) of state and they are- King (Swami), Council of Ministers (Amatya) Nation (Rastra), Capital (Durg), Treasury (Kosa), Armed Forces (Bala) and friends and allies (Mitra). We can not think of state if any one of these organs is absent. In a sense all organs are crucial to statehood, yet they have a descending significance if looked at comparatively. The king occupies the foremost position in the body politic because if the kingship is taken away, all the rest can not subsist. It makes no sense to talk of a headless body. Thus preceding organ of state is more important than the following. All the organs of state are important, yet all are not equal in importance.

Manu says that king was created out of eight divine particles – Indra, Agni, Vayu, Yam, Surya, Chandra, Varun and Kuber. Just as these divine forces sustain the universe, so the king should exercise his various powers and channelize his various forces to sustain the state. The king is to uphold Dharma by protecting the good and penalizing the wicked. He has been bestowed with rod of authority (Danda) to keep his kingdom in peace and order. But Manu says that it is only a virtuous king who can wield the Danda truly and effectively. But the onerous and complex task of governing the state can not be performed by the king single-handedly and therefore Manu speaks about a council of ministers to aid and advice the king. He says that a large body of ministers frustrate the very purpose of deliberation, and he therefore advocates a small council of ministers who are wise, virtuous, experienced and trustworthy. He also dwells upon geo-politics because climate, natural resources, quality of soil etc critically affect the strength of the state. A state, in order to be great should be nature's favourite, though moral endowments of the citizens are no less important. Manusmriti is also important from the viewpoint of political economy. We find an elaborate exposition of the principles of fiscal policy, items and rates of taxation and extraordinary measures to cope with natural calamities. The king's right of taxation is limited in the most important sources of revenue to a fixed percentage as a maximum and in other directions often by the right of various bodies representing community to a voice in the matter. Matters pertaining to military organization and war are also discussed in the *Manusmriti*, and while going through the laws of war propounded in it, one is struck by Manu's great emphasis on observing highest ethical standards while waging war. Manu has very significant things to say with regard to major aspects of foreign policy and diplomacy and in external relations, he considers the role of ambassadors and spies as very crucial in the formulation of sound policy.

Manu's social and political thought has drawn widespread criticism from the marxists, the feminists, the liberals and other modern ideologies. In India, B.R. Ambedkar and other Dalit thinkers have been highly critical of the social order enunciated by Manu. There is no doubt that ideas and ideals of the *Manusmriti* do not fit in with modern secular-democratic worldview. It is rather a clash of principles, and the chasm between the two is almost unbridgeable. The social and political theory of *Manusmriti*, rooted as it is in supremacy of transcendental principles, will naturally shock a modern reader who is a believer in scientific rationalism.

In the extract from chapter VII of the *Manusmriti*, we find an exposition of King's duties as well as the intellectual and moral requirements of king so that he is able to discharge them. The main function of king is to serve and assist the maintenance of the sound law of life of the society, king being the upholder of Dharma which in turn sustains and upholds the cosmos. Society aims at the right satisfaction of the vital, economic and other needs of human being but according to their right law and subject and subordinated to the ethical principles. All the members and groups of state have their Dharma determined for them by their nature and by their relation to the whole society and must be assured free and proper exercise of it, but king has to restrain transgressions, deviations and encroachments from their right working and true limits. To ensure that society remains normal and good by observance of Dharma is a sacred duty of king, and for this purpose the king has to be constantly vigilant.

This sacred obligation can be discharged only by a king who is self-controlled. Manu lays great emphasis on 'the divinity of king' i.e., he should be endowed with divine qualities, intellectual and moral virtues so that he may wield the rod of authority without fear or favour. He should well versed in Shastras so that his reason is purified, and ignoble desires and passions do not overshadow his judgment. He should be sufficiently strong so that external or internal enemies do not disturb the peace of land. In order to keep the king on the right track, Manu also expounds the daily routine of king. The whole emphasis of *Manusmriti* is, as Prof. Kewal Motwani has said, on 'the divinity of king, and not on the divine rights of king'. The Indian tradition of political thought does not recognize any theory of divine rights of king as expounded in modern times by some British and French monarchs and many political philosophers. A king who deflects from the path of duty gets destroyed. To quote Manu, "A king properly wielding the rod prospers in all three-virtue, pleasure and wealth, but a sensual, unfair and base king verily perishes by it."

That the king is subject to sovereignty of Dharma is evident from many other provisions. King is not the source of Law but is limited to the issue of administrative decrees. His right of taxation is limited, Though the king is in person supreme court, but here too his role is one of executor. He is to administer the law faithfully as interpreted and explained by legists learned in these matters. Thus the Indian theory of kingship is one of limited or constitutional monarchy and as Sri Aurobindo has pointed out, the monarchy in India had no resemblance to ancient Persian monarchy or to monarchies of Western and Central Asia or the Roman imperial government or later European autocracies.

Kingship

I shall declare the laws for kings, how a sovereign should be occupied, and what his origin is, and how his supreme perfection is effected. Protection of all this (his realm) according to justice is to be done by a Kshatriya who has duly received the Vedic initiation. For, this world being without a king, it trembles everywhere from fear; the Lord, then, created a king for the protection of all this (world). Having taken eternal elements from

Indra, Wind, Yama, the Sun, from Fire and Varuna, the Moon and Kuber. Because a king is formed from parts of these chiefs of the gods, therefore he excels in glory all beings. And he burns, like the Sun, the eyes and minds, nor can any one on earth even behold him. He is Fire and Wind; he (is) the Sun, the Moon, the King of Justice; he (is) Kuber, he Varuna, he great Indra in grandeur. Though a child, a king is not to be despised as a human being, for he is a powerful divinity in man's form.

Fire burns only the individual who approaches it carelessly; the fire of the king burns the race, with their cattle and accumulation of wealth. He having truly considered the matter, his power, and the place and time, again and again takes, in order to the perfection of justice, all forms. In whose favour best good fortune abides, in whose heroism victory, in whose wrath death, he indeed consists of all glory. But he who hates him out of folly perishes certainly; for the king quickly turns his mind to his destruction. Therefore let the king never alter the rule, either the law he arranges for those he loves, or the punishment, for those he dislikes. On his account *Isvara* formerly created Punishment, his son, as the protector of all beings, consisting of the glory of Brahma, criminal law. From fear of him, all beings, immovable and movable, are fit for enjoyment, and wander not from their law. Having truly considered him (Punishment), as well as place and time, and his power and knowledge, the king should suitably punish evil-doing men. He, Punishment, (is) a royal person, he (is) a guide and ruler; he is said to be the surety for the law of the four orders. Punishment rules all men; punishment alone protects them; punishment is watchful while they sleep; the wise know punishment to be justice. Inflicted properly after consideration, punishment delights all people; but, inflicted without consideration, it altogether destroys them. If the king did not untiringly inflict punishment on those to be punished, the stronger would roast the weak like fish on a spit. The crow would eat the sacrificial cake, and the dog would likewise lick the offering; there would be no lordship in any one; all would be upside down. The whole world is mastered by punishment; a pure man is hard to find : from fear of punishment, indeed, all the world is fit for enjoyment.

Gods, devils, gandharvas, evil demons, birds, and snakes-even they, ruled by punishment, become fit for enjoyment. All castes would b e perverted, all landmarks would be broken down, there would be mutiny in all the world from perversion of punishment. Where dark, red-eyed Punishment, destroying sin, advances, there the people are not confounded, if the leader discerns well. The wise declare a truth-speaking king, one who acts after consideration, discerning, wise in virtue, pleasure, and wealth, to be the (proper) inflictor of this punishment. A king properly inflicting it (punishment) prospers in all three-virtue, pleasure, and wealth; but a sensual, unfair, and base king verily perishes by punishment. For punishment, very glorious, and hard to be borne by the undisciplined, destroys a king, together with his kin, when he has indeed departed from justice. Also it destroys his castle, and kingdom, and land, with immovable and movable things, and vexes the Munis gone to heaven, and the gods also. It punishment cannot justly be inflicted by a king who is without a helper, who is foolish, covetous, undisciplined, and devoted to sensual objects. By a king who is pure, truthful, who exactly follows the treatises, who has good helpers and is prudent, may punishment be inflicted. He should act justly in his own kingdom and be very severe to enemies, straightforward to loving friends, patient to Brahmans. The fame of a king who does so, though he live by gleaning, is spread in the world like a drop of oil on water. But the fame of a king the opposite of this in conduct, of unconquered self, is congealed in the world like a drop of ghee in water. The king is created the protector of the castes and orders, each being devoted to its own duty in order.

What is to be done by him with his ministers to protect the people, that I shall declare to you duly in order. The king, having arisen early, should reerence Brahmans learned in the Vedas and wise, and he should stand firm by their decision; and he must ever honour old Brahmans who know the Veda and are pure; for one who honours the old is worshipped even by evil demons. From them he should always learn good conduct, though disciplined; for a well-behaved king never perishes. Many kings with their attendants have perished from want of good conduct; and even dwellers in the forest have gained kingdoms by discipline. Vena was ruined by bad conduct, and also the king Nahusa, and Sudas Paijavana, also Sumukha and Nimi.

But Prthu by good conduct got a kingdom, and Manu and Kuvera got lordship over wealth, and Gadhi's son got even Brahmanhood. He should learn the threefold knowledge of the Vedas from those who possess the knowledge of the three Vedas, and the eternal art of policy, logic, and knowledge of self; but business from the people. Let him day and night apply himself to the conquest of his organs; for one whose organs are conquered is able to bring the people under control. Let him avoid with effort ten vices which arise from lust, and eight which arise from anger; these end ill. For a king devoted to vices which spring from lust is deprived of his wealth and virtue; but if addicted to those which arise form anger, of his self. Sport, dice, sleeping by day, gossip, women, liquor, song, dance, and music, and vain wandering about, are the tenfold class of vices arising from lust.

Malice, violence, injury, envy, calumny, mischief to property, abuse and assault are the eightfold class of vices arising form anger. But covetousness, which all bards have recognized as the root of both those, he should overcome with effort; for both those classes of vices spring from it. Drink, dice, women also, and hunting, let him know to be, in order, the worst four in the class arising from lust. Let him know infliction of violence, also abuse, and mischief to property to be the worst three in the class arising from anger. Of this class of seven everywhere prevailing, a self-possessed king should know the prior sin to be the worse. Of vice and death, vice is said to be the worst; a vicious man, when dead, sinks down and a virtuous man goes to heaven.

The king should appoint seven or eight carefully examined ministers, who are hereditary, learned in the treatises, brave, skilled in the use of weapons, and well-descended. Even an easy deed is difficult to be effected by one only, especially by one without a helper; still more a very prosperous kingdom is hard to rule. With them he should ever deliberate ordinary matters of peace and war, the condition of the kingdom, wealth, protection, and the pacification of acquired territory. Having separately got from each of them his opinion, and then from them all, let him arrange distinguished from all. But let the king think over most important designs referring to the six matters with a learned Brahman distinguished from all. Always trusting him, the king should devolve on him all matters; having determined them with him, he should then begin the affair. He should also appoint other ministers, pure, discerning, firm, gatherers of wealth properly, well-tried.

As many men as by whom the business to be done for him may be effected, so many, unwearied, clever, discerning, let him appoint. Of them he should appoint over his gains the brave, clever, and well-descended; the pure, over mines; the fearful, in the interior of the palace. He should also appoint an ambassador learned in all the treatises, who understands gestures, expression, and acts, pure, clever, well-descended. The ambassador of a king is praised who is liked, pure, clever, with a good memory, who knows place and time, personable, fearless, eloquent. The army is dependent on the minister; disciplinary administration on the army; the treasury and kingdom on the prince; peace and the opposite on the ambassador.

For, verily, the ambassador alone unites, and divides also the united; the ambassador conducts that business by which they are divided or not. In affairs he the ambassador should know by his obscure signs and acts the emotions, intentions, and efforts of him the other king, and should learn what he intends to do from his dependents. And having known truly from the ambassador all that is intended by the other king, the king should so make effort that he does not vex himself. He should inhabit a country with waste ground, supplied with grain, inhabit by Aryas chiefly, not marshy, delightful, with subdued neighbouring kings, yielding a living. Let him dwell in a town fortified by a desert, or by earth, or by water, or even by trees, by armed men, or by mountains. But let him with all efforts occupy a hill-fort; for a hill-fort by its many good qualities is the best of them. The first three of them, beasts, rats, and water animals occupy; the last three, monkeys, men, and immortals, in order.

As enemies hurt them not when they have occupied their forts, so enemies hurt not a king in his fort. One archer on the wall fights a hundred below; a hundred, ten thousand; therefore a fort is directed. That fort should be furnished with weapons, with wealth, grain, and animals to ride, with Brahmans, artisans, machines, fodder, and water. In the middle of it he should have a well-built house made for himself, protected, suitable for all seasons, beautiful, with water and trees. Having occupied it, he should marry a wife of the same caste, with good marks, born of a great family, dear, endowed with beauty and good qualities. And he should appoint a domestic priest, and chose a sacrificial priest; these should perform the domestic and sacrificial rites for him.

The king should offer by various sacrifices with proper gifts to the priests, and should also give, for virtue sake, to Brahmans both means of enjoyment and wealth. He should casue to be collected by fit persons the yearly tribute from the kingdom, and should be thoroughly conversant with the holy texts in the world; he should behave to men as a father. He should appoint several clever superintendents in different places; they should inspect all the acts of the men doing his work. He should reverence Brahmans returned from their Guru's family, for that is laid down as the undecaying Brahmanic treasure of kings. Neither thieves nor enemies take it, and it perishes not'; therefore this undecaying treasure is to be deposited by a king with Brahmans. What is offered in a Brahman's mouth is better than *agnihotras;* it never is spilled, nor dries up, nor perishes.

A gift to a non-Brahman produces equal fruit; to one who calls himself a Brahman, twofold; to a learned Brahman, a hundrd thousand-(fold); to a student of the Vedas, endless recompense. For the fruit, small or great, of a gift to one specially fiot and given with faith also, is obtained after death. A king challenged by (kings of) equal, greater, or less power, giving protection to his people and remembering his duty as a Kshatriya, may not cease from battle. Never ceasing from battle, protection also of the people, and obedience to Brahmans are the chief cause of bliss to kings. Kings who, desirous to slay one another, fight with their greatest strength in battles and without turning away, go tho heaven. One should not, fighting in battle, slay enemies by concealed weapons, nor with barbed or poisoned weapons, nor with fire-kindled arrows.

Nor should one mounted slay and enemy down on the ground, a eunuch, a suppliant, one with loosened hair, one seated, one who says "I am thy prisoner. Nor one asleep, one without armour, one naked, one without weapons, one not fighting, a looker-on, one engaged with another. Nor one who has his arms broken, a distressed man, one badly hit, one afraid, one who has fled; remembering virtue, one should not slay them. But he who in fear flying is killed by others, whatever ill has been done by (his) chief, he acquires all that; and whatever good the slain coward has acquired for the future life, the chief takes all that from him. He who captures car and horses, elephants, umbrella, wealth, grain, women, property, and base metals, of him is that. 'But they must give a special portion of the booty to the king;' such is the Vedic revelation; and that which is not separately captured is to be given by the king to all the soldiers.

This real and eternal law for soldiers has been declared; from this law a Kshatriya slaying enemies in battle should not fall away. He should also desire to gain what (he has) not gained, and should with effort guard what is gained; he should also increase what is preserved, and bestow on the worthy what is increased. He should know this fourfold rule to be useful for human objects, (and), unwearied, should ever properly effect its accomplishment. He should desire to get by force what he has not got; he should guard with care what he has got; what is guarded, he should increase by interest; what is increased, he should bestow in gifts.

He should ever have his sceptre erect, his manliness evident; what is to be concealed, concealed; he should ever be seeking out his enemy's weak points. The whole world trembles at a king with ever-erect sceptre; therefore let him subdue all beings by his very sceptre. He should indeed act guilelessly, never by gule; but he, self-guarded, should be aware of the frauds used by his enemy. Let not another know his weak point, but let him know the other's weak point; like a tortoise, he should protect his members, and guard his own defect. Like a crane, he should meditate gain; like a lion, he should advance; like a jackal, he should rush on; like a hare, he should fly. These who are the opponents of him thus victorious, he should bring under his power by conciliation and the like expedients. But if they do not stand firm by the three first means, he must surely bring them into subjection by gradual force, having conquered them.

Of the four expedients, conciliation and the like, the learned ever praise conciliation and force for the increase of a kingdom. As a cultivator pulls up the grass and protects the grain, so a prince should protect his kingdom and should slay (his) opponents. If the king, through folly, harasses by carelessness his own kingdom, he, with his kin, soon loses his kingdom and life. As the lives of living beings perish from harassing the body, so the lives even of kings perish from harassing the kingdom. Let him ever follow this system for the protection of his kingdom; for a king whose kingdom is well protected gains happiness. As a protection of the kingdom, let him station in the middle of two, three, five, or a hundred towns and army division properly commanded.

Let him appoint a chief of a town, as well as a chief of ten towns, a lord of twenty, a lord of a hundred, and also a chief of a thousand. Let the head of a town frequently of his own accord acquaint the lord of ten town with the evils arisen in the town; let the lord of ten towns acquaint the lord of twenty. But the lord of twenty should give notice of all that to the lord of a hundred, and the lord of a hundred should, of his own accord, acquaint the chief of a thousand. What food, drink, and fuel are to be daily given by the inhabitants of a town to the king, let the head of the town take. Now a lord over ten (towns) should enjoy two ploughs' land; and a lord over twenty towns ten ploughs' land; the superintendent of a hundred towns, a town; the lord of a thousand, a city. As for the affairs of those (towns), and also those to be done separately, let another faithful minister of the king, unwearied, see to them.

And he should make in every city an overseer of all matters, exalted in position, terrible in appearance, like a planet among the stars. He should of himself ever visit all those chiefs, and discover duly their behavior in their provinces by his spies. For those servants appointed by the king for protection (are) mostly takers of the property of others (and) cheats; from them he should protect these people. Those sinful-minded servants who take property from suitors, the king, having taken all their property, should banish. He should arrange daily a maintenance for women employed in the king's affairs, and for his messengers, according to their position and work. A *pana* is to be given as salary of the lowest, six to the highest, with clothes every six months, and a *drone* of grain every month.

The king should make the traders pay taxes, after having considered the purchase and sale of their goods, the journey they have made, the food and condiments they use, and the means for security they employ. Having considered (the matter), let the king ever arrange the taxes in (his) kingdom, so that the king and the business-men may get profit. As the leech, calf, and insect eat little by little their food, so yearly taxes are to be taken little by little from the kingdom by the king. A fiftieth pat of cattle and gold is to be taken by the king; the eighth part of grain, or the sixth or twelfth. He may also take a sixth part of trees, meat, honey, (and) ghee; also of perfumes, medicines, and liquids, and of flowers, roots, and fruits. He may also take a sixth part of trees, meat, honey, and ghee; also of perfumes, medicines, and liquids, and of flowers, roots, and fruits.

And of leaves, herbs, and grass, of hides, and of rattan work; of earthen pots, and of all stoneware. Though dying from hunger, a king may not take taxes from a learned priest; and a learned priest living in (his) jurisdiction must not perish from hunger. Now if in any king's territory a learned priest perishes with hunger, his kingdom will soon perish with hunger. Knowing his learning and behavior, let him arrange for him a proper maintenance; and protect him wholly, as a father his own son. Protected by the king, the religious duty which he does daily increases the life of the king, his wealth, and the kingdom also. Let the king cause the low people in (his) kingdom who live by trade to pay something called tax every year.

Let the king cause skilled workmen and artisans also, and Shudras living by their own labour, to work for him a single day in each month. Let him not cut off his root and (the root of) others through much covetousness; for cutting off his root, he would torment himself and them. The king, considering the matter, should be severe and mild also by turns; a king both severe and mild is approved. When wearied of regarding the affairs of men, let him put in that place the chief of the ministers, knowing law, discerning, subdued, born of a good family. Having thus disposed of all this to be done by himself, devoted, and also not careless, he should protect the people. That king is dead and lives not, from whose kingdom the people crying out are carried off by savages, while he with (his) ministers look on. The chief duty of a Kshatriya is simply the protection of the people, for a king who receives the recompense mentioned is bound by law.

Having risen in the last watch of the night, purified (and) composed, having sacrificed by fire, and having reverenced the Brahmans, let him enter his splendid assembly-room. Standing there, after he has pleased all the people, he may dismiss them. Having dismissed all the people, he should consult with his ministers. Having gone up a mountain-back, or gone privately to the roof-terrace, or in a solitary wood, let him consult unperceived. Whose deliberations the low people, having come together, do not know-that prince, though deprived of treasure, enjoys the whole earth. At deliberation time he should expel the foolish, dumb, blind, and deaf; birds; the aged; women; the impure, diseased, and deformed.

The despised disclose counsel, so also do birds, and especially women; therefore among these let him be careful. At noon or midnight let him, having reposed and overcome his weariness, think on duty, pleasure, and wealth, with those ministers, or all alone; and on the attainment of these things when mutually opposed, and on the giving of his daughters (in marriage), and on the protection of his sons. Also on ambassadors (and) messengers, and the result of his acts also; on the behavior of the harem, and the doings of his spies. On all the eightfold acts of a kind, and on the fivefold class (of spies) exactly; on affection and disaffection also, and on the behavior of neighbouring states. Let him stenuously watch the behaviour of a king of middle position, and the attempts of an aggressive power desireous to conquer, the conduct of one who is neutral, and of his enemy. Those elements are the root, in short, of the surrounding country; and eight others are reckoned: those twelve are said to be the concern of a king.

And there are five other elements, (viz.) ministers, kingdoms, forts, wealth, forces; these, told separately, (amount), in brief, to seventy-two. A king should know the next king to him to be an enemy, as also the adherents of that enemy; the one next to the enemy (to be) a friend; the one beyond both to be neutral. All those he should gain by conciliation and the like means, separate or together; also by valour and policy. He should ever think of the six tactics of a king, alliance, war, marching, encampments, stratagems, and recourse to protection. Having considered what is to be done, he should employ encampment, marching, alliance, war, stratagems, and recourse to protection.

But a king should know that alliances are of two kinds, as is also war; both marching and encampment also, and stratagem; and recourse to protection is also said to be of two kinds. Alliance, connected with present or future gain, is to be known as of two kinds : (first) when one acts in conjunction, and second the opposite also. War is said to be of two kinds: first when made of one's own accord, in season or out of season, on account of one's object, and (second) also (when made) on occasion of injury to a friend. Expeditions are said to be of two kinds; first when the king marches alone, some affair admitting of no delay having unexpectedly arisen; and second when he is accompanied by an ally. Encamping is said to be of two kinds; first when the king is by degrees weakened by chance or by former deeds, and second to help an ally. Stratagem is declared to be of two kinds by those who know the sixfold characteristics of tactics: the placing first of the army, and second of the king to gain his ends.

Recourse is said to be of two kinds: first when a king is oppressed by enemies and takes refuge to save his wealth, and second when he is among friends and takes refuge in order to forestall danger. Whenever a king infers a sure increase of power of himself in future, and at the present time suffers little annoyance, then let him have recourse to an alliance. Whenever he thinks all the elements of the state very exalted, likewise himself very mighty, then let him make war. Whenever he thinks his own force pleased in disposition and prosperous, and that of the enemy the opposite, then let him march against the enemy. But whenever he is feeble in carriage and force, then he should encamp strenuously, conciliating the enemy by degrees.

Whenever a king considers the enemy in every respect more powerful than himself, then, having divided his army, let him accomplish his own objects. But whenever he is most accessible to the enemy's forces, let him then quickly resort to a virtuous and powerful prince. Let him ever, with all his might, have recourse as to a Guru, to him who can effect control of disobedient elements in his state and of the enemy's forces. If even then he perceive injury caused by his taking refuge, he should, even in that position, fearlessly fight a good battle alone. A prince skilled in polity should by all means so arrange that friends, neutrals, and enemies may not be his superiors. Let him truly consider the future and present of all matters, and the good and bad sides of all past deeds. He who knows the good and bad to come, who quickly decides as to be present, and who knows the result of past actions, is never overpowered by enemies.

Let him so manage all that neither friends, neutrals, (nor) foes may prevail over him; that is polity in brief. When a chief begins an expedition against the kingdom of his enemy, he should then march gradually against the enemy's city in this system. Let a king go on an expedition on the clear month Margacirsha, or about the time of the two months Phalguna and Caitra, according to his forces. Or even at other times, when he sees certain victory, let him set out against the enemy, waging war, or when also his enemy is in trouble. Having made arrangement at home, and for the expedition in due form, having collected supplies also, and having properly placed his spies. Having prepared the threefold way and sixfold forces, let him gradually advance by military rule to the enemy's city.

Let him be more than ordinary watchful, both of an ally who secretly favours the enemy, and also of a man who has returned to him after going away to the enemy, for such an one is an enemy more than ordinary dangerous. He should march upon the road with the troops distributed like a staff, or a wagon, or a boar, or a

Makara, or a needle, or a Garuda. And from whence he may suspect danger, to that point let him expand his forces; and let him ever himself be in the centre of a body distributed like a lotus. Let him place his general and commanders in all parts, and whence he fears danger there let him arrange his force to the front. And let him on all sides place fit bodies of men, distinguished by uniform, clever in standing firm and in fighting, brave, unchanging. Let him make a few fight in serried rank; at his will he may spread about many. And thus having arranged them in the needle, or also the thunderbolt form, let him cause them to fight.

He should fight with chariots and horses on level (ground), so with boats and elephants on marshes; on ground covered by trees (and) shrubs, with bows; on cleared ground, with weapons, swords and shields. Let him cause Kuruksetras, Matsyas, Pancalas, and natives of Curasena, and tall and light men also, to fight in the van. Having arranged his forces, let him cheer them up, and let him properly try them; and he should find out their deeds when they are fighting the enemy. Having obstructed the enemy, let him encamp and harass his kingdom, and ever spoil his fodder, food, water, and fuel. Let him also burst tanks, enclosures, as well as trenches; let him assail him, and also terrify him by night.

Let him bring over those that can be seduced, and let him be aware of what is done by the enemy, and let him fight, desirous of victory, and without fear, when a fortunate time occurs. He should endeavour to overcome his enemy by alliances, bribery, and treachery-all together or separate-never by battle. For since victory or defeat in battle is seen to be not permanent between two forces fighting, therefore he should avoid a battle. But in case the three expedients already mentioned do not suit, let (him), prepared, fight, so that he may conquer his enemies. Having conquered, let him worship the gods and righteous Brahmans also; let him grant immunities, and proclaim indemnities. But having completely known the intention of all of them, let (him) station there as ruler one of that race, and give precise directions.

And let him make authoritative their laws as declared, and let him honour him the new king with jewels, together with the chief persons in the country. The taking of desired things produces disaffection, but liberality is productive of loyalty; either is proper if used in season. All this action depends on divine or human design; but of the two, the divine is unthinkable; in human affairs, action is known. Or he may act with the conquered, having carefully made an alliance with him, and considering an ally, gold, territory, as the triple fruit of a victory. And, considering his heel-catcher, as well as the attacker of that heel-catcher in the adjacent region, let him reap the fruit of the expedition from friend and from foe.

A (conquering) sovereign prospers not so much by gain of gold and territory as by gaining a firm ally, though now insignificant, yet capable in the future. An insignificant ally, who knows duty and is grateful and contented, devoted and firm in his endeavours, is preferred. The wise declare an enemy who is discerning, of (high) race, brave, clever, liberal also, grateful and firm, to be a difficulty. Nobility, knowledge of men, heroism, mercifulness, and constant magnanimity are the fruit of virtues of a neutral. A king should, to save himself, unhesitating, abandon even a prosperous land, furnishing grain, and plentiful in cattle. Let him preserve wealth against misfortune; let him preserve his wife even by wealth; let him ever save himself, even at the cost of wife (and) wealth. Let a wise king, seeing all calamities arisen together in excess, apply, together or separate, all means. The doer, what is to be done, and the means, as a whole-keeping in mind those three, let him strive for the accomplishment of the business.

Let the king, after he has thus considered all this business together with the ministers, taken exercise and bathed, enter at noon the harem to eat. There let him eat food well tested by faithful attendants, who are skilled in times and not to be seduced, which has been enchanted by *mantras* which counteract poison. Let (him) use all his (useful) articles with drugs destructive of poison; and let him, ever attentive, wear gems destructive of poison. Let attentive women, who have been tested, and pure in dress and ornaments, attend him with fans, water and perfumes. Thus let him take care of vehicles, couches, seats, food; of baths, anointing also, and all ornaments.

Having eaten, he should also sport with women in the harem; having sported, he should, according to the time, again think of business. Dressed, he should again inspect the armed forces, and all vehicles, weapons, ornaments. Having performed the evening devotion, bearing arms, let him hear in the inner apartment what has been done by the reporters of secrets and also the spies. Having dismissed these people, having gone to another private apartment, surrounded by women, let him again enter the harem for food. Having there again eaten something, cheered by instrumental music, let him go to sleep in due time, and rise with fatigue gone. A healthy king should pursue this system; unwell, he may depute all that to his dependents.

(From *The Ordinances of Manu,* translated by AC Burnell, Orient Books Reprint Corporation, New Delhi, 1971, pp 148-177)

2

Kautilya

Life and Times

Kautilya, also known as Chankaya and Vishnugupta, wrote the *Arthashastra* not later than 150AD though the date has not been conclusively established. A master strategist who was well-versed in the Vedas and adept at creating intrigues and devising political stratagems, Kautilya's genius is reflected in his *Arthashastra* which is the most comprehensive treatise of statecraft of classical times.

Kautilya had a long mythology woven around him, particularly in literary productions. At one level he became the personification of the etymology of his name kutila. But he also became a kind of great legislator, the savior of India from internal dissension and external attack. While his teaching came to signify ruthlessness in a political cause, the opposite cautionary massage could also be drawn. The *Arthashastra* had the misforture to be known more than read, to be quoted more than understood. The publication of the Shamashastry edition in 1909 had energized not just the history of political thought, but the study of history as well. In retrospect, the output occasioned by the text is staggering in its scope and intensity.

The text contains fifteen books which in *Arthashastra* is an extraordinary detailed manual on statecraft and the science of living by one of classical India's greatest minds. It covers numerous topics viz., the king; a complete code of law; foreign policy; secret and occult practices and so on. The *Arthashastra* is written mainly in prose but also incorporates 380 shlokas.

Artha, literally wealth, is one of four supreme aims - artha, kama, dharma and moksha-prescribed by Hindu tradition. However, it has a much wider significance and the material well-being of indiviausl is just a part of it. In accordance with this, Kautilya's *Arthashastra* maintains that the state or government of a country has a vital role to play in maintaining the material status of both the nation and its people. Therefore, a significant part of the *Arthashastra* has to do with the science of economics. When it deals with the science of politics, the *Arthashastra* describes in details the art of government in its widest sense—the maintenance of law and order as also of an efficient administrative machinery.

The Arthashastra concedes man's desire for wealth and man's corruptible nature. These cannot be eliminated. But ideal managers will minimize corruption. Kautilya enumerates the various qualities a good manager should have and the type of character he should strive and develop—friendliness, ability to deal with others, professional and communication skills, ability to create management competencies in others. He should receive good training from the elderly and experienced. He should be a willing learner.

Both Kautilya and his master work the *Arthashastra* are much misunderstood. Popularly known as Chanakya, he is maligned and often ridiculed as a teacher of unethical, not to say immoral practices and as an advocate of the theory that 'the ends justify the means.' 'Chanakyan' has entered Indian vocabulary as the equivalent of 'Machiavellian'. Most people know little of what Kautilya actually said in the *Arthashastra*. The only thing they can recall is the 'mandala' theory, based on the principles; 'every neighboruing state is an enemy and the enemy's enemy is a friend.'

This popular view is not only simplest but untrue. Only scholars of ancient Indian history are aware of the range and depth of the *Arthashastra*. It is a pioneering work on statecraft in all its aspects, written at least one thousand five hundred years ago.

Unfortunately, the greatness of Kautilya remains unappreciated for want of a modern translation.

Kautilya's ideas on the social, political and economic structure of the ideal state are relevant even today. Who was Kautilya, this mastermind, who could write a definitive treatise on economics and government, at a time when large parts of the world were steeped in intellectual darkness? All sources of Indian tradition – Brahmanical, Buddhist and Jain – agree that Kautilya also referred to as Vishnugupta destroyed the Nanda dynasty and installed Chandragupta Maurya on the throne of Magadha. The name Kautilya denotes that he is of the kutila gotra; Chanakya shows him to be the son of Chanaka and Vishnugupta was his personal name.

Except for one incident, little is known about his early life. One legend has it that he was a Kerala Brahmin, impoverished, lean and unprepossessing, who somehow found himself in the court of the Nanda king at Pataliputra. Another is that he was a North-Indian Brahmin, born and educated in the famous university town of Taxila, who came to Pataliputra to win laurels in philosophic disputation. Kautilya, says one Buddhist source, was known for his proficiency in the three Vedas, in the mantras, skill in stratagem, dexterity in intrigue and policy, but also for his physical ugliness, disgusting complexion, deformity of legs and other limbs. According to Buddhist and Jain traditions, his parents noticed that Kautilya was born with a full set of teeth, a mark of a future king. They had the teeth removed making him uglier because either the father or the mother did not want him to become a king. He became a king-maker instead.

Dhana Nanda, the king of whose court Kautilya came, was known to be not only base-born but miserly. Curtius reports that Porus, who defeated Alexander, wrote to him that the Nanda king was not merely a man originally of no distinction, but even of the very meanest condition. His father was in fact a barber. The father became the lover of the queen of the country, assassinated the king and, while acting as a guardian to the royal children, had them put to death. On the top of his ignoble origins, Dhana Nanda was also hated by his subjects for his avarice. This arrogant king insulated Kautilya who had come to Pataliputra to display his knowledge, ordering him to leave a feast after he had started eating. The furious and humiliated Kautilya vowed not to tie his forelock knot again until he had destroyed the Nanda dynasty root and branch. He wandered disguised as an ascetic searching for a suitable person who would help him to achieve his objective.

Kautilya came upon the boy Chandragupta of royal line but fostered by a cowherd, playing with his companions on the village grounds. The boy was acting the role of a king, dispensing justice and giving orders to his 'ministers'. On Kautilya asking him for alms, the 'king' grandly gave away a herd of someone else's cows. Kautilya was so impressed with the boy's leadership qualities that he bought the boy then and there for a thousand panas, took him to Taxila and gave him an education fit for a future king.

Together Kautilya and Chandragupta set about attacking the Nanda kingdom only to meet with failure at first. Legend has it that the right tactics for destroying a powerful kingdom came to them when they saw a woman with whom they had taken shelter scolding her son 'you are just like Chandragupta' because he had got his fingers burnt by starting to eat from the center of a hot dish. They changed their tactics and began the conquest from the frontiers. Chandragupta then entered into an alliance with the king of a mountain kingdom. Though the young Maurya and his supporters were inferior in armed strength, they began by harassing the outlying areas. Garrisons were stationed in each conquered state to prevent a revolt behind them.

One story about the conquest is that when Chandragupta failed to conquer a town he was besieging, Kautilya entered it disguised as a beggar and predicted that the siege would be lifted if the people removed the idols from a temple. The gullible population did so and the besiegers pretended to withdraw. When the citizens were celebrating their supposed liberty, the attackers returned to take them by surprise. Gradually Chandragupta converged towards Pataliputra, besieged it, drove out Dhana Nanda and was installed as the king of Magadha. Kautilya then retired from active life and reflected on all that he had learnt. Having found earlier works on statecraft unsatisfactory in many respects, he composed his own definitive work.

The memory of the mythical Kautilya is also present in modern India, where the popularized saga of Kautilya's life was made into an immensely popular television historical soap opera series in the early 1990s, 'Chanakya'. The numerious episodes portray Chanakya's shrewdness and cunning realpolitik. Kautilya lives too in the names of streets and neighborhoods in Delhi; the diplomatic neighborhood is called *Chanakyapuri*, and one can find *Kautilya Marg*. Before the rediscovery of the *Arthashastra* his name continued to live in Sanskrit literature; one of the greatest of ancient Sanskrit plays that have come down to us is the *Mudraraksasa*, 'the minister's seal', written in the 6th century AD by Visakhadatta, a high official in the Indian court. The play recounts how over 800 years before Kautilya brilliantly and ruthlessly consolidates the power of the first Mauryan emperor, Chandragupta. A leading economic columnist in India's leading weekly news magazine writes under the pseudonym of Kautilya, a publishing house has its name as *Chanakya* and independent India's first prime minister, Jawaharlal Nehru thought Kautilya to be a far more penetrating political thinker than Machiavelli.

That in the almost 100 years since its rediscovery in 1909 nearly 4500 articles have been written on it by Indian, German, British and other scholars and researchers, the *Arthashastra* deserve a prominent place in the history of political therght. Four years earlier, Rudrapatnam Shastry had discovered the palm leaf manuscript that would define his legacy. But while he recognized the significance of the text, even he could not have anticipated the revolution in Indian self-image his discovery would bring about. The text became a focal point with which to contest every cliche that had been used to define India. Shortly after Kautilya's treatise was rediscovered and translated into western languages in the early 1900s, the great social thinker Max Weber marveled that 'in contrast with this document, Machiavelli's prince is harmless'. According to the great indologist Heinrich Zimer, 'Kautilya brought the whole historical period into being of which Ashoka's reign was the apogee.'

Kautilya's views on foreign policy of a king in very progressive, dynamic and creatively fascinating, success of a king's foreign policy initiatives depends on power, which is not to be measured purely in terms of military power. Intellectual power and morale are two other aspects. By projecting his power by using the appropriate foreign policy, a king makes progress, thus contributing to further increase in his power. There is thus a dynamic relationship between power and progress, mediated by the right policy, executed through the instruments of the circle of states.

The six methods of foreign policy are then defined; why one policy should be chosen in preference to another depends entirely on whether the chosen method helps the king to make progress. Hence, each of the six methods are evaluated in terms of the situations in which their use will result in progress. The analysis of five of the six methods is clear cut. However, in making peace, there is the special case of the enemy; is there any situation, when peace with the enemy is advisable? Kautilya is of the view that peace can be made with the enemy, purely as a temporary measure, provided that his long-term objective of conquest is thereby facilitated. This is not as duplicitous as it sounds because the enmity is inherent in the geography of the situation; by definition, two kings are enemies when they share a common border. Peace is only a stage enabling the conqueror to build up his strength before attempting to conquer the enemy. We must also bear in mind that whatever is said about the would-be conqueror also applies to the enemy, who would think of the 'conqueror' as his own enemy, whether in front or in the rear. It is assumed that he too will use the period of peace to increase his strength.

The other part of the dynamic equation is relative power. The choice of policy is dependent on the power of the king against whom it is directed. There are three logical possibilities. The other king may be stronger, weaker or of equal strength. Kautilya analyses this question thoroughly by stating a general principle and then modifying it to suit reality.

We then proceed to a definition of the terms by designating the role of different participating kings. For convenience, we designate one king as 'the conqueror' and define all other relationships as perceived by him. These relationships are based on the fundamental principle that two states sharing a common border are intrinsically hostile to each other. However, the nature of the hostility may be different for different neighbours; some may deserve only to be weakened while others have to be crushed. Some neighbours may even be friendly and some, after conquest, may become vassals. The basic principle automatically leads to a sequence of enemies and allies. There exist other interested kings in the environment, such as the Middle king and the Neutral king.

The complete list of the kings, defined in terms of their relationships to the conqueror is as follows:

ari	-	antagonist
mitra	-	friend, ally
ari's mitra	-	enemy's ally
mitra's mitra	-	friend of the ally
ari's mitra's-mitra	-	enemy's ally's friend
udasina	-	neutral king
madhyama	-	middle king

Every king has his own circle of allies. Since the conqueror, his enemy, the Middle king and the Neutral king are all independent actors, there are four circles. It must, however, be emphasized that the circle of kings is not meant to be imagined geographically as a series of concentric circles, though they may be symbolically represented as such. The nomenclature defines relationships in a dynamic situation, which may create opportunities for some and expose others to danger.

Foreign Policy

A potential conqueror [i.e., a king who wishes to enlarge his territory by conquest] is defined as a king who, having excellent personal qualities, resources and constituents of his state, follows good polities.

The Antagonists

Any king, whose kingdom shares a common border with that of the conqueror is an antagonist.

Neighbouring kings, who are deemed to be antagonists, are of different kinds:

(i) a powerful antagonistic neighbour having excellent personal qualities, resources and constituents is an enemy.

(ii) One who is afflicted by a calamity to one or more of his constituents is a vulnerable adversary;

(iii) One who is weak or without support is a destroyable antagonist and

(iv) One who has support is an antagonist who can be weakened or harassed.

Among the kings with contiguous territories, a natural enemy is one who is of the same family or of equally high birth as the conqueror; an 'antagonist by intent' is one who is opposed to the conqueror or is induced to be so.

An enemy who has any of the following characteristics is easily defeated: one not born of a royal family, greedy, vicious or whimsical, without energy or enthusiasm, trusting in fate, with a habit of behaving unjustly, always doing harm to others, with a mean mantriparishad, with unhappy subjects, powerless, or helpless.

The Group of Friends

A king whose territory has a common boundary with that of an antagonist [i.e., one whose territory has no common border with that of the conqueror] is an ally.

Like enemies, allies are also of different kinds. A 'natural ally' is one who is of equally noble birth or is closely related to the conqueror on the father's or mother's side; an 'ally by intent' is one who needs the conqueror's help for wealth or personal safety.

The Sequence of Enemies and Allies

Thus, in front [i.e., the direction of the conqueror's target for conquest] lie the enemy, the conqueror's ally, the enemy's ally, the ally's ally, the enemy's ally's ally and so on, depending on the contiguity of territories. Likewise, behind lie the enemy in the rear, the ally in the rear, the rear enemy's ally, the rear ally's ally and so on.

The Middle King

A Middle King is one whose territory is contiguous to those of the conqueror and the conqueror's enemy, who is powerful enough to help them whether they are untied or not or to destroy them individually when they are disunited.

The Neutral King

A Neutral king is one (i) whose territory is not contiguous with those of the conqueror, the conqueror's enemy or the middle King [i.e., totally outside the area of hostilities], (ii) who is stronger than these three and (iii) who is powerful enough to help any of three, whether they are united or not, or to destroy them individually when they are disunited.

The Circle of Kings

The would-be conqueror, the ally and the friend of the ally are the three basic constituents of the first circle of kings. They, along with the other constituent elements of their states [the ministers, the countryside, the fortified cities, the treasuries and the armies] together make up the eighteen elements of this circle. Likewise, the enemy, the Middle and the Neutral kings have each a circle of eighteen elements. Thus, there are four circles, with seventy-two constituents, made up of twelve kings, and sixty other elements [five for each king]. Each of the seventy-two elements has its own strength and may be weakened due to a calamity.

Types of Enemies

It is necessary to note that kings capable of harassing the conqueror in the rear and impeding his movements are of three kinds: the group of his neighbours behind him and the two groups on either side of him.

The Intervening King

A weak king situated between the conqueror and the enemy is called the intervening king. He becomes an impediment to the strong only when he can seek refuge in a fort or in the forest.

Power and Its Objectives

Strength of power; happiness is the objective of using power.

Power and success are interrelated. Power is of three kinds; so is the success resulting from its use. Intellectual strength provides the power of good counsel; a prosperous treasury and a strong army provide physical power and valour is the basis for morale and energetic action. The success resulting from each one is, correspondingly, intellectual, physical and psychological.

To the extent a conqueror is better endowed than his enemy in the three kinds of power, to the extent he will be stronger and more successful. If he is less well endowed, he will be weaker. Two kings of commensurate power are equal.

Hence, the conqueror shall always endeavour to add to his own power and increase his own happiness. If he is unable to improve his own qualities, he shall endeavour to increase the power of the human constituents of his state, keeping in mind their integrity as well as their importance to the work about to be undertaken. He shall also endeavour to reduce the power of his traitors and enemies.

Use of Circle of States by the Conqueror

The conqueror shall think of the circle of states as a wheel – himself at the hub and his allies, drawn to him by the spokes though separated by intervening territory, as its rim.

The enemy, however strong he may be, becomes vulnerable to harassment and destruction, when he is squeezed between the conqueror and his allies.

In order to further his own interests, the conqueror shall establish, both in the front and in the rear, a circle of kings made up of excellent allies.

He shall always station envoys and clandestine agents in all states of the circle. These shall cultivate those acting against the interests of the conqueror and, while maintaining their own secrecy, destroy repeatedly such inimical persons.

He who cannot maintain secrecy will undoubtedly find his efforts destroyed like a broken boat in a sea, even if temporarily there are some appearances of successes.

The conqueror may find himself in the role of the frontal attacker, an attacker in the rear, or a victim of aggression, how each situation should be dealt with is given below.

When the conqueror initiates his attack, he shall make:

in the rear

(i) his ally-in-the rear to engage his enemy-in-the-rear;

(ii) his rear ally's friend to engage the rear enemy's ally'

in the front;

(iii) his ally to engage the enemy's ally' and

(iv) the friend the ally to engage the enemy's ally's friend.

When the conqueror plays the role of an attacker in the rear, he shall first make his own ally in the rear of engage his own enemy-in-the rear [in order to safeguard his own rear]. He shall then go to the help of his ally by attaching in the rear the enemy.

When the conqueror finds himself under attack, he shall get his ally to attack the rear of the enemy and the friend of his ally to attack the rear of the enemy's ally in the rear.

The Six Methods

The would-be conqueror shall apply the six methods of foreign policy as appropriate to the various constituent elements of his circle of states with the aim of progressing from a state of decline to one of neither decline nor progress and from this state to one of progress.

The king who understands the interdependence of the six methods of foreign policy, as explained in this treatise, will bind other rulers by the chains of his intellect and can play with them as he pleases.

The Six Methods

Some teachers say that the six methods are: making peace, waging war, doing neither, preparing for war, seeking protection, and adopting a dual policy. Vatavyadhi however, says that there are only two methods – waging war and making peace, because the others are only derivatives of these two. Kautilya agrees with the view that there are indeed six different methods because each one is applicable in a different set of circumstances.

1. *Making peace* is entering into an agreement with specific conditions [i.e., concluding a treaty]. A king shall make peace when he finds himself in relative decline compared to his enemy.
2. Active hostilities is *waging war.* A king superior to his enemy in power shall attack him.
3. Being indifferent to a situation is *staying quiet.* When a king considers that neither he nor his enemy can harm the other, he shall remain quiet.
4. Augmenting one's own power is *preparing for war.* A king with special advantages shall make preparations for war.
5. Getting the protection of another is *seeking support.* A king depleted in power shall seek help.
6. Dual policy is making peace with one king and war with another. A king whose aim can be achieved only with the help of another shall pursue a *dual policy.*

Achieving Progress

1. By Making Peace

A king shall make peace with the enemy when:

(i) he and the enemy both achieve equal progress in equal time;

(ii) both decline equally in equal time; or

(iii) there is no change in their respective situations during the same period of time.

The king can achieve progress by making peace with his enemy if he thinks that he can use the period of peace so that:

(i) his gain through productive undertakings would be so great as to enable him to destroy those of the enemy;

(ii) he can enjoy the additional gain (a) from his own works [not spent in waging war], (b) those arising from works undertaken by the enemy and (c) those accruing from the confidence generated by the peace;

(iii) he can ruin the enemy's undertakings by using secret methods or occult practices;

(iv) he can entice away the people implementing the enemy's projects by offering them higher remuneration, favours or remissions of taxes;

(v) the enemy, being allied with a much stronger king, will undergo a decline;

(vi) he can manage to prolong the war between the enemy and another king, because of which the enemy had made the peace with the conqueror;

(vii) he can harass the countryside of another of his enemies;

(viii) he can acquire [parts] of the enemy's territory attacked by another and thereby gain the profits of the enemy's undertaking;

(ix) he can be safe from attach by the enemy who finds himself in a difficult situation due to the destruction of his undertakings;

(x) he can expect to improve his situation to start profitable undertaking elsewhere with another king;

(xi) he can sow dissension between the enemy and the enemy's allies and make them his own allies; and

(xii) he can, by judicious use of favours and punishments, make the enemy's own allies turn against him and eventually destroy him.

2. Through War

A king can achieve progress by waging war if:

(i) he is confident of repelling an enemy attack because of having (a) [superior forces such as] martial races and fighting guilds or (b) [impregnable defences such as] a mountain, forest or river fort with only one approach;

(ii) he can destroy the enemy's undertakings from the security of an impregnable fort on the border of his kingdom;

(iii) the enemy's undertakings are on the verge of collapse, having been weakened by a calamity; or (iv) a part of the enemy's country can be absorbed while he is busy fighting elsewhere.

3. By Doing Neither

A king can achieve progress without war of suing for peace if:

(i) neither the king nor his enemy can ruin each other's undertakings; or

(ii) the enemy is involved in a calamity or a life and death struggle permitting the king to concentrate on augmenting his own resources.

4. By Preparing for War

A king can make progress while preparing for war when he can bring about the ruin of the enemy's undertakings after making sure that his own will be well-protected.

5. By Seeking Protection

If a king is unable to ruin the enemy's undertakings and is also unable to protect his own from the enemy's attacks, he shall seek the help of a stronger king. [Under his protection] he shall first avert his decline and then move towards progress.

6. By Dual Policy

A king shall adopt a dual policy if he can promote his own undertakings by having peace with one [enemy] and [at the same time] ruin those of another by waging war.

Comparative Merits of the Six Methods

When the degree of progress is the same in pursuing peace and waging war, peace is to be preferred. For, in war, there are disadvantages such as losses, expenses and absence from home.

For the same reason, a policy of neither peace nor war is to be preferred to making preparations for war.

As between adopting a dual policy and seeking the protection of a stronger king, the dual policy is to be preferred. For, in adopting the dual policy, one gives importance to one's own undertakings and, thereby, promotes one's own interests. One who seeks the protection of another serves only the other's interests, not his own.

General Principles

The would-be conqueror shall apply the six methods with due regard to his power.

He shall make peace with an equally powerful or stronger king; he shall wage war against a weaker king.

[He shall not wage war against a stronger king] because he who fights against a stronger king is crushed like a foot soldier fighting an elephant. A fight with an equal brings losses to both sides, just like the destruction of two unbaked mudpots hitting each other.

Like a stone striking a mudpot, a more powerful king gains decisive victory over a weaker one.

(1) When a peace offer is rejected:

A king, whose offer of peace is rejected by a more powerful king, shall adopt the policies recommended either for one surrendering his troops or for a weaker king

A king, whose offer of peace is rejected by an equally powerful king, shall harass the other to the same extent that he is harassed. Just as unheated pieces of iron cannot be welded together, there can be no union without heat [brought about by friction].

(ii) Making peace with a weaker king:

Peace shall be made with a weaker king who is submissive in all respects. if he is ill-treated anger and resentment will make him fight bravely like a forest fire; he will also be supported by his circle of kings.

When a king at war with another finds that the enemy's principal constituents, though greedy, impoverished and rebellious, still do not come over to his side for fear of the war, he shall make peace, even if he is the stronger of the two; he shall at least reduce the intensity of the war.

When two kings are both affected by calamities, the more powerful shall make peace if his troubles are greater and if the other is likely to get over his lighter troubles easily and thus is in a position to launch an attack.

(iii) Waging war though weaker:

When two kings are at peace with each other, even a weaker king shall go to war against the stronger if he finds that the enemy's principal constituents, though greedy, impoverished and rebellious, are afraid of coming over to his side for fear of being handed back to their king.

(iv) Neither making peace nor waging war:

Even a powerful king shall refrain from any peacemaking of warlike activity, if by taking action there will neither be an increase in his own strength nor a decrease in that of the enemy.

(v) Weaker king preparing for war:

Even a weak shall make preparations for war , if the enemy is affícted by irremediable calamities.

(vi) Powerful king seeking protection:

Even a powerful king shall seek protection, if he faces an immediate danger or an irremediable calamity.

(vii) Powerful king adopting dual policy:

Even a powerful king shall adopt the dual policy, if he can obtain his objectives by making peace on one side and waging war on the other.

(viii) The last four methods towards an equal king:

A king shall adopt the four policies [of inaction, preparing for war, seeking help and dual policy] towards an equally powerful king in circumstances similar to the four mentioned immediately above [namely, no advantage, calamity to the other king, calamity to oneself and specific advantages].

Peace

The four aspects of making peace by treaty are : wanting to make peace where none exists, respecting the provisions of a treaty already concluded, violating a treaty and renegotiating a broken treaty.

Desire to make peace: Examining (i) the prospects of a new treaty keeping in mind the method of conciliation etc.,(ii) the consequences of such a treaty and (iii) the provisions determining the obligations of equal, stronger and weaker parties according to their strength are aspects of the desire to make peace.

Respecting a treaty means (i) the observance, on both sides, of the spirit of the treaty on the basis of mutual respect and advantage (ii) the implementation of the provisions of the treaty as agreed upon and (iii) the protection of the alliance by ensuring that no dissension creeps in between the parties.

Violation of a treaty is breaking it, after establishing, though spies and secret agents, that the other party is not respecting it.

A treaty is renegotiated when there is a reconciliation with a vassal or ally who had, through some fault, violated a treaty.

When the benefit accruing to kings under a treaty, irrespective of their status as the weaker, equal or stronger king, is fair to each one, peace by the agreement shall be the preferred course of action; if the benefits are to be unfairly distributed, war is preferable.

War

The three kinds of war are; open war, secret war and undeclared war.

Open war is fighting at a specified time and place.

Secret war is – terrorizing, sudden assault, threatening in one direction while attacking in another, sudden assault without specifying time or place, attacking an enemy when he makes a mistake or is suffering from a calamity, and appearing to yield in one place but attacking suddenly in another.

Undeclared war is using secret agents and occult practices against the enemy.

Types of Pauses

Prolonged inaction, inaction for a specific purpose and deliberately not taking action are three similar types of neither waging war nor making peace.

Sthana-settled with nuance of not actively pursuing preparations for war or peace;

Asana-sitting as if ready to jump up when the conditions are ripe;

Upekshana- ignoring one's ability to act.

The difference between them: prolonged inaction is necessary when waiting for one of the constituents of the king's state, which is not at its best, to recover. Inaction for a purpose is waiting for the right opportunity. When the conqueror and the enemy are both incapable of harming each other though each may want to conquer the other, the best policy is to pause after declaring war or offering peace and not actively pursue it.

A king shall declare war and then pause when he finds that:

(i) with his own troops, or with nose of the ally or by using jungle tribes he can weaken a king equal in strength to him or one more powerful; he shall, however, first ensure the safety of the frontier and the interior;

(ii) his own subjects are brave, united and prosperous, able to carry on their work without hindrance and capable of harming those of the enemy;

(iii) the enemy's subjects will come over to his side voluntarily or after instigation because they are greedy, impoverished, rebellious or harassed by the enemy's troops, robbers or jungle tribes;

(iv) while his own economy is prosperous, that of the enemy is miserable and, therefore, the enemy's people are likely to come over to his side when afflicted by famine;

(v) while the enemy's economy is prosperous, his own is miserable and his subjects are likely to go over to the enemy unless there is a war and he can promise them the plunder of the enemy's grain, cattle and gold;

(vi) he can prevent the import into his country of the enemy's goods which harm his economy;

(vii) because of the war, he can divert to his own country the valuable goods now going to the enemy by a trade route, or

(viii) because of the war, the enemy will be unable to suppress the traitors, enemies or jungle tribes in his territories or be compelled to deal with them while fighting the war.

If for reasons country to those given above the consequences of waiting after proclaiming war are unfavourable, the king shall make peace and wait.

Setting out on a Campaign

After the king has adequately increased his strength [during a period of waiting after declaring war] he shall set out on a campaign against the enemy, choosing a time when the enemy does not have all his forces fully mobilized.

He shall set out on a campaign when he finds that:

(i) the enemy is suffering from a calamity;

(ii) the enemy's troubles with one constituent of his state cannot be compensated by the other constituents;

(iii) the enemy's subjects have become impoverished, discouraged or disunited due to oppression by the troops or ill-treatment by their monarch and thus have become susceptible to enticement to desert; or

(iv) the enemy's draught animals, men, stores and fortifications have been weakened due to fire, floods, disease, epidemics or famine.

Seeking Help

Amity with a more powerful monarch carries great danger for kings, except when one is actually at war with an enemy.

A king shall seek the protection of one who is stronger than the neighbouring enemy.

Should a king seek the help of a king who loves him or a king who is loved by him? The best alliance is that made with one who loves him.

Dual Policy

The conqueror shall outmanoeuvre the second element of the Circle of Kings [i.e., the enemy] as follows. He shall induce a neighbouring ruler to undertake a simultaneous expedition, each attacking the enemy from a different direction, on the understanding that the spoils will be divided equally. If the neighbour agrees to equal division, a treaty shall be concluded; if he does not, he shall be treated as hostile.

The conqueror may take the help of the second member of the circle of kings [i.e. the natural enemy] in order to attack another neighbouring king if he considers that:

(i) there is no danger of an attack by the enemy in the rear;

(ii) the conqueror will have twice the number of troops at his disposal; or if the second king will

(iii) prevent an attack by the enemy in the rear;

(iv) not go to the help of the third king being attacked;

(v) provide supplies and reinforcements to the conqueror while denying them to the third king;

(vi) help remove the impediments and dangers coming in the way of the expedition;

(vii) use his army against the forts and forest refuges of the king under attack;

(viii) place the king under attack in mortal peril or force him to sue for peace;

(ix) help to create confidence among other enemies, as a result of being rewarded for his services.

(From *The Arthashastra* (ed) by L.N. Rangarajan, Penguin Books, New Delhi, 1992 pp. 533-579)

3

Rammohan Roy

Life and Times

Rammohan Roy (1772-1833) was born on 22 May 1772 in an orthodox Brahmin family at Radhanagar in Bengal, which was then beginning to come under the direct administration of the British East India Company. He was contemporary of Hegel (1770-1831) and was seventeen years old when the French Revolution began. His father, Ramakant Roy, was a revenue official and dependent land-holder under the Maharani of Burdwan. Soon after the 1793 Permanent Settlement of Land Revenue by the British, he bought several mahals and became an independent zamindar.

Rammohan's early education included the study of Persian and Arabic at Patna, where he read the Koran and the works of Plato. He went to Banaras, where he studied Sanskrit and read the ancient Hindu scriptures, especially the Vedas and the Upanishads. Returning to his village at the age of sixteen, he wrote a rational critique of the Hindu idol worship. This displeased his father greatly and Rammohan had to leave his home. His travelled to, among other places, Tibet, where he secured a first-hand knowledge of the Buddhism, and Banaras, where he undertook further studies of the Sanskrit texts of the Advaita-Vedanta school. In 1803, Rammohan Roy went to Murshidabad after the death of his father. From 1803 to 1814, he worked for the East India Company as the personal diwan, first of Woodforde and then of

Digby. The association with these English civil servants. especially Digby, was instrumental in Roy's study of modern Western thought. In 1814, he resigned from his job and moved to Calcutta in order to devote his life to religious, social and political reforms. By that time he had acquired ownership of some taluks under the 1793 Permanent Settlement. He also had a money business in North Calcutta. After shifting to Calcutta in 1818, he came into close contact with the British free-traders and invested his money in the Agency House of Mackintosh and Company. He also renewed his interactions with the scholars of the Fort William College and the Diwani Adalat in Calcutta, with whom he had been in contact with the course of his business dealings in Calcutta prior to 1803. Notable among his English friends in Calcutta were James Young, a merchant and follower of Jeremy Bentham, David Hare, a philanthropist, and J.S. Buckingham the radical editor of Calcutta Journal. The writings of David Locke, John Hume, Jeremy Bentham and the Christian Unitarians exerted much influence on Rammohan.

His studies of Hindu theology and metaphysics failed to generate in his mind and heart any devout reverence for orthodox Hinduism. Due to his critical intellectualism and social rationalism, he became one of the founders of the Bengal renaissance. The Renaissance in Bengal was a great creative and complex movement and it included persons like Rammohan Roy, Devendra Nath Tagore, Ishwar Chandra Gupta, Madhusudan Datta, Akshay Kumar Datta, Ishwar Chandra Vidyasagar, Ramakrishna Paramhansa, Vivekananda, Hemchandra Banerjee, Bankim Chandra Chatterjee, Rabindranath Tagore and Aurobindo Ghosh and several others. But Rammohan Roy was the earliest spokesman of the Bengal Renaissance. As a religious and social leader he appeared as a gigantic, almost extraordinary, personality.

In 1815 Rammohan came to Calcutta and in 1816 started the *Atmiya Sabha*. In Calcutta he came in contact with Christian missionaries of the Unitarian School. In 1818 Rammohan began his celebrated crusade for the abolition of Sati and in 1829 Lord William Bentinck, the then British Governor-General of India, rendered Sati illegal. The year 1829 may be taken as an important landmark in the social history of India. Rammohan Roy thus won immortal fame in his crusade to free Hindu women from the dark and inhuman practice of Sati.

In 1827 Rammohan formed the British India Unitarian Association and on 20 August 1818 he founded the Brahmo Samaj. The formal Depening of the Brahmo Samaj was made on 23 January 1830. On 15 November 1830, he sailed for England to be present there to counteract the possible nullification of the Act banning 'Sati' due to powerful propaganda mounted by the orthodox Brahmins against the Act. Incidentally, it may also be noted that Rammohan was given the title of 'Raja' by the titular Mughal Emperor of Delhi, whose grievances the former was to present before the British king. In England, Rammohan was well-received by the king and the Directors of the East India Company. In England, he met distinguished persons. Bentham hailed him as a collaborator in the service of humanity. He made friendship with Lord Brougham who was opposed to slavery and advocated popular education. While Rammohan was in England, the first Reform Act was passed and he hailed it as the victory of liberty, justice and right over oppression, injustice and wrong. Among his important activities in England was the presentation of the memorandum to the Select Committee of the House of Commons on the Revenue and Judicial Systems of India. He fell ill and died at Bristol on 27 December 1833.

Rammohan Roy born in a century was an era of darkness and desolation for our country. It was perhaps the darkest age in which Indian history. An old, decadent society and polity was in the process of crumbling down and no ray of light and hope was visible anywhere. The country had lost its link with the foundational values of its being and was crawling under a crippling load of obscurantism and irrationalism. All the vital forces of society have been cancerised and paralysed. Religious and educational institutions, rural and urban life, agriculture and industry, law and administration were in a state of utter chaos. Suffocating superstition and decadent tradition blocked any progress. In this situation of abject slavery to circumstances and dark gloom of degeneration came forth a light in the emergence of Rammohan Roy the father of the modem age in India. In this holy land there arose a conflict of three different cultures, three civilizations, the Hindu, the Muslim and the Christian. Rammohan was the first to evolve a synthesis between the three and thus ushered in the modern era which was marked with the gradual evolution of a composite nationality and synthetic culture for India. He indicated in his clear and synthetic vision, the solution to the larger problem of cosmopolitan culture and civilization. He was the harbinger of civilizational dialogue.

Rammohan was perhaps the only person of his time who realised completely the significance and importance of the modem age. He understood, as nobody else had done before his time, that human progress lay not in separation of national independence but in the fraternity of inter-dependence of individuals and nations evolved through rational synthesis of cultural and political interaction and exchange. He applied this principle of universal humanism in realms of social, religious, literary and political affairs, with his great depth of scholarship and clarity of vision. He never subjected himself to abject slavery of circumstances and endeavoured most strenuously to make his own people realise the innermost truths of their own culture and civilization and at the same time recognise the common links with the essential truths of other civilizations and cultures. Keeping this objective in view he made amazing contributions to original thinking in matters of social and political reform, women's emancipation, freedom of speech and the press, judicial and administrative reforms, scientific education and freedom from every kind of oppression and exploitation.

The Rights of Women

Advocate. I alluded, to the real reason for our anxiety to persuade widows to follow their husbands, and for our endeavours to burn them pressed down with ropes: *viz.*, that women are by nature of inferior understanding, without resolution, unworthy of trust, subject to passions, and void of virtuous knowledge; they, according to the precepts of the *Shastras,* are not allowed to marry again after the demise of their husbands, and consequently despair at once of all worldly pleasure; hence it is evident, that death to these unfortunate widows is preferable to existence; for the great difficulty which a widow may experience by living a purely ascetic life, as prescribed by the *Shastras,* is obvious; therefore, if she does not perform conceremation, it is probable that she may be guilty of such acts as many bring disgrace upon her paternal and maternal relations, and those that may be connected with her husband. Under these circumstances, we instruct them from their early life in the idea of conceremation, holding out to them heavenly enjoyments in company with their husbands, as well as the beatitude of their relations, both by birth and marriage, and their reputation in this world. From this many of them, on the death of their husbands, become desirous of accompanying them; but to remove every chance of their trying to escape from the blazing fire, in burning them we first the them down to the pile.

Opponent. The reason you have now assigned for burning widows alive in indeed you true motive, as we are well aware; but the faults which you have imputed to women are not planted in their constituted by nature; it would be, therefore, grossly criminal to condemn that sex to death merely as a precaution. By ascribing to them all sorts of improper conduct, you have indeed successfully persuaded the Hindu community to look down upon them as contemptible and mischievous creatures, whence they have been subjected to constant miseries. I have, therefore, to offer a few remarks on this head.

Women are in general inferior to men in bodily strength and energy; consequently the male part of the community, taking advantage of their corporeal weakness, have denied to them those excellent merits that they are entitled to by nature, and afterwards they are apt to say that women are naturally incapable of acquiring those merits. But if we give the subject consideration, we may easily ascertain whether or not your accusation against them is consistent with justice. As to their inferiority in point of understanding, when did you ever afford them a fair opportunity of exhibiting their natural capacity? How then can you accuse them of want of understanding? If, after instruction in knowledge and wisdom, a person cannot comprehend or retain what has been taught him, we may consider him as deficient; but as you keep women generally void of education and acquirements, you cannot, therefore, in justice pronounce on their inferiority. On the contrary, Lilavati, Bhanumati, the wife of the prince of Karnat, and that of Kalidasa, are celebrated for their thorough knowledge of all the *Shastras:* moreover in the *Brihadaranyaka Upanishad* of the *Yajur Veda* it is clearly stated that Yajnavalkya imparted divine knowledge of the most difficult nature to his wife Maitreyi, who was able to follow and completely attain it!

Secondly. You charge them with want of resolution, at which I feel exceedingly surprised: for we constantly perceive, in a country where the name of death makes the male shudder, that the female, from her firmness of mind, offers to burn with the corpse of her deceased husband; and yet you accuse those women of deficiency in point of resolution.

Thirdly. With regard to their trustworthiness, let us look minutely into the conduct of both sexes, and we may be enabled to ascertain which of them is the most frequently guilty of betraying friends. If we enumerate such women in each village or town as have been deceived by men, and such men as have been betrayed by women, I presume that the number of the deceived women would be found ten times greater than that of the betrayed men. Men are, in general, able to read and write, and manage public affairs, by which means they easily promulgate such faults as women occasionally commit, but never consider as criminal the misconduct of men towards women. One fault they have, it must be acknowledge; which is, by considering others equally void of duplicity as themselves, to give their confidence too readily, from which they suffer much misery, even so far that some of them are misled to suffer themselves to be burnt to death.

In the fourth place, with respect to their subjection to the passions, this may be judged of by the custom of marriage as to the respective sexes; for one man may marry two or three, sometimes even ten wives and upwards; while a woman, who marries but one husband, desires at his death to follow him, forsaking all worldly enjoyments, or to remain leading the austere life of an ascetic.

Fifthly. The accusation of the want of virtuous knowledge is an injustice. Observe what pain, what slighting, what contempt, and what affections their virtue enables them to support! How many Kulin Brahmans are there who marry ten or fifteen wives for the sake of money, that never see the greater number of them after the day of marriage, and visit others only three or four times in the course of their life. Still amongst those women, most, even without seeing or receiving any support from their husbands, living dependent on their fathers or brothers, and suffering much distress, continue to preserve their virtue; and when Brahmans, or those of other tribes, bring their wives to live with them, what misery do the women not suffer? At marriage the wife is recognized as half of her husband, but in after – conduct they are treated worse than inferior animals. For the woman is employed to do the work of a slave in the house, such as, in her turn, to clean the place very early in the morning, whether cold or wet, to scour the dishes, to wash the floor, to cook night and day, to prepare and serve food for her husband, father, mother-in-law, sisters-in-law, brothers-in-law, and friends and connections! (for amongst Hindus more than in other tribes relations long reside together, and on this account quarrels are more common amongst brothers respecting their worldly affairs).

If in the preparation of serving up of the rituals they commit the smallest fault, what insult do they not received from their husband, their mother-in-law, and the younger brothers of their husband? After all the male part of the family have satisfied themselves, the women content themselves with what may be let, whether sufficient in quantity or not. Whether Brahmans or Kayasthas are not wealthy, their women are obliged to attend to their cows, and to prepare the cow-dung for firing. In the afternoon they fetch water from the river or tank, and at night perform the office of menial servants in making the beds. In case of any fault of mission in the performance of those labours they receive injurious treatment. Should the husband acquire wealth, he indulges in criminal amours to her perfect knowledge and almost under her eyes, and does not see her perhaps once a month. As long as the husband is poor, she suffers every kind of trouble, and when he becomes rich, she is altogether heart-broken. All this pain and affliction their virtue alone enables them to support. Where a husband takes two of three wives to live with him, they are subjected to mental miseries and constant quarrels. Even this distressed situation they virtually endure. Sometimes it happens that the husband, from a preference for one of his wives, behaves cruelly to another. Amongst the lower classes, and those even of the better class who have not associated with good company, the wife, on the slightest fault, or even on bare suspicion of her misconduct, is chastised as a thief. Respect to virtue and their reputation generally makes them forgive even this treatment. If unable to bear such cruel usage, a wife leaves her husband's house to live separately from him, then the influence of the husband with the magisterial authority is generally sufficient to place her again in his hands; when, in revenge for her quitting him, he seizes every pretext to torment her in various ways, and sometimes even puts her privately to death. These are facts occurring every day, and not to be denied. What I lament is, that, seeing the women thus dependent and exposed to every misery, you feel for them no compassion, that might exempt them from being tied down and burnt to death.

(From *The Selected Works of Raja Rammohan Roy*. Publication Division, Govt. of India, New Delhi, 1977 pp. 121-133).

Freedom of the Press

Your Lordship may have learned from the works of the Christian Missionaries, and also from other sources, that ever since the art of printing has become generally known among the natives of Calcutta, numerous Publications have been circulated in the Bengalee Language, which by introducing free discussion among the natives and inducing them to reflect and inquire after knowledge, have already served greatly to improve their minds and ameliorate their condition. This desirable object has been chiefly promoted by the establishment of four native newspapers, two in the Bengalee and two in the Persian languages, published for the purpose of communicating to those residing in the interior of the country, accounts of whatever occurs worthy of notice at the

Presidency or in the country, and also the interesting and valuable intelligence of what is passing in England and in other parts of the world, conveyed through the English newspapers or other channels.

While your Memorialists were indulging the hope that Government, from a conviction of the manifold advantages of being put in possession of full and impartial information regarding what is passing in all parts of the country, would encourage the establishment of newspapers in the cities and districts under the special patronage and protection of Government, that they might furnish the supreme authorities in Calcutta with an accurate account of local occurrences and reports of judicial proceedings, they have the misfortune to observe, that on the contrary, his Excellency the Governor General in Council has lately promulgated a Rule and Ordinance imposing severe restraints on the Press and prohibiting all periodical publications even at the Presidency and in the native languages, unless sanctioned by a licence from Government, which is to be revocable at pleasure whenever it shall appear to Government that a publication has contained anything of an unsuitable character.

Those natives who are in more favourable circumstances and of respectable character, have such an invincible prejudice against making a voluntary affidavit, or undergoing the solemnities of an oath, that they will never think of establishing a publication which can only be supported by a series of oaths and affidavits, abhorrent to their feelings and derogatory to their reputation amongst their countrymen.

After this Rule and Ordinance shall have been carried into execution, your Memorialists are therefore extremely sorry to observe, that a complete stop will be put to the diffusion of knowledge and the consequent mental improvement now going on, either by translations into the popular dialect of this country from the learned languages of the East, or by the circulation of literary intelligence drawn from foreign publications. And the same cause will also prevent those natives who are better versed in the laws and customs of the British Nation, from communicating to their fellow subjects a knowledge of the admirable system of Government established by the British, and the peculiar excellences of the means they have adopted for the strict and impartial administration of justice. Another evil of equal importance in the eyes of a just ruler is, that it will also preclude the Natives from making the Government readily acquainted with the errors and injustice that may be committed by its executive officers in the various parts of this extensive country; and it will also preclude the natives from communicating frankly and honestly to their gracious sovereign in England and his Council, the real condition of his Majesty's faithful subjects in this distant part of his dominions and the treatment they experience from the local Government; since information cannot in future be conveyed to England, as it has heretofore been, either by the translations from the native publications inserted in the English newspapers printed here and sent to Europe, or by the English publications which the natives themselves had in contemplation to establish, before this Rule and Ordinance was proposed.

After this sudden deprivation of one of the most precious of their rights, which has been freely allowed them since the Establishment of the British Power, a right which they do not have, and cannot be charged with having ever abused, the inhabitants of Calcutta would be no longer justified in boasting, that they are fortunately placed by Providence under the protection of the whole British Nation or that the King of England and Lords and Commons are their legislators, and that they are secured in the enjoyment of the same civil and religious privileges that every Briton is entitled to in England.

Your Memorialists are persuaded that the British Government is not disposed to adopt the political maxim so often acted upon by Asiatic princes, that the more a people are kept in darkness, their rulers will derive the greater advantages from them; since, by reference to history, it is found that this was but a short-sighted policy which did not ultimately answer the purpose of its authors. On the contrary, it rather proved disadvantageous to them; for we find that as often as an ignorant people, when an opportunity offered, have revolted against their rulers, all sorts of barbarous excesses and cruelties have been the consequence; whereas a people naturally disposed to peace and ease, when placed under a good Government from which they experience just and liberal treatment, must become the more attached to it, in proportion as they become enlightened and the great body of the people are taught to appreciate the value of the blessings they enjoy under its Rule.

Every good ruler, who is convinced of the imperfection of human nature, and reverences the eternal Governor of the world, must be conscious of the great liability to error in managing the affairs of a vast empire; and therefore he will be anxious to afford every individual the readiest means of bringing to his notice whatever may require his interference. To secure this important object, the unrestrained liberty of publication is the only effectual means that can be employed. And should it ever be abused, the established law of the land is very properly armed with efficient powers to punish those who may be found guilty of misrepresenting the conduct or character of Government, which are effectually guarded by the same laws to which individuals must look for protection of their reputation and good name.

Your Memorialists conclude by humbly entreating your Lordship to take this Memorial into your gracious consideration; and that you will be pleased by not registering the above rule and Ordinance, to permit the natives of this country to continue in possession of the civil rights and privileges which they and their fathers have so long enjoyed under the auspices of the British nation, whose kindness, and confidence, they are not aware of having done anything to forfeit.

(From *The Selected Works of Raja Rammohan Roy.* Publication, Division, Govt. of India, 1977. pp 94-97)

When the Govpernor General refused to heed the protest, Rammohan chose to appeal directly to the King of England. This second memorial, was more analytical in tone, outlining moral and political reasons why the freedom of the press had to be safeguarded.

Men in power hostile to the liberty of the Press, which is a disagreeable check upon their conduct, when unable to discover any real evil arising from its existence, have attempted to make the world imagine that it might, in some possible contingency, afford the menns of combination against the Government, but not to mention that extraordinary emergencies would warrant measures which in ordinary times are totally unjustifiable, your Majesty is well aware, that a free press has never yet caused a revolution in any part of the world because, while men can easily represent the grievances arising from the conduct of the local authorities to the supreme Government, and thus get them redressed, the grounds of discontent that excite revolution are removed; whereas, where no freedom of the press existed, and grievances consequently remained unrepresented and unredressed, innumerable revolutions have taken place in all parts of the globe, or if prevented by the armed force of the Government, the people continued ready for insurrection.

It is well known that despotic Governments naturally desire the suppression of any freedom of expression which might tend to expose their acts to the obloquy which ever attends the exercise of tyranny or oppression, and the argument they constantly resort to, is, that the spread of knowledge is dangerous to the existence of all legitimate authority, since, as a people become enlightened, they will discover that by a unity of effort, the many may easily shake off the yoke of the few, and thus become emancipated from the restraints of power altogether, forgetting the lesson derived from history, that in countries which have made the smallest advance in civilization, anarchy and revolution are most prevalent—while on the other hand, in nations the most enlightened, any revolt against governments which have guarded inviolate the rights of the governed, is most rare, and that the resistance of a people advanced in knowledge, has ever been—not against the existence—but against the abuses of the Governing power. Canada, during the late war with America, afforded a memorable instance of the truth of this argument. The enlightened inhabitants of that colony, finding that their rights and privileges had been secured to them, their complaints listened to, and their grievances redressed by the British Government, resisted every attempt of the United States to seduce them from their allegiance to it. In fact, it may be fearlessly averred, that the more enlightened a people become, the less likely are they to revolt against the governing power, as long as it is exercised with justice tempered with mercy, and the rights and privileges of the governed are held sacred from any invasion.

While therefore the existence of a free Press is equally necessary for the sake of the Governors and the governed, it is possible a national feeling may lead the British people to suppose, that in- two points, the peculiar situation of this country requires a modification of the laws enacted for the control of the Press in England. First, that for the sake of greater security and to preserve the union existing between England and this country, it might be necessary to enact a penalty to be inflicted on such persons as might endeavour to excite hatred in the minds of the Natives of India against the English nation. Secondly, that a penalty should be inflicted on such as might seditiously attempt to excite hostilities with neighbouring or friendly states. Although your Majesty's faithful subjects are not aware that anything has yet occurred to call for the precautions thus anticipated, yet should such or any other limitations of the liberty of the Press be deemed necessary, they are perfectly willing to submit to additional penalties to be legally inflicted. But they must humbly enter their protest .against the injustice of robbing them of their long standing privileges, by the introduction of numerous arbitrary restrictions, totally uncalled for by the circumstances of the country—and whatever may be their intention, calculated to suppress truth, protect abuses—and encourage oppression.

The publication of truth and the natural expression of men's sentiments through the medium of the Press, entail no burden on the State, and should it appear to your Majesty and the enlightened men placed about your throne, that this precious privilege which is so essential to the well-being of your faithful subjects, could not safely be entrusted to the natives of India, although they have given such unquestionable proofs of their loyalty and attachment, subject only to' the restraints wisely imposed upon the Press by the laws of England, your faithful subjects entreat on behalf of their countrymen, that your Majesty will be graciously pleased to grant it, subject to such severer restraints and heavier penalties as may be deemed necessary; but legal restraints, not those of arbitrary power—and penalties to be inflicted after trial and conviction according to the forms of the laws of England, not at the will and pleasure of one or two individuals without investigation or without hearing any defence or going through any of the forms prescribed by law, to ensure the equitable administration .of justice.

Notwithstanding the despotic .power of the Mogul princes who formerly ruled over this country, and that their conduct was often cruel and arbitrary, yet the wise and virtuous among them always employed two intelligencers at the residence of their Nawabs or Lord Lieutenants, *akhbar-navees*, or news-writer who published an account of whatever happened, and a *khoofea-navees*, or confidential correspondent who sent a private and particular account of every occurrence worthy of notice; and although these Lord Lieutenants were often particular friends or near relations to the Prince, he did not trust entirely to themselves for a faithful and impartial report of their administration, and degraded them when they appeared to deserve it, either for their own faults or for their negligence in not checking the delinquencies of their subordinate officers; which shows that even the Mogul Princes, although their form of Government admitted of nothing better, were convinced that in a country so rich and so replete with temptations, a restraint of some kind was absolutely necessary, to prevent the abuses that are so liable to flow from the possession of power.

The country still abounds in wealth, and its inhabitants are still addicted to the same corrupt means of compassing their ends, to which from having long lived under arbitrary Government, they have become naturally habituated; and if its present Rulers have brought with them purer principles from the land of their birth which may better withstand the influence of long residence amid the numerous temptations to which they are exposed; on the other hand, from the seat of the Supreme government being placed at an immense distance and the channel of communication entirely in their own hands, they are left more at liberty to follow their own interests, and looking forward to the quiet and secure enjoyment of their wealth in their native land, they may care little for the character they leave behind them in a remote country, among a people for whose opinion they have no regard. Your Majesty's faithful subjects, therefore, humbly presume, that the existence of a restraint of some kind, is absolutely necessary to preserve your faithful subjects from the abuses of uncontrolled power.

It might be urged on the other hand, that persons who feel aggrieved, may transmit representations to the Court of Directors of the East India Company, and thus obtain redress; but the natives of this country are generally ignorant of this mode of proceeding; and with neither friends in England nor knowledge of the country, they could entertain no hope of success, since they know that the transmission of their representations, depends in point of time, upon the pleasure of the local Government, which will probably, in order to counteract their influence, accompany them with observations, the nature of which would be totally unknown to the complainants, discouragements which in fact have operated as complete preventives, so that no instance of such a representation from the Natives of Bengal has ever been known.

In conclusion, your Majesty's faithful subjects humbly beseech your Majesty, first, to cause the Rule and Ordinance and Regulation before mentioned, which has been registered by the Judge of your Majesty's Court, to be rescinded; and prohibit any authority in this country from assuming the legislative power, or prerogatives of your Majesty and the High Council of the Realm, to narrow the privileges and destroy the rights of your Majesty's faithful subjects, who 'claim your protection, and are willing to submit to such laws, as your Majesty with the advice of your Council, shall be graciously pleased to enact.

Secondly, your Majesty's faithful subjects humbly pray, that your Majesty will be pleased to confirm to them the privilege they have so long enjoyed, of expressing their sentiments through the medium of the Press, subject to such legal restraints as may be thought necessary or that your Majesty will be graciously pleased to appoint a commission of intelligent and independent Gentlemen, to inquire into the real condition of the millions Providence has placed under your high protection.

Your Majesty's faithful subjects from the distance of almost half the globe, appeal to your Majesty's heart by the sympathy which forms a paternal tie between you and the lowest of your subjects, not to overlook their condition; they appeal to you by the honour of that great nation which under your Royal auspices has obtained the glorious title of Liberator of Europe, not to permit the possibility of millions of your subjects being wantonly trampled on and oppressed; they lastly appeal to you by the glory of your Crown on which the eyes of the world are fixed, not to consign the natives of India to perpetual oppression and degradation.

(From *The Selected Works of Raja Rammohan Roy.* Publication, Division, Govt. of India, 1977. pp 109-119)

Plea for Modern Education

Humbly reluctant as the natives of India are to obtrude upon the notice of Government the sentiments they entertain on any public measure, there are circumstances when silence would be carrying this respectful feeling to culpable excess. The present rulers of India, coming from a distance of many thousand miles to govern a people whose language, literature, manners, customs, and ideas are almost entirely new and strange to them, cannot easily become so intimately acquainted with their real circumstances, as the natives of the country are themselves. We should therefore be guilty of a gross dereliction of duty to ourselves, and afford our Rulers just ground of complaint at our apathy, did we omit on occasions of importance like the present to supply them with such accurate information as might enable them to devise and adopt measures calculated to be beneficial to the country, and thus second by our local knowledge and experience their declared benevolent intentions for its improvement. The establishment of a new. School in Calcutta evinces the laudable desire of Government to improve the natives of India by education. When this Seminary of learning was proposed, we understood that the Government in England had ordered a considerable sum of money to be annually devoted to the instruction of its Indian subjects. We were filled with sanguine hopes that this sum would be laid out in employing European gentlemen of talents and education to instruct the natives of India in Mathematics, Natural Philosophy, Chemistry, Anatomy and other usefuls sciences, which the nations of Europe have carried to a degree of perfection that has raised them above the inhabitants of other parts of the world.

While we looked forward with pleasing hope to the dawn of knowledge thus promised to the rising generation, our hearts were filled with mingled feelings of delight and gratitude; we already offered up thanks to Providence for inspiring the most generous and enlightened of the nations of the West with the glorious ambitions of planting in Asia the arts and sciences of modern Europe.

We now find that the Government are establishing a Sanskrit school under Hindu pundits to impart such knowledge as is already current in India. This seminary (similar in character to those which existed in Europe before the time of Lord Bacon) can only be expected to load the minds of youth with grammatical niceties and metaphysical distinctions of little or no practicable use to the possessors or to society. The pupils will there acquire what was known two thousand years ago, with the addition of vain and empty subtleties since produced by speculative men, such as is already commonly taught in all parts of India.

The Sanskrit language, so difficult that almost a life time is necessary for its perfect acquisition, is well known to have been for ages a lamentable check on the diffusion of knowledge; and the learning concealed under the almost impervious veil is far from sufficient to reward the labour of acquiring it. But if it were thought necessary to perpetuate this language for the sake of the portion of the valuable information it contains, this might be much more easily accomplished by other means than the establishment of a new Sanskrit College; for there have been always and are now numerous professors of Sanskrit in the different parts of the country, engaged in teaching this language as well as the other branches of literature which are to be the object of the new Seminary. Therefore their more diligent cultivation, if desirable, would be effectually promoted by holding out premiums and granting certain allowances to those most eminent professors who have already undertaken on their own account to teach them, and would by such rewards be stimulated to still greater exertions.

From these considerations, as the sum set apart for the instruction of the natives of India was intended by the Government in England for the improvement of its Indian subjects, I beg leave to state, with due deference to your Lordship's exalted situation, that if the plan now adopted be followed, it will completely defeat the object proposed; since no improvement can be expected from inducing young men to consume a dozen of years of the most valuable period of their lives in acquiring the niceties of the Vyakaran or Sanskrit grammar. For instance, in learning to discuss such points as the following: Khad signifying to eat, khaduty, he or she or it eats. Query, whether does the word khaduti taken as a whole, convey the "meaning he, she, or it eats, or are separate parts of this meaning conveyed by distinct portions of the word? As if in the English language it were asked, how much meaning is there in the eat, how much 'in the 5? And is the whole meaning of the word conveyed by those two portions of it distinctly, or by them taken jointly?

Neither can such improvement arise from such speculations as the following, which are the themes suggested by the Vedant:- in what manner is the soul absorbed into the deity? What relation does it bear to the divine essence? Nor will youths be fitted to be better members of society by the Vedantic doctrines, which teach them to believe that all visible things have no real existence; that as father, brother, etc., have no actual entity, they consequently deserve no real affection, and therefore the sooner we escape from them and leave the world the better. Again, no essential benefit can be derived by the student from knowing what it is that makes the killer of a goat sinless on pronouncing certain passages of the Vedas and what is the real nature and operative influence of passages of Veda, etc.

Again the student cannot be said to have improved his mind after he has learned into how many ideal classes the objects in the Universe are divided, and what speculative relation the soul bears to the body, the body to the soul, the eye to the ear, etc.

In order to enable your Lordship to appreciate the utility of encouraging such imaginary learning as above characterized, I beg your Lordship will be pleased to compare the state of science and literature in Europe before the time of Lord Bacon, with the progress of knowledge made since he wrote.

If it had been intended to keep the British nation in ignorance of real knowledge the Baconian philosophy would not have been allowed to displace the system of the schoolmen, which was the best calculated to perpetuate ignorance. In the same manner, the Sanskrit system of education would be best calculated to keep this country in darkness, if such had been the policy of the British Legislature. But as the improvement of the native population is the object of the Government, it will consequently promote a more liberal and enlightened system of instruction, embracing mathematics, natural philosophy, chemistry and anatomy, with other useful sciences which may be accomplished with the sum proposed by employing a few gentlemen of talents and learning educated in Europe, and providing a college furnished with the necessary books, instruments and other apparatus.

In representing this subject to your Lordship I conceive myself discharging a solemn duty which I owe to my countrymen and also to that enlightened Sovereign and Legislature which have extended their benevolent cares to this distant land, actuated by a desire to improve its inhabitants, and I therefore humbly trust you will excuse the liberty I have taken in thus expressing my sentiments to your Lordship.

(From *The Selected Works of Raja Rammohan Roy.* Publication, Division, Govt. of India, 1977. pp 300-303)

4

Jotirao Phule

Life and Times

Jotirao Phule (1827-1890) was born in 1827, less than a decade after the advent of the East India Company in his native Maharashtra. He belonged to the low caste of Malis, who had traditionally cultivated flamers fruits and vegetables. Phule's family had supplied flowers to the court of the Peshwas, these grown on a holding of thirty-five acres granted them by the rulers. They were thus not poor, but not really affluent either.

Jotirao studied in a school in the town of Poona (now called Pune), run by Scottish missionaries. Here he mixed with boys of other castes, including Untouchables. As a young man, he visited and was powerfully impressed by a school for girls run by American missionaries in the town of Ahmednagar. These experiences inspired him them still in his twenties to start a school for girls o low castes himself. He also opened several other schools, which admitted children from the Untouchable castes of Mangs and Mahars.

An autodidact, Phule seems to have been influenced by Thomas Paine as a young man. In 1855 he wrote a play about the inequities of the caste system. In view of the dominance of Brahmins over book production and publishing in western India, the play was published only after the playwringht's death. By now Phule was convinced that Western education, with its rationalist outlook, could play a key role in the emancipation of the low castes and the concomitant undermining of Brahmin power.

Although his teachers seem to have seen a potential convert, Phule resisted the pressure to become a Christian. As with Rammohan Roy, the encounter with missionaries helped him fashion a critique of orthodox Hunduism. Like Roy, again, he came to profess a deism which held that there was single Creator who provided the moral touchstone for society as a whole.

From the 1860s, Phule's interest shifted from managing his schools to wieder programmes of social reform, such as widow remarriage. Meanwhile, he was also active in business, selling hardware to factories in and around Poona. He was also successful as a contractor for road works and bridges. The money he made from these enterprises was ploughed back into his social activates.

By the 1870s, Phule was a figure of some influence and importance in Maharashtra. His profile was enhanced by a series of powerful tracts that he published, which spoke out against the stranglehold of Brahmins over the social, economic, political and spiritual life of western India. These were sometimes written in the from of a dialogue between the reformer and one of his adversaries. Through a wily and unscrupulous operator who acted always to exploit and suppress the peasant and the labourer. Likewise, in a reinterpretation of the career of the warrior-king Shivaji, he represented the warrior as relying, in his campaigns and for his victories, on his peasant armies rather than as the conventional historiography had it on his Brahmin ministers and advisers.

In 1873 Phule helped found the *Satyashodak Samaj*, the Society of Truth-Seekers. To qualify as a member, an individual had to get fifty letters of support and nomination. Some of the rules of the society were typical of reformers of the time—the vow not to consume alcohol, for example. Others were daringly precocious, such as the obligation to spread education among women and low castes. The samaj also promoted marriages that would take place without the involvement of Brahmin priests.

Phule's status and achievements were recognized by his nomination to the Municipal Council of Poona in 1876. He, in turn, looked with favour upon the British Raj, which held the balance of power between the different communities, and which—so he thought— could be persuaded to recognize that it was not the Brahmins but the more numerous cultivating castes who were the real representatives of Indian society and the real carriers of its history.

Under Phule's direction, the *Satyashodak Samaj* lobbied the government to promote policies that would benefit the fanners and labourers who came under the caste category of 'Shudras'. As the sarnaj's first published report put it, the organization was founded 'in order to free the Shudra people from slavery to Brahmins, Bhats, Joshis, priests and others. For thousands of years, these people have heedlessly despised and exploited the Shudras, with the aid of their cunningly-devised books. This action was taken, therefore, so that through good advice and the spread of education, the Shudras might be got to understand their real rights, and freed both in religious and more general matters from the false and self-interested books of the Brahmins'. The British, believed Phule, had a historic mission 'to liberate the disabled Shudras from the slavery of the crafty Aryas [i.e., upper castes]'.

Jotirao Phule was a remarkable social activist as well as a gifted writer. By the time of his death in 1890, he had published polemics, plays, songs and ballads. In 1883 Phule wrote *Shetkaryacha Asud* (The Cultivator's Whipcord), a powerful and still resonant description of the plight and poverty of the majority of Indians who were agriculturists. This is a continuous saga of woe, the stream of consciousness style and the lack of paragraphs heightening the intensity and impact. I present three excerpts from a recent translation of the book.

Phule as liberal thinker did not belong to the Ranade school or a believe in Ranade's frame work. The strategy of the capitalist path of development and the high caste plitics of the Ranade school could not appeal to him. He opposed the elitism of the Ranade school and put forward and alternative liberal framework for the liberation of the sudras and atisudras, the low and downtrodden castes.

In his philosophical outlook, Phule was influenced by the revolutionary liberalism of Thomas Paine. Phule's book *Sarvajanik Satyadharma Pustak,* restated the libral principles contained in Paine's *Rights of Man.* Phule stated that all men and women are born free and equally capable of enjoying rights. The creator has made men and omen possessed of equal human rights and no man or group of man could suppress other men. The creator has bestowed upon all men and women equal religious and political liberties. They should, therefore, have equality before law and equality of opportunity for entry into the civil service or municipal administration.

When Phule looked at the position of the sudras and atisudras in the light of these principles of liberalism, he found that these social groups were slaves for generations. They were deprived of human liberty. This slavery was sustained by Brahminical rules. The Brahmins, according to Phule, cunningly devised mythologies, established an intolerable caste system and formulated cruel and inhuman laws. He exposed the falsehood and selfish motives behind of Hindu mythology and the cunningness of the codes of conduct propagated by the Brahmins in their own interest. For centuries the masses were kept in chains. The sudras and atisudras, according to Phule, experienced greater hardships and oppression than the slaves in America.

Phule observed that what little improvement had occurred in the contemporary position of the masses was due of British rule. While Ranade wanted larger state support to higher education, Phule blamed the British government for diverting large funds to higher education at the cost of the education of the masses. Phule argued that it was an injustice to neglect the education of the masses as a greater portion of, the revenue came from the peasantry. He wanted to restructure and reorganise the whole educational system for the upliftment of the masses. He realized that, due to their education, the Brahmins were able to monopolise the administration from the top to the bottom. He forcefully argued that the Brahmins should be appointed in government services in proportion of their number and that due share should be given to the other castes. The sudras should be given education to qualify themselves for positions in government.

Phule criticized the various organizations established by the liberals of the Ranade school. The Prarthana Samaj, he said was used by the Brahmins to confuse the sudras and atisudras. He pointed out that though the Sarvajanik Sabha was claimed to be a public organisation, it was, in fact, monopolized by the Brahmins; he did not find in it any Kunbi, Mali, Dhangar, Koli or Bhil. The Sabha's demand for more seats for the Hindu was misleading because only Brahmins reaped the advantage. The same was true of the Indian National Congress. He hoped that no sudra would join the Congress because the Brahmins would deceive the sudras at any moment. He exhorted the lower castes to acquire education and political unity.

While Ranade was proud of the Hindu tradition, Phule wanted to break with it. He criticized Hindu religion, its mythology and sacred books like the *Smritis* and the *Vedas*. He maintained that the history of Hinduism was the history of Brahmin hegemony over the sudras. The Protestant Hindu saints, whose role Ranade had eulogized, were also criticized by Phule for their limited pro-Brahmin vision. He wanted to substitute Hinduism with 'Sarvajanik Ishwar Pranit Satya'.

British rule, Phule believed, was meant by the Creator to rescue the sudras from slavery. Owing to English education, true knowledge was being imparted to the ignorant sudras and thereby they were becoming conscious of their rights and had begun to think of complete freedom from the cruel system of savery. Phule wanted the sudras to exploit the golden opportunity given by British rule to get themselves emancipated from Brahmin domination.

Phule's views on the economy were also different from the Ranade. The former's views were guided by concerns for the peasants and the masses. He thought that they were being exploited by the Brahmin elite and feudal ruler. He concentrated on the problems of agriculture while the elitist liberals and favoured industrialization. In this way, Phule's liberalism was radical, that of the Ranades school was moderated and elitist.

The Condition of the Peasantry

One day a farmer was walking towards his village from the Collector's tent in the breezy mangrove beside the river, striding in anger and grinding his teeth. He seemed about forty and a little demoralised. He had a white twisted turban on his head, which was tied down with a cloth, he was wearing a double half-shirt made of khadi and old curled Satara boots. The boot heels were strong and thick, but he was walking a little oddly because they had developed cracks in a few places. He had a beard and moustache, which were hiding his front teeth.

The face was a little rounded though. After reaching home around two in die afternoon, he went to the kitchen and taking a sheet off the peg, he spread it on the ground and with a rolled up blanket under his head, lay down to sleep, covering his face with a handkerchief. But he could not sleep, thinking of his meeting with the Collector—'He was still busy with his breakfast and tea, and he did n allow me to putting his h, to himself thus.

'Unlike other villagers, I have not warmed the hands of the *bhat* [upper-caste] servants and so they have spoken to the white officer and doubled my tax, and in the same year the rain was indifferent and my fields and gardens were burnt out, and them suddenly Father died. There were a lot of expenses for the rituals. So in the first year, I assured the garden-plot to the Brahman moneylender, registered it in his name as well, for the money to pay the taxes with. Later he calculated the interest, doubling and tripling it, and took over may garden-plot. The moneylender's uncle is a clerk in the revenue office, his cousin is the Collector's secretary, his brother-in-law is the munsif and his father-in-law the taluk's police officer, and moreover, most of the people in the government offices are his caste relations so if I had argued with him, they would have troubled me no end and reduced me to a dry summer, on the smallest excuses. Thus in the second year, I sold off the few ornaments women of my house had on their bodies and put all that money into paying the taxes and later borrowed money every year from Gujarati and Marwadi moneylenders to pay for that. Now the have filed suits against me, which have been lying in the court for so many years. I have paid so much in bribes to the court officers, peons, scribes, lawyers and all, that I am at the end of my tether. Now sometimes one finds government servants who do not take bribes, but they are even more useless than those who do, because they are nonchalant and do not care about the p-oor farmer at all, and the clever lawyers take money from us, in the name of these servants and put the bite on us regularly.

And if we do not do that then we have to accept the orders secured by the moneylenders. Now no moneylender lets me stand at his door! I paid off the tax installments last year with my newly-married elder daughter's ornaments and now her father-in-law does not let her live in his house. Oh, how unfortunate I am that I sold off her ornaments to avoid a calamity and ruined her marriage in the process! And now, how do I pay this year's tax? There is no money to buy new *mot* the old ones are torn and the sugarcane is drying up. The corn has also gone to waste. The cattle-feed is about to finish, as is all the dried grass and fodder. The bullocks are weak because they do not get enough to eat. The women's clothes are in tatters and they are forced to wear ancient bedsheets bought for marriage. The children have to go about half-naked and feel ashamed of meeting people. Because the grain in the house is nearly over, we are surviving on sweet radishes. I do not have enough money to feed our mother with good food as she prepares to die. What shall I do? How will I be able to till the land if I sell the bullock? I cannot think of starting a business because I cannot read or write at all. If I leave my province and go to alien places, I have no skill which will help me fill my belly. If I swallow a potion made of roots, the able children might be able to survive somehow, but who will look after the old woman and along with my little ones, look after my wife? At whose doors can they knock if they need help? Where will they beg?' Thus finally sighing, he fell asleep weeping. Later when I come out, wiping my tears and look around, I see that his house is single-storeyed and tile-roofed. Beside the house, there is a covered shed for cattle. There are two or three bullocks, old and ruminating and a few large empty containers are pushed into a corner and outside, in the courtyard, there stands an old cart for eight bullocks. On it, there is a broken basket. On the left, a square platform is made and beside it, there is place for storing water and on t lat there are a few clay pots filled with water and beside it, there is a crudely tiled bathing place, with a half-wall on three sides. Outside it, water has collected in a small ditch and it is filled with insects and worms. Beyond, under the white *chafa* tree, there ate a few children dancing, half-naked, with all manner of stains on their bodies, noses running, sweating and stinking, playing with lumps of mud.

One of them is playing at being a shopkeeper, with anklets of seeds on her feet, pretending to sell arrack [country liquor]. Many of the children giving her pebbles and seeds is coins are shuffling about, falling on each other, pretending to be drunk. Behind the house stands a cattle shed made with wooden beams and pillars. In it lies a buffalo who has just calved and a wretched mare. There are all manner of insects sticking to the walls. (11 the cracks of the roof knots of hair are stuck all over, collected from the head while combing. Beside this, is a chicken-run. There is a waste-heap beyond and large green flies are buzzing over it because little children have been shitting there. Beside that, because the heaps of grass and fodder are finished, lie small heaps of leaves. In the other corner cow-pats are stacked, beside it, under the tree, there are broken implements lying about and a *vilayati dhattura* grows under them, and a mangy bitch who's just littered lies there, growling at passers-by. Beside it lies a heap of waste fodder, and in the remaining area sits a youngish woman, with her back to the house, arranging cow-pats. She is upto her knees in the dung, pounding it with her feet. In the kitchen itself there is uneven flooring and one sees the waste from grinding and cleaning and cleaned vegetables lying about here and there. Here is a heap of pith thrown about, and there a heap of rotting onions. A stale stink rises from them. In the middle, and ancient women is lying on a sheet, groaning. Beside her head lies a plate of food – a bowl of crushed *bhakri* softened in the liquid of the dal, and [a] jug of water. In the cradle a little baby is weeping loudly. Besides all this, at places one finds a line of a child's piss, at some other place a patch of white ash where a child's turd has been cleaned up. Several corners of the house are red and dark from tobacco spit. In one corner sits a large grinder, to be drawn by three or four women, in another there is a large mortar and pestle and in the corner near the door under the broom, all the dirt pushed there after sweeping the floor, and on top, a rag which was used to clean a baby's arise. There beside the cooking fire stands a dirty frying pan and the milk pot. Beside it, the cat has covered up its shit with ash. The walls are covered with stains left from squishing bugs and insects on them, and fingers wiping off snot. In a small cabinet is the oil pot, tooth powder, a horn comb, a rickety mirror, and on a ledge three or four stone lamps are stacked for the night. An oil stain spreads from them onto the ground.

Maybe once in a year all the grease is scraped away. In another cabinet beside the flour basket are placed pieces of stale *bhakri,* in a third cabinet there are green chilies, garlic, coriander, and baskets of mangoes, on which flies eat from one side and excrete from the other. And in the fourth stands a heap of old and torn footwear. A Flintstone lies beside them. Old and worn bed sheets hang from one peg, and on another, bedcovers. If you look up you can see that the tiles of the roof have not been changed for three or four years, and with grass ropes rats have made holes in it. There are no windows or ventilators of any kind anywhere in the whole house to let in fresh air. The beams and corners and supports and pillars are tarred with black smoke, and in most empty spaces spiders have [woven] most artistic and delicate webs, like mosquito nets, on which a thousand baby spiders are playing. On the under gird of the roof, on the beams, on pillars the poisonous shells of insects and spiders are sticking, and especially on wooden spaces there are heaps of dust mixed with rat shit and cockroach shit and for years a broom has not touched them for lack of time. Suddenly, the kind of dust storm which rises because of the heat before the summer rains, swept through the house, and as the dust rose and filled the house with the wind streaming in through the gaps in the roof tiles, the poisonous dust filled the snoring farmer's open mouth, and he woke up coughing. The poisonous cough so troubled him that he nearly fainted and he started moaning and thrashing about. His sick old mother somehow managed to stumble upto him, and putting a blanket roll under his head, cupping his chin, staring into his eyes, said, 'Oh lord! Please open your eyes. So many times have I given money to [God] so that [the Devil] should not harm you, and that too sometimes without your knowledge, selling off grain, and have made the Brahman sit with his rosary in front of [the deity] and fed so many Brahman women! Dear child, so many times have I spent money without telling you so that the gods will be pleased with you. Why did not that god speak through the Collector's mouth today, and allow you to pay the taxes in installments? O you cunning brahmans, from the very birth of my dear child you have threatened me with ill-favored stars and taken money from me, where is all the virtue that you collected? O, you have cheated me so much in the name of *dharma* that with that money I could have saved my child's neck!

Now let us turn to the present condition of the farmer. Since our generous and kind government began to rule in this brahmanic nation, they have started killing bullocks and cows and calves, without any proper ritual, and have started eating them . . . One of the important resources of the farmer is diminishing. On top of that, because of the lack of rain there was a drought, and the cattle were destroyed by lack of fodder. Secondly, because of the rules of the Forest Department and the inadequacy of pastures, the cattle could not be fed, their off-spring became weak and cattle was seized by diseases, and thousands died, and the farmers had to uproot their pegs. Next, because there was not enough cattle to labour on their farms, the fanner could not take proper care of his fields, and the yield has decreased. Moreover, our cunning government, through its brahman employees, has carried out surveys every thirty years and have established levies and taxes as they willed, and the farmer, losing his courage, has not properly tilled his lands, and therefore millions of farmers have not been able to feed themselves or cover themselves. As the farmers weakened further because of this, they started dying by the thousands in epidemics. There was drought to add to the misery, and thousands of farmers died of starvation, but in spite of all this, their numbers did increase, and that led to the tilling of the same lands in increasing proportion, and the lands could not be rested. So the yield of the lands decreased. Moreover, every year vast amounts of grain, cotton, leather, wool were being exported to alien countries, and because of the inadequate information or because of their own rough nature itself, the white engineers and doctors and employees wasted large amounts of manure into the sea, and now most of the lands are close to being fallow. O, these foreign white engineers, in cahoots with white doctors devise schemes to make money, and sell the goods manufactured by craftsmen from their own countries, waste unlimited amounts of local people's money, and then make sure that there are buildings named after them.

Later if all the local citizens are ruined along with these buildings, why should they care? Having made money and acquired fame, they are done. Sometimes it does not rain one year and there is not enough crop. Sometimes because there are not enough bullocks, the crop suffers. Sometimes because the moneylender does not lend money in time to buy fresh seeds or sometimes because the farmer uses seeds bought last year, the crop suffers. If for these heavenly or earthly reasons, the farmer does not get a sufficient yield, and goes alone to the brahman employee's house to tell him of his condition and of his crops, he finds the brahman, newly bathed, sitting with stripes of holy ash on his body, enveloped in incense-smoke, engrossed in worship, some other [brahman] sitting with an old and dirty book, reading it, and someone else counting the beads, while thinking of women. Hearing his footsteps, without opening his eyes the brahman asks, 'Who is it?' Farmer: 'My lord it's me, a farmer.' Brahman: 'Why have you come at this holy hour? If you have brought vegetables and stuff, hand it in inside, without touching the children. Come to the office in the afternoon and make an application in your name, then I will talk to the officer myself Now go.' Then the farmer turns and walks straight to the Collector's tent in the mangrove, and saluting the butlers, the jamadar [sergeant] and the sepoy, and standing at a distance from the tent-door, what he sees is that some white officer dressed in a Mughal manner, with a velvet carpet under his feet, bathed in lavender perfume, is busy eating, some other is lying face down on a couch and is busy reading rosy descriptions in a book and is therefore disinterested, so the sepoys rudely turn the fanner back and he cannot even tell his woes and plaints to the white officers. Therefore there is not any manner in which the farmer can convey his condition to the white officers, who are inured in their customary luxury, status, attendants; or to black officers who are engrossed in their wealth, their higher caste and colour, and their rituals of purity (neither is there any interaction between the women and children of white and black officers and the ignorant women and children of the farmers' houses to establish a communication). Both these officers are so completely different from the farmer, and such alien people will survey the farmer's lands, and give him relief? Or how else? Let that be.

But when the ignorant farmer borrows money to pay the taxes, these brahmans dress up as bhats [priests] and blocking his path, give him all manner of blessings and surely extract some money from him. If there is timely rainfall, and the farmer gets a reasonable crop, since the cowardly employees of our brave government have disallowed use of firearms and other weapons to the farmer, he cannot protect his crop from wild boar and pigs. Of the remaining crop, the Brahman, the Marwadi moneylenders, Gujarati traders and brokers from other castes keep an eye on the crop and grab whatever they can of it. Not only this, but even the Gujarati Brahman cooks in traders' households have started claiming some amount of jaggery. Let that be. Eventually when the farmer returns from the market and enters the town gate, a few hoodlums and the patil [headman] demand to be given drink and if he does not, then we can be sure that after a few days, he will receive a summons of some kind or other. What a just kingdom this is, wealthy in knowledge! But in this just kingdom, there was a time when it was possible to travel from the southern most point to the northern most, carrying gold, without being challenged. But at present, the goddess of wealth cannot find food and clothes in the houses of the fanner, deprived of education and clothes, and has therefore gone away to her father, the ocean, and beyond the seas, the English people have shed laziness, following her wishes, and have become industrious and hard working, and have started treating all women young and old with equality, so she has not become a domestic servant in their houses. And now even though they speak sweetly to all the farmers, and collect money as they will, they avoid educating the farmer. The main reason behind this must be that they realize that the moment the farmer educates himself and acquires knowledge, he will carry his whip on his shoulder, and he will bring the goddess of wealth back to his own home, and make her stay there happily. Because if this ever happens, the English will have to scream and yell, and travel to America, and somehow manage to fill their bellies by working hard day and night.

Now I will go to the cool mountains of [the imperial summer capital] Simla, and resting there for some time I will call upon our government beyond the seas, and in the presence of our supremely kind Governor, suggest measures for improving the farmers' condition: Now our good and law-abiding government should keep aside the greed of money and appoint detective doctors to keep an eye on the farmer's behaviour, and if the fanner misbehaves and loses his health, or begins to steal and do other sinful things, then arrangements must be made for proper punishment, without that they will not become moral. Unless laws are passed forbidding the farmer from marrying more than one woman and forbidding him from marrying his children at an early age, their off-spring will not turn out strong. Because the white employees are ill informed there is a disproportionate number of *bhat* brahmins appointed, and therefore they do not have to slave in the farms, and their women do not have to fill their bellies by frequenting the market with produce.

Moreover, because the farmer is ignorant, the *bhat* brahmins benefit immensely from caste distinctions and hierarchies. Thus the brahmins, employed in government jobs, and the mythologists, storytellers, teachers in schools strive day and night, using all their cunning, to prevent the breakdown of these distinctions and hierarchies. Therefore until the farmers' children become able enough to manage positions in government, not more than the proportionate number of brahmins should be employed in government jobs, and the remaining posts should be given to Mussalman or [non-brahmin] Hindu or Britons. It is only then that they [the brahmins] will stop obstructing the education of the farmer. This their artifice, has become invisible to white eyes because in most government departments, it is the brahmans who are employed. Thus the Brahmin caste becomes more and more educated, and wealthy whereas the farmer becomes poorer and eventually pauperized, and sometimes takes part in the brahman's rebellions and loses his life. Moreover the brahmans have so impressed their cunning religion on the minds of the farmers that they think it virtuous to plead guilty for murders that they have committed on the say of the brahmans. This wastes the energies and labour of the police and the Justice Department. Therefore in order to educate the farmers' children, there should be teachers from their own castes, who can hold the plough properly, weed the farm and do other things as well.

A law should be made which will ensure that children are sent to the schools run by such teachers, and for the first few years, some lower and easier divisions should be created, enticing them with degrees equal to those of brahmins, and unless other castes are prevented from forcing the farmer to perform rituals in their marriages, the farmers' children will not be interested in education. And when there are such educated and qualified patils [headmen] in all villages, the cunning *bhat* kulkarnis [Brahmin accountants] will not be able to make the farmers fight amongst themselves and file cases against each other, and that will benefit our government immensely, since in a short time the farmer will be able to pay more tax than now, and the unjustifiable swellings in the police and justice departments can then be reduced. Also, the government should for a time believe that there are no *bhat* brahmans to be employed, and as capable people come up from amongst the farmers, they should be employed in other government offices in big and small positions, and trained to do these jobs. Until this happens, the farmers' feet will not find the ground, and the government's revenue will never increase.

Let that be. Now I will suggest measures for improving the lands of the farmer. The benevolent government should educate all the fanners, and until they become mature enough to use machines to do the usual things on the farms like European farmers, all the white people and the Mussalmatis should slaughter goats and sheep instead of slaughtering cows and oxen; or they should import cattle and slaughter and eat them here, because otherwise there will not be sufficient supply of cattle for the farms, and there will not be enough compost and other fertilizer as well, and so neither the farmer, nor the government will benefit. The essences of leaf, grass, flower, dead insects and animals, is washed away by summer rain, therefore our industrious government should, as and when convenient, use the white and black soldiers and the extra manpower in the police department to construct small dams and bunds in such a way that this water would seep into the ground, and only later go and meet streams and rivers. This would make the land very fertile, and the soldiers in general, having got used to working in [the] open air, will also improve their health and become strong.

Even if they labour to the value of one anna every day, this will mean an increase in the government's earnings to the tune of twenty-five lakh [rupees] per year, because our careful government has, including the police department, at least two lakh sepoys. Similarly the government should, in all the hills and valleys, build lakes wherever possible, so that the small dams in the lower areas will fill with water, and the wells too will have a supply of water and the land for fruit and flower and vegetables will be used, and the government too will benefit along with the farmer. Therefore the government should maintain these bunds in good condition, especially in the backwaters. The government should conduct surveys of all the lands in its territory, employing water specialists, and wherever it is found that there is enough water to be drawn from more than one source, these places should be clearly marked in the maps of the towns, and the government should give some awards to farmers who dig wells without its assistance. Also, the government should allow the farmer to collect alt the silt arid other things extracted from rivers and lakes, as in the olden times, and it should also return all the cow pastures to the villages, which it has included in its 'forest'; it should, however, make sure that no firewood is collected, or land tilled in the areas that belong to it, and it should also forbid the cutting of wood for selling as wood for construction and destroy the oppressive Forest Department. Our own government should, spending money from its own coffers, purchase breeds of good sheep from several countries, bring them here, and when they are bred here, their droppings will make for a good supply of fertilizer and their wool will benefit the shudra farmer. If the government does not have the courage to allow the farmer to possess old guns in order to protect his farms from wild beasts, then the government should assign that job to our clean black police department, and if a farmer's crop is devastated by wild boar, then the loss should be made up from the salaries of the sensor officers or from the government's coffers—and until such a law us passed, the farmer will not be able to sleep peacefully at night and he will not be able to labour fully on his farm during the day.

If the government sincerely wishes to improve the condition of the ignorant shudra farmer, and increase its own yield, it should hold annual tests and competitions of greatest yield and greatest skill and give awards to the best farmers. Calculating the yield average every three years, the best farmers should be given titles, and if the educated children of the fanner, along with good maintenance of their own farms, also learn some iron-work and carpentry and give exams in those subjects, the government should take them abroad, for them to see the agricultural schools there, so that the farmer will immediately improve his farming and be happy. In general, the shudra and atishudra [Untouchable] farmer is slaving on his farms, along with women and children, day and night, until he is exhausted, and paying the various taxes, funds, etc., but our charitable government does not even think of educating the fanners' children enough to enable them to read a book on farming or relevant notices in newspapers, and while lakhs of farmers do not have enough cloth and enough food, our government spends inordinate amounts of money on the salaries and pensions of people in the army, the police, the justice departments, who are employed to protect and ensure the farmer's happiness and security. What should we say to this!!! Many of the black and white employees become too weak and blind to work for the government, and cheating even some very good European doctors, manage to get pensions, the white employees escape to England, and from amongst the black employees, many become suddenly young, as if Jesus Christ himself has roused them from the dead, and polishing their moustaches with wax and blacking, find employment in municipalities or in offices of big traders and earn thousands of rupees. Our watchful government should, without changing the salaries of any of the army carriage bearers, or construction workers, iron-workers, carpenters, the casual employee etc., slowly reduce all the inordinately increased salaries of all the black and white employees and slowly reduce the pensions as well. Unless the things written above are thought of, the foundations of the government will not be strengthened, and the farmers' fated penury will not change, and the days of his starvation will never end.

(From *Seleded Writings of Jotirao Phule* (ed) G.P. Deshpande, Leftworld Book, pp-157-163, 167-169, 179-182)

5

Swami Vivekananda

Life and Times

In the nineteenth century India was reborn in Ramakrishna (1836-1886), who was as aptly pointed out by Romain Rolland, 'the consummation of two thousand years of spiritual life of three hundred million people. Re-birth, in the case of a nation does not, however, necessarily mean repetition of the past only or revival of the old. It is also 'springing up anew'. The seed is a product of the past, but the sapling is a new one. And it is evident in the life of Vivekananda (1863-1902), the great disciple of Ramakrishna how India, five thousand years or more old, emerged anew in the nineteenth century. Actually in Vivekananda nineteenth century Indian Renaissance found its culmination. He represented the spirit of the time and his dynamic philosophy promised to fulfil the aspirations of the renascent nation as well as that of the humanity as a whole, promising a new era of radiant hope, peace, prosperity and progress.

In the nineteenth century when Vivekananda was born, everything in this country was in the melting pot. The British rule, over a century old at the time, was instrumental in bringing this ancient land into contact with the technologically and materially advanced West. The consequence was a serious cultural confusion. The conflict of ideologies was at its zenith-religion or science?

reason or faith? theism or atheism? polytheism or monism? secularism or spirituality? economic prosperity or asceticism? ancient or modern values? Which way to turn? Which one to choose? The vexed people hardly knew the answer. Exponents of each of these conflicting ideals put forward equally formidable arguments in favour of their own pet theories.

Inspite of the seeming chaos and confusion, a new spirit was lurking somewhere underneath. A new awakening was coming. A new awareness of national identity, of the greatness of the national ideals, was emerging. New currents of thought generated reform movements seeking to eradicate the social evils and superstitions which like a cancerous growth was eating up the vitality of the nation. The reformers were enamoured by the Western social pattern and hence they tried to recast our society after the Western mode. They considered the British rule in India a blessing. But all these moves could not put an end to the turmoil, it rather accentuated it since the protagonists of the status quo sought to idealise every social institution that was considered an evil and every prejudice that was sought to be eradicated. Similarly, the reformers committed errors in holding religion of the land responsible for all the social evils that prevailed at the time. And the reformists and the anti-reformists were equal in strength.

On the political front, struggles and strife was the order of the day. The native princes were overthrown one by one by the British and there was no peace and security for the masses. In the turmoil on the political front they were the worst sufferers. On the economic front, there were burning problems, these were the consequences of the colonial exploitative economic policies of the imperialistic rulers. Under the patronage of the rulers the competition from the technologically advanced West shocked the very foundation of the age-old economic system of this country based on flourishing urban handicrafts and isolated village communities. The results were devastating famines, decline of the handicrafts, mass movements of population from the rural to the urban areas leading to increased pressure of population on land and decline of agricultural productivity, accentuating in its turn spreading of poverty all over the land. Inspite of the efforts of some benevolent Christian missionaries and philanthropists to spread English education in this country, this was the time chosen by their other compatriots to buy the soul of India and impose Christianity on the land. India revolted under this pressure and there broke out mutiny, mass uprising, agrarian revolt and turmoils of every possible variety even in the remotest corner of the country. Thus India was caught in the currents and cross-currents of devastating tempests on every front—social, economic, political, cultural and religious. Obviously, this was one of the most critical periods in her long and chequered history.

Naren, as Vivekananda was called at the time, them a young boy only, was caught in the tempests of the day and felt involved in every burning question since he had a very sensitive mind and his heart bled to find a solution. Even as a boy in his teens Naren had a rare intellect, 'the fire of genius burnt in his eyes', and above all there was a born seeker of truth in him. He devoured Western philosophy, history, science, sociology and political economy and grew all the more restless since the answer he sought was not to be found therein. The Western intellectualism of the time which emerged after the European revolutions was bourgeois intellectualism, wedded to secularism and mechanistic and deterministic science. This hollow intellectualism failed to satisfy the deeper spiritual urges of young Naren. At last a chance meeting with Ramakrishna brought him face to face with what he had been seeking for—a bold, direct and a sensible assertion of the Ultimate truth.

Ramakrishna was apparently ignorant of the burning question of the day. He had hardly any formal education, being born in a poor Brahmin family, dependent on agriculture, in a distant village in the district of Hoogly in West Bengal, India. He was brought up in the traditional way in his rural home. But when he was engaged as a priest in the Kali temple of Dakshineswar near Calcutta, he had the opportunity to learn by listening to various Sanskrit scholars and spiritually enlightened persons, monks and nuns who used to visit the place for pilgrimage. For twelve long years Ramakrishna rigorously practised religion strictly according to the various schools of Hinduism and even according to Islam and

Christianity under the guidance of enlightened persons. But every time he had the same realisation of fathomless God. At last he was convinced that all the religions of the world were equally true and they all converged to the same goal. He had the direct perception of the Vedantic truth that every living being is Brahman, that 'Jiva is Shiva' as he expressed it.

And when Vivekananda received from his master the fiery message—'Jiva is Shiva' emerging from his Advaita realisation, 'that everything in this universe is Brahman,' he saw a new light. He had the genius to realise that this was a message which could revolutionise the world. Yet, he was a to see more, learn more, have more experiences of life, for realising the full significance of this fiery message for society.

He gathered these experiences after he had completed his spiritual training under Ramakrishna. He realised that 'God is in various forms in this world[1] and that 'loving service to mankind is the true worship of God'. After the passing away of his Master, he undertook mostly on the soles of his feet, journey through the length and breadth of this vast subcontinent. While covering miles after miles through the vast countryside, he mingled his life with those of the peasants in the field, the cobblers at their jobs, the artisans in their cottages, petty traders in the marts and markets, the tribals living in the forests and hills, and shared their oppressions, sufferings and miseries. In the course of his pilgrimage throughout India he stopped also at the newly growing industrial cities, where the new proletariat class was just emerging, and saw with his own eyes their inhuman conditions. He realised that the common people living on the fruits of their labour were exploited and persecuted by the upper class elites, the zamindars, the priests and the imperialist foreign rulers. He saw also how these common men and women were great in their simple life of labour with sparks of divinity in them. The problems and misery of these living men and women engulfed him and he carried 'a soul of fire' for the rest of his life. He stated often 'My aim is not Ramakrishna, nor Vedanta, but the masses'.

India was at this time passing through perhaps the worst crisis in her economic history—the period of those devastating famines which took place in one or other part of the country almost every year beginning from 1770, the year of the great Bengal famine when people died in millions, up on 1900, as a result of which not only millions and millions died out of starvation, but millions turned paupers. These famines were the direct result of the new land revenue arrangements and overall economic policy of the British which upset the established system of production and distribution leading to the decline of both agriculture and industries.

Vivekananda visited the native princes and tried to make them conscious of the appaling conditions of the poor masses and of the misrule of the foreigners. Very soon he was totally disillusioned of the upper class 'who was more dead than alive'. He gave up all hope of the upper class playing any vital role in the regeneration of India. He realised by this time that the landed aristocracy along with the priestly class were equally responsible with the foreign rulers for the ruthless exploitation of the masses, their degradation and their appalling poverty and ignorance. For two long years during his Indian itinerary he had no peace of mind. He literally cried in agony—'A country where millions of people live on flowers of Mahua plant and a million or so of Brahmins suck the blood out of these poor people, without even the least efforts for their amelioration is that a country or hell?'

This direct contact with the masses led him to realise also the inherent unity of the people of India in spite of their endless diversity. At last when his long itinerary ended at Kanyakumari in 1893, he had himself become the living embodiment of 'the conscience of India', its unity and destiny, and the world was to witness all this in him very soon. He was to attend the Parliament of Religions at Chicago in September 1893 at the behest of his own inward urge. He came to realise unconsciously that he had a mission for the West just as he had a mission for the East. He proclaimed it in Hyderabad publicly and when arrangements for his departure were being made he declared that he was going, 'on behalf of the people and the poor'.

On his way to the West he visited China and he saw with his own eyes how the masses in that great country with a glorious civilisation was crushing under the tyranny of feudalism and foreign imperialism and his heart bled for them. On his way eastward he paid a visit also to Japan, which was making headway in the path of economic prosperity and he wished India could also do the same.

When finally he arrived at Chicago to champion the cause of the oppressed people, the poor, in his unfortunate motherland, he had no idea that the West was also waiting for his arrival. The West was spiritually starved amidst its spectacular achievements in the field of science, technology and economic prosperity. He realised that if India needed science and technology for her economic development, the West needed spiritual sustenance for happiness and peace. Advancement of knowledge in the field of science had posed a serious challenge to the long cherished religious doctrines and dogmas resulting in the loss of faith in religion among the elites. This and other intriguing problems of a material civilisation, which had firmly established itself in the West demanded a solution. Taking up the challenge Vivekananda preached that 'Religion was not dogma or doctrines' but 'the realisation of spirit as spirit', that 'all the sciences were manifestation of religion' and that 'Art, Science and Religion are but the three different ways of expressing a single truth'.

He found also that if the East was groaning under the tyranny of the priests, the West was groaning under the tyranny of the Shylocks. He felt that the West was 'sitting on a volcano and the eruption could take place any moment'. He saw clearly that the political slogans—'Democracy', 'Rights', 'Liberty' and 'Equality'—were meaningless high sounding words, 'mere void full of poisonous gas'. And he showed how Vedanta could serve as the broad base for building up a lasting unity between varieties of peoples, races, cultures, religions and ideologies and that only it could make a communistic society lasting. He emphasized that 'the one essential attitude for all people was the affirmation of their substantive divinity, not a s a background philosophy or theory but as a living, immediately relevant fact'. This was exactly the message that was needed—the savants and the thinkers felt so.

Meanwhile, he did not forget the long suffering masses of India and his motherland. His fiery letters written from America to his Indian followers are full of his plans and directives for the regeneration of the country and her masses. Returning to India in 1897 he formulated a comprehensive programme of mass education, of economic regeneration for amelioration of poverty and a 'root and branch reform' of society. It was a plan for a revolution through social service.

He founded the Ramakrishna Mission on May 1, 1897 to carry on the two-fold mission of regenerating India and working for the harmony, peace and prosperity of mankind as a whole and for that matter he wanted spreading of the Vedantic ideas, illustrated in the life of Ramakrishna. The method of action of the newly formed body was to include also training men so as to make them competent to teach such knowledge of sciences that were conducive to the material and spiritual welfare of the masses. He wrote on July 9, 1897 'the movement is begun. It will never stop', and sometimes later 'only one idea was burning in my brain—to start the machine for elevating the Indian masses and that I have succeeded in doing it'.

Earlier on his return from the West, he traversed once again through out the length and breadth of India, from Kanyakumari to Kashmir, giving his a call of unity to the people. Vivekananda tried to bring unity of hundred sects of Hinduism, unity within the vast ocean of all religious thought and all rivers past and present, Western and Eastern. India rang with his voice and this call brought forth a new awakening in India based on its cultural distinctiveness inherited from the past and a new aspiration to vindicate its prestige as free nation. The nationalist spirit charged with dynamism was ushered in with full force to rock the citadel of foreign power. And thousands rushed to sacrifice their lives at the altar of the freedom of the motherland.

This was different type of national awakening that was ushered in by Vivekananda—different in character and import from the earlier awakening that was brought by Ram Mohan Roy. It is true that Ram Mohan Roy stopped the rot in the national life and its downhill rush towards degradation that characterised the period when he was born. It is also true that his advent marked the line of demarcation between the dark middle age and the modem era of 'enlightenment' by opting for English education and by adopting a rational-critical attitude in matters religious and social. But as it has been very importantly pointed out by Romain Rolland that Ram Mohan's Universal Religion' fell short of true universalism since he failed to recognise religious realities in the form of polytheism professed by world's two-third population scattered all over the world.

Again Ram Mohan's social reform measures never sought to touch the basic problems of our masses—poverty, ignorance and illiteracy. To be brief, Ram Mohan had no programme of mass education or mass uplift whatsoever. Although his great contribution towards abolishing the abhorrent 'Sati' rites would be remembered eternally by a grateful nation, it cannot be overlooked that he did not utter a single world against the exploitation of the masses by the landed aristocracy. Nor did he raise his voice against British imperialism. His arguments justifying European settlement in India so that our society could be remoulded after the Western pattern did never appeal to the nation. India having a rich heritage to be proud of a glorious past achievements in the fields both temporal and spiritual, refused to subscribe to the idea of foreign domination in their social life.

Romain holland, evaluating Ram Mohan's role in our national awakening rightly observes, "and herein lies the difference between the awakening of Ramakrishna-Vivekananda and of Ram Mohan and Brahmo Samaj—in these days India refuses allegiance to the imperious civilisation of the West, she defended her own ideas, she has stepped into her age-long heritage with the firm intention not to sacrifice any part of it." Thus it is clear that Ram Mohan's programme of reforms failed to fulfil the aspirations of the awakened nation. This new awakening was brought by Vivekananda who declared 'India had glorious past, but its future is to be still more glorious", and that 'India would be the central force in the incoming new era. The sociological studies of Sorokin and the historical investigations of Arnold Toynbee support this view to a large extent since they were convinced that the next era will the era of predominance of the East.

Vivekananda's second visit to the West completely disillusioned him of the glamourous materialistic prosperity of the West and its apparent democracy, as this time 'the brutal face of Imperialism of the West' was fully unveiled to him and he was 'full of rapatious hatred'. During his two visits to the West he mixed not only with the elites and the wealthy but also with the labourers, artisans and farmers and felt their pulse. He studied-carefully that labour-capital strifes that were mounting at the time in the West and just emerging in India. He noticed the emergence of the socialistic movements which he hailed but was aware of their deficiencies unmistakably. He met the social revolutionaries of the West and scrutinized their methods—the political .method and violent revolutions and all that, which found wanting as instruments of social welfare. And he had the courage and the genius to offer to the suffering world an alternative to the political .method, which he discovered in Indian history. His study of Indian history revealed to him that in India, politics was never an active age. of social change. All social changes in India came in the form of spiritual upheavals.

He saw also with his deep historical insight that the coming age \vas to be the 'Age of Man' when the toiling masses would come to attain supremacy in society. He discovered in Vedanta—more precisely in its doctrine of the 'divinity of man' received from his great master, Ramakrishna through his message 'Jiva is Shiva',—a philosophy of revolutionising society, for the redemption of the rights of the common mail. Vedanta was, however, remoulded by him to convert it into a revolutionary weapon for the vindication of the rights of man as man.

Vivekananda is generally known to-day as great religious leader. If we leave out Ramakrishna, his illustrious guru, he was undoubtedly the greatest figure in the field of religion and spirituality in the modern epoch. In truth, he was the only 'Man of God' in the experience of the modem West, to whom Christ was then merely a legendary figure. Marie Louise Burke observes in a revealing statement about him— 'Never before had the people of

America seen one in whom spiritual truths had been fully raslised'. Sister Nivedita, the celebrated Western disciple of Vivekananda, sounding the same note said—'In him I found the heir to the spiritual discoveries and religious struggles of innumerable teachers and saints in the past of India and the world. Ela Wheeler Wilcox, the famous American journalist and poet added in the same strain—'I believe him to be the incarnation of some great spirit—perhaps Buddha, perhaps Christ.'

From all these evidences it is clear that Vivekananda was one of the greatest religious leaders of all times like Buddha, like Christ. But this was not the entire truth about him. He was at the same time one of the greatest intellectuals and learned men of all times. How learned he was is evident from the following remarks of some outstanding personalities of different periods. Prof. John Henry Wright of Harvard University himself an outstanding scholar, observed—"This young man of thirty is more learned than all our professors put together". Reverend Dr. Mills said about him, "a man gigantic intellect indeed to whom the greatest of our professors made children." Speaking about Vivekananda's outstanding book Raja-yoga, Tolstoy, the Russian sarvant, remarked "so far humanity has frequently gone backwards from this true and lofty and clear concept of the principles of life and never surpassed it."

Vivekananda's vast knowledge was not confined to religious texts, scriptures and philosophies only. He had complete command over the natural and social sciences as well. At the end of the first volume of her outstanding work on Vivekananda. Mane Louise Burke observes—"He understood and studied the modem civilization with the combined insight of a sociologist, psychologist, historian philosopher and a mystic". Vivekananda had a good grasp of even a secular subject like economics, is evident from the fact that before he became famous at the Parliament of Religions he lectured at a meeting of the distinguished economists of the American Social Science Association on purely an economic topic. The fact is that he was not only interested in social science but was a master of it. He read August Comte, Herbert Spencer, James Mill, John Stuart Mill and a lot of other social scientists, while he was still a student. At the age of eighteen only he was in correspondence with Spencer in the course of which he is said have disputed one of Spencer's theories. It is further stated by his biographers that Spencer was mush impressed by the originality and rationality of young Naren's viewpoint.

The growing democratism and along with it the criticism of bourgeois relations combined with religious-moralist preaching were specially perceptibly seen in the views of Vivekananda. His personal destiny was unusual, but reflected in it were some characteristic features of India of that time. Narendranath Datta (such was the secular name of Swami Vivekananda) was born in the family of a highly educated and seemingly rich attorney of Calcutta. His father Viswanath Datta passed away, leaving behind only debts, when Narendranath was still studying in a college where he displayed extraordinary capabilities. The family was on the verge of poverty, and the young boy had to pass through days of semi-starvation. Still earlier, ideological quests associated, as was only usual in the India of that time, with questions of religion, had brought Datta to Ramakrishna whose cottage in a temple near Calcutta attracted some intelligentsia. Now he came still closer to Ramakrishna and later became a sort of his disciple and 'renounced the worldly life'.

In 1891 he went wondering all over India as a sannyasi, adopting the name of Vivekananda. During these wanderings of about two years, he suffered, 'the sharpest pain on seeing the monstrous poverty and suffering of the common people'. Apparently, it was then that he conceived his naive plan of turning to the rich countries of the West for material aid to India in exchange for her spiritual values. This led to his journey to the U.S.A which he undertook on modest means provided by an Indian prince. The immediate purpose of his journey was to take part in the World's Parliament of Religions at Chicago in 1893. In his speeches Vivekananda rebuffed the attacks of the missionaries on the beliefs of the Indians and showed that Indian religious-philosophical and ethical conceptions were not inferior to such types of systems existing in Europe and America. His brilliant speeches, imbued with humanist spirit and affirming national dignity of India, attracted attention in the West, and in India these were construed as a national success.

His stay in the U.S.A and Europe in 1893-1896 brought a turning point in many of his views, and on returning home he devoted himself to active preaching work. He set up a socio-religious body of its own type with the features of a religious fraternity—the Ramakrishna Mission, which, as per his ideas, was to carry out the work of enlightening the people. In 1899-1900 he once again visited the U.S.A. and Europe.

In the West Vivekananda was known mainly as a religious philosopher, a moralist-preacher, and yogi. But his interests were not confined simply to religious and philosophical problems, and his work was not merely to moralist preaching and popularization of yogic practices. He was associated with social and political problems of India herself, which concerned him as thinker and social leader. The social-political views of Vivekananda played an extremely important role in the development of Indian social thought and growth of national liberation movement and influenced not simply one generation of its participants, specially in Bengal. Vivekananda, with a greater awareness than Bankimchandra, rejected the notions of the British power being a blessing for India. He saw in colonial dominance not only the manifestation of national oppression in general but also a main obstacle in the material and cultural development of India, a cause for the monstrous poverty of the Indian masses.

Vivekananda also sensed most acutely the weight of political oppression by colonial powers, as also the need for fighting against it. He wrote: 'A few hundred of modernized and half-educated people who have lost their nationality,— this is all that modem British India can. boast of, and nothing more.... The monstrous hunger, involving millions of lives, has become an inevitable consequence of the British power India could feed five time more people than her present population if everything would not have been taken from the people right at the roots. . . . Lately the country is being dominated by terror. The British soldiers kill our men and use force on our women—for this they are sent back home on a pension which, like the passage money, is also paid to them at our expense. . .. 'Freedom is the first prerequisite of growth and development. . . . 'O India! will this shameless cowardice really give your freedom which can be worthy only of a hero! The demands of the poor will never be satisfied.'

The most important, progressive feature of socio-political views of Vivekananda was that he considered national liberation of India and democratic social emancipation of its masses as mutually related and the two fold goal. He regarded the education of the working people as the first step on the way to this goal, called upon the youth to go 'to the people' and try to work in this direction. Here are a number of Vivekananda's statements on the masses and on the need of awakening them: 'Our aristocratic ancestors went treading the common masses of our country under foot till they became helpless, till under this torment the poor people nearly forgot that they were human being's. He further says 'I consider that the great national sin is the neglect of the masses, and that is one of the causes of our downfall. No amount of politics would be of any avail until the masses in India are once more well educated well fed, and well cared for. They pay for our education, they build our temples, but in return they get kicks. They are practically our slaves. If we want to regenerate India, we must work for them. 'The most important thing which 1 wish once again to remind you about, is the need for practical work, and practical work consists above all in that you must go to the suffering millions of Indians and take them with you.' He urges upon the Indians 'Go to their huts, from door to door, at noon and in the evening, at any time, and open their eyes. Give them ideas, open their eyes to the world surrounding them, and then they will themselves bring about their salvation. Your task is to give the masses their rights, and let them defend these. The only hope of India is from the masses. The upper classes are physically and morally dead.' Although Vivekananda saw the 'only hope' of India in the common people, he considered the middle class the leading force of social movement, obviously having in mind mainly the intelligentsia. He contrasts this middle class to the rich. He asks 'Mention to me any country where the rich persons ever helped anyone. It is the middle classes in all countries who carry out great tasks. I expect nothing from the rich people of India.'

In his own way Vivekananda already realized the class character of the position of the propertied classes or, rather, of their top hierarchy, in the work of national liberation. While Bankimchandra still hoped that zamindars would also play some positive role in this, Vivekananda clearly had no such expectations. He regraded the national freedom itself not only impossible without political mobilization of the masses but also unthinkable without their social emancipation. He was upset, like also Bankimchandra, over political ineffectiveness of liberal leaders in the face of colonial power. He saw in their position a class interest hostile to the working masses. He wrote: 'Our young fools hold meetings to gain more power from the British. They only laugh. He who is not ready to give freedom to others is not worth of it. Suppose that the British hand over to you all power. What then? You will use it to hold the people at the low level. Then let this freedom be not there. They thirst for power in order to enslave.' The social views which, together with a criticism of colonial regime and feudalism, also contained a criticism of the bourgeois structure, started spreading in the progressive social circles of India back in the late nineteenth century. This aspect of development of Indian social thoughts of the new times has been studied very little, particularly because the emergence of anti-capitalist tendency had a purely secondary position and did not play any independent role.

The growing democratic movement of national liberation in India was objectively directed not against exploitation in general but against its two concrete historical forms—colonial and feudal exploitation and the respective political and social relations. It was primarily against the colonial power. The capitalist relations nonetheless had already started asserting themselves in the Indian society, revealing the contradictions inherent in it; and the British power and colonial exploitation were nothing but the origin of capitalist structure, though outside India. In the second half of the nineteenth century, some Indians were already familiar with the ideas of socialist movement developing in the West and this influenced their social views. Such conditions in the late nineteenth and early twentieth centuries, led a number of Indian thinkers and social leaders to make a definite criticism of the bourgeois society. This criticism was still subjective—'sentimental' and 'moralist', and resulted only in purely 'Utopian' social formulations. But, at the same time, it was directly associated with the development of national liberation and democratic tendencies, and expressed these tendencies in its own way and even contributed quite a great deal to their growth. In other words, the criticism of bourgeois society by progressive Indian thinkers and leaders of the Indian national liberation movement in the nineteenth and twentieth centuries was itself an auxiliary of its own kind to their essentially bourgeois-democratic programme of liquidation of colonial subjugation of the country and feudal oppression, which in the conditions of that time would indeed have meant not overcoming but instead developing fast and more broadly the bourgeois relations.

Hinduism

Sisters and Brothers of America,

It fills my heart with joy unspeakable to rise in response to the warm and cordial welcome which you have given us. I thank you in the name of the most ancient order of monks in the world; I thank you in the name of the mother of religions; and I thank you in the name of millions and millions of Hindus people of all classes and sects.

My thanks, also, to some of the speakers on this platform who, referring to the delegates from the Orient, have told you that these men from far-off nations may well claim the honour of bearing to different lands the idea of toleration. I am proud to belong to a religion which has taught the world both tolerance and universal acceptance. We believe not only in universal toleration, but we accept all religions as true. I am proud to belong to a nation which has sheltered the persecuted and the refugees of all religions and all nations of the earth. I am proud to tell you that we have gathered in our bosom the purest remnant of the Israelites, who came to Southern India and took refuge with us in the very year in which their holy temple was shattered to prices by Roman tyranny. I am proud to belong to the religion which has sheltered and is still fostering the remnant of the grand Zoroastrian nation. I will quote to you, breathren, a few lines from a hymn which I remember to have repeated from my earliest boyhood, which is every day repeated by millions of human beings: "As the different streams having their sources in different places all mingle their water in the sea, so, O Lord, the different paths which men take through different tendencies, various though they appear, crooked or straight, all lead to Thee."

The present convention, which is one of the most august assemblies ever held, is in itself a vindication, a declaration to the world of the wonderful doctrine preached in the Gita: "Whosoever comes to Me, through whatsoever form, I reach him; all men are struggling through paths which in the end lead to me." Sectarianism, bigotry, and its horrible descendant, fanaticism, have long possessed this beautiful earth. They have filled the earth with violence, drenched it often and often with human blood, destroyed civilization and sent whole nations to despair. Had it not been for these horrible demons, human society would be far more advanced than it is now? But their time is come; and I fervently hope that the bell that tolled this morning in honour of this convention may be the death-knell of all fanaticism, of all persecutions with the sword or with the pen, and of all uncharitable feelings between persons wending their way to the same goal.

I will tell you a little story. You have heard the eloquent speaker who has just finished say, "Let us cease from abusing each other," and he was very sorry that there should be always so much variance.

But I think I should tell you a story which would illustrate the cause of this variance. A frog lived in a well. It had lived there for a long time. It was born there and brought up there, and yet was a little, small frog. Of course the evolutionists were not there then to tell us whether the frog lost its eves or not, but, for our story's sake, we must take it for granted that it had its evyes, and that it every day cleansed the water of all the worms and bacilli that lived in it with an energy that would do credit to our modern bacteriologists. In this way it went on and became a little sleek and fat. Well, one day another frog that lived in the sea came and fell into the well.

"Where are you from?"

"I am from the sea."

"The sea! How big is that? It is as big as my well?" and he took a leap from one side of the well to the other.

"My friend," said the frog of the sea, "how do you compare the sea with your little well?"

Then the frog took another leap and asked, "Is your sea so big?"

Then the frog took another leap and asked, "Is your sea so big?"

"What nonsense you speak, to compare that sea with your well!"

"Well, then," said the frog of the well, "nothing can be bigger than my well; there can be nothing bigger than this; this fellow is a liar, so turn him out."

That has been the difficulty all the while.

I am a Hindu. I am sitting in my own little well and thinking that the whole world is my little well. The Christian sits in his little well and thinks the whole world is his well. The Mohammedan sits in his little well and thinks that is the whole world. I have to thank you of America for the great attempt you are making to break down the barriers of this little world of ours, and hope that, in the future, the Lord will help you to accomplish your purpose.

Three religions now stand in the world which have come down to us from time prehistoric – Hinduism, Zoroastrianism and Judaism. They have all received tremendous shocks and all of them prove by their survival their internal strength. But while Judaism failed to absorb Christianity and was driven out of its place of birth by its all-conquering daughter, and a handful of Parsees is all that remains to tell the tale of their grand religion, sect after sect arose in India and seemed to shake the religion of the Vedas to its very foundations, but like the waters of the seashore in a tremendous earthquake it receded only for a while, only to return in an all-absorbing flood, a thousand times more vigorous, and when the tumult of the rush was over, these sects were all sucked in, absorbed, and assimilated into the immense body of the mother faith.

From the high spiritual fights of the Vedanta philosophy, of which the latest discoveries of science seem like echoes, to the low ideas of idolatry with its multifarious mythology, the agnosticism of the Buddhists, and the atheism of the Jains, each and all have a place in the Hindu's religion.

Where then, the question arises, where is the common centre to which all these widely diverging radii converge? Where is the common basis upon which all these seemingly hopeless contradictions rest? And this is the question I shall attempt to answer.

The Hindus have received their religion through revelation, the Vedas. They hold that the Vedas are without beginning and without end. It may sound ludicrous to this audience, how a book can be without beginning or end. But by the Vedas no books are meant. They mean the accumulated treasury of spiritual laws discovered by different persons in different times. Just as the law of gravitation existed before its discovery, and would exist if all humanity forgot it, so is it with the laws that govern the spiritual world. The moral, ethical, and spiritual relations between soul and soul and between individual spirits and the Father of all spirits, were there before their discovery, and would remain even if we forgot them.

The discovers of these laws are called Rights, and we honour them as perfected beings. I am glad to tell this audience that some of the very greatest of them were women. Here it may be said that these laws as laws may be without end, but they must have had a beginning. The Vedas teach us that creation is without beginning or end. Science is said to have proved that the sum total of cosmic energy is always the same. Then, if there was time when nothing existed, where was all this manifested energy? Some say it was in a potential form in God. In that case God is sometimes potential and sometimes kinetic, which would make Him mutable. Everything mutable is a compound, and everything compound must undergo that change which is called destruction. So God would die, which is absurd. Therefore there never was a time when there was no creation.

If I may be allowed to use a simile, creation and creator are two lines, without beginning and without end, running parallel to each other. God is the ever active providence, by whose power systems after systems are being evolved out of chaos, made to run for a time and again destroyed. This is what the Brahmin boy repeats every day : "*The sun and the moon, the Lord created like the suns and moons of previous cycles.*" And this agrees with modern science.

Here I stand and if I shut my eyes, and try to conceive my existence, "I", "I", "I", what is the idea before me? The idea of a body. Am I, then, nothing but a combination of material substances? The Vedas declare, "No". I am a spirit living in a body. I am not the body. The body will die, but I shall not die. Here am I in this body; it will fall, but I shall go on living. I had also a past. The soul was not created, for creation means a combination which means a certain future dissolution. If then the soul was created, it must die. Some are born happy, enjoy perfect health, with beautiful body, mental vigour and all wants supplied. Others are born miserable, some are without hands or feet, others again are idiots and only drag on a wretched existence. Why, if they are all created, why does a just and merciful God create one happy and another unhappy, why is He so partial? Nor would it mend matters in the least to hold that those who are miserable in this life will be happy in a future one. Why should a man be miserable even here in the reign of a just and merciful God?

In the second place, the idea of a creator God does not explain the anomaly, but simply expresses the cruel fiat of an all-powerful being. There must have been causes, then, before his birth, to make a man miserable or happy and those were his past actions.

Are not all the tendencies of the mind and the body accounted for by inherited aptitude? Here are tow parallel lines of existence – one of the mind, the other of matter. If matter and its transformations answer for all that we have, there is no necessity for supposing the existence of a soul. But it cannot be proved that thought has been evolved out of matter and if a philosophical monism is inevitable, spiritual monism is certainly logical and no less desirable than a materialistic monism; but neither of these is necessary here.

We cannot deny that bodies acquire certain tendencies from heredity, but those tendencies only mean the physical configuration, through which a peculiar mind alone can act in a peculiar way. There are other tendencies peculiar to a soul caused by its past actions. And a soul with a certain tendency would by the laws of affinity take birth in a body which is the fittest instrument for the display of that tendency. This is in accord with science, for science wants to explain everything by habit, and habit is got through repetitions. So repetitions are necessary to explain the natural habits of a new-born soul. And since they were not obtained in this present life, they must have come down from past lives.

There is another suggestion. Taking all these for granted, how is it that I do not remember anything of my past life? This can be easily explained. I am now speaking English. It is not my mother tongue, in fact no wards of my mother tongue are now present in my consciousness; but let me try to bring them up, and they rush in. that shows that consciousness is only the surface of the mental ocean, and within its depths are stored up all our experiences. They and struggle, they would come up and you would be conscious even of your past life.

This is direct and demonstrative evidence. Verification is the perfect proof of a theory, and here is the challenge thrown to the would by the Rishis. We have discovered the secret by which the very depths of the ocean of memory can be stirred up – try it and you would get a complete reminiscence of your past life.

So then the Hindu believes that he is a spirit. Him the sword cannot pierce – him the fire cannot burn – him the water cannot melt – him the air cannot dry. The Hindu believes that every soul is a circle whose circumference is nowhere, but whose centre is located in the body, and that death means the change of this centre from body to body. Nor is the soul bound by the conditions of matter. In this very essence it is free, unbounded, holy, pure, and perfect. But somehow or other it finds itself tied down to matter, and thinks of itself as matter.

Why should the free, perfect, and pure being be thus under the thralldom of matter, is the next question. How can the perfect soul be deluded into the belief that it is imperfect? We have been told that the Hindus shirk the question and say that no such question can be there. Some thinkers want to answer it by positing one or more quasi-perfect beings, and use being scientific names to fill up the gap. But naming is not explaining. The question remains the same. How can the perfect become the quasi-perfect; how can the pure, the absolute, change even a microscopic particle of its nature? But the Hindus is sincere. He does not want to take shelter under sophistry. He is brave enough to face the question in a manly fashion; and his answer is: "I do not know. I do not know how the perfect being, the soul, came to think of itself as imperfect, as joined to and conditioned by matter." But the fact is a fact for all that. It is a fact in everybody's consciousness that one thinks of oneself as the body. The Hindus does not attempt to explain why one thinks one is the body. The answer that it is the will of God is no explanation. This is nothing more than what the Hindu says, "I do not know".

Well, then, the human soul is eternal and immortal, perfect and infinite, and death means only a change of centre from one body to another. The present is determined by our past actions, and the future by the present. The soul will go on evolving up or reverting back from birth to birth and death to death. But here is another question : Is man a tiny boat in a tempest, raised one moment on the foamy crest of a billow and dashed down into a yawning chasm the next, rolling to and fro at the mercy of good and bad actions – a powerless, helpless wreck in an ever-raging, every-rushing, uncompromising current of cause and effect; a little moth placed under the wheel of causation which rolls on crushing everything in its way and waits not for the widow's tears or the orphan's cry? The heart sinks at the idea, yet this is the law of Nature. Is there no hope? Is there no hope? Is there no escape? – was the cry that went up from the bottom of the heart of despair. It reached the throne of mercy, and words of hope and consolation came down and inspired a Vedic sage, and he stood up before the world and in trumpet voice proclaimed the glad tidings: "Hear, ye children of immortal bliss! Even ye that reside in higher spheres! I have found the Ancient

One who is beyond all darkness, all delusion: knowing Him alone you shall be saved from death over again." "Children of immortal bliss" - what a sweet, what a hopeful name! Allow me to call you brethren, by that sweet name – heirs of immortal bliss – yea, the Hindu refuses to call you sinners. Ye are the Children of God, the sharers of immortal bliss, holy and perfect beings. Ye divinities on earth – sinners! It is a sin to call a man so; it is a standing libel on human nature. Come up, O lions, and shake off the delusion that you are sheep; you are souls immortal, spirits free, blest and eternal; ye are not matter, ye are not bodies; matter is your servant, not you the servant of matter.

Thus it is that the Vedas proclaim not a dreadful combination of unforgiving laws, not an endless prison of cause and effect, but that at the head of all these laws, in and through every particle of matter and force, stands One "by whose command the wind blows, the fire burns, the clouds rain, and death stalks upon the earth."

And what is His nature?

He is everywhere, the pure and formless One, the Almighty and the All-merciful. "Thou art our father, Thou art our mother, Thou art our beloved friend, Thou art the source of all strength; give us strength. Thou art He that beareth the Lurdens of the universe; help me bear the little burden of this life." Thus sang the Rishis of the Vedas. And how to worship Him? Through love. "He is to be worshipped as the one beloved, dearer than everything in this and the next life."

This is the doctrine of love declared in the Vedas, and let us see how it is fully developed and taught by Krishna, whom the Hindus believe to have been God incarnate on earth.

He taught that a man ought to live in this world like a lotus leaf, which grows in water but is never moistened by water; so a man ought to live in the world – his heart to God and his hands to work.

It is good to love God for hope of reward in this or the next world, but it is better to love God for love's sake, and the prayer goes: "Lord, I do not want wealth, nor children, nor learning. If it be Thy will, I shall go from birth to birth, but grant me this, that I may love Thee without the hope of reward – love, unselfishly for love's sake." One of the disciples of Krishna, the then Emperor of India, was driven from his kingdom by his enemies and had to take shelter with his queen in a forest in the Himalayas, and there one day the queen asked him how it was that he, the most virtuous of men, should suffer so much misery. Yudhishthira answered, "Behold, my queen, the Himalayas, how grand and beautiful they are; I love them. They do not give me anything, but my nature is to love the grand, the beautiful, therefore I love them. Similarly, I love the Lord. He is the source of all beauty, of all sublimity. He is the only object to be loved; my nature is to love Him, and therefore I love. I do not pray for anything; I do not ask for anything. Let Him place me wherever He likes. I must love Him for love's sake. I cannot trade in love."

The Vedas teach that the soul is divine, only held in the bondage of matter; perfection will be reached when this bond will burst, and the word they use for it is therefore, Mukti – freedom, freedom from the bonds of imperfection, freedom death and misery.

And this bondage can only fall off through the mercy of God, and this mercy comes on the pure. So purity is the condition of His mercy. How does that mercy act? He reveals Himself to the pure heart; the pure and the stainless see God, yea, even in this life; then and then only all the crookedness of the heart is made straight. Then all doubt ceases. He is no more the freak of a terrible law of causation. This is the very centre, the very vital conception of Hinduism. The Hindu does not want to live upon words and theories. If there are existences beyond the ordinary sensuous existence, he wants to come face to face with them. If there is a soul in him which is not matter, if there is an all-merciful universal Soul, he will go to Him direct. He must see Him, and that alone can destroy all doubts. So the best proof a Hindu sage gives about the soul, about God, is : "I have seen the soul; I have seen God." And that is the only condition of perfection. The Hindu religion does not consist in struggles and attempts to believe a certain doctrine or dogma, but in realizing – not in believing, but in being and becoming.

Thus the whole object of their system is by constant struggle to become perfect, to become divine, to reach God and see God, and this reaching God, seeing God, becoming perfect even as the Father in Heaven is perfect, constitutes the religion of the Hindus.

And what becomes of a man when he attains perfection? He lives a life of bliss infinite. He enjoys infinite and perfect bliss, having obtained the only thing in which man ought to have pleasure, namely God, and enjoys the bliss with God.

So far all the Hindus are agreed. This is the common religion of all the sects of India; but, then, perfection is absolute, and the absolute cannot be two or three. It cannot have any qualities. It cannot be an individual. And so when a soul becomes perfect and absolute, it must become one with Brahman, and it would only realize the Lord as the perfection, the reality, of its own nature and existence, the existence absolute, knowledge absolute, and bliss absolute. We have often and often read this called the losing of individuality and becoming a stock or a stone.

"He jests at scars that never felt a wound."

I tell you it is nothing of the kind. If it is happiness to enjoy the consciousness of this small body, it must be greater happiness to enjoy the consciousness of two bodies, the measure of happiness increasing with the consciousness of an increasing number of bodies, the aim, the ultimate of happiness being reached when it would become a universal consciousness.

Therefore, to gain this infinite universal individuality, this miserable little prison-individuality must go. Then alone can death cease when I am one with life, then alone can misery cease when I am one with happiness itself, then alone can all errors cease when I am one with knowledge itself; and this is the necessary scientific conclusion. Science has proved to me that physical individuality is a delusion, that really my body is one little continuously changing body in an unbroken ocean of matter; and Advaita (unity) is the necessary conclusion with my other counterpart, soul.

Science is nothing but the finding of unity. As soon as science would reach perfect unity, it would stop from further progress, because it would reach the goal. Thus Chemistry could not progress farther when it would discover one element our of which all others could be made. Physics would stop when it would be able to fulfil its services in discovering one energy of which all the others are but manifestations, and the science of religion become perfect when it would discover Him who is the one life in a universe of death, Him who is the constant basis of an ever-changing world. One who is the only Soul of which all souls are but delusive manifestations. Thus is it, through multiplicity and duality, that the ultimate unity is reached. Religion can go no farther. This is the goal of all science.

All science is bound to come to this conclusion in the long run. Manifestation, and not creation, is the word of science today, and the Hindu is only glad that what he has been cherishing in his bosom for ages is going to be taught in more forcible language, and with further light from the latest conclusions of science.

Descend we now from the aspirations of philosophy to the religion of the ignorant. At the very outset, I may tell you that there is no *polytheism* in India. In every temple, if one stands by and listens, one will find the worshippers applying all the attributes of God, including omnipresence, to the images. It is not polytheism, nor would the name henotheism explain the situation. "The rose called by any other name would smell as sweet." Names are not explanations.

I remember, as a boy, hearing a Christian missionary preach to a crowd in India. Among other sweet thins he was telling them was that if he gave a blow to their idol with his stick, what could it do? One of his hearers sharply answered, "If I abuse your God, what can He do?" "You would be punished," said the preacher, "when you die." "So my idol will punish you when you die," retorted the Hindu.

The tree is known by its fruits. When I have seen amongst them that are called idolaters, men, the like of whom in morality and spirituality and love I have never seen anywhere, I stop and ask myself, "Can sin beget holiness?"

Superstition is a great enemy of man, but bigotry is worse. Why does a Christian go to church? Why is the cross holy? Why is the face turned toward the sky in prayer? Why are there so many images in the Catholic Church? Why are there so many images in the minds of Protestants when they pray? My brethren, we can no more think about anything without a mental image than we can live without breathing. By the law of association, the material image calls up the mental idea and *vice versa.* This is why the Hindu uses an external symbol when he worships. He will tell you, it helps to keep his mind fixed on the Being to whom he prays. He knows as well as you do that the image is not God, is not omnipresent. After all, how much does omnipresence mean to almost the whole world? It stands merely as a word, a symbol. Has God superficial area? If not, when we repeat that word "omnipresent", we think of the extended sky or of space, that is all.

As we find that somehow or other, by the laws of our mental constitution, we have to associate our ideas of infinity with the image of the blue sky, or of the sea, so we naturally connect our idea of holiness with the image of a church, a mosque, or a cross. The Hindus have associated the idea of holiness, purity, truth, omnipresence, and such other ideas with different images and forms. But with this difference that while some people devote their whole lives to their idol of a church and never rise higher, because with them religion means an intellectual assent to certain doctrines and doing good to their fellows, the whole religion of the Hindu is centred in realization. Man is to become divine by realizing the divine. Idols or temples or churches or books are only the supports, the helps, of his spiritual childhood: but on and on he must progress.

He must not stop anywhere. "External worship, material worship," say the scriptures, "is the lowest stage; struggling to rise high, mental prayer is the next stage, but the highest stage is when the Lord has been realized." Mark, the same earnest man who is kneeling before the idol tells you, "Him the sun cannot express, nor the moon, nor the stars, the lightning cannot express Him, nor what we speak of as fire; through Him they shine." But he does not abuse any one's idol or call its worship sin. He recognizes in it a necessary stage of life. *"The child is father of the man."* Would it be right for an old man to say that childhood is a sin or youth a sin?

If a man can realize his divine nature with the help of an image, would it be right to call that a sin? Nor even when he has passed that stage, should be call it an error. To the Hindu, man is not traveling from error to truth, but from truth to truth, from lower to higher truth. To him all the religions, from the lowest fetishism to the highest absolution, mean so many attempts of the human soul to grasp and realize the Infinite, each determined by the conditions of its birth and association, and each of these marks a stage of progress; and every soul is a young eagle soaring higher and higher, gathering more and more strength, till it reaches the Glorious Sun.

Unity in variety is the plan of nature, and the Hindu has recognized it. Every other religion lays down certain fixed dogmas, and tries to force society to adopt them. It places before society only one coat which must fit Jack and John and Henry, all alike. If it does not fit John or Henry, he must go without a coat to cover his body. The Hindus have discovered that the absolute can only be realized, or thought of, or stated, through the relative, and the images, crosses, and crescents are simply so many symbols – so many pegs to hang the spiritual ideas on. It is not that this help is necessary for every one, but those that do not need it have no right to say that it is wrong. Nor is it compulsory in Hinduism.

One thing I must tell you. Idolatry in India does not mean anything horrible. It is not the mother of harlots. On the other hand, it is the attempt of undeveloped minds to grasp high spiritual truths. The Hindus have their faults, they sometimes have their exceptions; but mark this, they are always for punishing their own bodies, and never for cutting the throats of their neighbours. If the Hindus fanatic burns himself on the pyre, he never lights the fire of Inquisition. And even this cannot be laid at the door of his religion any more than the burning of witches can be laid at the door of Christianity.

To the Hindus, then, the whole world of religions is only a traveling, a coming up, of different men and women, through various conditions and circumstances, to the same goal. Every religion is only evolving a God out of the material man, and the same God is the inspirer of all of them. Why, then, are there so many contradictions? They are only apparent, says the Hindu. The contradictions come from the same truth adapting itself to the varying circumstances of different natures.

It is the same light coming through glasses of different colours. And these little variations are necessary for purposes of adaptation. But in the heart of everything the same truth reigns. The Lord has declared to the Hindu in His incarnation as Krishna, *"I am in every religion as the thread through a string of pearls. Wherever thou seest extraordinary holiness and extraordinary power raising and purifying humanity, know thou that I am there."* And what has been the result? I challenge the world to find, throughout the whole system of Sanskrit philosophy, any such expression as that the Hindu alone will be saved and not others. Says Vyasa, *"We find perfect men even beyond the pale of our caste and creed."* One thing more. How, then, can the Hindu, whose whole fabric of thought centres in God, believe in Buddhism which is agnostic, or in Jainism which is atheistic?

The Buddhists or the Jains do not depend upon God; but the whole force of their religion is directed to the great central truth in every religion, to evolve a God out of man. They have not seen the Father, but they have seen the Son. And he that hath seen the Son hath seen the Father also.

This, brethren, is a short sketch of the religious ideas of the Hindus. The Hindus may have failed to carry out all his plans, but if there is ever to be a universal religion, it must be one which will have no location in place or time; which will be infinite like the God it will preach, and whose sun will shine upon the followers of Krishna and of Christ, on saints and sinners alike; which will not be Brahminic or Buddhistic, Christian or Mohamedan, but the sum total of all these, and still have infinite space for development ; which in its catholicity will embrace in its infinite arms, and find a place for, every human being, from the lowest groveling savage not far removed from the brute, to the highest man towering by the virtues of his head and heart almost above humanity, making society stand in awe of his and doubt his human nature. It will be a religion which will have no place for persecution or intolerance in its polity, which will recognize divinity in every man and woman, and whose whole scope, whose whole force, will be created in aiding humanity to realize its own true, divine nature.

Offer such a religion, and all the nations will follow you. Asoka's council was a council of the Buddhist faith. Akbar's, though more to the purpose, was only a parlour meeting. It was reserved for America to proclaim to all quarters of the globe that the Lord is in every religion.

May He who is the Brahman of the Hindu, the Ahura-Mazda of the Zoroastrians, the Buddha of the Buddhists, the Jehovah of the Jews, the Father in Heaven of the Christians, give strength to you to carry out your noble idea! The star arose in the East ; it traveled steadily towards the West, sometimes dimmed and sometimes effulgent, till it made a circuit of the world; and now it is again rising on the very horizon of the East, the borders of the Sanpo, a thousandfold more effulgent than it ever was before.

Hail, Columbia, motherland of liberty! It has been given to thee, who never dipped her hand in her neighbour's blood, who never found out that the shortest way of becoming rich was by robbing one's neighbours, it has been given to thee to march at the vanguard of civilization with the flag of harmony.

Buddhism, the Fulfilment of Hindusim

I am not a Buddhist, as you have heard, and yet I am. If China, or Japan or Ceylon follow the teachings of the Great Master, India worships him as God incarnate on earth. You have just now heard that I am going to criticism Buddhism, but by that I wish you to understand only this. Far be it from me to criticize him whom I worship as God incarnate on earth. But our views about Buddha are that he was not understood properly by his disciples. The religion between Hinduism (by Hinduism, I mean the religion of the Vedas) and what is called Buddhism at the present day is nearly the same as between Judaism and Christianity. Jesus Christ was a Jew, and Shakya Muni was a Hindu. The Jews rejected Jesus Christ, nay, crucified him, and the Hindus have accepted Shakya Muni as God and worship him. But the real difference that we Hindus want to show between modern Buddhism and what we should understand as the teachings of Lord Buddha lies principally in this. Shakya Muni came to fulfil and not to destroy. Only, in the case of Jesus, it was the old people, the Jews, who did not understand him, while in the case of Buddha, it was his own follows who did not realize the import of his teachings. As the Jew did not understand the fulfillment of the Old Testament, so the Buddhist did not understand the fulfillment of the truths of the Hindu religion. Again, I repeat, Shakya Muni came not to destroy, but he was the fulfillment, the logical conclusion, the logical development of the religion of the Hindus.

The religion of the Hindus is divided into two parts: the ceremonial and the spiritual. The spiritual portion is specially studied by the monks.

In that there is no caste. A man from the highest caste and a man from the lowest may become a monk in India, and the two castes become equal. In religion there is no caste; caste is simply a social institution. Shakya Muni himself was a monk, and it was his glory that he had the large-heartedness to bring out the truths from the hidden Vedas and throw them broadcast all over the world. He was the first being in the world who brought mission arising into practice – nay, he was the first to conceive the idea of proselytizing.

The great glory of the Master lay in his wonderful sympathy for everybody, especially for the ignorant and the poor. Some of his disciples were Brahmins. When Buddha was teaching, Sanskrit was no more the spoken language in India. It was then only in the books of the learned. Some of Buddha's Brahmins disciples wanted to translate his teachings into Sanskrit, but he distinctly told them, "I am for the poor, for the people; let me speak in the tongue of the people." And so to this day the great bulk of his teachings are in the vernacular of that day in India.

Whatever may be the position of philosophy, whatever may be the position of metaphysics, so long as there is such a thing as death in the world, so long as there is such a thing as weakness in the human heart, so long as there is a cry going out of the heart of man in his very weakness, there shall be a faith in God.

On the philosophic side the disciples of the Great Master dashed themselves against the eternal rocks of the Vedas and could not crush them, and on the other side they took away from the nation that eternal God to which every one, man or woman, clings so fondly. And the result was that Buddhism had to die a natural death in India. At the present day there is not one who calls oneself a Buddhist in India, the land of its birth.

But at the same time, Brahminism lost something – that reforming zeal, that wonderful sympathy and charity for everybody, that wonderful leaven which Buddhism had brought to the masses and which had rendered Indian society so great that a Greek historian who wrote about India of that time was lead to say that no Hindu was known to tell an untruth and no Hindu woman was known to be unchaste.

Hinduism cannot live without Buddhism, nor Buddhism without Hinduism. Then realize what the separation has shown to us, that the Buddhists cannot stand without the brain and philosophy of the Brahmins, nor the Brahmin without the heart of the Buddhist. This separation between the Buddhists and the Brahmins is the cause of the downfall of India. That is why India is populated by three hundred millions of beggars, and that is why India has been the slave of conquerors for the last thousand years. Let us then join the wonderful intellect of he Brahmins with the heart, the noble soul, the wonderful humanizing power of the Great Master.

(From *The Complete Works of Swami Vivekananda*, Vol-1, Advait Ashram, Calcutta, 1994. pp 1-24)

Social Classes and Political Power

A cloud of impenetrable darkness has at present equally enveloped us all. Now there is neither firmness of purpose nor boldness of enterprise, neither courage of heart nor strength of mind, neither aversion to maltreatment by others nor dislike for slavery, neither love in the heart nor hope nor manliness; but what we have in India are only deep-rooted envy and strong antipathy against one another, morbid desire to ruin by hook or by crook the weak, and to lick dog-like the feet of the strong. Now the highest satisfaction consists in the display of wealth and power, devotion in self-gratification, wisdom in the accumulation of transitory objects, Yoga in hideous diabolical practices, work in the slavery of others, civilisation in base imitation of foreign nations, eloquence in the use of abusive language, the merit of literature in extravagant flatteries of the rich or in the diffusion of ghastly obscenities! What to speak separately of the distinct Shudra class of such a land, where the whole population has virtually come down to the level of the Shudra? The Shudras of countries other than India have become, it seems, a little awake; but they are wanting in proper education and have only the mutual hatred of men of their own class—a trait common to Shudras. What avails it if they greatly outnumber the other classes? That unity, by which ten men collect the strength of a million, is yet far away from the Shudra; hence, according to the law of nature, the Shudras invariably form the subject race.

But there is hope. In the mighty course of time, the Brahmin and the other higher castes, too, are being brought down to the lower status of the Shudras, and the Shudras are being raised to higher ranks. Europe, once the land of Shudras enslaved by Rome, is now filled with Kshatriya valour. Even before our eyes, powerful China, with Fast strides, is going down to Shudra-hood, while insignificant Japan, rising with the sudden start of a rocket, is throwing off her Shudra nature and is invading by degrees the rights of the higher castes.

Yet, a time will come when there will be the rising the Shudra class, *with their Shudrahood;* that is to say, not like that as at present when the Shudras are becoming great by acquiring the characteristic qualities of the Vaishya or the Kshatriya, but a time will come when the Shudras of every country, with their inborn Shudra nature and habits—not becoming in essence Vaishya or Kshatriya, but remaining as Shudras—will gain absolute supremacy in every society. The first glow of the dawn of this new power has already begun to break slowly upon the Western world, and the thoughtful are at their wits' end to reflect upon the final issue of this fresh phenomenon. Socialism, Anarchism, Nihilism, and other like sects are the vanguard of the social revolution that is to follow. As the result of grinding pressure and tyranny, from time out of mind, the Shudras, as a rule, are either meanly servile, licking dog-like the feet of the higher class, or otherwise are as inhuman as brute beasts.

In spite of the spread of education in the west, there is a great hindrance in the way of the rising, of the Shudra class, and that is the recognition of caste as determined by the inherence of more or less good or bad qualities. By this very qualitative caste system which obtained in y India in ancient days, the Shudra class was kept down, bound hand and foot. In the first place, scarcely any opportunity was given to the Shudra for the accumulation of wealth or the earning of proper knowledge and education, to add to this disadvantage, if ever a man of extraordinary pans and genius were born of the Shudra class, the influential higher sections of the society forthwith showered titular honours on him and lifted him up to their own circle. His wealth and [he power of his wisdom were employed for the benefit of an alien caste — and his own caste-people reaped no benefits of his attainments; and not only so, the good-for-nothing people, the scum and refuse of the higher castes, were cast off and teardown into the Shudra class to swell their number. Vasishtha, Narada, Satyakama Jabala, Vyasa, Kripa, Drona, Kama, and others of questionable parentage were raised to the position of a Brahmin or a Kshatriya, in virtue of their superior learning or valour; but it remains to be seen how the prostitute, maidservant, fisherman, or the charioteer class was benefited by these upliftings. Again, on the other hand, the fallen from the Brahmin, the Kshatriya, or the Vaishya class were always brought down to fill the ranks of the Shudras.

In modern India, no one born of Shudra parents, be he a millionaire or a great Pandit, has ever the right to leave his own society, with the result that the power of his wealth, intellect, or wisdom, remaining confined within his own caste limits, is being employed for the betterment of his own community. This hereditary caste system of India, being thus unable to overstep its own bounds, is slowly but surely conducing to the advancement of the people moving within the same circle. The improvement of the lower classes of India will go on, in this way, so long as India will be under a government dealing with its subjects irrespective of their caste and position.

Whether the leadership of society be in the hands of those who monopolise learning or wield the power of riches or arms, the source of its power is always the subject masses. By so much as the class in power severs itself from this source, by so much is it sure to become weak. But such is the strange irony of fate, such is the queer working of Maya that they from whom this power is directly or indirectly drawn, by fair means or foul—by deceit, stratagem, force, or by voluntary gift—they soon cease to be taken into account by the leading class. When in course of time, the priestly power totally estrange itself from the subject masses, the real dynamo of it power, it was overthrown by the then kingly power taking its stand on the strength of the subject people; again, the kingly power, judging itself to be perfectly independent, created a gaping chasm between itself and the subject people, only to be itself destroyed or become a mere puppet in the hands of the Vaishyas, who now succeeded in securing a relatively greater co-operation of the mass of the people. The Vaishyas have now gained their end; so they no longer deign to count on help from the subject people and are trying their best to dissociate themselves from them; consequently, here is being sown the seed of the destruction of this power as well.

Though themselves the reservoir of all powers, the subject masses, creating an eternal distance between one another, have been deprived of all their legitimate rights; and they will remain so as long as this sort of relation continues.

(From *The Complete Works of Swami Vivekananda,* Vol-IV, Advait Ashram, Calcutta, 1994. pp 467-471)

Socialism

Human society is in turn governed by the four castes—the priests, the soldiers, the traders, and the labourers. Each state has its glories as well as its defects. When the priest (Brahmin) rules, there is a tremendous exclusiveness on hereditary grounds; the persons of the priests and their descendants are hemmed in with all sorts of safeguards—none but they have any knowledge—none but they have the right to impart that knowledge. Its glory is that at this period is laid the foundation of sciences. The priests cultivate the mind, for through the mind they govern.

The military (Kshatriya) rule is tyrannical and cruel, but they are not exclusive; and during that period arts and social culture attain their height.

The commercial (Vaishya) rule comes next. It is awful in its silent crushing and blood-sucking power. Its advantage is, as the trader himself goes everywhere, he is a good disseminator of ideas collected during the two previous states. They are still less exclusive than the military, but culture begins to decay.

Last will come the labourer (Shudra) rule. Its advantages will be the distribution of physical comforts—its disadvantages, (perhaps) the lowering of culture. There will be a great distribution of ordinary education, but extraordinary geniuses will be less and less.

If it is possible to form a state in which the knowledge of the priest period, the culture of the military, the distributive spirit of the commercial, and the ideal of equality of the last can all be kept intact, minus their evils, it will be an ideal state. But is it possible?

Yet the first three have had their day. Now is the time for the last—they must have it—none can resist it. I do not know all the difficulties about the gold or silver standards (nobody seems to know much as to that), but this much I see that the gold standard has been making the poor poorer, and the rich richer. Bryan was right when he said, "We refuse to be crucified on a cross of gold." The silver standard will give the poor a better chance in this unequal fight.

I am a socialist not because I think it is a perfect system, but half a loaf is better than, no bread.

The other systems have been tried and found wanting. Let this one be tried—if for nothing else, for the novelty of the thing. A redistribution of pain and pleasure is better than always the same persons having pains and pleasures. The sum total of good and evil in the world remains ever the same. The yoke will be lifted from shoulder to/shoulder by new systems, that is all.

Let every dog have his day in this miserable world, so that after this experience of so-called happiness they may all come to the Lord and give up this vanity of a world and governments and all other botherations.

With love to you all,

(From *The Complete Works of Swami Vivekananda*, Vol-VI, Advait Ashram, Calcutta, 1994. pp 380-382)

6

Mahadev Govinda Ranade

Life and Times

The last two decades of the 19th century famously called 'the moderate era of Indian politics' was an epoch full of events and thought-currents of various sorts, prompting analysts to describe it as 'a multiple situation forever on the move'. One of the foremost thinkers of the period was Mahadev Govinda Ranade (1842-1901) historian, economist, politician, reformer and judge whom many regarded as the 'Socrates of Maharastra' for his mighty and versatile intellect. If ever the theoretical foundations of Indian liberalism were explored and explicated by anybody, it was M.G. Ranade more than anybody else. Other liberals like Naoroji or Gokhale or R.C. Dutt were either too involved in practical politics or too concerned with the economic dimensions of the Indian problem. Ranade's philosophical bent of mind naturally and spontaneously interested him in the complex issues of Indian polity and economy. He concluded that solution to these problems did not rest with classical liberal principles and classical liberalism had to be indianized to make it relevant to our situation.

Ranade was born at Nasik in 1842. One of the outstanding students of Bombay University, he began his career as a teacher in the university but later joined the judiciary and rose up to the position of judge at the Bombay High Court in 1893. He was closely involved with a number of social, religious, educational and economic institutions of Poona and Bombay. His association with the Prathna Samaj, Social Conference, Poona Sarvajanik Sabha, Indian National Congress and Industrial Conference was very close and significant. He was also the editor of an Anglo-Marathi weekly *Indu Prakash*. Ranade was the author of important works like *Rise of Maratha Power* and *Essays on Indian Economics*.

Ranade was a deeply religious man who believed in the omnipotence and immanence of God. He said that faith in the moral government of a perfect Being and the immortality of soul has made civilized man what he was at present found to be, and mankind could be saved only by this faith. History is the manifestation of the Divine Will and so also are the workings of external nature. This spark of Divine is reflected in man in the form of conscience. God's unbounded love and compassion for man have come down to us in the prophets' vision, in preachers' eloquence, in philosophers' wisdom and in martyr's self-surrender, and with their help and inspiration man can attain moral and spiritual perfection. Though influenced by the theistic philosophies of Frazer and Joseph Butler, his metaphysical views were rooted in Indian tradition. The philosophy of Upnishads and the Bhakti cult of Tukaram, Namdev, Eknath had a lasting impact on his ideas. Himself a great reciter of the poems (Abhangas) of Tukaram, he had immense faith in the reinvigorating and chastening power of prayers.

Conscience being the divine voice in man, the real freedom of man emanated from following its dictates. Neglect and over-dependence on external laws and customs very often benumb this faculty of conscience, but if we live a life of self-control and save ourselves from the temptations of petty interests and small comforts, purity and tranquility of mind is restored. The obedience to this inner law constitutes true freedom of man by the side of which the authority of government and laws and customs of society pale into insignificance. Thus the freedom of man is the moral freedom, it is the freedom flowing from man's higher powers. Thus freedom is also another name for duty and responsibility. Man does not possess the freedom to transgress the moral order nor can he be indifferent to the good and freedom of others. Ranade's ideas have close affinity with those of Kant.

Ranade thought that social life of India was in the grip of irrationality and unfreedom because external authority rather than the voice of conscience ruled the roost. People did not try to excel in the secular departments of life because of the sway of the unfounded prejudices and degrading superstitions. They were too self-centric to feel the need of developing contacts with outside world. He felt that caste-system was a great impediment to the establishment of liberal society. Caste and sex have been the sources of domination and oppression. Ranade pleaded for the eradication of social evils like untouchability, child-marriage, low status of woman etc. He along with K.T. Telang, R.G. Bhandarkar and others played a leading role in the movement for social reform in the western India, and in order to create an awareness for social reform, he started the practice of holding social conferences along with the annual sessions of Indian National Congress Ranade considered social reforms the need of hour while the nationalist school led by Tilak gave priority to political reforms.

Ranade's approach to the issue was based upon the organic concept of society. He thought that religious, political, economic spheres of society are closely intertwined and interdependent. One can not be progressive in one sphere and status quoist in the other. He said, 'You can not be liberal by halves'. Therefore reforms in different fields should go hand-in-hand and it is pointless to argue what should precede and what should follow. To quote him, "You cannot have a good social system when you find yourself low in the scale of political rights, nor can you be fit to exercise political rights and privileges unless your social system is based on reason and justice. You can not have a good economic system when your social arrangements are imperfect. If your religious ideas are low and groveling, you can not succeed in social, economic and political spheres. This interdependence is not an accident but is the law of our nature. Like the members of our body you can not have the strength in the hands and feet if your internal organs are in disorder. What applies to human body holds good of the collective humanity we call society or state."

Ranade believed that social transformation was a slow and gradual process. He rejected revolutionary or rebellious methods because orderly and lasting improvements were the result of slow and organic evolution. He underlined the need to use legislation, executive action, education and persuasion to bring about the desired social change. Force and coercion are to be avoided as far as possible. He also favoured what he called 'the method of tradition'. He thought that the reformers should convince the people that religious or social reforms they were advocating had scriptural sanction and what they were striving for was the restoration of the purity of ideals and institutions as contained in the Shrutis or Smritis. Many social or religious practices of Hindu society are distortions and perversions of the original principles. By trying to recast Hindu society we are neither interfering with nor undermining the religious principles of the Hindus. Himself a devout Hindu, Ranade believed that by following the method of tradition we could move forward without alienating or angering conservative elements of Hindu society. M.N. Roy was beside the mark when he praised Ranade for "boldly declaring war on the banefulness of the old religious corruptions and social customs". Ranade was reformer but he refrained from radicalism. Befitting a judge, he trode the path with judiciousness and sobriety.

The cautious approach of Ranade is also reflected in his appraisal of the British Empire. He saw in the British conquest of India not only a calamity to be lamented but on opportunity to be seized. He was of the view that certain weaknesses of both Hindus and Muslims helped the Britishers to gain a foothold in India. Both of them had been wanting "in the love of municipal freedom, in the exercise of virtues necessary for civic life and in aptitude for mechanical skills, in the love of science and research, in the love of daring and adventurous discovery, the resolution to master difficulties and in chivalrous respect for womankind." The loss of independence was not only the cause but also the consequence of the degeneration of the Indian society. He felt that we had to make the most of the new situation by "reactivating the ancient but ossified civilization which had been cutoff for centuries from an invigorating contact with the rest of the world." The British Empire can assist us here by initiating a disciplining and transforming process. Ranade saw the guiding hand of Providence in bringing the two countries together.

Ranade found the key to fruitful cooperation between the two countries in the liberal ideology of England. Ranade is the finest exponent of Indian liberalism, though he realized the need to modify classical liberalism so as to make it an effective tool to re-structure Indian society and economy. The complex nature of Indian society and its problems are not amenable to the analysis and solutions of the British liberals like Adam Smith, Ricardo or Mill. Rather the ideas and prescriptions of German historical school of Adam Muller, and Friedrich List are more relevant to the Indian situation. He argued that average Indian is not 'the Economic man' of the classical economists nor is he driven by the imperatives of profit which is the basis of capitalist economy. To quote him, "with us, the individual man is the very antipodes of the economical man. The family and caste are more powerful than the individual in determining his position in life. Self-interest in the shape of desire of wealth is not absent but it is not the only nor principal motto....There is neither the desire nor the aptitude for free and unlimited competition except within pre-determined groups or grooves. Neither capital nor labour is mobile and enterprising....In a society so constituted, the tendencies assumed as axiomatic are not only inoperative but are actually deflected from their proper direction." Thus Ranade considered political economy not as a science of abstract truths but a historical and dynamic one dealing with particular cultures. He asserted that 'universalism and perpetualism in economic doctrines were both unscientific and untrue.'

India's poverty saddened him, and like Gokhale, R.C. Dutt and Dadabhai Naoroji, he tried to go to the root causes of this wretchedness. Dependence of people only on agriculture was major cause though he knew full well that the advent of foreign capital, enterprise and skill had paralysed the indigenous industries, thus widening the scope of poverty. Besides, the harsh system of credit and congestion of population in certain areas also contributed to the economic degeneration. However, he considered the theory of 'drain' of Dadabhai Naoroji only partially true as far as appalling economic condition of India was concerned.

Ranade pleaded for structural reforms in the field of agriculture and industry. He felt immediate need of reforming the land revenue system so that ryots could be relieved from the morass of indebtedness. He also favoured the reorganization of rural credit on the pattern obtaining in the countries of continental Europe. Believing in 'industrialize or perish', he urged state initiative in matter of industrialization. He favoured cheap government loans to private entrepreneurs for the development of iron, coal, paper, glass and oil industries. He also favoured the flow of capital in agrarian industries.

Ranade was in favour of a balanced economic growth where three vital sectors-commerce, manufacture and agriculture should develop simultaneously. At the same time he thought that state had to play a key role in India's economic development and the policies of free-trade and non-intervention were not suited to India. He regarded state as 'the national organ to take care of national needs' in all matters in which individual and corporative efforts are not likely to be so effective and economical as the national effort. But Ranade was not a statist- a champion of complete governmental control of economy. He was for active and limited state interventions. He stood for an economic order in which private enterprise and effort was aided and regulated by the state.

Ranade is rightly regarded as the exponent of economic nationalism. The concern for India's economic regeneration was uppermost in his mind and he was very clear that this could not be brought about by the dogmatic assumptions of the classical school. Theory should illuminate reality and not distort it. Cultural or historical conditions of India must be taken into account while formulating policies for her socio-economic reconstruction. He wanted a cautious blending of the new and the old, of science and history and of individual initiative and state support. Gokhale once said that while he "cherished more lovingly and reverently the past of this land than anybody else, his vision was to interpret to the people the new order of things...... to point out its meaning, the opportunity it offered, the responsibilities it imposed and the rich harvest that was to be gathered." He was a reformer whose comprehensive gaze ranged over the entire edifice from summit to base and whose agenda included all parts of it-political, social, economic, moral and educational.

> The following extract is a lecture delivered in the Deccan College, Poona in 1892. The lecture is a sufficient testimony to his erudition and independence. A reader can not but be struck by his deep grounding in the contemporary economic theory and also his wisdom and foresight to separate wheat from the chaff. That he was able to see through the limitations of the classical liberalism long before socialists and communitarians appeared on the scene, speaks volumes for his genius.

Colonialism and Indian Political Economy

In the beginning of this year before a similar gathering in Bombay, a master-hand sketched the outlines of the influence of Nature on Literature and Politics, and in a few bold touches showed how, from time to time, the aberrations and evil tendencies observable in English thought and action were counteracted and corrected by an appeal to, and a diligent Study of, the standard of Nature-the final source of all true knowledge, and the only guide to wise conduct. The same master-hand drew also the moral to be learned from such a Study,-the moral being that our growth could only be in strict correspondence to our aptitudes and surroundings, and that we should be on our guard against precipitation and hot-house culture, which can never lead to permanently beneficial results. There can be no doubt that the Historical line of Thought so developed is to some extent the chief characteristic feature of the latter half of the present Century. It occurred to me at the time that if the Law of Relativity and correspondence holds good in politics and social science generally, it ought to hold good equally in all kindred subjects, including, among others, the science of national wealth, or as it is more popularly described, Political Economy. As a matter of fact, however what do we see about us? The same teachers and statesmen, who warn us against certain tendencies in our political aspirations, forget this salutary caution when the question at issue is one of Indian economics. They seem to hold that the truths of economic science, as they have been expounded in our most popular English Text-books, are absolutely and demonstrably true, and must be accepted as guides of conduct for all time and place whatever might be the stage of National advance. Ethnical, social, juristic, ethical or economical differences in the environments are not regarded as having any influence in modifying the practical application of these truths. If free trade is good for England, it must be equally beneficial to all countries, and prohibitive or protective duties, bounties and subsidies, restrictions and regulative control, are absolute evils, and no thought need be given to the relative differences civilization, or the possession of natural advantages, or disadvantages in matter of situation, climate, soil, national aptitudes and wants. If factory Legislation is good in our country, it must be equally needed to protect labourers everywhere. If laws in restraint of usury are out of place in centers of commercial and manufacturing activity, they must be equally pernicious in backward, antiquated, and agricultural communities. If the State finds no occasion to help credit institutions in England, the demand for such help, in countries where the spirit of private enterprise is feeble, is also held to be preposterous. If the government of advanced countries do not undertake certain functions with a view to direct industry and help enterprise, the government out here is equally precluded from taking any new line of departure in these matter. If direct taxes suit English conditions of life and property, they must be equally suitable to Indian conditions, and Octroi and transit duties must be kept down rigorously as sources of our local or municipal income.

I might multiply these instances without number, but those given above will, I hope, serve to illustrate my present purpose. Even if Statesmen had stooped here, there would have been some extenuation for the line of conduct adopted by them. The absolute truths of Political Economy, however, are appealed to as a justification for a curious change of front. Men, who come from a country where private property in land is most absolute, develop on their arrival here a taste for socialistic doctrines. The State aspires to relegate all private property in land into mere superior and inferior holding. A love for capitalist farming on a large scale give way to a taste for *petit culture* by poor tenants. In England the landlords as such pay no special tax to the State, but here Land is taxed on the ground that there is an unearned increment based on the Theory of Economical Rent, and that this unearned increment belongs of special right to the State. While the nationalization of land is but a socialist dream in England and Europe, it is in full swing here, and furnishes a scientific justification for periodical revisions and enhancements. Status and privilege form still the very cornerstone of English social arrangements, but here every member of society is only a mobile atom, without any differences marking him off from others, so far as the State is concerned. The middle class is the backbone of English supremacy, but here there is no room for a middle class between the state and the poor tax-payers. This change of front is a curious study by itself. For my present purposes, it is not necessary to cite more instances. Of course, if Political Economy is a science of general and absolute truths, like physics or astronomy, the tendency noted above to push its principles to their logical conclusions in all times and places, even when English statesmen halt midway in their practical application of these principles, is intelligible, and may be even wise. There can be no doubt that those who thus give effect to these principles honestly believe in the scientific and absolute character of these economical conclusions. But it is certainly a fair subject for consideration whether this belief is well-founded. If in politics and social science, time and place and circumstances, the endowments and aptitudes of men, their habits and customs, their laws and institutions, and their previous history, have to be taken into account, it must be strange indeed, that in the economical aspect of our life, one set of general principles should hold good everywhere for all time and place, and for all stages of civilization. This conflict was one of the reasons which induced me to take up this subject for consideration on the present occasion.

Another reason which influenced me in the choice of this subject was the fact that at this time, when an appeal is being made to the popular will in two great communities to declare itself, the questions at issue are more economical than political in their character. The dream of Cobden and Right, of Ricardo and Mill, that the civilized world would, in a few years, with one accord embrace their principles, has not been realized. In America the issues are solely economical. One party favours Free Trade, the other favours Protection. One party favours Silver Legislation, the other denounces it. In England also, as you are aware, the present

Prime Minister has declared himself in favour of what is called fair trade, which is a modification dictated by political and Economical considerations of the extreme doctrine of Free Trade with a view to restrict the freedom to those who reciprocate it, and the Liberals have denounced this lapse from orthodoxy as unpardonable heresy. Even in Ireland, the political issue is really at its base an economical dispute, which centers round the question of the extent of the rights of private property and free contract as between the landlords and the tenants. Similarly, here in our own country, the Currency Association is also running a tilt against economical theorists, and boldly denies the universally of the equation of supply and demand as the best and only regulator of the exchange values of the precious metals. On the continent of Europe, and in the English Colonies, the same protest is being practically urged against the extreme rigour of the current theories of orthodox Political Economy. The Americans dispute the rights of the Chinese to settle in their country, the Australians fear the same scare, and even in England, legislation was contemplated against the immigration of alien Jews, on the ground that they were likely to under-bid the indigenous labourer. The Trades Unions and strikes, and the knights of labour, of which we have heard so much recently, furnish another form of this same general protest. This conflict of practice with theory, not in one, but all points, not in one place or country, but all over the world, which distinguishes contemporary history, furnishes another reason which appeared to me to justify a reconsideration of the question on broader lines than those you will find enunciated in the ordinary textbooks.

In justice to some of these writers, it must be admitted that they have taken good care to prevent many of the misapprehensions which are popularly entertained about the absolute and general character of the economical doctrines taught by them. Mr. John Stuart Mill, for instance, states in his preface that "for practical purposes, Political Economy is inseparably intertwined with many other branches of social philosophy. Except in matter of mere detail, there are perhaps no practical questions, even among those which approach nearest to the character of purely Economical questions, which admit being decided on economical premises alone." You will also recollect that one characteristic feature of Mr. Mill's work is his frank recognition of an essential difference between the Laws relating to the production of Wealth, which he deems to be Universal and not arbitrary, and those which regulate its distribution. The laws of distribution, Mr. Mills admits, are partly of human institution. Mr. Mill, and Mr. Cairns more clearly even than Mr. Mill, affirmed the hypothetical character of the Science. Mr. Mill contented himself with suggesting the necessity of verification to establish the soundness of the hypothetical demonstration, but Mr. Cairns went further, and asserted that "economical laws are not assertions respecting the character or sequence of phenomena, and that they can neither be established or refuted by statistical or documentary evidence." It is true this was not the position of the earlier teachers, Adam Smith, Ricardo, senior James Mill, McCulloch, and Malthus, who never doubted that in all their reasoning they were dealing with human beings as they actually exist.

Adam Smith, for instance, believed that Nature had made provision for social well-being by that principle of the human constitution which prompts every man to better his condition, and in aiming at individual good, every man is led by an invisible hand to promote general good. Human institutions only interfere with this tendency, and when all restraints are removed, the obvious and simple system of natural liberty establishes, itself. Ricardo and Malthus were, if possible, still more dogmatic and absolute in their assertion of these necessary tendencies, and made no allowances, or at the best gave scanty recognition to, the one-sided character of their premises. Mr. Senior seriously thought that the whole science could, like geometry, be reduced from four axiomatic propositions. It will be useful at this stage to note the general features of these assumptions of the earlier Economists, which they believed to be as necessarily and universally true as the First Law of mechanics, that bodies move in straight lines, or the First Law of physics, that they attract each other directly according to their mass, and inversely according to their distance. These assumptions may be thus briefly stated:- (1) that national economy is essentially Individualistic and has no separate collective aspect; (2) that the individual, or typical economical man, has no desire but that of promoting his own Self-interest, or at least that this is his strongest motive power; (3) that this self-interest is best promoted by the largest production of wealth, i.e. articles with value in Exchange, at the least trouble; (4) that such pursuit of private gain by each individual promotes best the general good; (5) that the free and unlimited competition of individuals in the race and struggle of life is the only safe and natural regulator; (6) that all customary and State Regulation is an encroachment on natural liberty; (7) that every individual knows best his Interest, and has the capacity and desire of acting according to this know ledge; (8) that there is perfect Freedom and Equality in the power of contract between individuals and individuals; (9) that capital and labour are always free and ready to move from one employment to another, where better remuneration is expected; (10) that there is a universal tendency of profits and wages to seek a common level; (11) that population tends to outstrip the means of subsistence; (12) and that demand and supply always tend mutually to adjust each other.

These assumptions lie at the root of all dogmatical treatment of the subject. It need not be said that they are literally true of no existing community. To the extent that they are approximately true of any state of society, the assumptions furnish valid explanations of its economical statics. Even then they furnish no suggestion as to its dynamical progress or development. As these assumptions do not absolutely hold good of even the most advanced societies, it is obvious that in societies like ours, they are chiefly conspicuous by their absence. With us an average individual man is, to a large extent, the very antipodes of the Economical man. The family and the caste are more powerful than the Individual in determining his position in life. Self-interest in the shape of the desire of wealth is not absent, but it is not the only nor principal motor. The pursuit of wealth is not the only ideal aimed at. There is neither the desire not the aptitude for free and unlimited competition except within certain predetermined grooves or groups. Custom and state regulation are far more powerful than competition, and status more decisive in its influence than contract. Neither capital nor labour is mobile, and enterprising and intelligent enough to shift from place to place. Wages and Profit are fixed, and not elastic and responsive to change of circumstances. Population follows its own law, being cut down by disease and famine, while production is almost stationary, the bumper harvest of one year being needed to provide against the uncertainties of alternate bad Seasons. In a Society so constituted, the tendencies assumed as axiomatic, are not only inoperative, but are actually deflected from their proper direction. You might as well talk of the tendency of mountains to be washed away into the sea, or of the valleys to fill up, or of the Sun to get cold, as reasons for our practical conduct within a measurable distance of time.

This hypothetical character of the entire fabric of doctrinal economy has been more or less freely recognized, as stated above, by Mr. Mill, Mr. Cairns and other Teachers of Political Economy; and in our own time, Mr. Bagehot has gone so far as to assert that the traditional system rested on assumptions which were not only not true generally, but were true only of the present day. He calls it the Science of Business done in large and trading Communities. It does not explain the economic life of earlier times, or of our own times in other Nations. It is insular, and has not obtained general recognition, by reason of its being chiefly a convenient series of deductions from assumed axioms which are in many times and places not true, and are only true in England, where Capital and labour can freely transport themselves from one employment to another. Mr. sidgwick, another contemporary writer, has expressed the view that the abstract method is useful only for the statical study of Economy, and that its conclusions, even within this province, are only by hypothetically valid. In the dynamical study of the progress of wealth the value of the deductive method is almost nil. Mr. Cliff Leslie has expressed himself in stronger terms. The Economy of every Nation, according to this writer, is the result of a long growth in which there has been continuity and change, and the economic side of this change is only a particular aspect. The laws of social progress in Wealth must be sought in the history of the general social evolution which is different in different countries. Professor Jevons was filled with such despair by the sterile character of the hypothetical system that he thought the only way to cure its defects was to fling away, once and for ever, preposterous assumptions of the Ricardian School. It will be thus seen that in the land of its birth and highest development, the claims of political economy as ordinarily taught in the text books, have been seriously questioned, and its value as a guide to practical conduct greatly discounted.

You will naturally desire to know how this revulsion of thought has been brought about tin the course of a hundred years. It becomes necessary in this connection to take a retrospective view of the progress of the Science in Western Europe during the past two or three hundred years. Such a retrospect will help us to judge for our self how far the development of the Scientific theory of Political Economy can be regarded as even now complete. The ancient conception of Political Economy had regard chiefly to laying down the practical rules of prudent conduct for each private individual who desired to be rich. The conception of it as a Principle of Social Polity was more or less ignored. The general feeling in those days was that manual labour was below the dignity of a Free man. Such work was done by slaves, or as we would in this country describe them, by the lower castes. A free-man could only devote his attention to agriculture, commerce and manufactures were later developments.

This circumstance also explains the interdict on Usury which was a common feature of all ancient Institutes, excepting those of our own country, which in this respect were more advanced than the Greek, or Mahomedan, or Christian notions on the subject. Gradually slaves became serfs, and then free men, who worked for wages. These serfs, seeking refuge in ancient coast towns and Roman colonies, developed them into the free commercial cities of the Middle Ages about the times of the crusades, and later on into great manufacturing centres. The discoveries of the 15th century gave a stimulus to trade, and later on to colonization. The large imports of Gold and Silver helped to encourage the greater circulation of money. The gradual rise of European monarchies, and the decay of the Church and the nobility, removed the pressure of Feudal ideas, and raised the status of those who were engaged in commerce. The Republics of Italy developed banking and credit. It was when the national activity of Europe took such a varied form, stimulating agriculture, commerce, manufactures, banking, currency, exchange, co-operation, taxation, colonization, and foreign conquests, that the ground was prepared for a systematic study of the theory of the laws which regulated economical arrangements, and made nations prosperous and strong, or the reverse. And the first speculative explanation attempted is known in history as the mercantile theory. It is too much the practice of text-writers to cry down this theory as one which confounded wealth with money and bullion, and made the possession of precious metals the test of national prosperity. This is however, an utterly unfair and one-sided view of the subject. The leading feature of the system was that it set a higher value on commerce and manufactures, than on agriculture, and on foreign over home trade. It encouraged exports, but desired to check imports with a view not to retain money so much as to develop home manufactures. Lastly, it prescribed the directive control of the state in the way of stimulating domestic manufactures and encouraging commerce.

Each State competed with the rest in foreign markets, and sought to secure the most advantageous terms, and it sought also to extend its colonies and dependencies with a view to increase the sphere of open markets, for its produce. It is enough to state that men like Colbert, and Oliver Cromwell, Raleigh and Childe, could not have encouraged a system which had not some solid justification in the then circumstances of Europe. Cromwell's navigation laws have admittedly been the foundation of England's naval supremacy, and Colbert made France in his day the most prosperous State on the continent. He had a keen perception that State protection and control were but crutches to teach the nation to walk, and that they should be thrown away when the necessary advance had been made. It was under the influence of the same, ideas that the great East India companies of Holland, France, and England were formed, and received the support of their respective Governments. Charters and monopolies, bounties and subsidies, were freedly granted under the influence of the same ideas, and State help and regulation did their work remarkably well.

In the next century the natural progress of events made nations alive to the abuses of the old system, and men began to feel the necessity of freedom in the economical as well as in the political field. This work of destructive and negative criticism began in England with the teachings of Hobbes and Locke but was more earnestly taken up in France previous to the Revolution. The enormous abuses of State control and direction, of monopolies and restrictions, led to a reaction in favour of a theory which was founded on the idea of natural liberty. In this negative philosophy individual man was moreover conceived as being solely guided by private interest, which it was supposed he understood better for himself than others could do for him, and the removal of all restrictions and prohibitions became the watch-word of this School. The previous preponderance of State support in favour of commerce and manufactures was condemned and a preference for Agriculture as the only true source of all Wealth was developed into a mania. In grasping the conception that money alone was not wealth, and that all wealth is created by human labour applied to natural agents, people ran to the other extreme of classifying commerce and manufactures along with service and professions under the head of unproductive labour. In protesting against protection and prohibition, the extreme view went so far as to hold that Government itself was only a necessary evil, and that the State had no concern with industry, and must confine itself to its sole function of keeping the public peace. This conception of the domain of natural liberty in economics was but a part and parcel of the great movement of Freedom which culminated in the French Revolution. Quesnay, Guorney, and the great statesman Turgot, were the advocates of this New School of thought which is know as the School of the Physiocrats.

Next in order of time we have Adam Smith, who was the direct product of the French negative School of Quesnay, but he improved upon his model and exposed the weakness of that School in two important respects. He established the fact that agriculture was not the only source of wealth, and that manufactures and commerce were equally efficient in this respect, and that Nature helped man equally in all the three departments. While accepting the *laissez faire* doctrine of free trade as a general principal, Mr. Smith was alive to the fact that restrictive navigation laws had helped greatly to ensure English commercial supremacy, and he justified these laws on the express ground that defense was of more importance than opulence, and he advocated what are known as fair trade views, i.e., views which permit retaliation by way of differential duties against non-reciprocating countries, on condition that such retaliation produces its desired consequences. He also approved of temporary concessions by way of monopolies to chartered companies in enterprises which involved risk and expense. Adam Smith never separated economical from social considerations, and thus occupied a position of advantage, which his Successors gave up by their too absolute assertion of his doctrines. I have already spoken of the rigid character of the system of Ricardo, Malthus, James Mill, Torrens, Mac Cullocch and others, and shown how this dogmatic feature provoked a reaction in England, at first faintly represented in the protests of John Stuart Mill and Mr. Cairns, but more decidedly formulated by Bagehot, Leslie and Jevons. This strong reaction of feeling among English writers was due to the influence of the great French and German teachers.

August Comte was the first who denied the name of science to the doctrines taught by the deductive school, and he elaborated his own system of the historical method of research, and these hints were taken up by the German and English thinkers of our day. Sismondi was the first economical writer who gave expression to the dissatisfaction felt in France at the conclusions of the English economists. He charged the individualistic school with tendencies by which the rich became richer, and the poor were made poorer. He protested against the abuses of the *lissez faire* policy and invoked Government intervention for protecting the masses against the classes, and the weaker races against the pressure of the stronger and more advanced nations under the regime of competition. Sismondi declared that the State was not merely an agency for keeping peace, but that it was an organization for securing the progress of the people as widely as possible, and for extending the benefits of the social union to all. Another French writer, Dunoyer, defined liberty not as a mere negation of restraint, but a positive effort to increase efficiency of labour in all its grades.

Two American thinkers, Hamilton and Carey, sounded the same note of difference in more distinct terms, Hamilton was one of the fathers of the American constitution, and he stated that the English doctrine of absolute freedom was practicable only if all nations accepted free trade views simultaneously, and he suggested a scheme of protective duties which were later on adopted as the leading feature of American state tariff. The Hayleybury Professor Jones had before Carey attacked the Ricardian theory of rent as being true only of Farmers' rents, and as wholly inapplicable to the Indian Ryots' rent or the Metayer or Cottier rents. Carey went further, and denied that there was any Economic rent proper, and contended that Rent was only a remuneration, in the same way as profits, of past invested capital or labour. Carey justified protection to domestic agriculture on the ground that the waste products of land must return to the soil to restore its powers, and this restoration was not possible where raw products were exported to and consumed by distant countries. Like the French Sismondi, Carey regarded the State as a co-ordinating power in society, which checked the tendency of individuals to seek immediate gain at the sacrifice of permanent national interests, and he asserted that Protection was justified as being the only means by which the obstacles, thrown in the way of younger and less advanced communities by more advanced nations could be removed. The immediate loss to the nation was, like the sum spent on the education of youth by individuals, which more than repays itself in the long run.

Like the French and American writers, the Italian economists of the modern period, Gioga and Ludovico, also advocated State regulation of industry, and asserted the doctrine of relativity as being an essential factor of all true economic theory. The work of positive exposition was, however, most successfully taken up by the German professors. Miller first suggested that Adam Smith's system, as elaborated by his more dogmatic disciples, was essentially English and insular. It succeeded in England, because the national life of England was preserved intact by its favoured situation and past history and conservative instincts, while it was unsuitable to the continental countries, because, with them the preservation of the national existence was a subject of greater importance than mere individual prosperity. It was the writings of List, which gave the fullest expression to this rebellion against the orthodox creed. He urged that the permanent interests of nations were not always in harmony with the present benefit of individuals. National well-being does not consist only in the creation of the highest quantity of wealth measured in exchange value independently of all variety of quality in that wealth, but in the full and many-sided development of all productive powers. The nation's economic education is of far more importance than the present gain of its individual members, as represented by the quantity of wealth measured by its value in exchange. In a sound and normal condition, all the three departments of national activity must be fully developed. Commerce and manufactures are, if possible, more vital in their bearing on the education of the intelligence and skill and enterprise of the Nation than Agriculture. In a purely agricultural country there is a tendency to stagnation and absence of enterprise and the retention of antiquated prejudices. The function of the State is to help those influences which tend to secure national progress through the several stages of growth, and adopt free trade or protection as circumstances may require. In this view free trade may be good for a country like England, but not for America and Germany.

The subsequent German teachers further elaborated this historical view, and under the stimulus of the success of comparative method in philology and jurisprudence, proposed to reconstruct economy by the help of the new method. Raw, Knieys, Roscher, Hildebrand, Wagner and others worked on these lines. Their influence made itself felt on English thought, and Leslie and Jevons were directly influenced by these teachings. They advocated that Economy was only one branch of Sociology, and like all Social Sciences, it must be studied both in its statical and dynamical conditions, and that the basis of a hypothetical economic man, guided solely by one motive of self-interest, must be given up, and man as he is, both selfish and altruistic, possessing rights as well as being bound by duties, must be studied in history, both ancient and modern. In brief, this German school regards that Universalism and Perpetualism in economic doctrine are both unscientific and untrue.

This resume of the past and contemporary history of the growth of economic sciences in England, France, Germany, Italy and America will satisfy the student that modern European thought does not at all countenance the view of the English writers of the Ricardian School, that the principles of the science, as they have enunciated them in their text books, are universally and necessarily true for all times and places, and for all stages of advancement modern thought is veering to the conclusion that the individual and his Interest are not the centre round which the Theory should revolve, that the rue centre is the body politic of which that individual is a member, and that collective defence and well-being, social education and discipline, and the duties, and not merely the interests, of men, must be taken into account, if the theory is not to be merely Utopian. The method to be followed is not the deductive but the historical method, which takes account of the past in its forecast of the future; and relativity, and not absoluteness, characterizes the conclusions of economical science. There are those who seek to get over this difficulty by differentiating the science from what they are disposed to call the art of economy. This divorce of theory and practice is, however, a mischievous error, which relegates the science to the sterility of an ideal dream or a puzzle, and condemns the art to the position of a rule of the thumb. Theory is only enlarged practice, practice is theory studied in its relation to proximate causes. The practice is predetermined by the theory which tests its truth, and adopts it to different conditions by reason of its grasp of the deep-seated, permanent, and varied basal truths. I hope thus to have shown that the nature of the subject itself as a branch of social science which is best-studied historically and not deductively, the actual practice of the most civilized nnations and the history of the growth of its theory given above, alike establish the doctrine of relativity, and the predominant claim of collective welfare over individual interests, as the principal features in which the highest minds of the present day chiefly differ from the economical writers of the Old school, with their a *priori* conclusions based on individual self-interest and unrestricted competition.

We have next to consider the bearings of this enlarged view of the science in its Indian aspects. The characteristics of our social life are the prevalence of status over contract, of combination over competition. Our habits of mind are conservative to a fault. The aptitudes of climate and soil facilitate the production of raw materials. Labour is cheap and plentiful, but unsteady, unthrifty, and unskilled. Capital is scarce, immobile, and unenterprising. Cooperation on a large scale of either capital or labour is unknown. Agriculture is the chief support of nearly the whole population, and this agriculture is carried on under conditions of uncertain rainfall. Commerce and manufactures on a large scale are but recent importations, and all industry is carried on, on the system of petty farming, retail dealing, and job working by poor people on borrowed capital. There is an almost complete absence of a landed gentry or wealthy middle class. The land is a monopoly of the State. The desire for accumulation is very weak, peace and security having been almost unknown over large areas for any length of time till within the last century. Our laws and institutions favour a low standard of life, and encourage subdivision and not concentration of wealth. The religious ideals of life condemn the ardent pursuit of wealth as a mistake to be avoided as far as possible. These are old legacies and inherited weaknesses, stagnation and dependence, depression and poverty-these are written in broad characters on the face of the land and its people. To these must be added the economical drain of wealth and talents which foreign subjection has entailed on the country.

As a compensation against all these depressing influences, We have to set off the advantage of a free contact with a race which has opened the country to the commerce of the world, and by its superior skill and resources has developed communications in a way previously unknown. If we wish to realize our situation fully, we may not overlook this factor, because it represents the beam of light which alone illumines prevailing darkness. It cannot well be a mere accident that the destinies of this country have been entrusted to the guidance of a nation whose characteristic strength is opposed to all our weaknesses, whose enterprise, chiefly in commerce and manufactures, knows no bounds, whose capital overflows the world, among whom contract has largely superseded status, and competition and co-operation play a predominant part, whose vient of life is full of hope, and whose powers of organization have never been surpassed.

The first point which illustrates the divergence between the orthodox English doctrine and the enlarged views I have attempted to set forth, as characterizing the more developed modern European thought on the subject, relates to the so-called system of the territorial division of labour by which the orthodox economists assign to the backward torrid zone reigions of Asia the duty of producing raw materials, and claim for the advanced European temperate zone countries the work of transport and manufactures, as a division of labour in production which is fraught with the highest advantage to all, and is almost a providential dispensation, against which it would be foolish to rebel. Of course, as far as the natural advantages of climate and situation force our hands, economically backward races must submit to such an arrangement, but it is fairly open to question whether there is any such inevitable necessity which justifies a line of separation, which has a tendency to accentuate natural deficiencies, and make them a source of permanent weakness.

(i) In the first place, the torrid zone people may fairly appeal to past history, when their skilled products found a ready market in temperate kingdoms, and excited such jealousy as to dicate prohibitive sumptuary laws both in ancient Rome and in modern England. (ii) They may also urge that the natural fitness of things requires that the manufactures should spring up where the raw materials grow, and where besides, there is demand for the manufactured produce, rather than that bulky goods should be transported many thousands of miles over land and sea, and re-consigned the same way back. (iii) The differences in favour of temperate regions are all modern growths due to the employment of steam machinery, and the abundance of cheap iron and coal. This is a real advantage, and has to be faced, but if it can be faced, there is no natural incongruity in an arrangement by which industry would return to its ancient home with a double saving in time and cost. (iv) Neither Mr. Adam Smith, nor even Mr. John Stuart Mill, recommend absolute freedom in such matter. Adam Smith was a fair trader, and Mr. Mill distinctly recognizes an exception to the general rule of free trade, where time is required to see whether new industries are or are not adapted to natural resources of new countries. The late controversy between Mr. Blaine and Mr. Gladstone chiefly turned upon this point, Mr. Blaine contending that, with a large continental country like America, with all shades of climate and soil and position, the conditions of the problem were different from those of an isolated small territory like England. The Australian colonies also justify their departure from the orthodox policy on this same ground. India may fairly claim the benefit of the experience and practice of these self-governmenting communities, and demand breathing time. (v) It is further to be noted that such a division of production, if permanently stereotyped, consigns Asia to an industry which is under the bane of the law of diminshing returns, while the West of Europe appropriates to itself those forms of Industry which are not subject to any such law. The orthodox view thus condemns the poor to grow still poorer, and helps the rich to become richer-'it give much to him that, and taketh away from him that hath not the little that he hath.' (vi) Lastly, people forget that the agricultural industry in the torrid regions has to work under the disadvantage of an uncertain rainfall, and suffer from famine visitations, which, when they come, paralyze production, and condemn millions to violent or slow death. A due co-ordination of the three-fold forms of industrial activity, even if it be not immediately most advantageous to individuals in any one period, is a permanent national insurance against current dangers, and as such is economically the most beneficial course in the interests of the community.

(2) The point noticed above has reference chiefly to foreign trade. In domestic interchange also, the same law operates, and every nation which desires economical advances has to take care that its urban population bear an increasing ratio to its rural masses with every advance it seeks to make. Mr. John Stuart Mill has expressly laid down that no agriculture can be really productive which is divorced from a neighboring non-agricultural market represented by thriving towns and cities. Under native rulers there was a sort of rude adjustment made in this direction, when the Courts of the petty sovereigns afforded so many centres of urban activity in industries patronized by the Court and its dependents. Mr. Mill suggests that in the absence of such near markets, the next available substitute is a large export trade to foreign countries. This substitute cannot, however, be accepted as really answering the purpose in view. The progress of ruralization in modern India means its rustication, i.e., a loss of power, and intelligence, and self-dependence, and is a distinctly retrograde move. The growth of the sea ports and of the few ministry and railway stations is not enough to counterbalance the enormous loss that has been inflicted

by this retrograde movement. Every class of artisans, the spinners, weavers and the dyers, the oilsmen, the paper-markers, the silk and sugar and metal workers, etc., who are unable to bear up against Western competition, resort to the land, leave the towns and go into the country, and are lost in the mass of helpless people who are unable to bear up against scarcity and famine.

(3) The highest statesmanship may well feel against at this rapid change, and I know as a matter of fact that this subject weighs heavily on the conscience of the British administrators in India. They, however, feel powerless to act under the influence of the all-pervading doctrine that these matters lie outside the province of Government A regular system of immigration from thickly populated poor agricultural tracts to sparely peopled new and virgin districts is a desideration. The halting efforts made in this direction produce no good, for the concessions are not liberal enough, and there is no prescience about it. The ancient rulers who settled waste districts, and founded towns with flourishing and extensive Industries, made no difficulty about granting the most liberal concessions. Anticipating Mr. Wakefield's colonization proposals, whole village communities with their varied elements of life were encouraged to move *en masse*, and were made comfortable in their new places, powerful guilds of traders and artisans from distant places were similarly induced to settle in new towns by free gifts of lands and houses and privileges. Stray settler attracted by a few years' leases can never accomplish the end the rulers have in view, and such attempts are bound to fail. A Colbert or a Peter the Great is wanted to give effect to such a scheme, and the ordinary doctrines of *laissez faire* must be set aside in view of the great interests at stake.

(4) Conquest, consolidation, and conciliation have had their heroes in British history. Systematic colonization and the promotion of varied culture are the next stages of development; and it may be hoped that, before long, with Africa and Australia and the East and West Indies literally starving for Indian labour, and Burma, at our door, opened up the ravages of periodical famines, carrying away our thousands and million for want of work when agriculture fails will become impossible, as soon as the policy of let-alone is

given up, and an active effort made in all directions to stimulate productions both of raw and manufactured products. If the State can legitimately undertake from borrowed funds the construction or subsidization of railroads and canals, if it can afford to sell the fee simple of waste lands at nominal rates to European settlers on the hills, the road is certainly open for a further development of this same industrial effort on new lines. The Dutch Government have shown the way in Java, and with less selfish motives the same method might well be tried in regard at least, to the industries allied with agriculture, sugar refining, oil pressing, tobacco curing, silk rearing, etc., all of which can certainly be made to thrive in this torrid land under skilled supervision.

Proceeding next to the department of distribution, the enlarged view of political economy stated above does not accept the position of the unearned increment as a leading feature of the law of rent in India. The unearned increment theory fits in only where landed property continues for generations in the possession of the same family. If the land changes hand, the incoming purchaser buys it at its market value, and he enjoys no unearned advantage, and the so-called rent is but a return by way of fair profits on his investment. The English conditions of landlordism, where the land under a complicated system of entails, and settlements and primogeniture, continues in the same family for generations, allow free play to the law of the unearned increment. Here, in this country lands and houses are not so tied up, and they change hands frequently and largely. In every twenty years, the registration returns show that the value of sales comes up to the total value of landed property. In one generation, property thus changes hands, and frequently and largely. In one generation, property thus changes hands, and when new men come in as purchasers for value, they do not enjoy any unearned increment of the of the past, but have to pay full value for the differential advantages of superior productiveness and vicinity. In the same way the Ricardian theory that economic rent does not enter as an element of price, admitted does not apply when all occupied land has to pay monopoly rent to the State landlord. There is no competition among landlords in this country, for there is only one true landlord, and the so-called land tax is not a tax on rents proper but frequently encroaches upon the profits and wages of the poor peasant, who has to submit perforce to a loss of status and accommodate himself to a lower standard of life as pressure increases.

Lastly, the advanced theory expounded by the modern school fully justifies the attempts made by the Government here and in England to check the abuse of competition among poor tenants by conferring fixity of tenure, by adjusting rents judicially for a term of years, and imposing limitations on its increase. In this matter the tenants of Government claim the same consideration as those of private Zamindars. The justification for this active interference is as valid in regard to agricultural labourers and tenants, as it is in the case of factory labourers and miner in Europe. These people are unable to combine for self-protection, or at least their combination is not so effective as that of the employers of labour, and when their efforts fail to obtain regular redress, disorder and misery result as consequences, and threaten public peace and general well-being. In the same spirit, the regulation of the freedom of contract in regard to the fixing of rates of interest in transactions between the poor disunited indebted classes and the money lenders, and the protection of immovable property from being sold away for improvident debts, not secured on the same, are all legitimate forms of protection of the weak against the strong, and do not effect the real freedom of distribution. The advanced theory concedes freedom where the parties are equally matched in intelligence and resources; when this is not the case, all talk of equality and freedom adds insult to the injury. It is in this spirit that the distribution of produce among the needy many and the powerful few has to be arranged, i.e., in a spirit of equity and fair play, and the orthodox views of finality in such matters must be reconsidered in all the relations of life.

Lastly comes the great department of governmental interference. The meddlesomeness of the mercantile system provoked a reaction against State control and guidance towards the end of the last century in favour of natural liberty. The doctrines of this negative school have now in their turn been abused by a too logical extension of its principles. There is a decided reaction in Europe against the *laissez faire* system. Even in England, the recent factory legislation, the qualified reorganization by law of Trade-Unionism, the Poor Law System, and the Irish Land Settlement, are all instances which indicate the same change of view. Speaking roughly, the province of State interference and control is practically being extended so as to restore the good points of the mercantile system without its absurdities. The State is now more and more recognized as the national organ for taking care of national needs in all matters in which individual and cooperative efforts are not likely to be so effective and economic as national effort. This is the correct view to take of the true functions of a State. To relegate them to the simple duty of maintaining peace and order is really to deprive the community of many of the advantages of the social union. Education, both liberal and technical, post and telegraphs, railway and canal communications, the pioneering of new enterprise, the insurance of risky undertakings, all these function are usefully discharged by the State. The question is one of time, fitness, and expediency, not one of liberty and rights. In our own country, the State has similarly enlarged its functions with advantage.

The very fact that the rulers belong to a race with superior advantages imposes this duty on them of attempting things which no native rulers, past or present, could as well achieve, or possibly even think of. This obligation is made more peremptory by the fact that the State claims to be the sole landlord, and is certainly the largest capitalist in the country. While the State in India has done much in this way in the working of iron and coal fields, and in the experiments made about cotton and tobacco, and in tea and coffee and cinchona plantations, it must be admitted that, as compared with its resources and the needs of the country, these attempts are as nothing by the side of what has been attempted with success in France, Germany and other countries, but which, unhappily, has not been attempted in this country. Even if political consideration forbid independent action in matter of differential duties, the pioneering of new enterprise is a duty which the Government might more system tically undertake with advantage. In truth, there is no difference of principle between lending such support and guidance by the free use of its credit and superior organization in pioneering industrial undertakings or subsidizing private cooperative effort, and its guaranteeing minimum interest to railway companies. The building up of national, not merely State, credit on broad foundations by helping people to acquire confidence in a free and largely ramified banking system, so advantageously worked in Europe under different forms, has also not been attempted here. There is, lastly, the duty cast on it of utilizing indigenous resources, and organizing them in a way to produce in India in state factories all products of skill which the State departments require in the way of stores. These are only a few of the many directions in which far more than exchange and frontier difficulties, the highest statesmanship will have a field all its own for consideration and action. They will, no doubt, receive such consideration if only the minds of the rulers were once thoroughly freed form the fear of offending the so-called maxims of rigid economical science. It is time that a new departure should take place in this connection. And it is with a view to drawing public attention to this necessity that I have ventured to place before you the results of modern economic thought. In this, as in other matters, the conditions of Indian life are more faithfully reproduced in some of the continental countries and in America than in England. If the attempt I have made leads to a healthy and full discussion of the change of policy I advocate, I shall regard myself amply repaid for my trouble.

(From *Essays on Indian Economics*, G.A. Nata Sen, Madras, 1920, pp 1-24)

7

Bal Gangadhar Tilak

Life and Times

The later half of the 19th century was a period of ferment. In the noontime of the British Empire, dark clouds of resistance and re-awakening gathered on the horizon, and of this spirit of resistance and re-awakening there was no better embodiment than Bal Gangadhar Tilak (1856-1920). Born just one year before the India war of independence of 1857, Tilak was to carry forward and fortify with steadfast devotion and rare courage the struggle against the British Empire and when he departed from the scene in 1920, the work was half-accomplished. The inspired, determined and mobilized nation could no longer be thrown back to its knees. If he rejected the constitutionalism of the moderates, if he frowned upon the social reforms, it was because he clearly understood the imperatives of real politic and while he considered reformism as costly distraction, he looked upon the constitutionalism as momentous self-deception. Tilak steered clear both of social progressivism and political gradualism because both appeared to him irrelevant to the immediate task of inspiring and mobilizing people for Swaraj. A pen-portrait by a British journalist Henry Nevinson sums up his charismatic personality thus – "I recognize in him the personal attraction that the extremists always have, the freedom from hesitation and half-measures, the delight in conflict, the reckless disregard of the self. When to this attraction, his own people could add his personal and intimate acquaintance with all classes among then down to the poorest villagers and his steady maintenance of all that they hold most dear in religious belief and customary observances, I could not wonder at his influence among them."

Bal Gangadhar Tilak was born in Ratnagiri district of Maharastra on 23rd July, 1856. His teacher-father was well-versed in Sanskrit and Mathematics, and love of Sanskrit and with that love of Indian culture and tradition naturally flowed to him. After graduating from Deccan college, Poona in 1876, he along with some of his friends started New English School in Poona not only to impart education to the youth but to infuse in them a sense of service for the motherland. To educate the people at large, he also started an English-language weekly *'Maratha'* and a Marathi weekly *'Kesari'*. His editorship of these journals involved him deeply in social and political affairs of Maharastra in particular and India in general. In the last decade of the 19th century, he started participating in the annual conferences of the Indian National Congress. Between 1891 to 1898, the political situation of Maharastra was aggravated by the callous attitude of government in tackling famine and plague, and Tilak severely criticized the insensitivity of the government towards the sufferings of the people. It was also during this period that as a result of Tilak's inspiration and efforts, people started celebrating Ganapti and Shivaji festivals on large scale. Through these celebrations Tilak was able to create great awakening among the people against the alien government and a sense of pride in their own culture and traditions The British government arrested him in 1897 on the charge of causing disaffection among the people against the government through his writings and other public activities. He was sentenced to 18 months of rigorous imprisonment.

Where Moderates like Gokhale asked young men to serve, Tilak asked them to protest and if necessary, go to prison. In this respect, the sarcasm and sharpness of Tilak's writings are in contrast to the understated reasonableness of Gokhale. As the Poona militant put it in a speech, of 1897, 'God has not conferred upon foreigners the grant inscribed on a copperplate to the kingdom of India.' In a speech in Calcutta in 1906 Tilak insisted that 'love of nation is one's first duty. Next comes religion . . .' Claiming that 'no nation can equal India' in the antiquity of its history and the depth of its cultural traditions, he tended to believe that India was (as his biographer Stanley Wolpert puts it) 'God's chosen nation'.

In 1908 Tilak was charged again with sedition and with intensifying racial animosity between Indians and the British. He was defended by the brilliant Bombay lawyer Muhammad Ali Jinnah. The defence could not completely annul the evidence contained in Tilak's polemical articles. In the event, he was sentenced to six years in prison and deported to Burma. When they heard of the sentence, the textile workers of Bombay downed tools in a spontaneous strike that shut down seventy mills. While in Mandalay prison, Tilak wrote a major and still influential work on the meanings of the Bhagavad Gita.

Tilak came out of jail in 1914, run-down in health and spirit. The fire of his early years was now much attenuated. He was more accommodative of British rule: where he had once thundered that 'swaraj is my birthright and I shall have it', he was willing to settle for Dominion status within the British Empire, rather than full independence. However, he continued to be active in politics, forming a Home Rule League in 1916. The same year he was charged once more with sedition. He was defended once again by Jinnah, this time successfully, and acquitted of the charges.

Tilak was a militant, populist leader, who did a great deal to encourage young Indians to join the national movement. On the negative side, the Hindu tenor of his speeches and writings may have alienated Indian Muslims. For much of his career, he insisted that political freedom must take precedence over all else, including or even especially social reform. This credo is manifest in an excerpt from a speech of 1916, which carries on a long-running debate with the recently deceased Gokhale: 'If there is no swarajya there is no use labouring for the spread of female education, there is no use trying to secure industrial development and social reform also can avail but little . . . Power is the primary necessity and where there is power, there alone resides wisdom; wisdom never resides apart from power.'

Bal Gangadhar Tilak died in Bombay in August 1920.

Tilak's popularity soared high with each passing day and from 1898 to 1908 he was at the peak of his political carrer. He along with Lala Lajpat Rai and Bipin Chandra Pal fromed a trio which in the backdrop of the partition of Bengal, popularized a four-fold programme of action, i.e. Swaraj (Self-government), Swadeshi (use of indigenous goods), Bahishkar (Boycott of foreign goods) and Rastriya Shiksha (National Education). Tilak made a whirlwind four of the country and his slogan 'Swaraj is my birth right and I shall have it' fired the popular imagination in such a way that national agenda and popular mood was radically transformed, making the moderates irrelevant. His campaign to have the Indian National Congress resort to passive resistance led to the split in the party and he along with his extremist colleagues and followers parted company from the Congress.

The infuriated British government was looking for opportunity to do away with Tilak politically. In the wake of revolutionary activities in Bengal and Maharastra he was charged with sedition and convicted in July 1908 for a fine of Rs. 1000 and transportation for six years. Tilak was sent to Mandalay prison of Burma. However neither the confinement nor the inhospitable climate of the place could weaken the indomitable spirit of Tilak; rather it came as a spur to his natural love of scholarship. Tilak wrote his timeless treatise *Gita Rahasya* which is a commentary on *Bhagvat Gita* and a gem of scholarship.

In 1914, he was set free form the prison. The first world was had begun and the extremists led by Tilak thought it advisable to close rank with moderates in this new situation. In 1916, he started Home Rule league along the lines of the Irish Home Rule Movement in order to further the cause of Swaraj. He also played a leading role in bringing about the Lucknow Pact of 1916 between the Congress and Muslim League. In 1918-19 he was in England for about Thirteen months contesting a court case against Valentine Chirol, a British Journalist who had sought to defame him in his writings. However he used this opportunity to advance the cause of Swaraj by inter-acting with the British politicians and addressing various section of the people. The valiant fighter passed away on 1st August 1920 leaving behind a rich and powerful legacy of service and sacrifice. Mahatma Gandhi rightly observed, "No man preached the gopel of Swaraj with the consistency and insistence of Lokmanya."

A scholar-statesman, Tilak's political thought was rooted in the spiritual and cultural traditions of India. Vedas represented to him the distilled wisdom capable of accomplishing the temporal and transcendental good. The Sanatana Dharma has been the bedrock of the ideas and institutions that have sustained India through the ages. In 'Gita Rahasya' he explicated the Indian vision of man and society and said that in sublimity and comprehensiveness, it surpassed the modern liberal-utilitarian viewpoints which were severally limited and hopelessly partial materialism, howsoever sophisticated, can not adequately understand and explain the multi-dimensionality of human existence. Similarly, moral theories based upon the vague concepts like conscience can also not lead us far. It is only by taking refuge of spiritual worldview that a proper concept of human good in all its aspects and dimensions can be had. The ancient civilization of India could rise to great heights in all walks of life-temporal and transcendental because of its proper understanding of totality and unity of cosmic existence. Any renovation of India in particular and world in general hinges upon the recovery of this central principle.

Man's yearning for the divine centre is the essential feature of his nature. Being a part of Brahma, he cannot but strive for his union with him. The part will naturally strive to be united with the whole because this alone ensures his fulfillment and freedom. As he put it, "the divine instinct of freedom never aged. Freedom is the very life of the individual soul which Vedanta declares to be not separate from God but identical with Him." This spiritual Swaraj-'a life centered in Self and dependent upon Self', can not be the award of a people who have not enjoyed it in the world. Thus spiritual Swaraj demands the presence of political Swaraj. Every nation has its distinctive way of life, its distinctive institutions, laws and customs and it is possible to live according to them only if the nation is politically free. The alien government, since it can not properly understand and appreciate the ideals and institutions of the subject country, will only be obstructive and destructive of the realization of its full potentiality. Thus political 'Swaraj' becomes a birthright and a moral necessity. Its loss is a calamity. Once the vital spark of freedom is extinguished, a nation is reduced to vegetative life. In a speech at Nasik during the Home Rule Movement, he thus emphasized the vital significance of political freedom- "The privilege of being free does not need to be granted by some one else. What is called 'Atma' in religious philosophy is known as liberty in the science of politics. Atma exits every where, it does not need to be reborn. Similarly love of liberty exists in every heart and I am only awakening you to the consciousness of its existence." He did not agree with liberals like Ranade and Pherozeshah Mehta that good government could be a substitute for self-governemnt. He said that the British Empire was in India not to further the good and welfare of Indians but its own interests. Moreover, by depriving us of our freedom, it had already dealt a fatal blow to our identity and our good.

Like Edmund Burke and Mazzini, Tilak regarded nationalism as essentially a spiritual and cultural concept. Many objective and subjective factors like a common history and tradition, common territory and language, common heroes and memories-all these factors went into the formation of nationhood. These subjective and psychological bonds existing among the people are given expression to and strengthened through objective visible symbols like national festivals, national heroes, national flag etc. Accordingly, Tilak favored the celebration of Ganapati festival in a public manner so as to foster unity and pride among the people. Likewise he played a leading role in organizing Shivaji festivals. He had no doubt that Sanatana Dharma was the real source of unity in India and this unity, so necessary to fight the British rule, could be promoted through the use of religious and historical symbols.

While Tilak's use of these symbols to awaken and arouse the people across the country proved to be a master stroke as it touched the 'mystic chords of memory', he was greatly misunderstood and severely criticized for mixing religion and politics. The Muslim leadership and the British journalists like Valentine Chirol attacked Tilak and charged him with creating disunity and dissension between the major communities of India. Tilak was not impressed by their arguments and rejected their charge of being anti-Muslim. He said that his purpose was to organize Hindu community against the British Empire and not against the Muslims, and this could be done more effectively and successfully by appealing to the religious sentiments. As for the Shivaji Festival he said that Shivaji was not anti-Muslim but against the oppressive policies of an emperor who happened to be Muslim.

Commenting on Tilak's concept of nationalism, the Marxist thinker M.N. Roy said 'The theory of nationalism expressed in the person and preachings of Tilak ignored the social law that political nationalism in modern times could not exist without economic foundation.' However the criticism is misplaced. Tilak did raise the question of economic exploitation of India under the British rule and fully agreed with Dadabhai Naoroji's 'drain theory'. He played a key role in organizing peasants and workers against the economic policies of the British government. But he was clear that economic factor played a subsidiary role in uniting the people against an oppressive regime, the real Sources of unity are moral-spiritual. To strengthen these moral-spiritual sources of nationalism, Tilak also stressed the importance of the national education and national press.

The issue of social reform had also become very contentious in the public life of Maharastra. Heated debates and hot exchanges on issues like child marriage, widow-remarriage, women's education etc characterized the social scene. While Ranade, Gokhale, Agarkar, Bhandarkar were ardent supporters of social reforms, Tilak took a very cautious view in the matter. He said that he was not opposed to social reforms as such but he had doubts about the intentions and methodology of the advocates of reforms. His objections were mainly (i) Any reformism driven by western rationalistic-secular world-view can not have a correct perspective of our social institutions and practices. As he put it, 'We do not want to anglicize our institutions and so to denationalize them in the name of social and political reforms. (ii) People seeking liberation from an alien government should refrain from seeking their support in solving social questions. It is morally wrong and socially enervating to try to cleanse our social system through the support of a foreign government and not through our own judgment and resolve. (iii) Education and not legislation is the proper method of eradicating social evils.

While in social matters, Tilak was in favour of cautious and gradual approach, in political field he was thoroughly dissatisfied with constitutionalism and gradualism of the liberals. He scoffed at those who advocated constitutional methods to gain political goals and said that they did not know what the word "Constitution" means. A term which is applicable in the politics of a free nation like England, is wholly inapplicable in the politics of a subject nation which has only one constitution-the Indian penal code. In fighting an oppressive foreign government, not law but justice, morality and historical tradition should be our guiding principles. He espoused Swadeshi and Boycott as the most effective means to undermine the British Empire. Swadeshi is the positive expression of people's love of their motherland and their resolve to rear their own political, economic, legal and educational institutions and Boycott is the expression of non-cooperation with imperial government in all walks of life. As for the revolutionary methods being advocated and used by a section of political class of India, Tilak said that under present conditions, such methods were imprudent, but not unethical. He had the highest regard for the burning patriotism of revolutionaries like Shyamji Krishna Verma, Damodar Savarkar etc though he himself was no revolutionary like Lenin or Bakunin.

Tilak combined in himself the intellectual profundity of a theoretician and shrewdness of a strategist. His formidable presence transformed the Congress organization and the political landscape of the country. M.N. Buch has rightly said "Like Socrates, Tilak brought the political philosophy in India from heaven to earth, from the Council Hall or the Congress Mandap to the street and the market." But in the midst of his many political engagements, he could find leisure and detachment to plunge into his scholarly pursuits and his many writings like *Orian*, *Arctic Home of Vedas*, and *Gita Rahasya* are shining examples of it. Dr. S. Radhakrishnan regards him essentially a scholar and only circumstantially a politician. To quote him- "The field of politics to which Mr. Tilak devoted the best years of his life was not the one for which he was made. He was by nature a scholar and only by necessity a politician."

The following extract from *The Gita Rahasya* provides a peep into his stupendous grasp of the ancient scriptures as well as the contemporary currents of the European thought. He was well-versed in the Hindu scriptures and he was equally at home in the moral and political ideas and arguments of contemporary thinkers like Hobbes, Bentham, Butler, Mill, Kant, Spencer etc. The central question of *The Bhagavad Gita* is - what is duty and what is non-duty ? What makes an action right ? Tilak says that the problem concerning action and non-action can be looked at from three standpoints. While the Indian scriptures say that the metaphysical way is the most excellent way of resolving the question, the other two ways have been advocated by most of the Western philosophers and thinkers of modern times.

Tilak divides the materialistic or hedonistic philosophers into three categories- (i) The advocates of the self-interest (ii) The advocates of enlightened self-interest (iii) The advocates of the compatibility between self-interest and common interest. He examines the three viewpoints and exposes their contradictions and limitations. He then considers the best division of this school-benevolent materialist philosophers who maintain that one should decide about the doability or non-doability of all actions by judiciously weighing the material happiness of not only one human being but the majority of people. The utilitarianism of Bentham and Mill broadly belongs to this school of thought. Tilak argues that this view point, though superior to the three categories of materialistic or hedonistic school is thoroughly inadequate in as much as (i) The questions of morality can not properly be decided by reference to numbers and (ii) happiness is intrinsic, being the reward of purity of mind. Thus correct answers to the questions of duty and non-duty are to be sought at metaphysical level. When one ascends to this plane of consciousness, all one's doubts and dilemmas get resolved as happened with Arjun in the battlefield of Kurushetra.

The Materialistic Theory of Happiness (Âdhibhautika Sukhavâda)

As we have seen that stock precepts like : 'mahâjano yena gatah sa panthâh', i.e. 'follow the path which has been followed by venerable persons', or, 'ati sarvatra varjayet', i.e., 'do too much of nothing', do not satisfactorily explain : (i) why Manu and the other legislators laid down the rules of 'ahimsâ satyamasteya' (Non-Violence, Veracity, Not-stealing) etc., (ii) whether those rules are mutable or immutable, (iii) what their extent or the fundamental principle underlying them is, and (iv) which precept should be followed when two or more of them are equally in point and yet conflict with each other, it is now necessary for us to see whether or not there are any definite means for properly determining these questions, and deciding which is the most beneficial or meritorious path of duty, as also, in what way and from what point of view we can determine the relative importance or the greater or less worth of mutually conflicting principles of morality. I have in the last chapter explained that there are three ways of considering the questions involved in the exposition of action and non-action, namely, the positive, (âdhibhautika), the theological (âdhidaivika), and the metaphysical (âdhyatmika), just as in the case of the scientific exposition of other matters. According to our philosophers the most excellent of these ways is the metaphysical way. But, as it is necessary to carefully consider the other two methods in order to fully understand the importance of the metaphysical method, I have in this chapter first considered the fundamental materialistic principles underlying the examination of the question of action and non-action. The positive physical sciences which have made an immense growth in modern times have to deal principally with the external or visible properties of tangible objects.

Therefore, those persons who have spent their lives in studying the physical sciences, or who attach much importance to the critical methods particular to these sciences, get into the habit of always considering only the external effects of things; and their philosophical vision being thereby to a certain extent narrowed, they don't, in discussing any particular thing, attach much importance to causes which are metaphysical, or intangible, or invisible, or which have reference to the next world. But, although on that account, they leave out of consideration the metaphysical or the next-world point of view, yet, as codes of morality are necessary for the satisfactory regulation of the mutual relations of human beings and for public welfare, even these philosophers, who are indifferent about life after death or who have no faith in intangible or metaphysical knowledge, (and also necessarily no faith n God), look upon the science of proper action (Karma Yoga) as a most important science; and, therefore, there has been in the past and there is still going on, a considerable amount of discussion in the West, as to whether the science of proper and improper action can be satisfactorily dealt with in the same way as the physical sciences, that is to say, by means of arguments based on purely worldly and visible effects. As a result of this discussion, modern Western philosophers have made up their minds that the science of metaphysics is of no use whatsoever for the consideration of ethics, that the goodness or badness of any particular action must be determined by considering only those of its external effects which are actually visible to us, and that we can do so. Any act which a man performs, is performed by him either for obtaining happiness, or for warding off unhappiness.

One may even say that 'the happiness of all human beings' is the highest worldly goal, and if the ultimate visible resultant of all action is thus definite, the correct method of deciding Ethical problems, is to determine the moral value of all actions by weighing the greater or lesser possibilities of each action producing happiness or preventing unhappiness. If one judges the goodness or badness of any particular object in ordinary life by considering its external usefulness, e.g., if, we decide that that cow which has short horns and which is docile, and at the same time gives a large quantity of milk is the best cow, then on the same principle, we must also consider that action as the most meritorious one, from the ethical point of view, of which the external result of producing happiness or preventing unhappiness is the highest. If it is possible to decide the ethical value of any particular act in such an easy and scientific way, namely, by considering the greater or less value of its purely external and visible effects, one should not trouble about entering into the discussion of the self and non-self (*atmanatma*); "*arke cen madhu vindeta kimartham parvatam vrajet*", *i.e.*, " if one can get honey near at hand where he sits, then where is the sense of going into the hills to look for honey-combs?" I call this method of determining the morality of any particular Action by considering merely its external results the '*adhibhautika sukhavada*' (the materialistic theory of happiness), because, the happiness to be considered for determining the morality of any action is, according to this theory, actually visible and is external-that is, is such as arises from the contact of the organs with external objects, and consequently materialistic (*adhibhautika*)- and this school has likewise been brought into existence by those philosophers who consider the world from the purely positive or materialistic point of view. But, it is not possible to fully discuss this theory in this book. It would be necessary to write an independent book to even merely summarize the opinions of the different writer. I have, therefore, in this chapter collected together and given as precisely as possible as much general information about this materialistic school of ethics as is absolutely necessary for fully understanding the nature and importance of the science of proper action expounded in the Bhagavad Gita.

If any one wants to go deeper into the matter, he must study the original works of the Western philosophers. From my statement above, that materialistic philosophers are apathetic about the science of the atman or about the next world, one must not draw the conclusion that all the learned persons who subscribe to this path, are selfish, self-centered or immoral. There belong to this school high-minded philosophers like Comte, Spencer, Mill, and others, who most earnestly and enthusiastically preached that striving for the benefit of the whole world by making at least one's worldly outlook as comprehensive as possible (if one does not believe in the next world), is the highest duty of every man; and as their works are replete with the most noble and deep thoughts, they ought to be read by every one. Although the paths of the science of proper action are many, yet, so long as one has not given the go-bye to the external ideal of 'the benefit of the world', one must not ridicule a philosopher on the ground that his method of dealing with the philosophy of ethics is different from one's own. I shall now precisely and in their proper order, consider the various divisions into which the modern or ancient materialistic philosophers fall , as a result of differences of opinion between them as to whether the external material happiness which has to be considered for determining the ethical propriety or impropriety of an action is one's own happiness or the happiness of another, and whether of one person or of several persons; and I shall also consider to what extent these opinions are proper or faultless.

The first of these classes is of those who maintain the theory of pure selfish happiness. This school of thought says that there is no such thing as life after death or as philanthropy; that all Metaphysical sciences have been written by dishonest people to serve their own ends; that the only thing which is real in this world is one's own interest; and that, that act by which this self-interest can be achieved or whereby one can promote one's own material happiness is the most just, the most proper, and the most meritorious act. This opinion was, at a very early date, vociforously proclaimed in India by Carvaka. and the mischievous advice given by Jabali to Sri Rama at the end of the Ayodhyakanda of the *Ramayana,* as also the Kanikaniti in the *Mahabharata* pertains to this school of thought. The opinion of the illustrious Carvaka was that when the five primordial elements are fused together, they acquire the quality of an atman, and when the body is burnt, the atman is burnt with it; therefore, a wise man should not bother about the *Atman,* but should enjoy himself so long as life lasts, even borrowing money for the purpose, if necessary; one should *"rnam krtva ghrtam pipet"*, i.e., " borrow money and drink clarified butter", because there is nothing after death.

As Carvaka was born in India, he satisfied himself with prescribing the drinking of clarified butter *(ghrtam pibet)* otherwise, this canon would have been transformed into *'rnam krtga suram pibet'*, i.e., 'borrow money and drink wine'. This school says: "What is this *dharma* and this charity? All the objects which have been created in this world by the Paramesvara, -what did I say? I have made a mistake! Of course, there is no Paramesvara-all the things which I see in this world have come into existence only for my enjoyment, and as I can see no other purpose for them, there is, of course, no such purpose. When I am dead, the world is over; and therefore, so long as I am alive, I shall acquire all the various things which can be acquired, acquiring this to-day and that to-morrow, and thereby I shall satisfy all all my desires. If at all I go in for any religious austerity or charity, that will be only to increase my reputation and worth; and if I make a *rajasuya yajna* or an *asvamedha yajna,* that too will be for the sole purpose of establishing that my power is unchallenged in all directions. In short, the EGO, the 'I' is the only focus of this world, and this 'I' is the sum and substance of all morality; all the rest is false". The description of godless endowment *(asuri sampatti)* given in the 16th chapter of the Gita in the words: *"isvaro 'ham aham bhogi siddho' ham balavan sukhi"* (*Gi.*16.14), i.e., " I am the Isvara, I am the one who enjoys, and I am the *siddha* (perfect), the all-powerful, and the happy", applies quite appropriately to the opinions of persons who follow this philosophy. If instead of Sri Krisna, there had been some person like Jabali belonging to this sect for advising Arjuna, he would, in the first place, have slapped Arjuna on the face, and then said to him : " What a fool are you! When you have without effort got this golden opportunity of fighting and conquering everybody and enjoying all kinds of royal enjoyment and happiness, you are uttering the most foolish things, being lost in the futile confusion of ' shall I do this, or shall I do that'! You will not get such a chance again. What a fool are you to think of the atman and of relatives! Strike! and enjoy the empire of Hastinapura after having removed all the thorns from your path! In this lies your truest happiness. Is there anything in this world except one's visible material happiness?"

But, Arjuna was not anxious to hear such a disgustingly selfish, purely self-centred, and ungodlike advice; and he had already in advance, said to Sri Krisna: " If I had to acquire for myself (by this war), the kingdom even of the three worlds-to say nothing of the kingdom of this world-(that is, such physical pleasures), I do not desire for that purpose to kill the Kauravas. I do not mind if they slit open my throat'. Even a mere reference to this ungodlike self-centered and entirely selfish doctrine of material happiness, which

Arjuna had, in this way, denounced in advance, would amount to a refutation of it. This extremely low stage reached by the school of material happiness, which looks upon one's own physical pleasures as the highest ideal of man, and totally disregards what happens to other people, has been treated by all writers on the science of proper action, and even by ordinary people, as extremely immoral, objectionable and disdainable. Nay!, this theory does not even deserve the name of ethics or of an exposition of morality; and therefore, instead of wasting more time in considering this subject, we will now turn to the next class of materialistic philosophers.

Pure and naked selfishness or self-centeredness never succeeds in the world; because, although physical and material pleasures may be desirable to every one, yet, as is a matter of actual experience, if our happiness interferes with the happiness of others, those others will certainly do us harm. Therefore other materialistic philosophers maintain that although one's happiness or selfish purposes may be one's goal, yet, in as much as it is not possible for one to acquire such happiness, unless one makes some sacrifices for other people similar to those one oneself wants from them, one must long-sightedly take into account the happiness of others in order to obtain one's own happiness. I put these materialistic philosophers in the second class. It may be said that the materialistic exposition of Ethics truly begins at this point. Because, instead of saying like Carvaka, that no ethical limitations are necessary for the maintenance of society, persons belonging to this school have made an attempt to explain their own view as to why these limitations must be observed by everybody.

These people say that, if one minutely considers how the theory of Harmlessness came into this world, and why people follow that doctrine, there is no other reason at the root of it except the fear based on selfish considerations that, 'if I kill others, others will kill me, and then I will lose my happiness', and that all other moral precepts have come into existence as a result of this selfish fear in the same way as this law of harmlessness. If we suffer pain, we cry, and if others suffer pain, we feel pity for them. But why? Because the fear that we in our turn may have to suffer the same pain, that is, of course, the thought of our possible future unhappiness comes to our minds. Charity, generosity, pity, love, gratefulness, humbleness, friendship, and other qualities which at first sight appear to be for the benefit of others are, if we trace them to their origin, nothing but means of acquiring our own happiness or warding off our own unhappiness in another form. Everybody who soever helps others or gives in charity with the internal motive that if he found himself in the same position, other people should help him; and we love others, only in order that others should love us. At any rate, the selfish idea that other people should call us good is at the back of our minds. The expressions 'doing good to others' and ' the welfare of other' are words based on confusion of thought. What is real, is one's own selfish purpose; and one's own selfish purpose means obtaining one's own happiness or warding off one's own unhappiness. This amounts to saying that a mother suckles her baby not on account of love, but she does this selfish act in order to ease herself (as her breasts are full of milk and she feels the inconvenience of the pressure), or in order that the child, after growing up, should love her and give her happiness. The fact that people of this school of thought admit that it is necessary to long-sightedly observe such moral principles as will permit of the happiness of others-though that may be for obtaining one's own happiness- is the important difference between this school of thought and the school of Cârvâka. Nevertheless, the idea that a human being is nothing but a statue cast into the mould of selfish physical desires, which is the opinion of the Cârvâka school, has been left untouched by this school. This opinion has been supported in England by Hobbes and in France by Helvetius. But there are not to be found many followers of this school in England or anywhere else.

After the exposition of ethics by Hobbes had been published, it was refuted by philosophers like Butler, who proved that human nature as a whole is not absolutely selfish, and that there exist in a human being from birth such other qualities as humanity, love, gratitude etc., to a greater or less extant, side by side with selfishness; and therefore, in considering any act or any dealing from the ethical point of view, one should instead of considering only the qualities of selfishness or even of long-sighted selfishness, always consider the two inherent distinct tendencies of human beings, namely, 'selfishness', (svârtha) and the 'unselfishness', (parârtha). If even a cruel animal like a tigress is prepared to sacrifice her life for the sake of her cubs, it follows that saying that emotions of love and philanthropy come into existence in the human mind merely out of selfishness is futile, and that weighing between the duty and the non-duty merely from the point of view of long-sighted selfishness is scientifically incorrect. Our ancient writers had not lost sight of the fact that persons, whose intelligence has remained unpurified on account of their having remained wholly engrossed in family life, very often do whatever they do in this world for others, only with an eye to their own benefit. The saint Tukârâm has said: "the daughter-in-law weeps for the mother-in-law but the motive in her heart is quite different" (Gâ. 2583.2); and some of our philosophers have gone even beyond Helvetius. For instance, in commenting on the proposition laid down by Sri Samkarâchârya in his Brahma-Sutrabhâsya (Ve. Su.Sâm. Bhâ. 2.2.3) on the authority of the Gautama-Nyâyasutra (1.1.18) 'pravartanâ laksanâ dosâh', i.e., 'all human activity, whether selfish or unselfish, is faulty', Anandgiri says that: "We practice kindness or benevolence towards other only in order to remove that pain which result from the emotion of pity awakening in our hearts" This argument of Anandgiri is to be found in almost all our books on the path of renunciation, and all that is principally attempted to be proved from it is, that all actions are selfish, and, therefore, non-performance. But in the conversation between Yâjnavalkya and his wife Maitreyi, which appears twice in the Brhadâranyak-opanisad (Br. 2.4; 4.5), this very argument has been made use of in another and a strange way.

In answering the question of Maiteryi: "How can one acquire immortality?", Yâjnavalkya says to her: "O Maitreyi, the husband is loved by the wife, not for the sake of the husband, but for the sake of her own âtman; in the same way, the son is not loved by us for his own sake; we love him for our own sake. 'âtmanastu kâmâya sarvam priyam bhavati', i.e., 'We like all things for the sake of our Self (âtman)', and if all love is in this way based on Self, must we not, in the first place, find out what our âtman (Self) is ?" And, therefore, the concluding advice of Yâjnavalkya is "âtmâ vâ are drastavyah srotavyo manavyo nidihyâsitavyah", i.e., "See (first) what the âtma (Self) is, hear the âtman, and meditate and contemplate on the 'atman'. When the true form of 'atman' in this way been realized by following this advice, the whole world becomes Self-ised (âtma-maya), and the distinction between selfishness (svârtha) and unselfishness (parârtha) in the mind ceases to exist. Although this argument of Yâjnavalkya is apparently the same as that of Hobbes, yet, as can be easily seen, the inferences drawn by them respectively from that advice are contrary to each other. Hobbes attaches higher importance to selfishness, and, looking upon all philanthropy as long-sighted selfishness, says that there is nothing in this world except selfishness; whereas Yâjnavalkya, relying on the word 'sva' (one's own) in the phrase 'svârtha' (selfishness), shows, on the authority of that word, that from the metaphysical point of view, all created beings are harmoniously comprised in our Atman and our Atman is likewise harmoniously comprised in all created beings; and he, in that way, gets rid of the apparently dualistic (dvaita) conflict between the interest of oneself and the interest of others. These opinions of Yâjnavalkya and of the school of Renunciation will be considered in grater detail later on. I have referred here to the opinions of Yâjnavalkya and other only for the purpose of showing how our ancient writers have more or less praised or accepted as correct the principle that the ordinary tendency of human beings is selfish and that it is concerned with their own happiness', and drawn from it inferences which are quite contrary to those drawn by Hobbes.

Having thus proved that human nature is not purely selfish and is not governed wholly by the tamas quality, nor totally ungodly (as has been maintained by the English writer Hobbes and the French writer Helvetius), and that a benevolent (sâttvika) mental impulse forms part of human nature from birth along with the selfish impulse, and that doing good to others is not long-sighted selfishness, one has to give equal importance to the two principles of svârtha, i.e., one's own happiness and parârtha, i.e., the happiness of others, in building up the science of the doable and the not-doable (kâryâkârya-vyavasthiti). This is the third division of materialistic philosophers. Nevertheless, the materialistic view that both svârtha and parâtha deal only with worldly happiness, is also held by this school. The only difference is that people who belong to this school consider it their duty to take into account both self-interest (svârtha) and other's-interest (parârtha) in determining questions of morality, because they look upon the impulse of doing good to others as, as much an inherent impulse, as the selfish impulse. As normally there the actions which a man performs are primarily also beneficial to society. If one man accumulated wealth, that ultimately benefits the whole society; because, society being a collection of numerous individuals, if each individual in it benefits himself without harming others, that is bound to benefit the whole society. Therefore, this school of philosophers has laid down that if one can do good to others without neglecting one's own happiness, it is one's duty to do so. But, as this school does not admit the superiority of other's-interest and advises that one should each time, according to one's own lights, consider whether one's own interests or the interests of others are superior, it is difficult to decide to what extent one should sacrifice one's own happiness for the happiness of others when there is a conflict between self-interest and other's-interest, and there is very often a chance of a man falling a prey to considerations of his own interests. For instance, if self interest is considered to be as important as other's interest, it is difficult to decide by reference to the doctrines of this school of thought, whether or not one should, for the sake of truth, suffer considerable financial loss-to say nothing of the much more serious question whether or not one should, for the sake of truth, sacrifice one's life or lose one's kingdom. Persons belonging to this school may possibly praise a benevolent man who sacrifices his life for the advantage of another, but if they are themselves faced with a similar situation, these philosophers, who habitually sit on the two stools of self-interest and other's-interest, will certainly be dragged towards self-interest.

This school believes that they do not look upon other's-interest as a long-sighted variety of selfishness (as was done by Hobbes), but that they minutely weigh self-interest and other's-interest in a scale, and very skillfully decide in what self-interest lies; and, on that account, they glorify their doctrine by calling it the path of 'enlightened' (udatta) or 'wise' self-interest (but self-interest in any case). But see what Bhartrhari says that is, "those who do good to others, sacrificing their own interests are the truly good persons; those who strive for the good of others, without sacrificing self-interest, are ordinary persons; those who harm others, for their self-interest, must be looked upon not as human beings but as godless beings (râksasâh); but I do not know how to describe those who are worse than these, that is, those who needlessly harm the interests of others". In the same way in describing the most excellent form of regal morality, Kâlidâsa says that is, "you strive ever day for the welfare of others without considering your own happiness, or it may be said that such is your natural instinct or vocation". Neither Bhartrhari nor Kâlidâsa had to see how to discriminate between right action or wrong action (karmâkarma) or righteousness and unrighteousness (dharmâdharma) by adopting both th principles of self interest and other's interest into a science of right action (Karma Yoga), and judiciously weighing them. Nevertheless, the highest place which has been given by them to persons who sacrifice self-interest for other's-interest is justifiable even from the point of view of ethics. Persons belonging to this school of thought say, that although other's-interest may be superior to self-interest from the philosophical point of view, yet, in as much as we have not to consider what ideally pure morality is, but only how 'ordinary' persons should act in the ordinary affairs of the world, the prominence given by us to 'enlightened self-interest' is proper from the worldly point of view. But in my opinion there is no sense in this argument.

The weights and measures used in commerce are as a rule more or less inaccurate; but if, taking advantage of that fact, the greatest possible accuracy is not maintained in the standard weights and measures kept in public offices, shall we not blame the persons in authority? The same rule applies to the philosophy of Karma Yoga. Ethics has been formulated only in order to scientifically define the pure, complete, and constant form of morality; and, if any science of Ethics does not do this, it must be said to be useless. Sidgwick is not wrong in saying that 'enlightened self-interest' is the path of ordinary people. Bhartrhari says the same thing. But if one examines what the opinion of these ordinary people about the highest morality is, it will be seen that, even in their opinion, the importance given by Sidgwick to enlightened self-interest is wrong, and the path of spotless morality or the path followed by saints, is looked upon by them as something much better than the ordinary selfish path; and, that is what is intended to be conveyed by the stanzas of Bhartrhari quoted above.

I have so far dealt with the three divisions of the school of material happiness, namely, the purely selfish, the longsighted selfish, and the enlightened selfish (which is both the former ones combined), and I have pointed out what the principal shortcomings of their respective systems are. But this does not exhaust all the divisions of the material happiness school. The next division, that is to say, the best division of this school is the one of the benevolent (sâttvika) materialistic philosophers, who maintain that; one should decide the ethical doability or non-doability of all action by judiciously weighing the material happiness of only one human being, but of the entire human race. It is not possible that one and the same act will cause happiness to all persons in the world or in a society at one and the same time.

If one person looks upon a particular thing as productive of happiness, it produces unhappiness to another person. But, just as light is not considered objectionable on the ground that the owl does not like it, so also if a particular thing is not profitable to some persons, it cannot be said, even according to the Karma Yoga science, that it is not beneficial to all; and on that account, the words 'the happiness of all persons' (sarvabhutahita) have to be understood as meaning the 'greatest happiness (good) of the greatest number'. Inshort, the opinion of this school is that, "we must consider only such acts as ethically just and fit to be performed, as are conductive to the greatest good of the greatest number; and that, acting in that way is the true duty of every human being in this world." This doctrine of the school of material happiness is acceptable to the metaphysical school. Nay, I may even say that this principle was propounded by the metaphysicians in very ancient times, and the materialistic philosophers have now turned it to use in a particular way.

It is a well-known fact, as has been said by the Saint Tukârâm that, "saintly persons come to life only for the benefit of the world; they suffer in body in order to do good to others". Needless to say, there is no dispute about the correctness or the propriety of this principle. Even in the Bhagavadgitâ, in describing the characteristic features of saints (jnânin) who practice the perfect Yoga- of course, the Karma Yoga- the words "sarvabhutahite ratah" i.e., "they are engrossed in doing good to all created beings" have been clearly used twice (Gi. 5.25; 12.4); and it becomes quite clear from the statement from the *Mahâbhârata* quoted in the second chapter above: "yad bhutahitam atyantain tat satyam iti dhâramâ". (Vana 208. 4), i.e., "that is Truth according to dharma in which the highest benefit of all lies," that our ancient writers used to take into account this principle in deciding what is just (dharma) and what unjust (adharma). But, looking upon the promotion of the welfare of all created beings as the external characteristic feature of the conduct of jnânins, and occasionally making use of that principle in a broad way for determining what is just and what unjust, is something absolutely different from taking for granted that, that is the substance of ethics, and disregarding everything else, and erecting an immense structure of the science of ethics on that foundation alone.

Materialistic philosophers accept the latter course and maintain that ethics has nothing to do with metaphysics. It is, therefore, necessary for us to see now to what extent they are correct. There is a great deal of difference between the meanings of the two words 'happiness' (sukha) and 'benefit' (hita); but, although for the moment that difference is not taken into consideration and the word 'sarvabhutahita' is taken as meaning 'the greatest happiness of the greatest number', yet it will be seen, that numerous important difficulties arise, if we rely only on this principle for distinguishing the doable from the not-doable. Suppose, a materialist follower of this principle was advising Arjuna: what would he have told him? Would he not have said: If as a result of your becoming victorious in the Bhâratiya war, you bring about the greatest happiness of the greatest number, then it is your duty to fight, even if you might kill Bhisma. Apparently, this advice seems very easy.

But, if we go a little deeper, we realize its insufficiency and the difficulties involved in it. 'Greatest number' means how much? The Pândava army was of seven aksauhinis (a unit for measuring the numbers of soldiers). But, the Kaurava army was of eleven aksauhinis. Can one, therefore, argue that the Pândavas were in the wrong, on the ground that if the Pândavas had been defeated these eleven Kaurava aksuhinis would have become happy? To decide questions of morality merely on the basis of numbers would be wrong on any number of occasions, to say nothing of the Bhâratiya war. Even in ordinary life everyone believes, that that act which pleases even one good man is more truly a good act than the act which gives happiness to a hundred thousand evil-doers. In order to justify this belief, the happiness of one saint has to be given a higher value than the happiness of a hundred thousand evil-doors, and if one does that, the fundamental principle that 'the greatest external happiness of the greatest number is the only test of morality' becomes, to that extent, weak. One has, therefore, to say that numbers have no fixed bearing on morality. It must also be borne in mind that some thing which is ordinarily considered as productive of happiness by all persons is, by a far-sighted person, seen to be disadvantageous to all.

Take for example the cases of Socrates and Jesus Christ. Both of them were preaching to their countrymen what, in their respective opinions, was ultimately beneficial. But their countrymen denounced them as 'enemies of society', and put them to death. The people, as also their leaders, were acting on the principle of the 'greatest good of the greatest number'; but we do not now say that what the ordinary people then did was just. In short, even if we for a moment admit that 'greatest good of the greatest number' is the only fundamental principle of ethics, yet, we do not thereby solve to any extent the questions, in what lies the happiness of millions of persons, how that has to be ascertained, and by whom. On ordinary occasions, the task of finding this out may be left to those persons whose happiness or unhappiness is under consideration.

But, as it is not necessary to go so deep into the matter on ordinary occasions, and, as ordinary persons do not possess the mental grasp to understand and decide faultlessly in what their happiness lies on extraordinary and difficult occasions, putting into the hands of such uneducated persons the solitary ethical principle of 'the greatest good of the greatest number' is like placing a fire-brand into the hands of an evil spirit, as is apparent from the illustrations of the two leaders given above. There is no sense in the repartee: "our ethical principle is correct; what can we do if ignorant persons have wrongly applied it?" Because, although the principle may be correct, one must at the same time explains who are the proper persons to give effect to it, and when and how these persons do so, and other similar limitations of the principle. Otherwise, ordinary people will needlessly indulge in the fond belief that they are as capable of determining questions of morality as Socrates, and serious consequences are likely to follow.

This theory is open to other objections which are more serious than the two objections: (i) questions of morality cannot be properly decided by reference to numbers alone and (ii) there is no definite external measure for logically proving in what lies the greatest good of the greatest number, which I have mentioned above. For instance, only a little consideration will show that it is very often impossible to fully and satisfactorily decide whether a particular Action is just or unjust by considering merely its external effects. It is true that we decide whether a particular watch is good or bad, by seeing whether or not it shows correct time; but before applying this rule to human actions, one must bear in mind, that man is not merely a watch or a machine. It is true that all saints strive for the benefit of the world. But we cannot draw the definite converse conclusion that every person who strives for the benefit of the world must be a saint. One must also see what that man's frame of mind is. This is the great difference between a man and a machine; and therefore, if some one commits a crime unintentionally or by mistake, it is legally considered a pardonable offence. In short, we cannot arrive at a correct decision as to whether a particular act is good or bad, just or unjust, or moral or immoral by considering merely its external result or effect, that is, by considering whether or not that act will produce the greatest good of the greatest number. One has also necessarily to consider at the same time, the reason, the desire, or the motive of the doer of the act. There was once an occasion to construct a tramway for the benefit and happiness of all the citizens of a big city in America.

But there were delays in obtaining the requisite sanction from the proper authorities. Thereupon, the directors of the tramway company gave a bribe to the persons in authority, and the necessary sanction was immediately obtained; and, the construction of the tramway being complete soon afterwards, all the people in the city were in consequence considerably convenienced and benefited. Some time after that, the bribery was found out, and the manager of the tramway was criminally prosecuted. There was no unanimity in the first jury, so a second jury was empanelled and the second jury having found the manager guilty, he was convicted. In such a case, the principle of the greatest good of the greatest number Is useless by itself. The external effect of the briber, namely, that the tramway came to be constructed because the bribe was given, was the greatest good of the greatest number; yet, on that account, the fact that the bribe was given does not become legal. Though the external effects of the two several acts of giving in charity desirelessly in the belief that it is one's duty to do so (dâtavyam), and of giving in charity for the sake of reputation or for some other purpose are the same, yet, even the Bhagavadgita distinguishes between the two by saying, that the first gift is sâttvika (benevolent) and that the second gift is râjasa (desire-prompted) (Gi. 17.20-23); and the same gift, if made to an unworthy person is said to be tamasa and objectionable.

Even ordinary people consider a poor man's giving a few pies for a charitable purpose as of the same moral value, as the gift of a hundred rupees by a rich man. But, if the matter be considered by an external test like 'the greatest good of the greatest number' we will have to say that these two gifts are not of the same moral value. The great drawback of the Materialistic ethical principle of the 'greatest good of the greatest number' is, that it does not attach any importance to the motive or the reason of the doer, and if one says that the inner motive has to be taken into account, then the fundamental condition of the greatest external good of the greatest number being the only test of morality is not satisfied. As the Legislative Council or Assembly is a collection of many individuals, it is not necessary to ascertain what the state of their conscience was when we consider whether or not the laws made by them are proper; and it is enough if one considers only the external aspect of the laws, namely, whether or not the greatest good of the greatest number will result from them.

But, as will be clear from the illustrations given above, the same test does not apply to other cases. I do not say that the principle of 'the greatest good or happiness of the greatest number' is utterly useless. One cannot have a more excellent principle for considering external matter; but in considering whether a particular thing is morally just or unjust, it is very often necessary to consider several other things besides this external principle; and therefore, one cannot safely depend on this principle alone for determining questions of morality; and all that I say is, that it is necessary to ascertain and fix upon some principle, more definite and faultless than this. The same moral is conveyed by the statement: "The reason (buddhi) is of greater importance than the action" (Gi. 2. 49), made in the very beginning of the Gita. If one considers only the external action, it is often misleading. It is not impossible for a man to be subject to excessive anger, notwithstanding that he continues to perform his external actions of religious austerities. But on the other hand, if the heart is pure, the external act becomes immaterial, and the religious or moral value of an insignificant external act like the giving of dried boiled rice by Sudâmâ to Sri Krisna is considered by people to be as great as the public distribution of tons of food, which will give great happiness to a great number. Therefore, the well-known German philosopher Kant has treated the weighing of the external and visible effects of an act as of minor importance and has started his exposition of Ethics with a consideration of the purity of mind of the doer.

It is not that this shortcoming of the materialistic theory of happiness was not noticed by the principal supporters of that theory. Hume has clearly said that in as much as the acts of a person are considered a test of his morality as being the index of his disposition, it is impossible to decide that they are praiseworthy or unworthy merely from their external effects; and even Mill accepts the position that 'the morality of any act depends entirely upon the motive of the doer, that is to say, upon the reasoning on which he bases that act.' But, in order to support his own point of view, Mill has added a rider to this principle that, 'so long as the external act is the same, its moral value remains the same, whatever may have been the desire which prompted it'. This argument of Mill is only doctrinal.

Because, if the Reason (buddhi) is different, then, though two acts may be the same in appearance, yet they can never have the same value essentially. And Green, therefore, objects that the limitation: 'so long as there is no difference in the (external) act' etc. laid down by Mill, itself falls to the ground. The same is the opinion expressed in the Gitâ. Because, the Gitâ says that even if two persons have given the same amounts for the same charitable purpose- that is, even when their external act is just the same-it is possible that one gift will be sâttvika, and the other one will be râjasa or even tâmasa if the two persons have different reasons for the gift. But I shall deal in grater detail with this question later on, when I compare the Eastern and the Western opinions in the matter. All that I have to prove at the moment is, that even this refined form of the materialistic theory of happiness,-which depends only on the external results of an Action-falls short on the mark in determining questions of morality; and Mill's admission quoted above is, in my opinion, the best possible proof of that fact.

The greatest drawback of the theory of 'the greatest good of the greatest number' is that it does not take into consideration the reason (buddhi) of the doer. Because, the writings of Mill himself show that, even if his arguments are accepted, this principle of determining questions of morality merely by external results, is applicable only within specified limits, that is, is one-sided, and cannot be equally applied to all cases. But, there is a further objection to this theory, namely that, as the entire argument of the theory has been developed on the basis that other's-interest is superior to self-interest without explaining why or how it is so, the theory of 'enlightened self-interest' gets a chance of pushing itself forward. If both self interest and other's interest have come into existence with man, why should one look upon the good of the greatest number as more important than one's own interest? The answer, that other's interest should be protected because it involves the greatest good of the greatest number is not satisfactory; because the question itself is why I should bring about the greatest good of the greatest number. It is true that this question does not always arise, since one's interest, as a general rule, lies in promoting the interests of others.

But the difference between this last and fourth stage of the materialistic theory of happiness and its third stage is, that the followers of this last school believe that where there is a conflict between self-interest and other's-interest, the duty of everybody is to sacrifice self-interest and to strive for other's-interest, instead of following the path of 'enlightened self-interest'. Is not some explanation due in support of this particular feature of this materialistic theory of happiness? As one learned materialistic philosopher belonging to this school realized this difficulty, he has examined the activities of all living beings, from the minutest organisms to the human race, and come to the conclusion that in as much as the quality of maintaining one's own progeny or community just as one maintains oneself, and of helping one's fellows as much as possible without harming any one, is to be seen being gradually more and more developed from the stage of minute organisms to the human race, we must say that that is the principle feature of the mode of life of the living world. This feature is firstly noticed in the living world in the production of progeny and protecting it.

In those minute organisms in which the difference of the sexes has not been developed, the body of one organism is seen to grow until it breaks into two organisms; or, it may even be said that this minute organism sacrifices its own life for the sake of its progeny, that is to say, for the sake of another. In the same way, animals of both sexes in grades of life higher than that of these organisms, are seen to willingly sacrifice their own interests in the living world for the maintenance of their progeny; and this quality is seen to be always growing; so that, even in the most aboriginal societies, man is seen willingly helping, not only his own progeny, but also his tribe; and therefore, the highest duty in this world of man, who is the crown jewel of the living world, is to attempt to permanently do away with the present apparent conflict between self-interest and other's-interest by further developing this tendency of created beings of finding happiness in other's interest as if it was self-interest, which is observed to become stronger and stronger in the rising grades of creation. This argument is correct. There is nothing new in the principle that, as the virtue of philanthropy is to be seen even in the dumb world in the shape of protection of progeny, it is the highest duty of enlightened man to carry that virtue to its perfection.

Only, as the knowledge of the material sciences has now considerably increased, it is now possible to develops more systematically the materialistic demonstration of this principle. Although the point of view of our philosophers was metaphysical, yet, it has been stated in our ancient treatises that is, "doing good to others is meritorious, and doing harm to others, sinful; this is the sum and substance of the eighteen Purânas"; and, even Bhartrhari says that: "svârtho yasya parârtha eva sa pumân ekah satâm agranih", i.e., "that man with whom other's-interest has become self-interest is the best of good men:. But, when we consider the scale of life gradually rising from the minutest organisms to the human race, another question also arises, namely: is the virtue of philanthropy the only virtue which has been fully developed in the human race, or have other benevolent (sâttvika) virtues, such as justice, kindness, wisdom, far-sightedness, logic, courage, perseverance, forgiveness, control of the organs, etc., also been developed in man? When one thinks of this, one has to say that all virtues have been more fully developed in the human race than in any other living being. We will for the present refer to this aggregate of sâttvika qualities as 'humanness'. When in this way 'humanness' is seen to be superior to philanthropy, one has, in determining the propriety or impropriety or the morality of any particular Action, to examine that action from the point of view of its 'humanness'-that is, from the point of view of all those various qualities which are seen to be more developed in the human race than in other living beings-rather than from the point of view of its philanthropicalness. We must therefore, come to the conclusion, that it is better to call that action alone virtuous, or to say that that alone is morality, which will enhance the state of being human or the 'humanness', of all human beings, or which will be consistent with the dignity of such 'humanness', instead of merely relying on the virtue of philanthropy, and somehow or other getting rid of the matter. And when one accepts this comprehensive view-point, the consideration of 'the greatest good of the greatest number', becomes only an insignificant part of such view-point, and the doctrine that the righteousness or unrighteousness of all actions has to be tested only by that test falls to the ground, and we see that we have also to take 'humanness' into account. And when one considers minutely in what 'humanness', or 'the state of being human' consists, the question "âtmâ vâ are drastavyah" naturally crops up, as stated by Yajnavalkya. An American writer, who has written an exposition of Ethics, has given this comprehensive quality of 'humanness' the name of 'Atma'.

(From *Gita Rahasya,* R.B. Tilak, Lok Manya Tilak Mandir, Navayan Peeth, Poona, 1935. pp. 102-128)

Plea For A Militant Nationalism

Two new words have recently come into existence with regard to our politics, and they are Moderates and Extremists. These words have a specific relation to time, and they, therefore, will change with time. The Extremists of to-day will be Moderates to-morrow, just as the Moderates of to-day were Extremists yesterday. When the National Congress was first started and Mr. Dadabhai's [Naoroji] views, which now go for Moderates, were given to the public, he was styled an Extremist, so that you will see that the term Extremist is an expression of progress. We are Extremists to-day and our sons will call themselves Extremists and us Moderates. Every new party begins as Extremists and ends as Moderates. The sphere of practical politics is not unlimited. We cannot say what will or will not happen 1,000 years hence—perhaps during the long period, the whole of the white race will be swept away in another glacial period. We must, therefore, study the present and work out a programme to meet the present condition.

It is impossible to go into details within the time at my disposal. One thing is granted, viz., that this Government does not suit us. As has been said by an eminent statesman—the Government of one country by another can never be a successful, and therefore a permanent, Government. There is no difference of opinion about this fundamental proposition between the Old and New schools. One fact is that this alien Government has ruined the country. In the beginning, all of us were taken by surprise. We were almost, dazed. We thought that everything that the rulers did was for our good and that this English Government has descended from the clouds to save us from the invasion of Tamerlane and Chengis Khan, and, as they say, not only from foreign invasions but from internecine warfare, or the internal or external invasions, as they call it. We felt happy for a time, but it soon came to light that the peace which was established in this country did this as Mr. Dadabhai has said in one place—that we were prevented from going at each other's throats, so that a foreigner might go at the throats of us all.

Pax Britannica has been established in this country in order that a foreign Government may exploit the country. That this is the effect of this Pax Britannica is being gradually realized in these days. It was an unhappy circumstance that it was not realized sooner. We believed in the benevolent intentions of the Government, but in politics there is no benevolence. Benevolence is used to sugar-coat the declarations of self-interest, and we were in those days deceived by the apparent benevolent intentions under which rampant self-interest was concealed. That was our state then. But soon a change came over us. English education, growing poverty, and better familiarity with our rulers, opened our eyes and our leaders; especially, the venerable leader who presided over the recent Congress was the first to tell us that the drain from the country was mining it, and if the drain was to continue, there was some great disaster awaiting us. So terribly convinced was he of this that he went over from here to England and spent twenty-five years of his life in trying to convince the English people of the injustice that is being done to us. He worked very hard. He had conversations and interviews with Secretaries of State, with Members of Parliament—and with what result?

He has come here at the age of eighty-two to tell us that he is bitterly disappointed. Mr. Gokhale, I know, is not disappointed. He is a friend of mine and I believe that this is his honest conviction. Mr. Gokhale is not disappointed but is ready to wait another eighty years till he is disappointed like Mr. Dadabhai. He is young, younger than myself, and I can very well see that disappointment cannot come in a single interview, from interviews which have lasted only for a year or so. If Mr. Dadabhai is disappointed, what reason is there that Mr. Gokhale shall not, after twenty years? It is said there is a revival of Liberalism, but how long will it last? Next year it might be, they are out of power, and are we to wait till there is another revival of Liberalism, and then again if that goes down and a third revival of Liberalism takes place; and after all what can a Liberal Government do? I will quote the observation of the father of the Congress, Mr. A.O. Hume. This was made in 1893. Let the Government be Liberal or Conservative, rest sure that they will not yield to you willingly anything.

A Liberal Government means that the Government or the members of the Government are imbued with liberal principles because they want to have the administration of their country conducted on those principles. They are Liberals in England, but I have seen Liberals in England come out to India to get into conservative ways. Many of the civilian officers from schools and colleges, when they come out are very good Liberals. Coming in contact with Anglo-Indian women, they change their views, and by the time they leave India they are conservatives. This has been the experience all over. So liberal or conservative, the point is, is any one prepared to give you those rights and concessions which intellectually a philosopher may admit to be fit to be conceded or granted to a subject nation in course of time? It is intellectual perception. A philosopher and statesman cannot be forced to do it. I laughed when I read the proceedings of the meeting in Calcutta, congratulating people on the appointment of Mr. John Morley to the Secretaryship of State for India. Passages were read from Mr. Morley's books. Mr. Morley had said so and so in Mr. Gladstone's life; Mr. Morley had said this and had said that; he was the editor of a certain paper thirty years ago, and he said so and so. I asked myself if it would not have been better that some of the passages from the Bhagavad Gita were so quoted. The persons to whom I refer are gentlemen for whom I have the highest respect. But what I say is, that they utterly misunderstood the position or absolutely ignored the distinction between a philosopher and a statesman. A statesman is bound to look to the present circumstances and see what particular concessions arc absolutely necessary, and what is theoretically true or wrong. He has to take into consideration both the sides. There are the interested Anglo-Indians and the Secretary of State is the head of the Anglo-Indian bureaucracy whose mouthpiece he is. Do you mean to say that when the whole bureaucracy, the whole body of Anglo-Indians, is against you, the Secretary of

State will set aside the whole bureaucracy and give you rights? Has he the power? If he does, will he not be asked to walk away? So then it comes to this that the whole British electorate must be converted.

So you are going to convert all persons who [have] a right to vote in England, so as to get the majority on your side, and when this is done and when by that majority the Liberal Party is returned to Parliament bent upon doing good to India and it appoints a Secretary of State as good as Mr. Morley, then you hope to get something by the old methods. The new Party has realized this position. The whole electorate of Great Britain must be converted by lectures. You cannot touch their pocket or interest, and that man must be a fool indeed who would sacrifice his own interest on hearing a philosophical lecture! He will say, 'It is a very good lecture; but I am not going to sacrifice my interest.' I will tell you a story. One of my friends who had been lecturing in England delivered a lecture on the grievances of India. A man from the audience came and asked him how many of them there were. The lecturer replied, 'thirty crores'-. The inquirer replied, 'Then you do not deserve anything.' That is' the attitude with which an English workman looks at the question. You now depend on the Labour Party. Labourers have their own grievances, but they won't treat you any better. On the contrary they will treat you worse, because British labourers obtain their livelihood by sending us their goods. This is the real position. This position is gradually recognized. Younger people who have gone to England like Mr. Gokhale are not so disappointed though those who went with him were, like Mr. Lala Lajpat Rai. I am entering into personalities but I cannot place these facts in an intelligent manner, if I do not give the names, although all of them are my friends. This is then the state of things. The new party perceives that this is futile. To convert the whole electorate of England to your opinion and then to1 get indirect pressure to bear upon the members of Parliament, they in their turn to return a cabinet favourable to India and the whole Parliament, the Liberal Party and the cabinet to bring pressure on the bureaucracy to yield—we say this is hopeless. You can now understand the difference between the old and the new parties. Appeals to the bureaucracy are hopeless. On this point both the new and old parties are agreed. The old party, believes in appealing to the British nation and we do not. That being our position, it logically follows we must have some other method. There is another alternative. We are not going to sit down quiet. We shall have some other method by which to achieve what we want. We are not disappointed, we are not pessimists. It is the hope of achieving the goal by our own efforts that has brought into existence this new party.

There is no empire lost by a free grant of concessions by the rulers to the ruled. History does not record any such event. Empires are lost by luxury, by being too much bureaucratic or over-confident or from other reasons. But an empire has never come to an end by the rulers conceding power to the ruled.

You got the Queen's proclamation. But it was obtained without a Congress. They wanted to pacify you, as you had grown too turbulent, and you got that proclamation without a demand, without Congress and without constitutional agitation. That is a very good and generous declaration indeed. The Queen was very anxious that it should be couched in such terms as would create hopes in you. Now, all that anxiety did not proceed from constitutional agitation. It was after 1858 that constitutional agitation began. The result was, the proclamation remained a dead letter, because you could not get it enforced, the conditions under which it was made having disappeared. A promise was made but you proved too weak to have it enforced. That is the reason why it was not enforced. The bureaucracy got the upper hand and they established a system of administration in which it made it impossible for the proclamation to be acted up to. Is Mr. Morley going to fulfil it? The explanation of the proclamation is not the question. The question is what will compel him to fulfil it. This is the point at issue. I admit that we must ask; but we must ask with the consciousness that the demand cannot be refused. There is great difference between asking and petitioning. Your industries are ruined utterly, ruined by foreign rule; your wealth is going out of the country and you are reduced to the lowest level which no human being can occupy. In this state of things, is there any other remedy by which you can help yourself? The remedy is not petitioning but boycott. We say prepare your forces, organise your power, and then go to work so that they cannot refuse you what you demand.

A story in Mahabharata tells that Sri Krishna was sent to effect a compromise, but the Pandavas and Kauravas were both organizing their forces to meet the contingency of failure of a compromise. This is politics. Are you prepared in this way to fight if your demand is refused? If you are, be sure you will not be refused; but if you are not, nothing can be more certain than that your demand will be refused, and perhaps, for ever. We are not armed, and there is no necessity for arms either. We have a stronger weapon, a political weapon, in boycott. We have perceived one fact, that the whole of this administration, which is carried on by a handful of Englishmen, is carried on with our assistance. We are all in subordinate service. The whole Government is carried on with our assistance and they try to keep us in ignorance of our power of co-operation between ourselves by which that which is in our own hands at present can be claimed by us and administered by us. The point is to have the entire control in our hands. I want to have the key of my house, and not merely one stranger turned out of it. Self-Government is our goal; we want a control over our administrative machinery. We don't want to become clerks and willing instruments of our own oppression in the hands of an alien Government, and that Government is ruling over us not by its innate strength but by keeping us in ignorance and blindness to the perception of this fact.

Every Englishman knows that they are a mere handful in this country and it is the business of every one of them to befool you in believing that you are weak and they are strong. This is politics. We have been deceived by such policy so long. What the new party wants you to do is to realize the fact that your future rests entirely in your own hands. If you mean to be free, you can be free; if you do not mean to be free, you will fall and be for ever fallen. So many of you need not like arms; but if you have not the power of active resistance, have you not the power of self-denial and self-abstinence in such a way as not to assist this foreign Qovernment to rule over you? This is boycott and this is what is meant when we say, boycott is a political weapon. We shall not give them assistance to collect revenue and keep the peace. We shall not assist them in carrying on the administration of justice. We shall have our own courts, and when time comes we shall not pay taxes. Can you do that by your united efforts? If you can, you are free from to-morrow. Some gentlemen who spoke this evening referred to half'bread as against the whole bread. I say I want the whole bread and that immediately. But if I cannot get the whole, don't think that I have no patience.

I will take the half they give me and then try for the remainder. This is the line of thought and action in which you must train yourself. We have not raised this cry from a mere impulse. It is a reasoned impulse. Try to understand that reason and try to strengthen that impulse by your logical convictions. I do not ask you to blindly follow us. Think over the whole problem for yourselves. If you accept our advice, we feel sure, we can achieve our salvation thereby. This is the advice of the new party. Perhaps we have not obtained a full recognition of our principles. Old prejudices die very hard. Neither of us wanted to wreck the Congress, so we compromised, and were satisfied that our principles were recognised, though only to a certain extent. That does not mean that we have accepted the whole situation. We may have a step in advance next year, so that within a few years our principles will be recognised, and recognised to such an extent that the generations who come after us may consider us Moderates. This is the way in which a nation progresses. This is the way national sentiment progresses, and this is the lesson you have to learn from the struggle now going on. This is a lesson of progress, a lesson of helping yourself as much as possible, and if you really perceive the force of it, if you are convinced by these arguments, then and then only is it possible for you to effect your salvation from the alien rule under which you labour at this moment.

(From *Bal Gargadhar Tilak : His Writings and Speeches,* Ganesh and Co., Madras, 1918. pp 37-52)

8

Rabindranath Tagore

Life and Times

Rabindranath Tagore popularly known as Gurudev (1861-1941) was born on 7 May 1861. At some time towards the end of the seventeenth century, his forefathers migrated from their native lands to Govindpur, one of the three villages which later came to constitute Calcutta. In the course of time, the family came to acquire property and considerable business interests through the pursuit of commercial and banking activities. They had particularly benefited from the growing power of the British East India Company. Rabindranath's grandfather, Dwarkanath Tagore, lived lavishly and broke the Hindu religious ban of those times by travelling to Europe, just like his contemporary, Rammohan Roy, the nineteenth century social and religious reformer.

Rammohan Roy started a religious reform movement in 1828 that came to be known as the Brahma Samaj Movement. Rabindranath's grandfather supported Roy in his attempts at reforming Hindu society. Dwarkanath's son, Devendranath Tagore, also became a staunch supporter of the Brahma Samaj Movement. In order to encourage its spread, in 1863 he established a meditation centre and guest house on some land about 100 miles from Calcutta at a place called *Santiniketan*, the Abode of Peace.

Although deeply steeped in Hindu and Islamic traditions, Tagore's family contributed large sums of money for the introduction of Western education, including colleges for the study of science and medicine. This peculiar situation explains the combination of tradition and experiment that came to characterize Rabindranath Tagore's attitude to life.

Rabindranath's father was one of the leading figures of the newly awakened phase of Bengali society. He had been educated at one stage in Rammohan Roy's Anglo-Hindu school and had been greatly influenced by Roy's character, ideals and religious devotion. Devendranath Tagore was well versed in European philosophy and, though deeply religious, did not accept all aspects of Hinduism. He was to have a profound influence on his son's mental and practical attitudes.

Important changes were taking place in Bengal at the time Rabindranath was born. Iswar Chandra Vidyasagar had been attempting to reform the position of women in society. Schools using English as the language of teaching were being established, alongside the traditional Sanskrit schools. Vidyasagar had established Bengali-medium schools at different places in Bengal with little or limited government support. He had also established a centre to train teachers for these schools. Rabindranath attended this school and, as he says himself, owed his love of Bengali language and literature to it. He was also sent to a number of English-speaking schools, but he did not like their teaching style and had no wish to be taught in a foreign language.

Rabindranath was the fourteenth child of his parents. His brothers and sisters were poets, musicians, playwrights and novelists and the Tagore home was thus filled with musical, literary and dramatic pursuits. The family was also involved with diverse activities at the national level. He gradually withdrew from formal schooling when he was around 14 years old. The remainder of his education was carried out at home through his own personal efforts and with the help of tutors in various subjects. He also had lessons from professionals in wrestling, music and drawing. The manner of his early schooling was to leave a deep impression on him.

When Rabmdranath was 12, his father took him to Santiniketan, the meditation centre established in 1863. During their brief stay there, Devendranath gave his son lessons in Sanskrit, astronomy and the scriptures that formed the basis of his reformed religion. After these lessons were over, Rabindranath was free to roam among the fields and forests. This routine continued when father and son journeyed on and stayed at Dalhousie in the Himalayan foothills. After lessons in Sanskrit, English literature and religion, the would-be poet explored the mountains and forests. Life in close proximity to nature was unknown to him in the urban surroundings of Calcutta.

The close and affectionate contact between teacher and pupil that he felt when his father taught him was also completely absent in Calcutta. It was this childhood experience of the willing pupil enthusiastically following lessons given by his father in the manner of a noble teacher among agreeable surroundings that guided Rabindranath in establishing a school at Santiniketan in 1901. In 1878, when he was 17, he was sent to London by his father to qualify for the Indian Civil Service or as a lawyer. He took his matriculation examination and then joined University College, London. He came to like his lessons in English literature, and became exposed to British social life and Western music, both of which he enjoyed. But he returned home suddenly after some eighteen months without completing his education However, he did gain the impression that human nature was perhaps the same everywhere.

Back in India he continued with his personal education and his creative writing and music. His *Sandhya Sangeet* [Evening songs], a volume of Bengali verse, came out in 1882. It was at about this time that he had a kind of mystical experience that led him to appreciate the unity of all that exists and himself as an integral part of it. In the same year, he wrote his famous poem *Nirjharer Swapna Bhanga* [The awakening of the fountain]. He became aware of his unusual talent as a poet. Between 1884 and 1890 various volumes of his poems appeared, together with a profuse output of prose articles, criticism, plays and novels.

Tagore married when he was 23. At this stage, beyond his literary pursuits, he had begun sharing his father's religious responsibilities. In 1890 he made a second trip to the United Kingdom, but came back after a month to look after the family estates.

This responsibility opened up new vistas of inspiration for him. Whereas his previous literary work had been primarily based on imagination, he now came to acquire a direct and intimate experience of the wretched life led by the poor Bengali peasants. This new experience led to the composition of Galpaguccha (A bunch of stories, 1900), and the many letters he wrote to his niece, subsequently published as *Chhinnapatra* [Torn Letters] and *Chhinnapatravali* [A collection of torn letters], considered to be landmarks in the writing of Bengali prose and in describing the countryside of Bengal.

These conditions, he thought, cannot be changed by appealing to the religious sentiments of the landlord, policeman or money-lender. In human society, necessity is a greater force than charity. The first requirement therefore is that people should discover the bond that holds them together as a society. If there is one path likely to achieve this, it is education. Tagore realized from his own experience of the farmers' attitudes and their social behaviour that strength can be generated only in a self-reliant village society developing its own locus of power and its own momentum of growth. He turned again and again in various contexts to this theme of local self-reliance, local initiatives, local leadership and local self-government centring on co-operative ways of life. This could be the basis for reorganizing India's fragmented rural society, and could serve as an instrument of welfare. Tagore realized that education and village councils were the only available instruments of economic and social change, and that the villagers should obtain various forms of expert help from outside to accomplish this change.

As a young landlord managing his family's rural estates, Tagore came to realize the possibilities of introducing education and co-operation to transform rural life. Thus he began to turn his thoughts towards the problems of education He spoke publicly on 'The Vicissitudes of Education' in which he made a strong plea for the use of the mother-tongue. His first experiments in teaching also date from this period He started his own school in Selhdah, the headquarters of his estate, to which he sent his own children to be taught by teachers in various subjects, including an Englishman to teach them the English language. He also started organizing co-operatives, schools and hospitals in the villages of his estates and tried to introduce improved farming methods. All these efforts for rural reconstruction went on while he pursued his creative writing. Tagore called this the period of his Sadhana—preparation, reflection, austerity and self-education for an active social life. He lived either at Selhdah or on his houseboat on the river Padma visiting villages, talking to people and listening to their problems. Tagore's later educational experiments arose from this experience.

In 1901 he left Selhdah where he had undertaken these experiments and moved to Santiniketan where, with his father's consent, he started a boarding school. The Ashram School was inaugurated on 22 December 1901 with only a few pupils, his son being one of them, and with an equal number of teachers. It was to be run on the pattern of teachers and pupils living together amidst natural surroundings and willingly accepting an austere standard of living, often working with their own hands. Life at Santiniketan left its impression on the poet's literary work. He wrote about India's past and present, and stories of noble self-sacrifice He published more realistic novels such as *Choker Bali* [Eyesore] (1901), *Naukadubi* [The wreck] (1903) and *Gora* (1910). He was trying to discover the eternal India that succeeds in achieving unity amidst a bewildering diversity of races, cultures and religions.

In 1912 Tagore left for the United Kingdom once again. Some of his poems and writings had already been translated into English and had attracted the attention of the well-known English poet W.B. Yeats. He made such an impression on the British writers and intellectuals that he was at once accepted as a great poet and intellectual. He was awarded the Nobel Prize for Literature in November 1913 and came back to India after visiting the United States of America, delivering there his 'Sadhana' lectures (The Realization of Life, 1913). In 1916 Tagore went abroad again to Japan and then to the United States of America delivering lectures, published later in two volumes as *Nationalism* and *Personality*.

This international experience gave him a new idea, that he must bring his country into contact with the world at large. He felt that overemphasis on narrow nationalism led men and countries into paths of conflict. There should be an institution that emphasized the unity of the world's cultures and streams of knowledge. He considered Santiniketan to be that institution. He was thus already contemplating the foundation of *Visva Bharati,* an international centre of culture, and humanistic studies. The foundation stone of Visva Bharati was laid on 24 December 1918.

This period also saw a rise in Indian nationalism. There was resentment against an imitation of British lifestyles and against British rule, coupled with increased awareness and appreciation of India's cultural traditions. Tagore's educational and other writings of the period reflect this nationalist trend. His concern with educational reform grew in intensity after 1901, and more so after 1905. Dissatisfaction with the existing system of education led to a general concern with reform.

A tragic series of family bereavements probably caused Tagore's withdrawal from the growing national struggle for independence in the country. He retired to his Ashram School to concentrate on its development and on the task of village reconstruction that he had initiate at Selhdah. He wanted his students to think in terms of the whole of mankind. He wanted them to become universal men and women like himself and to overcome feelings of narrow nationalism in order that the world could live and grow in peace and fellowship.

The poet passed away in 1941. The two institutions specific to Tagore's educational ideas and experiments still survive in the form of Patha Bhawan (the school section) at Santiniketan and in the form of Sikshasastra and Sri Niketan—of course, they have been modified a good deal over this long stretch of time. They form the core of the Santiniketan ideal. Visva Bharati survives too; it is now a central university and has changed considerably. The emphasis that Tagore placed on the teaching of the fine arts and crafts, and on music, continues in the form of two separate autonomous institutions under the general supervision of Visva Bharati.

The myriad-minded Rabindranath Tagore long life of eighty years was marked by ceaseless and torrential flow of creativity manifested in the richness and variety of all kinds of literary forms, dance, drama, music, painting and original organizational activities. Touching the kindred points of heaven and earth he was a man of action and of contemplation, a seer and also a pioneer in cooperative movement, a writer of most profound poems and an author of children's text-books including books of science, a nationalist and internationalist, a man of royal grandeur like his grandfather, a prince, and an ascetic like his father, a 'maharshi'. He was both a poet and a painter, a dramatist and an actor, a philosopher and a social reformer, an educationist and a humanist. In his philosophy of life the best of the East and the West are reconciled into a harmonious whole enriching the quality and substance of life which he always saw steady and saw it whole. His life was marked as much by Shakespearean fecundity as by protean plasticity. His inclusive mind aspired after the Universal Man shining in the glory of creation.

Tagore's unfailing faith in man and divinity, his concern for women and solicitation for childcen, his sympathy for the poor and the downtrodden, his philosophical speculations and practical wisdom and the evolution of taste—all find expression in the all-encompassing sweep of his writings in a magnificent synthesis of philosophical profundity and aesthetic luxuriance. With the passage of time Tagore has only grown in stature and is now reckoned as an increasingly significant and complex personality. Whether seen as a great sentinel or a complete man, the finest exponent of the Bengal Renaissance or the harbinger of a new age, a majestic personality or a deeply scarred individual.

The West, Tagore appears to have come out of nowhere in 1912 and collected a Nobel prize without the least effort; to have travelled the world and enjoyed ,a worldwide homage for over two decades not granted to any other writer this century; and then to have evanesced until he is barely more than a name. But seen from Bengal he looks very different. Before 1912, Rabindranath was rejected by many, perhaps the majority of Bengalis as being a product of western influence; for the rest of his life he experienced a unique blend of vilification and only after his death m 1941 was he canonized as Bengal's greatest creative artist and raised to the Olympian pedestal he now occupies. No writer, living or dead, is today more actively worshipped in Bengal than Rabindranath Tagore.

From his own point of view, Tagore's predicament was even more contradictory. As an idealist he reserved his highest admiration for the humane spirit of the West he had first encountered in the liberalism of nineteenth-century Enlish literature and politics. 'Whatever may be the outward aspect of Europe's power, I have no doubt that at its core is the power of the spirit', he said before leaving Bengal in 1912. Like some other highly educated Bengalis of his time, until about 1920 Tagore believed British rule in India to be providential, necessary for the reform of a moribund, degenerate society. But as a patriot, particularly after 1900he needed to believe in the persistence of ancient India's spiritual values in contemporary India. In 1912, through his poems *Gitanjali* (Song Offerings), translated by himself, and through his personal presence in England - where people were even reminded of Christ - these two beliefs became harmonized in his mind. For a few brief years he brought East and West into receptive emotional and intellectual contact. Thereafter, with the First World War, the upsurge of the Indian nationalist movement, its suppression by the imperial government and the popularity of the non-cooperation movement led by Gandhi, neither belief proved tenable. Both, however, continued to coexist in Tagore's mind. As a direct consequence, he found himself obliged to defend Indian spirituality when abroad and the spirit of the West when in India. Not surprisingly he felt inwardly torn and often tortured.

Spiritual Freedom

There are injuries that attack our life; they hurt the harmony of life's functions through which is maintained the harmony of our physical self with the physical world; and these injuries are called diseases. There are also factors that oppress our intelligence. They injure the harmony of relationship between our rational mind and the universe of reason; and we call them stupidity, ignorance of insanity. They are uncontrolled exaggerations of passions that upset all balance in our personality. They obscure the harmony between the spirit of the individual man and the spirit of the universal Man; and we give them the name sin. In all these instances our realization of the universal Man, in his physical, rational and spiritual aspects, is obstructed, and our true freedom in the realms of matter, mind and spirit is made narrow or distorted.

All the higher religions of India speak of the training for *Mukti,* the liberation of the soul. In this self of ours we are conscious of individuality, and all its activities are engaged in the expression and enjoyment of our finite and individual nature. In our soul we are conscious of the transcendental truth in us, the Universal, the Supreme Man; and this soul the spiritual self, has its enjoyment in the renunciation of the individual self for the sake of the supreme soul. This renunciation is not in the negating of self, but in the dedication of it. The desire for it comes from an instinct which very often knows its own meaning vaguely and gropes for a name that would define its purpose. This purpose is in the realization of its unity with some objective ideal of perfections, some harmony of relationship between the individual and the infinite man. It is of this harmony, and not of a barren isolation that the Upanishad speaks, when it says that truth no longer remains hidden in him who finds himself in the All.

Once when I was on a visit to a remote Bengali village, mostly inhabited by Mahomedan cultivators, the villagers entertained me with an operatic performance the literature of which belonged to an obsolete religious sect that had wide influence centuries ago. Though the religion itself is dead, its voice still continues preaching its philosophy to a people, who, in spite of their different culture, are not tired of listening. It discussed according to its own doctrine the different elements, material and transcendental, that constitute human personality, comprehending the body, the self and the soul. Then came a dialogue, during the course of which was related the incident of a person who wanted to make a journey to Brindaban, the Garden of Bliss, but was prevented by a watchman who startled him with an accusation of theft. The thieving was proved when it was shown that inside his clothes he was secretly trying to smuggle into the garden the self, which only finds its fulfillment by its surrender. The culprit was caught with the incriminating bundle in his possession which barred for him his passage to the supreme goal. Under a tattered canopy, supported on bamboo poles and lighted by a few smoking kerosene lamps, the village crowd, occasionally interrupted by howls of jackals in the neighbouring paddy fields, attended with untried interest, till the small hours of the morning, the performance drama the discussed the ultimate meaning of all thing in a seemingly incongruous setting of dance, music and humorous dialogue.

This illustration will show how naturally, in India, poetry and philosophy have walked hand in hand, only because the latter has claimed it right to guide men to the practical path of their life's fulfillment. What is the fulfillment? It is our freedom in truth, which as for its prayer:

Lead us from the unreal to reality.

For *satyam is anandam,* the Real is Joy.

In the world of art, our consciousness being freed from the tangle of self interest, we gain an unobstructed vision of unity, the incarnation of the real, which is a joy for ever.

As in the world of art, so in the spiritual world, our soul waits for its freedom from the ego to reach that disinterested joy which is the source and goal of creation. It cries for its *mukti,* its freedom in the unity of truth. The idea of *mukti* has affected our lives in India, touched the springs of pure emotions and supplications; for its soars heavenward on the wings of poesy. We constantly hear men of scanty learning and simple faith singing in their prayer to Tara, the Goddess Redeemer:

'For what sin should I be compelled to remain in this dungeon of the world of appearance?'

They are afraid of being alienated from the world of truth, afraid of perpetual drifting amidst the froth and foam of things, of being tossed about by the tidal waves of pleasure and pain and never reaching the ultimate meaning of life. Of these men, one may be a carter driving his cart to market, another a fisherman playing his net. They may not be prompt with an intelligent answer if they are questioned about the deeper import of the song they sing, but they have no doubt in their mind, that the abiding cause of all misery is not so much in the lack of life's furniture as in the obscurity of life's significance. It is a common topic with such a decry an undue emphasis upon 'me' and 'mine', which falsifies the perspective the truth. For have they not often seen men, who are not above their own level in social position or intellectual acquirement, going out to seek truth, leaving everything that they have behind them?

They know that the object of these adventurers is not betterment in worldly wealth and power – it is *mukti,* freedom. They possibly know some poor fellow villager of their own craft, who remains in the world carrying on his daily vocation and yet has the reputation of being emancipated in the heart of the Eternal. I myself have come across a fisherman singing with an inward absorption of mind, while fishing all day in the Ganges, who was pointed out to me by my boatman, with awe, as a man of liberated spirit. He is out of reach of the conventional prices that are set upon men by society, and which classify them like toys arranged in the shop – windows according to the market standard of value.

When the figure of this fisherman comes to my mind, I cannot but think that their number is not small who with their lives sing to epic of the unfettered soul, but will never be known in history. These unsophisticated Indian peasants know that an Emperor is merely a decorated slave, remaining chained to his Empire, that a millionaire is kept pilloried by his fate in the golden cage of his wealth, while this fisherman is free in the realm of light. When, groping in the dark, we stumble against objects, we cling to them believing them to be our only hope. When light comes, we slacken our hold, finding them to be mere parts of the All to which we are related. The simple man of the village knows what freedom is – freedom from the isolation of self, from the isolation of things, which imparts a fierce intensity to our sense of possession. He knows that this freedom is not the mere negation of bondage, in the bareness of our belongings, but in some positive realization which gives pure joy to our being, and he sings: "To him who sinks into the deep, nothing remains unattained." He says again:

Let my two minds meet and combine,

And lead me to the city Wonderful.

When that one mind of our which wanders in search of things in the outer region of the varied, and the other which seeks the inward vision of unity, are no longer in conflict, they help us to realize the *ajab*, the *anirvachaniya*, the ineffable. The poet saint Kabir has also the same message when he sings:

By saying that Supreme Reality only dwells in the inner realm of spirit, we shame the outer world of matter; and also when we say that he is only in the outside, we do not speak the truth.

According to these singers, truth is in unity, and therefore freedom is in its realization. The texts of our daily worship and meditation are for training our mind to overcome the barrier of separateness from the rest of existence and to realize *advaitam*, the Supreme Unity which is *anantam*, infinitude. It is philosophical wisdom, having its universal tradition in the popular mind in India, that inspire our prayer, our daily spiritual practices. It has its constant urging for us to go beyond the world of appearances, in which facts as facts are alien to us, like the mere sounds of foreign music; it speaks to us of an emancipation in the inner truth of all things, where the endless *Many* reveal the *One*.

Freedom in the material world has also the same meaning expressed in its own language. When nature's phenomena appeared to us as irrelevant, as heterogeneous manifestations of an obscure and irrational caprice, we lived in an alien world never dreaming of our *swaraj* within its territory. Through the discovery of the harmony of its working with that of our reason, we realize our unity with it, and therefore our freedom.

Those who have been brought up in a misunderstanding of this world's process, not knowing that it is one with themselves through the relationship of knowledge and intelligence, are trained as cowards by a hopless faith in the ordinance of a destiny darkly dealing its blows. They submit without struggle when human rights are denied them, being accustomed to imagine themselves born as outlaws in a world constantly thrusting upon them incomprehensible surprises of accidents.

Also in the social or political field, the lack of freedom is based upon the spirit of alienation, on the imperfect realization of the One. There our bondage is in the tortured link of union. One may imagine that an individual who succeeds in dissociating himself from his fellow attains real freedom, inasmuch as all ties of relationship imply obligation to others. But we know that, thought it may sound paradoxical, it is true that in the human world only a perfect arrangement of interdependence gives rise to freedom. The most individualistic of human beings who own no responsibility are the savages who fail to attain their fullness of manifestation. They live immersed in obscurity, like an ill-lighted fire that cannot liberate itself from its envelope of smoke. Only those may attain their freedom from the segregation of an eclipsed life who have the power to cultivate mutual understanding and co-operation. The history of the growth of freedom is the history of the perfection of human relationship.

It has become possible for men to say that existence is evil, only because in our blindness we have missed something wherein our existence has its truth. If a bird tries to soar with only one of its wings, it is offended with the wind for buffeting it down to the dust. All broken truths are evil. They hurt because they suggest something they do not offer. Death does not hurt us, but disease does, because disease constantly reminds us of health and yet withholds it from us. And life in a half world is evil because it feigns finality when it is obviously incomplete, giving us the cup but not the draught of life. All tragedies result from truth remaining a fragment, its cycle not being completed. That cycle finds its end when the individual realize the universal and thus reaches freedom.

But because this freedom is in truth itself and not in an appearance of it, no hurried path of success, forcibly cut out by the greed of result, can be a true path. And an obscure village poet, unknown to the world of recognized respectability, sings:

O cruel man of urgent need, must you scorch with fire the mind which still is a bud? You will burst it into bits, destroy its perfume in your impatience. Do you not see that my Lord, the Supreme Teacher, takes ages to perfect the flower and never is in a fury of haste? But because of your terrible greed, you only rely on force, and what hope is there for you, O man of urgent need? 'Prithi', says Madan the poet, 'Hurt not the mind of my Teacher. Know that only he who follows the simple current and loses himself, can hear the voice, O man of urgent need.'

This poet knows that there is no external means of taking freedom by the throat. It is the inward process of losing ourselves that leads to it. Bondage in all its forms has its stronghold in the inner self and not in the outside world; it is in the dimming of our consciousness, in the narrowing of our perspective, in the wrong valuation of things.

Let me conclude this chapter with a song of the Bal sect in Bengal, over a century old, in which the poet sings of the eternal bond of union between the infinite and the finite soul, from which there can be no *mukti*, because love is ultimate, because it is an inter-relation which makes truth complete, because absolute independence is the blankness of utter servility. The song run thus:

It goes on blossoming for ages, the soul-lotus, in which I am bound, as well as thou, without escape. There is no end to the opening of its petals, and the honey in its has so much sweetness that thou, like an enchanted bee, canst never desert it, and therefore thou art bound, and I am, and *mukti* is nowhere.

(From The *Religion of Man*, Rupa and Co., New Delhi, 2002, pp 182-192)

Limits of Nationalism

Our real problem in India is not political. It is social. This is a condition not only prevailing in India, but among al nations. I do not believe in an exclusive political interest. Politics in the West have dominated western ideals, and we in India are trying to imitate you. We have to remember that in Europe, where peoples had their racial unity from the beginning, and where natural resources were insufficient for the inhabitants, the civilisation has naturally taken on the character of political and commercial aggressiveness. For on the one hand they had no internal complications, and on the other they had to deal with neighbours who were strong and rapacious. To have perfect combination among themselves and a watchful attitude of animosity against others was taken as the solution of their problems, in former days they organised and plundered; in the present age the same spirit continues—and they organise and exploit the whole world.

But from the earliest beginnings of history India has had her own problem constantly before her—it is the race problem. Each nation must be conscious of its mission, and we in India must realise that we cut a poor figure when we try to be political, simply because we have not yet been finally able to accomplish what was set before us by our providence. This problem of race unity which we have been trying to solve for so many years has likewise to be faced by you here in America. Many people in this country ask me what is happening to the caste distinctions in India. But when this question is asked me, it is usually done with a superior air. And I feel tempted to put the same question to our American critics with a slight modification: 'What have you done with the Red Indian and the Negro?' For you have not got over your attitude of caste towards them. You have used violent methods to keep aloof from other races, but until you have solved the question, here in America, you have no right to question India.

In spite of our great difficulty, however, India has done something. She has tried to make an adjustment of races, to acknowledge the real differences between them where these exist, and yet seek for some basis of unity. This basis has come through our saints, like Nanak, Kabir, Chaitanya and others, preaching one God to all races of India.

In finding the solution of our problem we shall lave helped to solve the world problem as well. What India has been, the whole world is now. The whole world is becoming one country through scientific facility. And the moment is arriving when you must also find a basis of unity which is not political. If India can offer to the world her solution, it will be a contribution to humanity. There is only one history—the history of man. All national histories are merely chapters in the larger one. And we are content in India to suffer for such a great cause.

Each individual has his self-love. Therefore his brute instinct leads him to fight with others in the sole pursuit of his self-interest. But man has also his higher instincts of sympathy and mutual help. The people who are lacking in this higher moral power and who therefore cannot combine in fellowship with one another must perish or live in a state of degradation. Only those peoples have survived and achieved civilisation who have this spirit of co-operation strong in them. So we find that from the beginning of history men had to choose between fighting with one another and combining, between serving their own interest or the common interest of all.

In our early history, when the geographical limits of each country and also the facilities of communication were small, this problem was comparatively small in dimension. It was sufficient for men to develop their sense of unity within their area of segregation. In those days they combined among themselves and fought against others. But it was this moral spirit of combination which was the true basis of their greatness, and this fostered their art, science and religion. At that early time the most important fact that man had to take count of was the fact of the members of one particular race of men coming in close contact with one another. Those who truly grasped this fact through their higher nature made their mark in history. The most important fact of the present age is that all the different races of men have come close together. And again we are confronted with two alternatives. The problem is whether the different groups of peoples shall go on fighting with one another or find out some true basis of reconciliation and mutual help whether it will be interminable competition or co-operation.

I have no hesitation in saying that those who are gifted with the moral power of love and vision of spiritual unity, who have the least feeling of enmity against aliens, and the sympathetic insight to place themselves in the position of others, will be the fittest to take their permanent place in the age that is lying before us, and those who are constantly developing their instincts for fight and intolerance of aliens will be eliminated. For this is the problem before us, and we have to prove our humanity by solving it through the help of our higher nature. The gigantic organisations for hurting others and warding off their blows, for making money by dragging others back, will not help us. On the contrary, by their crushing weight, their enormous cost and their deadening effect upon living humanity, they will seriously impede our freedom in the larger life of a higher civilisation. During the evolution of the Nation the moral culture of brotherhood was limited by geographical boundaries, because at that time those boundaries were true. Now they have become imaginary lines of tradition divested of the qualities of real obstacles. So the time has come when man's moral nature must deal with this great fact with all seriousness or perish. The first impulse of this change of circumstance has been the churning up of man's baser passions of greed and cruel hatred. If this persists indefinitely, and armaments go on exaggerating themselves to unimaginable absurdities, and machines and storehouses envelop this fair earth with their dirt and smoke and ugliness, then it will end in a conflagration of suicide. Therefore man will have to exert all his power of love and clarity of vision to make another great moral adjustment which will comprehend the whole world of men and not merely the fractional groups of nationality. The call has come to every individual in the present age to prepare himself and his surroundings for this dawn of a new era, when man shall discover his soul in the spiritual unity of all human beings.

If it is given at all to the West to struggle out of these tangles of the lower slopes to the spiritual summit of humanity then I cannot but think that it is the special mission of America to fulfil this hope of God and man. You are the country of expectation, desiring something else than what is. Europe has her subtle habits of mind and her conventions. But America, as yet, has come to no conclusions. I realise how much America is untrammeled by the traditions of the past, and I can appreciate that experimentalism is a sign of America's youth. The foundation of her glory is in the future, rather than in the past, and if one is gifted with the power of clairvoyance, one will be able to love the America that is to be.

America is destined to justify western civilisation to the East. Europe has lost faith in humanity, and has become distrustful and sickly. America, on the other hand, is not pessimistic or blase. You know, as a people, that there is such a thing as a better and a best, and that knowledge drives you on. There are habits that are not merely passive but aggressively arrogant. They are not like mere walls, but are like hedges of stinging nettles. Europe has been cultivating these hedges of habits for long years, till they have grown round her dense and strong arid high. The pride of her traditions has sent its roots deep into her heart. I do not wish to contend that it is unreasonable. But pride in every form breeds blindness at the end. Like all artificial stimulants its first effect is a heightening of consciousness, and then with the increasing dosage it muddles it and brings an exultation that is misleading. Europe has gradually grown hardened in her pride in all her outer and inner habits. She not only cannot forget that she is western, but she takes every opportunity to hurl this fact against others to humiliate them. This is why she is growing incapable of imparting to the East what is best in herself and of accepting in a right spirit the wisdom that the East has stored for centuries.

In America national habits and traditions have not had time to spread their clutching roots round your hearts. You have constantly felt and complained of your disadvantages when you compared your nomadic restlessness with the settled traditions of Europe—the Europe which can show her picture of greatness to the best advantage because she can fix it against the background of the past. But in this present age of transition, when a new era of civilisation is sending its trumpet-call to all peoples of the world across an unlimited future, this very freedom of detachment will enable you to accept its invitation and to achieve the goal for which Europe began her journey but lost herself mid-way. For she was tempted out of her path by her pride of power and greed of possession.

Not merely your freedom from habits of mind in individuals, but also the freedom of your history from all unclean entanglements, fits you in your career of holding the banner of civilisation of the future. All the great nations of Europe have their victims in other parts of the world. This not only deadens their moral sympathy but also their intellectual sympathy, which is so necessary for the understanding of races which are different from one's own. Englishmen can never truly understand India, because their minds are not disinterested with regard to that country. If you compare England with Germany or France you will find she has produced the smallest number of scholars who have studied Indian literature and philosophy with any amount of sympathetic insight or thoroughness. This attitude of apathy and contempt is natural where the relationship is abnormal and founded upon national selfishness and pride. But your history has been disinterested, and that is why you have been able to help Japan in her lessons in western civilisation, and that is why China can look upon you with the best confidence in this, her darkest period of danger. In fact you are carrying all the responsibility of a great future because you are untrammeled by the grasping miserliness of a past. Therefore, of all countries of the earth, America has to be fully conscious of this future; her vision must not be obscured and her faith in humanity must be strong with the strength of youth.

A parallelism exists between America and India— the parallelism of welding together into one body various races. In my country we have been seeking to find out something common to all races, which will prove their real unity. No nation looking for a mere political or commercial basis of unity will find such a solution sufficient. Men of thought and power will discover the spiritual unity, will realise it, and preach it. India has never had a real sense of nationalism. Even though from childhood I had been taught that idolatry of the Nation is almost better than reverence for God and humanity, 1 believe I have outgrown that teaching, and it is my conviction that my countrymen will truly gain their India by fighting against the education which teaches them that a country is greater than the ideals of humanity.

The educated Indian at present is trying to absorb some lessons from history contrary to the lessons of our ancestors. The East, in fact, is attempting to take ' unto itself a history, which is not the outcome of its own living. Japan, for example, thinks she is getting powerful through adopting western methods but, after she has exhausted her inheritance, only the borrowed weapons of civilisation will remain to her. She will not have developed herself from within. Europe has her past. Europe's strength therefore lies in her history. We in India must make up our minds that we cannot borrow other people's history, and that if we stifle our own we are committing suicide. When you borrow things that do not belong to your life, they only serve to crush your life. And therefore I believe that it does India no good to compete with western civilisation in its own field. But we shall be more than compensated if, in spite of the insults heaped upon us, we follow our own destiny.

There are lessons which impart information or train our minds for intellectual pursuits. These are simple and can be acquired and used with advantage. But there are others which affect our deeper nature and change our direction of life. Before we accept them and pay their value by selling our own inheritance, we must pause and think deeply. In man's history there come ages of fireworks which dazzle us by their force and movement. They laugh not only at our modest household lamps but also at the eternal stars. But let us not for that provocation be precipitate in our desire to dismiss our lamps. Let us patiently bear our present insult and realise that these fireworks have splendor but not permanence, because of the extreme explosiveness which is the cause of their power, and also of their exhaustion. They are spending a fatal quantity of energy and substance compared to their gain and production.

Anyhow, our ideals have been evolved through our own history, and even if we wished we could only make poor fireworks of them because their materials are different from yours, as is also their moral purpose. If we cherish the desire of paying our all to buy a political nationality it will be as absurd as if Switzerland had staked her existence on her ambition to build up a navy powerful enough to compete with that of England. The mistake that we make is in thinking that man's channel of greatness is only one—the one which has made itself painfully evident for the time being by its depth of insolence.

We must know for certain that there is a future before us and that future is waiting for those who are rich in moral ideals and not in mere things. And it is the privilege of man to work for fruits that are beyond his immediate reach, and to adjust his life not in slavish conformity to the examples of some present success or even to his own prudent past, limited in its aspiration, but to an infinite future bearing in its heart the ideals of our highest expectations.

We must recognise that it is providential that the West has come to India. And yet someone must show the East to the West, and convince the West that the East has her contribution to make to the history of civilisation. India is no beggar of the West. And yet even though the West may think she is, I am not for thrusting off western civilisation and becoming segregated in our independence. Let us have a deep association. If Providence wants England to be the channel of that communication, of that deeper association, I am willing to accept it with all humility. I have great faith in human nature, and I think the West will find its true mission. I speak bitterly of western civilisation when I am conscious that it is betraying its trust and thwarting its own purpose. The West must not make herself a curse to the world by using her power for her own selfish needs but, by teaching the ignorant and helping the weak, she should save herself from the worst danger that the strong is liable to incur by making the feeble acquire power enough to resist her intrusion. And also she must not make her materialism to be the final thing, but must ralise that she is doing a service in freeing the spiritual being from the tyranny of matter.

I am not against one nation in particular, but against the general idea of all nations. What is the Nation? It is the aspect of a whole people as an organised power. This organisation incessantly keeps up the insistence of the population on becoming strong and efficient. But this strenuous effort after strength and efficiency drains man's energy from his higher nature where he is self-sacrificing and creative. For thereby man's power of sacrifice is diverted from his ultimate object, which is moral, to the maintenance of this organisation, which is mechanical. Yet in this he feels all the satisfaction of moral exaltation and therefore becomes supremely dangerous to humanity. He feels relieved of the urging of his conscience when he can transfer his responsibility to this machine which is the creation of his intellect and not of his complete moral personality. By this device the people w.. freedom perpetuate slavery in a large portion of the world with the comfortable feeling of pride in having done its .duty; men who are naturally just can be cruelly unjust both in their act and their thought, accompanied by a feeling that they are helping the world to receive its deserts; men who are honest can blindly go on robbing others of their human rights for self-aggrandisement, all the while abusing the deprived for not deserving better treatment. We have seen in our everyday life invent small organisations of business and profession produce callousness of feeling in men who are not naturally bad, and we can well imagine what a moral havoc it is causing in a world where whole peoples are furiously organising themselves for gaining wealth and power.

Nationalism is a great menace. It is the particular thing which for years has been at the bottom of India's troubles. And inasmuch as we have been ruled and dominated by a nation that is strictly political in its attitude, we have tried to develop within ourselves, despite our inheritance from the past, a belief in our eventual political destiny.

(From *Nationalism*, Rupa and Co, New Delhi, 2005 pp. 75-87)

9

Gopal Krishna Gokhale

Life and Times

Gopal Krishna Gokhale (1866-1915) was born in 1866 in a village in coastal Maharashtra, the son of a police sub-inspector. He learnt his letters in a rural school, before proceeding to the inland town of Kolhapur, where he completed his matriculation. He was then admitted to the Deccan College in Poona, from where he shifted to Bombay's Elphinstone College. On being awarded his BA, he began to coach students, to pay back the loans his family had incurred to send him to college.

In 1884, two brilliant young Brahmin reformers, Gopal Ganesh Agarkar and Bal Gangadhar Tilak, founded the Deccan Education Society. The following year, Gokhale joined one of the society's schools as a teacher. In 1889, Ranade appointed him editor, of the quarterly journal of the *Poona Sarvajanik Sabha*. In the same year he attended his first session of the Indian National Congress. The next year Gokhale joined the faculty of Fergusson College in Poona, where he worked for the next two decades, teaching English literature, mathematics and political economy. By now, he had acquired a taste for British writers and thinkers, among them Edmund Burke and John Stuart Mill.

By the time he was in his mid-twenties, Gokhale was a regular fixture at the annual meetings of the Congress. At the Calcutta session in 1890, for example, he spoke on the inequities of the salt tax. In 1897, having just turned thirty, Gokhale made the first of several trips to London, where he usually stayed at the National Liberal Club. On this visit, he testified to a Royal Commission on poverty and famines in .his homeland. Meanwhile, in a speech in the seaside town of Hastings, he compared the relationship between Britain and India to that between a giant and a dwarf, where 'everything went to the giant and what was left went to the dwarf.

Gokhale was now a rising star in Indian politics. He was elected to the Bombay Legislative Council in 1899, and to its all-India counterpart, the Imperial Council, two years later. Between 1902 and 1906 he simultaneously served as the president of the Poona municipality. All this while, he continued taking classes in Fergusson College.

As befitting a teacher, Gokhale's speeches were rich in facts and subtle in argument. Favourite subjects included the excessive tax burden on the peasantry and the need for more and better schools to provide free and compulsory education for all regardless of caste, religion, or gender. He demanded more seats for Indians in the Imperial Council and asked also that the annual budget of the , Government of India be open for scrutiny and amendment in the light of criticism.

Meanwhile, through his work for the Congress, Gokhale had acquainted himself with different parts of India. His outlook was further broadened by a visit to South Africa, to study the condition of the Indian diaspora in that country.

In 1905 Gokhale founded the *Servants of India Society*, whose members dedicated themselves to serving the nation-in-the-making. These 'Servants of India' were required to 'work for the advancement of all Indians, regardless of caste or creed.' He visited the United Kingdom again the same year. When he spoke at

Cambridge, a young John Maynard Keynes told an Indian friend that Gokhale 'has feeling, but feeling guided and controlled by thought, and there is nothing in him which reminds us of the usual type of political agitators'. The year 1905 ended for Gokhale with him presiding in December over the Congress meeting in Banaras.

As a leader of the Congress, Gokhale tried hard to reach out to the Muslims. He was wholly free of sectarian prejudice himself. However, he was regarded as excessively pro-British by militants such as Bal Gangadhar Tilak. His was the classical liberal dilemma— too moderate for the radicals, yet too extreme for the Establishment. One viceroy, Lord Hardinge, called Gokhale 'the most dangerous enemy of British rule in this country'.

In 1914 Gokhale turned down the offer of knighthood. He died the following year, not yet fifty. He had already done a great deal for his country, then still a colony, and shown his compatriots many new directions. Summing up his life's work, his biographer B.R. Nanda remarks that Gokhale 'hated foreign rule, but he did not blame all the ills from which India suffered on the British. He wanted her to shake off the shackles of social and economic backwardness as well as of political subjection. He wanted to turn the encounter with the Raj into an opportunity for building a secular, modern and democratic society'.

Empowering the Depressed Classes

Mr. President and Gentlemen, the proposition which has been entrusted to me runs thus:-

That this Conference hold that the present degraded condition of the low castes is in itself and from the national point of view unsatisfactory, and is of opinion that every well-wisher of the country should consider it his duty to do all he can to raise their moral and social condition by trying to rouse self-respect in these classes and placing facilities for education and employment within their reach.

Gendemen, I hope I am not given to the use of unnecessarily strong language and yet I must say that this resolution is not as strongly worded as it should have been. The condition of the low castes—it is painful to call them low castes—is not only unsatisfactory as this resolution says—it is so deeply deplorable that it constitutes a grave blot on our social arrangements; and, further, the attitude of our educated men towards this class is profoundly painful and humiliating. I do not propose to deal with this subject as an antiquarian; I only want to make a few general observations from the standpoint of justice, humanity, and national self-interest. I think all fair-minded persons will have to admit that it is absolutely monstrous that a class of human beings, with bodies similar to our own, with brains that can think and with hearts that can feel, should be perpetually condemned to a low life of utter wretchedness, servitude and mental and moral degradation, and that permanent barriers should be placed in their way so that it should be impossible for them ever to overcome them and improve their lot. This is deeply revolting to our sense of justice. I believe one has only to put oneself mentally into their place to realize how grievous this injustice is. We may touch a cat, we may touch a dog, we may touch any other animal, but the touch of these human beings is pollution! And so complete is now the mental degradation of these people that they themselves see nothing in such treatment to resent, that they acquiesce in it as though nothing better than that was their due.

I remember a speech delivered seven or eight years ago by the late Mr. Ranade in Bombay, under the auspices of the Hindu Union Club. That was a time when public feeling ran high in India on the subject of the treatment which our people were receiving in South Africa. Our friend, Mr. Gandhi, had come here on a brief visit from South Africa and he was telling us how our people were treated in Natal and Cape Colony and the Transvaal—how they were not allowed to walk on foot-paths or travel in first-class carriages on the railway, how they were not admitted into hotels and so forth. Public feeling, in consequence, was deeply stirred, and we all felt that it was a mockery that we should be called British subjects, when we were treated like this in Great Britain's colonies. Mr. Ranade felt this just as keenly as any one else. He had been a never-failing adviser of Mr. Gandhi, and had carried on a regular correspondence with him. But it was Mr. Ranade's peculiar greatness that he always utilized occasions of excitement to give a proper turn to the national mind and cultivate its sense of proportion. And so, when every one was expressing himself in indignant terms about the treatment which our countrymen were receiving in South Africa, Mr. Ranade came forward to ask if we had no sins of our own to answer for in that direction. I do not exactly remember the title of his address. I think it was 'Turn the search-light inwards,' or some such thing. But I remember that it was a great speech—one of the greatest that I have ever been privileged to hear. He began in characteristic fashion, expressing deep sympathy with the Indians in South Africa in the struggle they were manfully carrying on. He rejoiced that the people of India had awakened to a sense of the position of their countrymen abroad, and he felt convinced that this awakening was a sign of the fact that the dead bones in the valley were once again becoming instinct with life. But he proceeded to ask:- Was this sympathy with the oppressed and down-trodden Indians to be confined to those of our countrymen only who had gone out of India? Or was it to be general and to be extended to all cases where there was oppression and injustice? It was easy, he said, to denounce foreigners, but those who did so were bound in common fairness to look into themselves and see if they were absolutely blameless in the matter. He then described the manner in which members of low caste were treated by our own community in different parts of India. It was a description, which filled the audience with feelings of deep shame and pain and indignation. And Mr. Ranade very justly asked whether it was for those who tolerated such disgraceful oppression and injustice in their own country to indulge in all that denunciation of the people of South Africa. This question, therefore, is in the first place a question of sheer justice.

Next, as I have already said, it is a question of humanity. It is sometimes urged that if we have our castes, the people in the West have their classes, and after all, there is not much difference between the two. A little reflection will, however, show that the analogy is quite fallacious. The classes of the West are a perfectly elastic institution, and not rigid or cast-iron like our castes. Mr. Chamberlain, who is the most masterful personage in the British Empire to-day, was at one time a shoemaker and then a screw-maker. Of course, he did not make shoes himself, but that was the trade by which he made money. Mr. Chamberlain to-day dines with Royalty, and mixes with the highest in the land on terms of absolute equality. Will a shoemaker ever be able to rise in India in the social scale in a similar fashion, no matter how gifted by nature he might be? A great writer has said that castes are eminently useful for the preservation of society, but that they are utterly unsuited for purposes of progress. And this I think is perfectly true. If you want to stand where you were a thousand years ago, the system of castes need not be modified in any material degree. If, however, you want to emerge out of the slough in which you have long remained sunk, it will not do for you to insist on a rigid adherence to caste. Modern civilization has accepted greater equality for all as its watchword, as against privilege and exclusiveness, which were the root-ideas of the old world. And the larger humanity of these days requires that we should acknowledge its claims by seeking the amelioration of the helpless condition of our down-trodden countrymen.

Finally, gentlemen, this is a question of national self-interest. How can we possibly realize our national aspirations, how can our country ever hope to take her place among the nations of the world, if we allow large numbers of our countrymen to remain sunk in ignorance, barbarism, and degradation? Unless these men are gradually raised to a higher level, morally and intellectually, how can they possibly understand our thoughts or share our hopes or co-operate with us in our efforts? Can you not realize that so far as the work of national elevation is concerned, the energy, which these classes might be expected to represent, is simply unavailable to us? I understand that that great thinker and observer—Swami Vivekananda—held this view very strongly. I think that there is npt. much hope for us as a nation unless the help of all classes, including those that are known as low castes, is forthcoming for the work that lies before us. Moreover, is it, I may ask, consistent with our own self-respect that these men should be kept out of our houses and shut out from all social intercourse as long as they remain within the pale of Hinduism, whereas the moment they put on a coat and a hat and a pair of trousers and call themselves Christians, we are prepared to shake hands with them and look upon them as quite respectable? No sensible man will say that this is a satisfactory state of things. Of course, no one expects that these classes will be lifted up at once morally and intellectually to a position of equality with their more-favoured countrymen.

This work is bound to be slow and can only be achieved by strenuous exertions for giving them education and finding for them honourable employment in life. And, gentlemen, it seems to me that, in the present state of India, no work can be higher or holier than this. I think if there is one question of social reform more than another that should stir the enthusiasm of our educated young men and inspire them with an unselfish purpose, it is this question of the degraded condition of our low castes. Cannot a few men—five per cent, four per cent, three, two, even one per cent—of the hundreds and hundreds of graduates that the University turns out every year, take it upon themselves to dedicate their lives to this sacred work of the elevation of low castes? My appeal is not to the old or the middle-aged—the grooves of their lives are fixed—but I think I may well address such an appeal to the young members of our community—to those who have not yet decided upon their future course and who entertain the noble aspiration of devoting to a worthy cause the education which they have received. What the country needs most at the present moment is a spirit of self-sacrifice on the part of our educated young men, and they may take it from me that they cannot spend their lives in a better cause than raising the moral and intellectual level of these unhappy low castes and promoting their general well-being.

(From *Speeches of Gopal Kishna Gokhale* G.A. Nata Sen, Madras, 1916, pp-1054-1059)

10

Mohandas Karamchand Gandhi

Life and Tiems

Mohandas Karamchand Gandhi (1869-1948) held no office in government, and led no terrorist gang or rebel military army. Yet his intentions and actions aroused the millions of Indians, shook the Empire, and provoked both ridicule and admiration among people throughout the world. This strange man for nearly fifty years challenged, first, the European masters of South Africa, then, the British masters of India, and, finally, even the basic tenets of orthodox politics. Gandhi was an extraordinary political strategist, and that an appreciation of this is necessary to understand the man and the movements with which he challenged the most vast Empire which the world had ever seen and contributed significantly to its dissolution. We need to continue to consider Gandhi's challenge to established political tenets, his refinements of non-violent struggle, and his perceptions of requirements for ending oppression, reconstructing society, and lifting dependency upon political violence.

Mohandas Karamchand Gandhi, the prominent leader of the Indian national liberation movement and the founder of the doctrine of Gandhism, was born on 2 October 1869 in the Gujarat principality of Porbandar. His world outlook was largely determined by his upbringing in a family that belonged to the Bania caste and strictly adhered to the religious precepts of Hinduism.

His father held a ministerial position in various principalities of the Kathiawar peninsula.

Educated in England, Mohandas Gandhi first practised law in Bombay (between 1891 and 1893) and then (between 1893 and 1914) in South Africa as a legal adviser with a Gujarat Trade Company. While in South Africa, he led the struggle against race discrimination and the oppression of Indians. It was then that he first advocated Satyagraha, the tactics of non-violent resistance. Upon his return to India in January 1915, he got increasingly closer with the Indian National Congress to become its member in 1919 and, later, one of its most prominent leaders. Between 1919 and 1922, he headed India's mass national liberation movement. Speaking at numerous meetings and rallies he called for a non-violent struggle against the British domination. Between 1923 and 1928 he called for the revival of home spinning and weaving, and the elimination of the institution of untouchability.

Between 1919 and 1947 he was the most influential political figure in the Indian National Congress. Under his ideological leadership, it developed into a mass party and gained popular backing. The involvement of the masses in the national liberation movement was his major achievement. Tremendously popular with the people, he was called Mahatma, or Great Soul. The years 1922-1924, 1930-1931, 1942-1944 saw him arrested and imprisoned. Both in prison and at large, he resorted to hunger strikes to protest against the British colonial rule. In 1942 he advanced the "Quit India" slogan that matched the anti-British sentiment of the. Indian public and was supported by the Congress.

Since August 1947, when the division of the country into two states—India and Pakistan—was followed by Hindu-Muslim conflicts instigated by imperialist forces and domestic reactionaries, he persistently called for the unity of the Hindus and the Muslims. On 30 January 1948 he was assassinated by Nathuram Godse, member of the Hindu chauvinist organisation. More than 40 years have elapsed since the assassination of the leader of the Indian anti-imperialist movement, Mohandas Karamchand Gandhi. The years of dramatic struggle to liberate the great nation from the colonial yoke are becoming part of increasingly remote history. The passion about the appraisal of the extraordinary particularly in the European eye—and controversial figure of the "rebellious fakir", as Winston Churchill, a vehement opponent of decolonisation, described Gandhi, have almost subsided. But there is a sustained interest in his ideological and political legacy, his role in Indian history, his view of India's past and future. For all the contradictions in his behaviour, he was a man of striking integrity. Less fiery now a days, the debate around him is sure to continue for a long time to come. Gandhi is associated with a whole era in his country's history, the era when modem India and the people who until recently largely determined its image, were in the making. It is natural for all the political forces and all the schools of socio-political thought to strive to formulate their attitude towards Gandhi. The interpretation of his legacy is one of the important hallmarks of every political platform.

It has long been recognised that history is made by the masses. However it is the individual that becomes the historical symbol of age. Gandhi, Jawaharlal Nehru and Indira Gandhi have come to be part of historical symbolism inherent in the political consciousness and political life of the Indian people. The symbolism has spread beyond the boundaries of that country because Gandhi's and Nehru's activities and legacy feature many of the qualities typical of the age marked by the liberation of colonial and dependent countries from foreign oppression.

Gandhism, a set of political, moral ethical and philosophical concepts advanced by Gandhi in course of Indian people's national liberation struggle is phenomenon associated, in national consciousness, with the many years of fighting for independence against the British imperialist rule. Gandhism is also a factor in today's ideological, political and class struggles. This explains the importance of studying Gandhism, its actual content and historical role.

Gandhi's distant ancestors were retail grocers. His grandfather and father, however, came to be ministers in tiny Gujrat principalities and family prospered. In the mid-19th century,

Porbandar was remote provincial town whose life was governed by ancient traditions. Jainism, India's most distinctly non-violent religion, was— and still is—predominant in Gujarat. Although Gandhi's parents belonged to the Vaishnava sect of Hinduism, they, too, were strongly influenced by Jainism. The family ardently observed all rites and traditions. As a child, Mohandas was engaged to be married three times. His first two fiancees died, and he was for the last time engaged at the age of seven. He was married at thirteen. Just as many other young people in his youth. Gandhi was sceptical about the traditional way of life. The desire to escape the Hindu conservatism prompted his decision to continue his education in England. The community saw it as a defiance of tradition, and the Bombay members of the Bania caste ostracised him.

From September 1889 to June 1891, Gandhi lived in London, studying law first with the Inner Temple and, since 1890, at the University of London. Here, after a brief period of absorption in the life of metropolitan elite, he became nostalgic and drawn to Indian national traditions. Whatever reminded him about them in England, attracted his attention—the vegetarian society, Islam, Christianity and the theosophy of Elena Blavatskaya and Annie Besant. Theosophy made him interested in the sacred scriptures of his own country.

Many of those from the colonies who came to London for an education embraced the metropolitan culture and lost touch with their native land and turned into foreigners in their own home countries. This was not the case with Gandhi. He never adopted the British mode of life and the liberal-bourgeois values and ways of the Victorian age. In London, the foundation for his negative attitude to "European civilization" was laid.

In 1893 Gandhi left for South Africa. He became a legal adviser for a Gujarat trade firm. That year acts of race discrimination against the! Indian emigres became specially blatant: Gandhi placed himself at the head of the anti-racist movement that emerged in the Indian civil disobedience. The long and bitter struggle led result, the position of the Indian emigres somewhat improved. More importantly, participation in the movement taught them dignity and determination to defend their civil rights.

Gandhi had never intended to stay in South Africa long. However, he spent twenty years of his life there. This period proved to be of decisive importance for the formation of his character and views. It is while in South Africa that he fully appreciated his own country's humanitarian culture and traditions. It is there that he challenged race discrimination and inequality and his world outlook was shaped by his dedication to non-violence and high moral principles. Although in his spiritual quest Gandhi proceeded from the principles of Hinduism and Jainism, he also relied on what was consonant with them in Western culture which he continuously studied since his days in England Particularly close to his heart were the ethical ideals of reformed Christianity free of dogmas and rites, the desire to turn away from bourgeois values and urban civilisation that isolate man from nature and to seek moral self-improvement in a natural environment. Hence his interest in Thomas Carlyle, Henry Thoreau and especially the great Russian writer Leo Tolstoy.

Gandhi's years in South Africa were marked by an intensive search for an ethical ideal which, in his view, was to be associated with social and political activity. This was a continuation of the work lie started in London, hut here, among the members of an oppressed Indian community, Gandhi concentrated not only on the issue of personal spiritual development, but also on that of social injustice and ways to combat it. He was attracted by the struggle against oppression and despotism, no matter where and how it was waged, because reconciling with injustice was organically alien to him. In this connection, significant is his interest in and sympathy for the first Russian revolution. In his articles he wrote about the .courage of Russian revolutionaries and their preparedness for resolute action. He was especially supportive of the general strike. "We too can resort to the Russian remedy against tyranny," he commented.

Although he was attracted by the revolutionary movement of the masses as a manifestation of fearlessness and commitment, in his personal quest he was inspired by the public stance of Leo Tolstoy. Gandhi's European friends encouraged his interest in the writings of the great humanist. He found Tolstoy's view of ethical and social issue to be strikingly consonant with his own and readily described himself as "a humble follower who had asked Tolstoy to express his solidarity with the Indian people oppressed by the British colonisers. On 1 October 1909, he sent him a letter describing the struggle waged by the Indians hit by race discrimination in Transvaal to assert their dignity by non-violent methods. He asked for the writer's permission to have his "Letter to a Hindoo" translated and circulated among them. In his reply, Tolstoy wished Gandhi every success and stressed the similarity of their principles. For Gandhi, Tolstoy's support was an important spiritual and ideological incentive. Throughout his life, Gandhi held Tolstoy in high esteem and remained grateful to him.' Lenin had every reason to mention, in his plan for the unfinished "Notes of a Publicist, a Hindu Tolstoy-follower". There can hardly be any doubt that he meant Gandhi. The activities of the latter attracted the attention of the founder of the world's first working people's state.

It goes without saying that there was a significant difference between Gandhi's and Tolstoy's views. This is primarily accounted for by their different areas of activity. Tolstoy was, above all, a writer and a moral philosopher, while Gandhi, a politician and public figure. Admittedly, Gandhi did a lot to adjust Tolstoy's individualistic, purely and classically personal doctrine to a public movement This called for a noticeable shift in emphases and for an elaboration on Tolstoy's ideas. With Tolstoy, it is non-resistance to evil by violence, with Gandhi, it is non-violent resistance; Tolstoy seeks personal improvement, Gandhi '.ids to this personal influence exerted on other people in the course of mass movement general ideals of good and justice. While Tolstoy's sublime abstraction is clear and well-balanced, Gandhi's political activity is marked by repeated compromise and deviation from the ideal.

It was in South Africa that Gandhi's invincible mettle as a public figure first manifested itself. For him moral improvement and social commitment were inseparable. Isolation, retirement into oneself and eternal self-contemplation were alien to him. Fighting against social and political injustice was part of his personal moral code. Combining ethics and politics was Gandhi's life-long preoccupation. Although he did not deem it possible to tolerate evil, he thought it to be immoral and contrary to the sublime spiritual goal to resort to all available means in fighting it. He found a way out in introducing non-violence in politics through the elaboration of the theory and practice of (non-violent) resistance—Satyagraha that was first tested as a public movement in South Africa. Gandhi developed into an outstanding politician and a great strategist of the Indian national liberation movement through paradoxically combining ethical idealism and political pragmatism. He first displayed the ability to do so while in South Africa.

Underlining the enormous significance of Mahatma Gandhi and his moral-political philosophy, Fred Dallamayr, the noted political scientist observes-'Gandhi was and remains a source of immense ferment unsettling all kinds of intellectual and political complacency'. Few would dispute that Gandhi was a path-breaker and path-finder, without flourish or fanfare he was able to point out the darkness beneath the glittering structure of modern civilization and shake the foundations of a mighty empire. He had enough moral courage, as prof. K. Raghvendra Rao has said, 'to take positions directly and uncompromisingly opposed to dominant currents of thought and practice.' He strove hard for India's freedom but did not tread the beaten path nor did he regard the attainment of freedom as the end of journey. He infact was straining his nerves to usher in a social order based on lofty ideals and moderate expectations. His foremost concern was to restore the sovereignty of moral law in human affairs.

Gandhi's life is a saga of experiments with truth. In the formative years of his childhood, the stories of *Ramayan* and *Mahabharat*, the Jain and Buddhist writings and nobility of character of persons like Raj Chandra Mehta made an abiding impact on him. Later on, the thoughtful works of Tolstoy, Ruskin, Thoreau, Emerson etc. touched his soul and played a great role in moulding Gandhi's whole outlook on life. In 1893, he went to South Africa in connection with a legal case but the plight of Indians because of the oppressive racist policies of the government so moved him that he decided to stay there and wage a non-violent struggle against the government. Thus South Africa became the testing ground of many of the ethical and political ideals and experiments that were to characterize his long and distinguished life. Returning to India in 1915, he joined the Indian national Congress and became a leading light of national struggle. That he was able to become a front line leader of congress within a few years speaks volumes for his magnetism and maturity. Subsequently, he was the moving spirit behind three moments movements- Non-cooperation movement, Civil Disobedience Movement and Quit India Movement which played a crucial past in leading India to freedom. But politics was only one aspect of his many-faceted life. Through various constructive programmes he sought to bring about qualitative change in social, economic and educational spheres. He tirelessly worked for India's freedom and he also worked unceasingly to make Indians worthy of their great and ancient civilization. India's freedom was his immediate goal, the restoration of a spiritual social order in India and in world was his ultimate goal. For him, Indian movement was not national but universal-human.

The science of politics is designated 'master science' in the traditional political thought not because of the superior might of state but because of supreme importance of the state in the attainment by individuals of the 'summum bonum' or the supreme good. Politics is thus not only a pre-requisite of human survival but of human salvation. But if political activity becomes autotelic, it degenerates into a game of power and passion. It is exactly to save politics from operating at sub-human level for inhuman purposes that the need to subordinate it to metaphysics arises.

This explains as well as establishes Gandhi's uniqueness among the modern political thinkers. The vast Gandhian edifice is erected not on the postulates of scientific materialism or scientific rationalism but on the truths of transcendental reason which he calls 'still small voice' and 'delicate divine music' 'God rules', he proclaimed, 'my every breath.' For him metaphysics defines as well as refines politics. Celestial city is the model and norm of the earthly city. It is the Supreme Being and the cosmic order on which he expends his chief thought and attention because he believed like Plato that'if the first principles are rightly laid down, all the rest will follow.' And it is because he finds modern civilization wholly deanchored from the first principles that he totally and finally rejects it.

Gandhian thinking strives to restore the sovereignty of moral law. He first desired the supreme good and then aspired political, social and economic good as a natural consequence of it. As he one wrote in *Harijan*, Man's ultimate aim is the realization of God and all his activities-social, political, religious have to be guided by the ultimate aim of vision of God'. In this way, he sought to radically alter or rather reverse the civilizational concerns of modern age and modern man. Like Socrates, he sought to practice 'true art of politics' which is ever concerned with moral development of all men and women and which is ' the means to the realization of the highest realizable in life'. Real politic was to him a profane thing deadly in its devices and effects in terms of human good and fulfillment. He disdained the prostitution of politics in the hands of the power-seekers since power is not the law of human species or the norm of human action. Politics without principles is brutality and a source of dehumanization. When he said that he was trying to introduce religion into politics, he was rendering unto politics its meaning and sanctity.

With this insistence on the integrality of politics and ethics, it is no wonder that Gandhi attaches immense importance to means. He does not subscribe to the pragmatist view which regards politics as a study in expediency. Both Machiavelli and Marx denied the existence of supra-historic moral principles. But for Gandhi perennial principles of morality are the ultimate test of individual or collective action. Since the doctrine 'end justifies the means' is a denial of unity and integrity of life and disruptive of 'holistic balance', it can never be the guide to action. No end, howsoever high and worthy, overrides the proscription of means recognized as immoral. And if this is so, Satyagrah is the only means for the resistance of an evil and the redressal of a wrong. It is the universal method of vigilance. It is steadfastness in truth that works wonders at the individual as well as social level. Satyagraha is the normal and natural way of conducting politics. He once declared, 'If violence and untruth are necessary for the advancement of my country, let my country go under.' Infact Gandhi was only re-echoing the old Latin adage 'Let justice be done though the world may perish.'

Gandhi's espousal of 'goodness politics' made him a devastating critic of state in its present form. If true progress is an exercise in self-discovery, state has not got much to do. According to Gandhi, a normal political order is one where everybody is his ruler. While holding on to 'the enlightened anarchy' as the ultimate ideal, in practice his concept of state is one of minimum state. Since modern state is highly centralized, it is most interfering without being least helpful. His own measures to transform the present state into a kingdom of God on earth aimed at progressive elimination of all the coercive apparatus of state and establishment of commonwealth of autonomous village republics based on love instead of coercion, service instead of exploitation, renunciation instead of acquisitiveness and on largest measure of local and individual initiative instead of centralization.

The nounmenalist politics of Mahatma Gandhi cannot go with major ideologies of our times, whether liberalism or marxian socialism. These partial ideologies are disruptive of holistic balance. Like politics, the criterion of true and sound economics is its moral adequacy, and an economics independent from ethics is dismal science. He once wrote in *Young India* - 'I must confess that I do not draw sharp or any distinction between economics and ethics. Economics that hurts the moral well-being of an individual or nation is immoral and therefore sinful'. Gandhi opposes industrialism because it sets in motion exploitation and domination at individual and collective levels. Industrialism thrives on self-interest and greed and because of its obsession with 'progress' ruthlessly exploits and destroys lower orders of nature. Though he regarded grinding poverty as morally and spiritually degrading, he did not think that material prosperity must necessarily issue in moral progress. He was opposed to both capitalism and socialism as both essentially believed in 'mammon worship'. His theory of trusteeship was the application of sound ethical principles in restructuring the conflict-ridden relationship between capital and labour. At a higher level, as Bhikhu Parekh has observed, 'It is an economic extension of Gandhi's philosophical concept of man as a trustee of all he has, including his powers, capacities, energy and time.'

The following extracts have been re-produced from Gandhi's *Hind Swaraj*. It is the seminal document of Gandhian creed. All his later writings and speeches are elaboration or reiteration of 'whole theory of life' propounded in it. Unsettling truths have been said in direct manner. Written in dialogue form, the book contains a radical critique of fundamental ideals and institutions of modernity, and Gandhi emerges as the spokesman for the non-modern or pre-modern or even the anti-modern ideas lodged in the intestines of the modern cosmos.

When Gandhi said that universe would disappear without the force of love, he was underlining the normal and natural way of conducting political affairs. This love-force or soul-force is the law of the human species, and any resort to brute force is an affront to human dignity. While resisting evil, one must keep in mind that evil-doer is also a part of spiritual fellowship, and though a deviant from the path of right out of ignorance or arrogance, he is all the same a human being, with a conscience and a soul, and therefore as amenable to force of love as anybody else. In resisting evil, use of force or violence is disruptive of that spiritual fellowship and that unity and integrity of life which forms the core of a true civilization. Resisting evil by evil only enlarges the kingdom of darkness because violence breeds greater violence, and is a sign of our moral and mental depravity. On the other hand, resisting evil by good is a sign of our humanity, our moral and spiritual strength. Therefore Gandhi says that a passive resister is never defeated though he may suffer setbacks. Passive resistance results in our own moral expansion as well as of those against whom it is applied. Passive-resistance aims at the victory of truth, not the victory of this or that side.

The weapon of passive resistance has been used since time immemorial in family, in community and in state, and if modern societies favour the force of arms to settle disputes, it is not an evidence of the ineffectiveness of the soul-force but of the brutalization of human relations and human affairs. Gandhi says that human species would have vanished long ago if brute force had been its law. Therefore political and social affairs must be conducted on the basis of love and non-violence. It is worthwhile, in this connection, to refer to important insight of Hannah Arednt who says that violence, being instrumental, cannot be the essence of political realm. It may destroy power but it cannot be the source of power. The Gandhian idea that ways of moral action and resistance could be transferred from the individual to collective plane and be used as powerful forms of political action is one that has awakened politicians from their dogmatic slumbers.

Brute Force

Reader: This is a new doctrine, that what is gained through fear is retained only while the fear lasts. Surely, what is given will not be withdrawn?

Editor: Not so. The Proclamation of 1857 was given at the end of a revolt, and for the purpose of preserving peace. When peace was secured and people became simple-minded its full effect was toned down. If I cease stealing for fear of punishment, I would recommence the operation as soon as the fear is withdrawn from me. This is almost a universal experience. We have assumed that we can get men to do things by force and, therefore, we use force.

Reader: Will you not admit that you are arguing against yourself? You know that what the English obtained in their own country they obtained by using brute force. I know you have argued that what they have obtained is useless, but that does nt affect my argument. They wanted useless things and they got them. My point is that their desire was fulfilled. What does it matter what means they adopted? Why should we not obtain our goal, which is good, by any means whatsoever, even by using violence? Shall I think of the means when I have to deal with a thief in the house? My duty is to drive him out anyhow. You seem to admit that we have received nothing, and that we shall receive nothing by petitioning. Why, then, may we not do so by using brute force? And, to retain what we may receive we shall keep up the fear by using the same force to the extent that it may be necessary. You will not find fault with a continuance of force to prevent a child from thrusting its foot into fire. Somehow or other we have to gain our end.

Editor: Your reasoning is plausible. It has deluded many. I have used similar arguments before now. But I think I know better now, and I shall endeavour to undeceive you. Let us first take the agreement that we are justified in gaining our end by using brute force because the English gained theirs by using similar means. It is perfectly true that they used brute force and that it is possible for us to do likewise, but by using similar means we can get only the same thing that they got. You will admit that we do not want that. Your belief that there is no connection between the means and the end is a great mistake. Through that mistake even men who have been considered religious have committed grievous crimes. Your reasoning is the same as saying that we can get a rose through planting a noxious weed. If I want to cross the ocean, I can do so only by means of a vessel; if I were to use a cart for that purpose, both the cart and I would soon find the bottom. "As is the God, so is the votary," is a maxim worth considering. Its meaning has been distorted and men have gone astray. The means may be likened to a seed, the end to a tree; and there is just the same inviolable connection between the means and the end as there is between the seed and the tree.

I am not likely to obtain the result flowing from the worship of God by laying myself prostrate before Satan. If, therefore, anyone were to say: "I want to worship God; it does not matter that I do so by means of Satan," it would be set down as ignorant folly. We reap exactly as we sow. The English in 1833 obtained greater voting power by violence. Did they by using brute force better appreciate their duty? They wanted the right of voting, which they obtained by using physical force. But real rights are a result of performance of duty; these rights they have not obtained. We, therefore, have before us in England the force of everybody wanting and insisting on his rights, nobody thinking of his duty. And, where everybody wants rights, who shall give them to whom? I do not wish to imply that they do no duties. They don't perform the duties corresponding to those rights; and as they do not perform that particular duty, namely, acquire fitness, their rights have proved a burden to them. In other words, what they have obtained is an exact result of the means they adopted. They used the means corresponding to the end. If I want to deprive you of your watch, I shall certainly have to fight for it; if I want to buy your watch, I shall have to pay you for it; and if I want a gift I shall have to plead for it; and, according to the means I employ, the watch is stolen property, my own property, or a donation. Thus we see three different results from three different means. Will you still say that means do not matter?

Now we shall take the example given by you of the thief to be driven out. I do not agree with you that the thief may be driven out by any means. If it is my father who has come to steal I shall use one kind of means. If it is an acquaintance I shall use another; and in the case of a perfect stranger I shall use a third. If it is a white man, you will perhaps say you will adopt with an Indian thief. If it is a weakling, the means will b e different from those to be adopted for dealing with an equal in physical strength; and if the thief is armed from top to toe, I shall simply remain quiet. Thus we have a variety of means between the father and the armed man. Again, I fancy that I should pretend to be sleeping whether the thief was my father or that strong armed man. The reason for this is that my father would also be armed and I should succumb to the strength possessed by either and allow my things to be stolen. The strength of my father would make me weep with pity; the strength of the armed man would rouse in me anger and we should become enemies. Such is the curious situation. From these examples we may not be able to agree as to the means to be adopted in each case. I myself seem clearly to see what should be done in all these cases, but the remedy may frighten you. I therefore hesitate to place it before you. For the time being I will leave you to guess it, and if you cannot, it is clear you will have to adopt different means in each case. You will also have seen that any means will not avail to drive away the thief. You will have to adopt means to fit each case. Hence it follows that your duty is *not* to drive away the thief by any means you like.

Let us proceed a little further. That well-armed man has stolen your property; you have harboured the thought of his act; you are filled with anger; you argue that you want to punish that rogue, not for your own sake, but for the good of your neighbours; you have collected a number of armed men, you want to take his house by assault; he is duly informed of it, he runs away; he too is incensed. He collects his brother robbers, and sends you a defiant message that he will commit robbery in broad daylight. You are strong, you do not fear him, you are prepared to receive him. Meanwhile, the robber pesters your neighbours. They complain before you. You reply that you are doing all for their sake, you do not mind that your own goods have been stolen. Your neighbours reply that the robber never pestered them before, and that he commenced his depredations only after you declared hostilities against him. You are between Scylla and Charybdis. You are full of pity for the poor men. What they say is true. What are you to do? You will be disgraced if you now leave the robber alone. You, therefore, tell the poor men: "Never mind. Come, my wealth is yours, I will give you arms, I will teach you how to use them; you should belabor the rogue; don't you leave him alone." And so the battle grows; the robbers increase in numbers; your neighbours have deliberately put themselves to inconvenience. Thus the result of wanting to take revenge upon the robber is that you have disturbed your own peace; you are in perpetual fear of being robbed and assaulted; your courage has given place to cowardice. If you will patiently examine the argument, you will see that I have not overdrawn the picture. This is one of the means.

Now let us examine the other. You set this armed robber down as an ignorant brother; you intend to reason with him at a suitable opportunity; you argue that he is, after all, a fellow-man; you do not know what prompted him to steal. You, therefore, decide that, when you can, you will destroy the man's motive for stealing. Whilst you are thus reasoning with yourself the man comes again to steal. Instead of being angry with him you take pity on him. You think that this stealing habit must be a disease with him. Henceforth, you, therefore, keep your doors and windows open, you change your sleeping-place, and you keep your things in a manner most accessible to him. The robber comes again and is confused as all this is new to him; nevertheless, he takes away your things. But his mind is agitated. He inquires about you in the village, he comes to learn about your broad and loving heart, he repents, he begs your pardon, returns you your things and leaves off the stealing habit. He becomes your servant, and you find for him honourable employment. This is the second method. Thus, you see,, different means have brought about totally different results. I do not wish to deduce from this that robbers will act in the above manner or that all will have the same pity and love like you, but I only with to show that fair means alone can produce fair results, and that, at least in the majority of cases, if not indeed in all, the force of love and pity is infinitely greater than the force of arms. There is harm n the exercise of brute force, never in that of pity.

Now we will take the question of petitioning. It is a fact beyond dispute that a petition, without the backing of force, is useless. However, the late Justice Ranade used to say that petitions served a useful purpose because they were a means of educating people. They give the latter and idea of their condition and warn the rulers. From this point of view, they are not altogether useless. A petition of an equal is a sign of courtesy; a petition from a slave is a symbol of his slavery. A petition backed by force is a petition from an equal and, when he transmits his demand in the form of a petition, it testifies to his nobility. Two kinds of force can back petitions. "We shall hurt if you do not give this," is one kind of force; it is the force of arms, whose evil results we have already examined. The second kind of force can thus be stated: "If you do not concede our demand, we shall be not longer your petitioners. You can govern us only so long as we remain the governed; we shall no longer have any dealings with you." The force implied in this may be described as love-force, soul-force, or, more popularly but less accurately, passive resistance. This force is indestructible. He who uses it perfectly understands his position. We have an ancient proverb which literally means: "One negative cures thirty-six diseases." The force of arms is powerless when matched against the force of love or the soul.

Now we shall take your last illustration, that of the child thrusting its foot into fire. It will not avail you. What do you really do to the child? Supposing that it can exert so much physical force that it renders you powerless and ruhes into fire, then you cannot prevent it. There are only two remedies open to you-either you must kill it in order to prevent it from perishing in the flames, or you must give your own life because you do not wish to see it perish before your very eyes. You will not kill it. If your heart is not quite full of pity, it is possible that you will not surrender yourself by preceding the child and going into the fire yourself. You, therefore, helplessly allow it to go into the flames. Thus, at any rate, you are not using physical force. I hope you will not consider that it is still physical force, though of a low order, when you would forcibly prevent the child from rushing towards the fire if you could. That force is of a different order and we have to understand what it is.

Remember that, in thus preventing the child, you are minding entirely its own interest, you are exercising authority for its sole benefit. Your example does not apply to the English. In using brute force against the English you consult entirely your own, that is the national, interest. There is no question here either of pity or of love. If you say that the actions of the English, being evil, represent fire, and that they proceed to their actions through ignorance, and that therefore they occupy the position of a child and that you want to protect such a child, then you will have to overtake every evil action of that kind by whomsoever committed and, as in the case of the evil child, you will have to sacrifice yourself. If you are capable of such immeasurable pity, I wish you well in its exercise.

Passive Resistance

Reader: Is there any historical evidence as to the success of what you have called soul-force or truth-force? No instance seems to have happened of any nation having risen through soul-force. I still think that the evil-doers will not cease doing evil without physical punishment.

Editor: The poet Tulsidas has said: "Of religion, pity, or love, is the root, as egotism of the body. Therefore, we should not abandon pity so long as we are alive." This appears to me to be a scientific truth. I believe in it as much as I believe in two and two being four. The force of love is the same as the force of the soul or truth. We have evidence of its working at every step. The universe would disappear without the existence of that force. But you ask for historical evidence. It is, therefore, necessary to know what history means. The Gujarati equivalent means: "It so happened". If that is the meaning of history, it is possible to give copious evidence. But, if it means the doings of kings and emperors, there can be no evidence of soul-force or passive resistance in such history. You cannot expect silver ore in a tin mine. History, as we know it, is a record of the wars of the world, and so there is a proverb among Englishmen that a nation which has no history, that is, no wars, is a happy nation. How kings played, how they became enemies of one another, how they murdered one another, is found accurately recorded in history, and if this were all that had happened in the world, it would have been ended long ago. If the story of the universe had commenced with wars, not a man would have been found alive today. Those people who have been warred against have disappeared as, for instance, he natives of Australia of whom hardly a man was left alive by the intruders. Mark, please, that these natives did not use soul-force in self-defence, and it does not require much foresight to know that the Australians will share the same fate as their victims. "Those that take the sword shall perish by the sword." With us the proverb is that professional swimmers will find a watery grave.

The fact that there are so many men still alive in the world shows that it is based not on the force of arms but on the force of truth or love. Therefore, the greatest and most unimpeachable evidence of the success of this force is to be found in the fact that, in spite of the wars of the world, it still lives on.

Thousands, indeed tens of thousands, depend for their existence on a very active working of this force. Little quarrels of millions of families in their daily lives disappear before the exercise of this force. Hundreds of nations live in peace. History does not and cannot take note of this fact. History is really a record of every interruption of the even working of the force of love or of the soul. Two brothers quarrel; one of them repents and re-awakens the love that was lying dormant in him; the two again begin to live in peace; nobody takes note of this. But if the two brothers, through the intervention of solicitors or some other reason take up arms or go to law-which is another form of the exhibition of brute force, - their doings would be immediately noticed in the pres, they would be the talk of their neighbours and would probably go down to history. And what is true of families and communities is true of nations. There is no reason to believe that there is one law for families and another for nations. History, then, is a record of an interruption of the course of nature. Soul-force, being natural, is not noted in history.

Reader: According to what you say, it is plain that instances of this kind of passive resistance are not to be found in history. It is necessary to understand this passive resistance more fully. It will be better, therefore, if you enlarge upon it.

Editor: Passive resistance is a method of securing rights by personal suffering; it is the reverse of resistance by arms. When I refuse to do a thing that is repugnant to my conscience, I use soul-force. For instance, the Government of the day has passed a law which is applicable to me. I do not like it. If by using violence I force the Government to repeal the law, I am employing what may be termed body-force. If I do not obey the law and accept the penalty for its breach, I use soul-force. It involves sacrifice of self.

Everybody admits that sacrifice of self is infinitely superior to sacrifice of others. Moreover, if this kind of force is used in a cause that is unjust, only the person using it suffers. He does not make others suffer for his mistakes. Men have before now done many things which were subsequently found to have been wrong. No man can claim that he is absolutely in the right or that a particular thing is wrong because he thinks so, but it is wrong for him so long as that is his deliberate judgement. It is therefore meet that he should not do that which he knows to be wrong, and suffer the consequence whatever it may be. This is the key to the use of soul-force.

Reader: You would then disregard laws-this is rank disloyalty. We have always been considered a la-abiding nation. You seem to be going even beyond the extremists. They say that we must obey the laws that have been passé, but that if the laws be bad, we must drive out the law-givers even by force.

Editor: Whether I go beyond them or whether I do not is a matter of no consequence to either of us. We simply want to find out what is right and to act accordingly. The real meaning of the statement that we are a law-abiding nation is that we are passive resisters. When we do not like certain laws, we do not break the heads of law-givers but we suffer and do not submit to the laws. That we should obey laws whether good or bad is a new-fangled notion. There was no such thing in former days. The people disregarded those laws they did not like and suffered the penalties for their breach. It is contrary to our manhood if we obey laws repugnant to our conscience. Such teaching is opposed to religion and means slavery. If the Government were to ask us to go about without any clothing, should we do so? If I were a passive resister, I would say to them that I would have nothing to do with their law. But we have so forgotten ourselves and become so compliant that we do not mind any degrading law.

A man who has realized his manhood, who fears only God, will fear no one else. Man-made laws are not necessarily binding on him. Even the Government does not expect any such thing form us. They do not say: " You must do such and such a thing," but they say " If you do not do it, we will punish you." We are sunk so low that we fancy that it is our duty and our religion to do what the law lays down. If man will only realize that it is unmanly to obey laws that are unjust, no man's tyranny will enslave him. This is the key to self-rule or home-rule.

It is a superstition and ungodly thing to believe that an act of a majority binds a minority. Many examples can be given in which acts of majorities will be found to have been wrong and those of minorities to have been right. All reforms owe their origin to the initiation of minorities in opposition to majorities. If among a band of robbers a knowledge of robbing is obligatory, is a pious man to accept the obligation? So long as the superstition that men should obey unjust laws exists, so long will their slavery exist. And a passive resister alone can remove such a superstition.

To use brute-force, to use gunpowder, is contrary to passive resistance, for it means that we want our opponent to do by force that which se desire but he does not. And if such a use of force is justifiable, surely he is entitled to do likewise by us. And so we should never come to an agreement. We may simply fancy like the blind horse moving in a circle round a mill, tat we are making progress. Those who believe that they are not bound to obey laws which are repugnant to their conscience have only the remedy of passive resistance open to them. Any other must lead to disaster.

Reader: From what you say I deduce that passive resistance is a splendid weapon of the weak, but that when they are strong they may take up arms.

Editor: This is gross ignorance. Passive resistance, that is, soul-force, is matchless. It is superior to the force of arms. How, then, can it be considered only a weapon of the weak? Physical-force men are strangers to the courage that is requisite in a passive resister. Do you believe that a coward can ever disobey a law that he dislikes? Extremists are considered to be advocates of brute force. Why do they, then, talk about obeying laws? I do not blame them. They can say nothing else. When they succeed in driving out the English and they themselves become governors, they will want you and me to obey their laws. And that is a fitting thing for their constitution. But a passive resister will say he will not obey a law that is against his conscience, even though he may be blown to pieces at the mouth of a cannon.

What do you think? Wherein is courage required – in blowing others to pieces from behind a cannon, or with a smiling face to approach a cannon and be blown to pieces? Who is the true warrior-he who keeps death always as a bosom-friend, or he who controls the death of others? Believe me that a man devoid of courage and manhood can never be a passive resister.

This however, I will admit: that even a man weak in body is capable of suffering this resistance. One man can offer it just as well as millions. Both men and women can indulge in it. It does not require the training of an army; it needs no jiu-jitsu. Control over the mind is alone necessary, and when that is attained, man is free like the king of the forest and his very glance withers the enemy.

Passive resistance is an all-sided sword, it can be used anyhow; it blesses him who uses it and him against whom it is used. Without drawing a drop of blood it produces far-reaching results. It never rusts and cannot be stolen. Competition between passive resisters does not exhaust. The sword of passive resistance does not require a scabbard. It is strange indeed that you should consider such a weapon to be a weapon merely of the weak.

Reader: You have said that passive resistance is a speciality of India. Have cannons never been used in India?

Editor: Evidently, in your opinion, India means its few princes. To me it means its teeming millions on whom depends the existence of its prices and our own.

Kings will always use their kingly weapons. To use force is bred in them. They want to command, but those who have to obey commands do not want guns; and these are in a majority throughout the world. They have to learn either body-force or soul-force. Where they learn the former, both the rulers and the ruled become like so many madmen; but where they learn soul-force the commands of the rulers do not go beyond the point of their swords, for true men disregard unjust commands. Peasants have never been subdued by the sword, and never will be. They do not know the use of the sword, and they are not frightened by the use of it by others. That nation is great which rests its head upon death as its pillow. Those who defy death are free from all fear. For those who are labouring under the delusive charms of brute-force, this picture is not overdrawn. The fact is that, in India, the nation at large has generally used passive resistance in all departments of life. We cease to co-operate with our rulers when they displease us. This is passive resistance.

I remember an instance when, in a small principality, the villagers were offended by some command issued by the prince. The former immediately began vacating the village. The prince became nervous, apologized to his subjects and withdrew his command. Many such instances can be found in India. Real Home Rule is possible only where passive resistance is the guiding force of the people. Any other rule is foreign rule.

Reader: Then you will say that it is not at all necessary for us to train the body?

Editor: I will certainly not say any such thing. It is difficult to become a passive resister unless the body is trained. As a rule, the mind, residing in a body that has become weakened by pampering, is also weak, and where there is no strength of mind there can be no strength of soul. We shall have to improve our physique by getting rid of infant marriages and luxurious living. If I were to ask a man with a shattered body to face a cannon's mouth I should make a laughing-stock of myself.

Reader: From what you say, then, it would appear that it is not a small thing to become a passive resister and, if that is so, I should like you to explain how a man may become one.

Editor: To become a passive resister is easy enough but it is also equally difficult. I have known a lad of fourteen years become a passive resister; I have known also sick people do likewise; and I have also known physically strong and otherwise happy people unable to take up passive resistance. After a great deal of experience it seems to me that those who want to become passive resisters for the service of the country have to observe perfect chastity, adopt poverty, follow truth, and cultivate fearlessness.

Chastity is one of the greatest disciplines without which the mind cannot attain requisite firmness. A man who is unchaste loses stamina, becomes emasculated and cowardly. He whose mind is given over to animal passions is not capable of any great effort. This can b e proved by innumerable instances. What, then, is a married person to do is the question that arises naturally; and yet it need not. When a husband and wife gratify the passions, it is no less an animal indulgence on that account. Such an indulgence, except for perpetuating the race, is strictly prohibited. But a passive resister has to avoid even that very limited indulgence because he can have no desire for progeny. A married man, therefore, can observe perfect chastity. This subject is not capable of being treated at greater length. Several questions arise: How is one to carry one's wife with one, what are her rights, and other similar questions. Yet those who wish to take part in a great work are bound to solve these puzzles.

Just as there is necessity for chastity, so is there for poverty. Pecuniary ambition and passive resistance cannot well o together. Those who have money are not expected to throw it away, but they are expected to be indifferent about it. They must be prepared to lose every penny rather than give up passive resistance.

Passive resistance has been described in the course of our discussion as truth-force. Truth, therefore, has necessarily to be followed and that at any cost. In this connection, academic questions such as whether a man may not lie in order to save a life, etc., arise, but these questions occur only to those who wish to justify lying. Those who want to follow truth every time are not placed in such a quandary; and if they are, they are still saved from a false position.

Passive resistance cannot proceed a step without fearlessness. Those alone can follow the path of passive resistance who are free from fear, whether as to their possessions, false honour, their relatives, the government, bodily injuries or death.

These observances are not to be abandoned in the belief that they are difficult. Nature has implanted in the human breast ability to cope with any difficulty or suffering that may come to man unprovoked. These qualities are worth having, even for those who do not wish to serve the country. Let there be no mistake, as those who want to train themselves in the use of arms are also obliged to have these qualities more or less. Everybody does not become a warrior for the wish. A would-be warrior will have to observe chastity and to be satisfied with poverty as his lot. A warrior without fearlessness cannot be conceived of. It may be thought that he would not need to be exactly truthful, but that quality follows real fearlessness. When a man abandons truth, he does so owing to fear in some shape or form. The above four attributes, then, need not frighten anyone. It may be as well here to not that a physical-force man has to have many other useless qualities which a passive resister never needs. And you will find that whatever extra effort a swordsman needs is due to lack of fearlessness. If he is an embodiment of the latter, the sword will drop from his hand that very moment. He does not need its support. One who is free from hatred requires no sword. A man with a stick suddenly came face to face with a lion and instinctively raised his weapon in self-defence. The man saw that he had only prated about fearlessness when there was none in him. That moment he dropped the stick and found himself free from all fear.

(From *Hind Swaraj,* pp 63-77, Navjivan Publishing House, Ahmedabad 1998.)

What is Swaraj?

Reader: I have now learnt what the Congress has done to make India one nation, how the Partition has caused an awakening, and how discontent and unrest have spread through the land. I would now like to know your views on Swaraj. I fear that our interpretation is not the same as yours.

Editor: It is quite possible that we do not attach the same meaning to the term. You and I and all Indians are impatient to obtain Swaraj, but we are certainly not decided as to what it is. To drive the English out of India is a thought heard from many mouths, but it does not seem that many have properly considered why it should be so. I must ask you a question. Do you think that it is necessary to drive away the English, if we get all we want?"

Reader: I should ask of them only one thing, that is: "Please leave our country." If, after they have complied with this request, there withdrawal from India means that they are still in India. I should have no objection. Then we would understand that, in their language, the word "gone" is equivalent to "remained".

Editor: Well the, let us suppose that the English have retired. What will you do then?

Reader: That question cannot be answered at this stage. The state after withdrawal will depend largely upon the manner of it.

If, as you assume, they retire, it seems to me we shall still keep their constitution and shall carry on the Government. If they simply retire for the asking we should have an army, etc., ready at hand. We should, therefore, have no difficulty in carrying on the Government.

Editor: You may think so: I do not. But I will not discuss the matter just now. I have to answer your question, and that I can do well by asking you several questions. Why do you want to drive away the English?

Reader: Because India has become impoverished by their Government. They take away our money from year to year. The most important posts are reserved for themselves. We are kept in a state of slavery. They behave insolently towards us and disregard our feelings.

Editor: If they do not take our money away, become gentle, and give us responsible posts, would you still consider their presence to be harmful?

Reader: That question is useless. It is similar to the question whether there is any harm in associating with a tiger if he changes his nature. Such a question is sheer waste of time. When a tiger changes his nature, Englishmen will change theirs. This is not possible, and to believe it to be possible is contrary to human experience.

Editor: Supposing we get self- Government similar to what the Canadians and the South Africans have, will it be good enough?

Reader: That question also is useless. We may get it when we have the same powers; we shall then hoist our own flag. As in Japan, so must India be. We must own our navy, our army, and we must have our own splendour, and then will India's voice ring through the world.

Editor: You have drawn the picture well. In effect it means this: that we want English rule without the Englishman. You want the tiger's nature, but not the tiger; that is to say, you would make India English. And when it becomes English, it will be called not Hindustan but *Englistan.* This is not the Swaraj that I want.

Reader: I have placed before you my idea of Swaraj as I think it should be. If the education we have received be of any use, if the works of Spencer, Mill and others be of any importance, and if the English Parliament be the mother of Parliaments. I certainly think that we should copy the English people, and this to such an extent that, just as they do not allow others to obtain a footing in their country, so we should not allow them or others to obtain it in ours. What they have done in their own country has not been done in any other country. It is, therefore, proper for us to import their institutions. But now I want to know your views.

Editor: There is need for patience. My views will develop of themselves in the course of this discourse. It is as difficult for me to understand the true nature of Swaraj as it seems to you to be easy. I shall therefore, for the time being, content myself with endeavouring to show that what you call Swaraj is not truly Swaraj.

(From *Hind Swaraj*, pp 26-28, Navjivan Publishing House, Ahmedabad, 1998.)

Civilization

Reader: Now you will have to explain what you mean by civilization.

Editor: It is not a question of what I mean. Several English writers refuse to call that civilization which passes under that name. Many books have been written upon that subject. Societies have been formed to cure the nation of the evils of civilization. A great English writer has written a work called *Civilization: Its Cause and Cure.* Therein he has called it a disease.

Reader: Why do we not know this generally?

Editor: The answer is very simple. We rarely find people arguing against themselves. Those who are intoxicated by modern civilization are not likely to write against it. Their care will be to find out facts and arguments in support of it, and this they do unconsciously, believing it to be true. A man whilst he is dreaming, believes in his dream; he is undeceived only when he is awakened from his sleep. A man labouring under the bane of civilization is like a dreaming man. What we usually read are the works of defenders of modern civilization, which undoubtedly claims among its votaries very brilliant and even some very good men. Their writings hypnotize us. And so, one by one, we are drawn into the vortex.

Reader: This seems to be very plausible. Now will you tell me something of what you have read and thought of this civilization?

Editor: Let us first consider what state of things is described by the word "civilization". Its true test lies in the fact that people living in it make bodily welfare the object of life. We will take some examples. The people of Europe today live in better-built houses than they did a hundred years ago. This is considered an emblem of civilization, and this is also a matter to promote bodily happiness. Formerly, they wore skins, and used spears as their weapons. Now, they wear long trousers, and, for embellishing their bodies, they wear a variety of clothing, and, instead of spears, they carry with them revolvers containing five or more chambers. If people of a certain country, who have hitherto not been in the habit of wearing much clothing, boots, etc. adopt European clothing, they are supposed to have become civilized out of savagery. Formerly, in Europe, people ploughed their lands mainly by manual labour. Now, one man can plough a vast tract by means of steam engines and can thus amass great wealth. This is called a sign of civilization. Formerly, one a few men wrote valuable books. Now, anybody writes and prints anything he likes and poisons people's minds. Formerly, men traveled in wagons. Now, anybody writes and prints anything he likes and poisons people's minds. Formerly, men traveling in wagons. Now, they fly through the air in trains at the rate of four hundred and more miles per day. This is considered the height of civilization.

It has been stated that, as men progress, they shall be able to travel in airship and reach any part of the world in a few hours. Men will not need the use of their hands and feet. They will press a button, and they will have their clothing by their side. They will press another button, and they will have their newspaper. A third, and a motor-car will be in waiting for them. They will have a variety of delicately dished up food. Everything will be done my machinery. Formerly, when people wanted to fight with one another, they measured between them their bodily strength; now it is possible to take away thousands of lives by one man working behind a gun from a hill. This is civilization. Formerly, men worked in the open air only as much as they liked. Now thousands of workmen meet together and for the sake of maintenance work in factories or mines. Their condition is worse than that of beasts. They are obliged to work, at the risk of their lives, at most dangerous occupations, for the sake of millionaires. Formerly, men were made slaves under physical compulsion. Now they are enslaved by temptation of money and of the luxuries that money can buy. There are now diseases of which people never dreamt before, and an army of doctors is engaged in finding out their cures, and so hospitals have increased. This is a test of civilization. Formerly, special messengers were required and much expense was incurred in order to send letters; today, anyone can abuse his fellow by means of a letter for one penny. True, at the same cost, one can send one's thanks also. Formerly, people had two or three meals consisting of home-made bread and vegetables; now, they require something to eat every two hours so that they have hardly leisure for anything else. What more need I say? All this you can ascertain from several authoritative books. These are all true tests of civilization. And if anyone speaks to the contrary, know that he is ignorant. This civilization takes note neither of morality nor of religion. Its votaries calmly state that their business is not to teach religion. Some even consider it to be a superstitious growth. Others put on the cloak of religion, and prate about morality. But, after twenty years' experience, I have come to the conclusion that immorality is often taught in the name of morality. Even a child can understand that in all I have described above there can be no inducement to morality. Civilization seeks to increase bodily comforts, and it fails miserably even in doing so.

This civilization is irreligion, and it has taken such a hold on the people in Europe that those who are in it appear to be half mad. They lack real physical strength or courage. They keep up their energy by intoxication. They can hardly be happy in solitude. Women, who should be the queens of households, wander in the streets or they slave away in factories. For the sake of a pittance, half a million women in England alone are labouring under trying circumstances in factories or similar institutions. This awful fact is one of the causes of the daily growing suffragette movement.

This civilization is such that one has only to be patient and it will be self-destroyed. According to the teaching of Mahommed this would be considered a Satanic civilization. Hinduism calls it the Black Age. I cannot give you an adequate conception of it. It is eating into the vitals of the English nation. It must be shunned. Parliaments are really emblems of slavery. If you will sufficiently think over this, you will entertain the same opinion and cease to blame the English. They rather deserve our sympathy. They are a shrewd nation and I therefore believe that they will cast off the evil. They are enterprising and industrious, and their mode of thought is not inherently immoral. Neither are they bad at heart. I therefore respect them. Civilization is not an incurable disease, but it should never be forgotten that the English people are at present afflicted by it.

(From *Hind Swaraj,* pp 31-34 Navjivan Publishing House, Ahmedabad, 1998)

What is True Civilization?

Reader: You have denounced railways, lawyers and doctors. I can see that you will discard all machinery. What, then, is civilization?

Editor: The answer to that question is not difficult. I believe that the civilization India has evolved is not to be beaten in the world. Nothing can equal the seeds sown by our ancestors. Rome went, Greece shared the same fate; the might of the Pharaohs was broken; Japan has become Westernized; of China nothing can be said; but India is still, somehow or other, sound at the foundation. The people of Europe learn their lessons from the writings of the. men of Greece or Rome, which exist no longer in their former glory. In trying to learn from the, the Europeans imagine that they will avoid the mistakes of Greece and Rome. Such is their pitiable condition. In the midst of all this India remains immovable and that is her glory. It is a charge against India that her people are so uncivilized, ignorant and stolid, that it is not possible to induce them to adopt any changes. It is a charge really against our merit. What we have tested and found true on the anvil of experience, we dare not change. Many thrust their advice upon India, and she remains steady. This is her beauty: it is the sheet-anchor of our hope.

Civilization is that mode of conduct which points out to man the path of duty. Performance of duty and observance of morality are convertible terms. To observe morality is to attain mastery over our mind and our passions. So doing, we know ourselves. The Gujarati equivalent for civilization means "good conduct".

If this definition be correct, then India, as so many writers have shown, has nothing to learn from anybody else, and this is as it should be. We notice that the mind is a restless bird; the more it gets the more it wants, and still remains unsatisfied. The more we indulge our passions the more unbridled they become. Our ancestors, therefore, set a limit to our indulgences. They saw that happiness was largely a mental condition. A man is not necessarily happy because he is rich, or unhappy because he is poor. The rich are often seen to be unhappy, the poor to be happy. Millions will always remain poor. Observing all this, our ancestors dissuaded us from luxuries and pleasures. We have managed with the same kind of plough as exited thousands of years ago. We have retained the same kind of cottages that we had in former times and our indigenous education remains the same as before. We have had no system of life-corroding competition. Each followed his own occupation or trade and charged a regulation wage. It was not that we did not know how to invent machinery, but our forefathers knew that, if we set our hearts after such things, we would become slaves and lose our moral fibre. They, therefore, after due deliberation decided that we should only do what we could with our hands and feet.

They saw that our real happiness and health consisted in a proper use of our hands and feet. They further reasoned that large cities were a snare and a useless encumbrance and that people would not be happy in them, that there would be gangs of thieves and robbers, prostitution and vice flourishing in them and that poor men would be robbed by rich men. They were, therefore, satisfied with small villages. They saw that kings and their swords were inferior to the sword of ethics, and they, therefore, held the sovereigns of the earth to be inferior to the Rishis and the Fakirs. A nation with a constitution like this is fitter to teach others than to learn from others. This nation had courts, lawyers and doctors, but they were all within bounds. Everybody knew that these professions were not particularly superior; moreover, these vakils and vaids did not rob people; they were considered people's dependants, not their masters. Justice was tolerably fair. The ordinary rule was to avoid courts. There were no touts to lure people into them. This evil, too, was noticeable only in and around capitals. The common people lived independently and followed their agricultural occupation. They enjoyed true Home Rule.

And where this cursed modern civilization has not reached, India remains as it was before. The inhabitants of that part of India will very properly laugh at your newfangled notions. The English do not rule over them, nor will you ever rule over them. Those in whose name we speak we do not know, nor do they know us. I would certainly advise you and those like you who love the motherland to go into the interior that has yet been not polluted by the railways and to live there for six months; you might then be patriotic and speak of Home Rule.

Now you see what I consider to be real civilization. Those who want to change conditions such as I have described are enemies of the country and are sinners.

Reader: It would be all right if India were exactly as you have described it, but it is also India where there are hundreds of child widows, where two year old babies are marred, where twelve year old girls are mothers and housewives, where women practise polyandry, where the practice of Niyoga obtains, where, in the name of religion, girls dedicate themselves to prostitution, and in the name of religion sheep and goats are killed. Do you consider these also symbols of the civilization that you have described?

Editor: You make a mistake. The defects that you have shown are defects. Nobody mistakes them for ancient civilization. They remain in spite of it. Attempts have always been made and will be made to remove them. We may utilize the new spirit that is born in us for purging ourselves of these evils. But what I have described to you as emblems of modern civilization are accepted as such by its votaries. The Indian civilization, as described by me, has been so described by its votaries. In no part of the world, and under no civilization, have all men attained perfection. The tendency of the Indian civilization is to elevate the moral being, that of the Western civilization is to propagate immorality. The latter is godless, the former is based on a belief in God. So understanding and so believing, it behoves every lover of India to cling to the old Indian civilization even as a child clings to the mother's breast.

(From *Hind Swaraj*, pp 54-57, Navjivan Publishing House, Ahmedabad 1998.)

11

Aurobindo Ghosh

Life and Times

Few of Indian national movement are so interesting and instructive personalities as Aurobindo Ghosh (1872-1950). The child, who at the tender age of eight was sent to England with clear instructions from his father that he should not know anything about the Indian ways of life was later hailed as the mighty prophet of Indian nationalism by his countrymen. Every phase of Aurobindo's life was extraordinary. His literary genius won him laurels from his teachers and friends in England; his ardent nationalism inspired the young and old in the country, and his spiritual accomplishments earned him adoration of the world. Dr. R.C. Majumdar, the doyen among the Indian historians has summed up his charisma in these words "As a child in Indian, a youth in England, a scholar and professor in Baroda, a fighter for his country's freedom, a thinker, poet, Yogi and Rishi, Sri Aurobindo was a transcendent splendour, an incomparable phenomenon."

Aurobindo was born on 15th August, 1872 at Calcutta. After his early education in India, his father Dr. Krishnadhan Ghosh sent him to England where he was admitted to St. Paul's School. From King's college in Cambridge he passed the classical tripos examination in the first division which entitled him to B.A. degree.

On his father's insistence he appeared for Indian Civil Service examination and got selected for the job, obtaining a position of distinction. Since he had no interest for the administrative life, he managed to get himself disqualified for the job by not clearing the riding test. During his stay in England, he had the opportunity to meet some Indian students of a secret society called 'Lotus and Dagger' which was wedded to liberation of India from the British rule. Through news papers and magazines, he closely watched the political development in India. Meanwhile, he had acquired a good command of Sanskrit and Bengali languages and had gone through Max Muller's translation of the Sacred Books of East series. Thus, love of motherland and the desire to serve her had sufficiently been aroused in Aurobindo when he set foot on the soil of India in January, 1893. From 1893 to 1906 he was in the service of the Baroda state, first in the Revenue Department and then as a professor and Vice-Principal of Baroda College. At Baroda college, he became the centre of respectful attention of his colleagues and students. The English principal Clark was greatly impressed by his lofty idealism and utter self-effacement. He once remarked to one of his colleagues "Did you notice his eyes? There is a mystic fire and light in them. They penetrate into the beyond. If Joan of Arc heared heavenly voices, Aurobindo probably sees heavenly visions."

After returning to India, Aurobindo keenly watched the politics and programmes of the Moderatos, and was thoroughly dissatisfied with them. In a series of articles in 1893 in '*Indu Prakash*', he attacked the leadership, timid moderation and begging and petitioning policy of the India National Congress. He asserted, "I say of the Congress this-that its aims are mistaken, that the spirit in which it proceeds towards their accomplishment is not a spirit of sincerity and whole heartedness; and the methods it has chosen are not the right methods and the leaders in whom it trusts are not the right sort of men to be leaders,-in brief that we are at present blind and led if not by the blind, then by the one-eyed...The national congress was not really national and had not in any way attempted to become national...The congress which represents not the mass of the population but a single and very limited class...could not honestly be called national." He rejected liberal's faith in the reasonableness of the Englishman and considered the British administrators to be the cast of the people with 'narrow hearts' and 'a commercial bent of mind'. It was unrealistic to expect that the British government was there in the India to do good to the Indians.

The partition of Bengal in 1905 forced Aurobindo to take a plunge in the politics of Bengal. He came to Calcutta and started a bangle newspaper *Yugantar*. He also became the joint editor of English daily *Bande Matram* which was started by B. C. Pal. Through thoughtful and inspiring articles in these news papers, Aurobindo played a key-role in transforming the mind of the people and preparing them for national struggle. Like Tilak and other extremist leaders, he advocated the boycott of foreign goods and the whole administrative apparatus of the imperial government. The British government regarded him "the most dangerous man we now have to reckon with". And sooner than later he was arrested in 1910 in connection with Alipore Bomb conspiracy. During the investigation and his famous trial, he spent a year in Alipore jail.

Aurobindo imprisonment paved the way for his extraordinary decision to leave the political scene. He had mystic experiences in jail and 'the leap in being' brought about a fundamental change in his life. After his acquittal and release through lack of evidence, he gave up politics and took the path of yoga. Leaving Calcutta for the French territory of Pondicherry, he founded an Ashram where he lived till his death in 1950. this period from 1910 to 1950 was devoted to self-realization through Integral Yoga. A political revolutionary was not engaged in the spiritual regeneration of India and the world. A poet and litterateur of the first rank, his great and numerous writings include *Sävitri, The Life Divine, The Synthesis of Yoga, Foundations of Indian Culture, The Human Cycle, The Ideal of Human Unity.*

Aurobindo's metaphysics is deeply rooted in the 'wisdom uncreate' of ancient Indian Sages and seers though certain currents of western thought also influenced him. His philosophy has three main aspects- nature of reality, evolution and integral yoga. Following Vedanta, he said that behind the appearances of the Universe, there is the Reality of Being and Consciousness, Self of all things one and eternal. All beings are the sparks of one great Divine Fire, but because of ignorance of their true self, they entertain a certain separativity of consciousness. It is possible by a certain psychological discipline to remove this veil of separative coconsciousness and become aware of our true self, the Divine with in all of us.

The phenomenal world is the reflection of 'Brahma; one Being and Consciousness is involved here in the Matter. Evolution is the method by which it liberates itself; consciousness appears in what seems to be inconscient and once having appeared, is self-impelled to grow higher and higher and at the same time to enlarge and develop towards greater perfection. Life is the first step of this release of consciousness; mind is the second; but the evolution does not finish with the mind, it awaits a release into something greater-a consciousness that is spiritual and supra-mental. The next step of the evolution must be towards the development of Super mind and spirit as the dominant power in the conscious being.

But while the former steps in evolution were taken by nature without a conscious will in plants and animals, in man Nature becomes able to evolve by a conscious will. But it is not by mental will in man that this can be wholly done because mind can go only upto a certain point. A conversion has to be made and for turning of the consciousness, ancient psychological discipline and practice of Yoga is the master key. This is 'the spiritual revolution' where by even the lowest dimensions of life, body and sole-consciousness are permuted by the descent and presence of 'Higher Light, Knowledge, Power, Force, Bliss, Purity' and that is the ascent into the Super mind. Aurobindo says that history is evolving towards this spiritual illumination. A new order of being and a new socio-political order is possible if man opens his life to the divine. "Such a consummation being no other than the Kingdom of Heaven within reproduced in the Kingdom of Heaven without, would also be the true fulfillment of the great dream cherished in different terms by the world's religions." Thus evolution or ascent through integral yoga obliterates the distinction between the natural and supernatural and bring about a unity of the two at a higher place. There is thus an intimate connection between Yoga, evolution and social change. To quote him, "The descent of super mind...will take up not only the whole characteristic experience which we recognize clearly as constituting the spiritual life but also all which we now exclude from that category but which is capable of divinization, not excluding whatever of the earth-nature and earth-life can be transformed by the touch of the super mind and taken up into the manifested life of the spirit. For a divine life on earth need not be a thing apart and exclusive having nothing to do with the common earthly existence; it will take up human life and human being, transform whatever can be transformed, spiritualize whatever can be spiritualized."

Aurobindo's social and political philosophy is integrally connected to his metaphysics. He says that character and quality of the social and political institutions will depend upon the stage of evolution of the human consciousness. To quote him, "This erring race of human beings dreams always of perfecting their environment by the machinery of the government and society, but it is only by the perfection of soul within that outer environment can be perfected." The rise and fall in human history may appear to be arbitrary and accidental but they are the working out of the divine will. The great men and women of history are the instruments of God to fulfill his purposes. In his book *The Human Cycle*, he dwelt upon the philosophical underpinnings of various stages of social evolution. Taking his cue from the German philosopher Karl Lamprcht, he said that there have been four major stages in the evolution of society-symbolic, typal, conventional and rationalistic-individualistic, and final stage of supermind is yet to come when the rational soul will attain its end.

The societies in their earliest stage are based upon a strong symbolic mentality that pervades its thought, institutions and customs. Human relationships are expressed in terms of religious symbols. Everything is regarded as sacred. The Vedic age, according to him, was the age of symbolism. The typal society evolves from the symbolic society when religion becomes a mystic sanction for ethical motive and discipline. When moral ideals and motives of discipline of various classes or varnas are institutionalized, we have a society organized according to the types (philosophers, administrators, producers) each with their own code of conduct and duties that provide the structural basis of society. When the outward expressions of societal types become more important that the ideals themselves, then conventional society comes into existence. In this social type, rigidity and formation become the order of the day, giving rise in course of time to a spirit of resistance and revolt. Out of the ashes of the conventional society emerges the rationalistic-individualistic society where the sovereignty of autonomous reason comes to prevail. Every form of authority is questioned and physical science becomes new standard of truth. The modern European society is the embodiment of this rationalistic-individualistic way of life. But he says that unrestrained use of individual reason without any recognizable standard of truth is dangerous as "it is likely to lead to a continual fluctuation and disorder of opinion rather than to progressive enfoldment of truth of things." While reason has made a contribution by breaking through the prison house of superstitions and conventions that shackled human mind and spirit, the modern society has led to barbarian mentality emphasizing the lower aspects of human nature.

But India-the nation that has to take the mankind to the supramental level of social evolution, to the integral society was in chains. Aurobindo said that India must get Swaraj firstly because freedom was the life-blood of a nation and secondly because a free India will be means of spiritual and moral regeneration of the world. Following the footsteps of Bankim Chandra, Tilak and Bipin Chandra Pal, he elaborates a concept of nationalism deeply metaphysical and religious in form and content. As he put it- "Nationalism is not a mere political programme. Nationalism is a religion that has come from God. It is a creed which you shall have to live. If you are going to be a nationalist, you must do it in religious spirit. You must remember that you are the instruments of God. It is a religion by which we are trying to realize God in the nation, in our fellow countrymen." A nationalist is a political 'Sanyasi' who in the service of his motherland gives up his own personal interests and comforts. He said that nationalism is a 'Sadhna', a 'Yajna' and a 'Tapa' and demands the whole of you. If this is so, what means are to be adopted for the national liberation? Since freedom is the life-breath of a nation any means must be taken to secure that life against those who wish to destroy it. Whether resistance should be active or passive is a question to be resolved on the basis of the pressures experienced. He said, "It is the nature of the pressure which determines he nature of resistance...where need for immediate liberty is urgent and it is a present question of national life or death on the instant, revolt is the only course. But where the oppression is legal and subtle in its methods and respects life, liberty and property and there is still breathing time, the circumstance demand that we should make the experiment of a method of resolute but peaceful resistance."

India's freedom though immediate and urgent goal was not the ultimate ideal for Aurobindo. His soul craved for the unity of human race by an inner oneness and not only by an external association of interest the resurgence of man out of merely animal and economic life or merely intellectual and aesthetic into the glories of the spiritual existence, the pouring of the power of the spirit into body and mind so that man may develop his manhood into that true supermanhood which shall exceed our present state. Human unity and man's self-transcendence can come only by living in the Spirit.

Rabindra Nath Tagore hailed Aurobindo as the "Voice incarnate of India's soul." The great poet was absolutely right. During his participation in the national struggle he with extraordinary fearlessness and fervour espoused the course of India's freedom. After withdrawing from polity, the light that emanated from his 'Sadhna' illuminated the hearts and souls of his countrymen and of the world. Aurobindo's life mirrored the political resolve and the spiritual depths of India at a very critical stage of her history.

The introduction is followed by two extracts from Aurobindo's writings. The first one dealing with the renaissance in India is first of the series of essays originally published in *Arya*. The second extract is massage broadcast by All India Radio, Tiruchchirapalli on 14th August 1947, i.e. on the eve of India's Independence. In the first extract, he distances himself from the prevalent understanding of European Renaissance and the general tendency to look upon the Indian Renaissance as the kindred phenomenon.

The other extract is the message of Aurobindo on the eve of India's independence. Commenting on this declaration, the Mother said that it is a most precious and revelatory autobiographical document which should be most carefully read by every Indian. Aurobindo here outlines the momentous significance of India's independence on August 15th, 1947 which date is also his date of birth. Aurobindo says that resurgence and liberation of other nations of Asia are in the pipeline; the unification of the world is also under way though forces of disruption are not fully eliminated. He is keen that more and more nations of the world are benefited by the spiritual treasure of India so that man is raised to higher and larger consciousness. For Aurobindo, political freedom should be the stepping-stone to moral and spiritual freedom.

The Renaissance in India

There has been recently some talk of a Renaissance in India. A number of illuminating essays with that general title and subject have been give to us by poet and subtle critic and thinker, Mr. James H. Cousins, and others have touched suggestively various sides of the growing movement towards a new life and a new thought that may well seem to justify the description. This Renaissance, this new birth in India, if it is a fact, must become a thing of immense importance both to herself and the world, to herself because of all that is meant for her in the recovery or the change of her time-old spirit and national ideals, to the world because of the possibilities involved in the rearising of a force that is in many respects unlike any other and its genius very different from the mentality and spirit that have hitherto governed the modern idea in mankind, although not so far away perhaps from that which is preparing to govern the future. It is rather the first point of view that I shall put forward at present : for the question what India means to make of her own life must precede the wider question what her new life may mean to the human race. Ant it is, besides, likely to become before long an issue of a pressing importance.

There is a first question, whether at all there is really a Renaissance in India. That depends a good deal on what we mean by the word; it depends also on the future, for the thing itself is only in its infancy and it is too early to say to what it may lead. The word carries the mind back to the turning-point of Eurpean culture to which it was first applied; that was not so much a reawakening as an overturn and reversal, a seizure of Christianised, Teutonised, feudalized Europe by the old Graeco-Latin spirit and form with all the complex and momentous results which came from it. That is certainly not a type of renaissance that is at all possible in India. There is a closer resemblance to the recent Celtic movement in Ireland, the attempt of a reawakened national spirit to find a new impulse of self-expression which shall give the spiritual force for a great reshaping and rebuilding : in Ireland this was discovered by a return to the Celtic spirit and culture after a long period of eclipsing English influences, and in India something of the same kind of movement is appearing and has especially taken a pronounced turn since the political outburst of 1905. But even here the analogy does not give the whole truth.

We have to see, moreover, that the whole is a present a great formless chaos of conflicting influences with a few luminous points of formation here and there where a new self-consciousness has come to the surface. But it cannot be said that these forms have yet a sufficient hold on the general mind of the people. They represent an advance movement; they are the voices of the vanguard, the torch-lights of the pioneers. On the whole, what we see is a giant Shakti who, awakening into a new world, a new and alien environment, finds herself shackled in all her limbs by a multitude of gross or minute bonds, bonds self-woven by her past, bonds recently imposed from outside, and is struggling to be free from them, to arise and proclaim herself, to cast abroad her spirit and set her seal on the world. We hear on every side a sound of the slow fraying of bonds, here and there a sharp tearing and snapping; but freedom of movement has not yet been attained. The eyes are not yet clear, the bud of the soul has only partly opened. The Titaness has not yet arisen.

Mr. Cousins puts the question in his book whether the word 'renaissance' at all applies since India has always been awake and stood in no need of reawakening. There is a certain truth behind that and to one coming in with a fresh mind from outside and struck by the living continuity of past and present India, it may be especially apparent; but that is not quite how we can see it who are her children and are still suffering from the bitter effects of the great decline which came to a head in the eighteenth and nineteenth centuries. Undoubtedly there was a period, a brief but very disastrous period of the dwindling of that great fire of life, even a moment of incipient disintegration, marked politically by the anarchy which gave European adventure its chance, inwardly by an increasing torpor of the creative spirit in religion and art,-science and philosophy and intellectual knowledge had long been dead or petrified into a mere scholastic Punditism,- all pointing to a nadir of setting energy, the evening-time from which, according to the Indian idea of the cycles, a new age has to start. It was that moment and the pressure of a superimposed European culture which followed it that made the reawakening necessary.

We have practically to take three facts into consideration, the great past of Indian culture and life with the moment of inadaptive torpor into which it had lapsed, the first period of the Western contact in which it seemed for a moment likely to perish by slow decomposition, and the ascending movement which first broke into some clarity of expression only a decade or two ago. Mr. Cousins has his eye fixed on Indian spirituality which has always maintained itself even in the decline of the national vitality; it was certainly that which saved India always at every critical moment of her destiny, and it has been the starting-point too of her renascence. Any other nation under the same pressure would have long ago perished soul and body. But certainly the outward members were becoming gangrened; the powers of renovation seemed for a moment to be beaten by the powers of stagnation, and stagnation is death. Now that the salvation, the reawakening has come, India will certainly keep her essential spirit, will keep her characteristic soul, but there is likely to be a great change of the body. The shaping for itself of a new body, of new philosophical, artistic, literary, cultural, political, social forms by the same soul rejuvenescent will, I should think, be the type of the Indian renascence,- forms not contradictory of the truths of life which the old expressed, but rather expressive of those truths restated, cured of defect, completed.

What was this ancient spirit and characteristic soul of India? European writers, struck by the general metaphysical bent of the Indian mind, by its strong religious instincts and religious idealism, by its other-worldliness, are inclined to write as if this were all the Indian spirit. An abstract, metaphysical, religious mind overpowered by the sense of the infinite, not apt for life, dreamy, unpractical, turning away form life and action as Maya, this, they said, is India; and for a time Indians in this, as in other matters, submissively echoed their new Western teachers and masters. They learned to speak with pride of their metaphysics, of their literature, of their religion, but in all else they were content to be learners and imitators. Since then Europe has discovered that there was too an Indian art of remarkable power and beauty; but the rest of what India meant it has hardly at all seen. But meanwhile the Indian mind began to emancipate itself and to look upon its past with a clear and self-discerning eye, and it very soon discovered that it had been misled into an entirely false self-view. All such one-sided appreciations indeed almost invariably turn out to be false. Was it not the general misconception about Germany at one time, because she was great in philosophy and music, but had blundered in life and been unable to make the most of its materials, that this was a nation of unpractical dreamers, idealists, erudite and sentimentalists, patient, docile and industrious certainly, but politically inapt,-"admirable, ridiculous Germany" ? Europe had a terrible awakening from that error. When the renascence of India is complete, she will have an awakening, not of the same brutal kind, certainly, but startling enough, as to the real nature and capacity of the Indian spirit.

Spirituality is indeed the master-key of the Indian mind; the sense of the infinite is native to it. India saw from the beginning,- and, even in her ages of reason and her age of increasing ignorance, she never lost hold of the insight,-that life cannot be rightly seen in the sole light, cannot be perfectly lived in the sole power of its externalities. She was alive to the greatness of material laws and forces; she had a keen eye for the importance of the physical sciences; she knew how to organize the arts of ordinary life. But she saw that the physical does not get its full sense until it stands in right relation to the supraphysical; she saw that the complexity of the universe could not be explained in the present terms of man or seen by his superficial sight, that there were other powers behind, other powers within man himself of which he is normally unaware, that he is conscious only of a small part of himself, that the invisible always surrounds the visible, the supersensible the sensible, even as infinity always surrounds the finite. She saw too that man has the power of exceeding himself, of becoming himself more entirely and profoundly than he is,-truths which have only recently begun to be seen in Europe and seem even now too great for its common intelligence. She saw the myriad gods beyond man, God beyond the gods, and beyond God His own ineffable eternity; she saw that there were ranges of life beyond our life, ranges of mind beyond our present mind and above these she saw the splendours of the spirit. Then with that calm audacity of her intuition which knew no fear or littleness and shrank from no act whether of spiritual or intellectual, ethical or vital courage, she declared that there was none of these things which man could not attain if he trained his will and knowledge; he could conquer these ranges of mind, become the spirit, become a god, become one with God, become the ineffable Brahman. And with the logical practicality and sense of science and organized method which distinguished her mentality, she set forth immediately to find out the way. Hence from long ages of this insight and practice there was ingrained in her spirituality, her powerful psychic tendency, her great yearning to grapple with the infinte and possess it, her ineradicable religious sense, her idealism, her Yoga, the constant turn of her art and her philosophy.

But this was not and could not be her whole mentality, her entire spirit; spirituality itself does not flourish on earth in the void, even as our mountain-tops do not rise like those of an enchantment of dream out of the clouds without a base. When we look at the past of India, what strikes us next is her stupendous vitality, her inexhaustible power of life and joy of life, her almost unimaginably prolific creativeness. For three thousand years at least,-it is indeed much longer,-she has been creating abundantly and incessantly, lavishly, with an inexhaustible many-sidedness, republics and kingdoms and empires, philosophies and cosmogonies and sciences and creeds and arts and poems and all kind of monuments, palaces and temples and public works, communities and societies and religious orders, laws and codes and rituals, physical science, psychic sciences, systems of Yoga, systems of politics and administration, arts spiritual, arts worldly, trades, industries, fine crafts,-the list is endless and in each item there is almost a plethora of activity. She creates and creates and is not satisfied and is not tired; she will not have an end of it, seems hardly to need a space for rest, a time for inertia and lying fallow. She expands too outside her borders; her ships cross the ocean and the fine superfluity of her wealth brims over to Judea and Egypt and Rome; her colonies spread her arts and epics and creeds in the Archipelago; her traces are found in the sands of Mesopotamia; her religions conquer China and Japan and spread westward as far as Palestine and Alexandria, and the figures of the Upanishads and the sayings of the Buddhists are reechoed on the lips of Christ. Everywhere, as on her soil, so in her works there is the teeming of a super-abundant energy of life. European critics complain that in her ancient architecture, sculpture and art there is no reticence, no holding back of riches, no blank spaces, that she labours to fill every rift with ore, occupy every inch with plenty. Well, but defect or no, that is the necessity of her superabundance of life, of the teeming of the infinite within her. She lavishes her riches because she must, as the Infinite fills every inch of space with the stirring of life and energy because it is the Infinite.

But this supreme spirituality and this prolific abundance of the energy and joy of life and creation do not make all that the spirit of India has been in its past. It is not a confused splendour of tropical vegetation under heavens of a pure sapphire infinity. It is only to eyes unaccustomed to such wealth that there seems to be a confusion in this crowding of space with rich forms of life, a luxurious disorder of excess or a wanton lack of measure, clear balance and design. For the third power of the ancient Indian spirit was a strong intellectuality, at once austere and rich, robust and minute, powerful and delicate, massive in principle and curious in detail. Its chief impulse was that of order and arrangement, but an order founded upon a seeking for the inner law and truth of things and having in view always the possibility of conscientious practice. India has been pre-eminently the land of the Dharma and the Shastra. She searched for the inner truth and law of each human or cosmic activity, its dharma; that found, she laboured to cast into elaborate form and detailed law of arrangement its application in fact and rule of life. Her first period was luminous with the discovery of the Spirit; her second completed the discovery of the Dharma; her third elaborated into detail the first simpler formulation of the Shastra; but none was exclusive, the three elements are always present.

In this third period the curious elaboration of all life into a science and an art assumes extraordinary proportions. The mere mass of the intellectual production during the period from Asoka well into the Mahomedan epoch is something truly prodigious, as can be seen at once if one studies the account which recent scholarship gives of it, and we must remember that scholarship as yet only deals with a fraction of what is still lying extant and what is extant is only a small percentage of what was once written and known. There is no historical parallel for such an intellectual labour and activity before the invention of printing and the facilities of modern science; yet all that mass of research and production and curiosity of detail was accomplished without these facilities and with no better record than the memory and for an aid the perishable palm-leaf. Nor was all this colossal literature confined to philosophy and theology, religion and Yoga, logic and rhetoric and grammar and linguistics, poetry and drama, medicine and astronomy and the sciences; it embraced all life, politics and society, all the arts from painting to dancing, all the sixty-four accomplishments, everything then known that could be useful to life or interesting to the mind, even, for instance, to such practical side minutiae as the breeding and training of horses and elephants, each of which had its Shastra and its art, its apparatus of technical terms, its copious literature. In each subject from the largest and most momentous to the smallest and most trivial there was expended the same all-embracing, opulent, minute and thorough intellectuality. On one side there is an insatiable curiosity, the desire of life to know itself in every detail, on the other a spirit of organization and scrupulous order, the desire of the mind to tread through life with a harmonized knowledge and in the right rhythm and measure. Thus an ingrained and dominant spirituality, an inexhaustible vital creativeness and gust of life and, mediating between them, a powerful, penetrating and scrupulous intelligence combined of the rational, ethical and aesthetic mind each at a high intensity of action, created the harmony of the ancient Indian culture.

Indeed without this opulent vitality and opulent intellectuality India could never have done so much as she did with her spiritual tendencies. It is a great error to suppose that spirituality flourishes best in an impoverished soil with the life half-killed and the intellect discouraged and intimidated. The spirituality that so flourished is something morbid, hectic and exposed to perilous reactions. It is when the race has lived most richly and thought most profoundly that spirituality finds its heights and its depths and its constant and many-sided fruition. In modern Europe it is after a long explosion of vital force and a stupendous activity of the intellect that spirituality has begun really to emerge and with some promise of being not, as it once was, the sorrowful physician of the malady of life, but the beginning of a large and profound clarity. The European eye is struck in Indian spiritual thought by the Buddhistic and illusionist denial of life. But it must be remembered that this is only one side of its philosophic tendency which assumed exaggerated proportions only in the period of decline. In itself too that was simply one result, in one direction, of a tendency of the Indian mind which is common to all its activities, the impulse to follow each motive, each specialization of motive even, spiritual, intellectual, ethical, vital, to its extreme point and to sound its utmost possibility. Part of its innate-direction was to seek in each not only for its fullness of detail, but for its infinite, its absolute, its profoundest depth or its highest pinnacle. It knew that without a "fine excess" we cannot break down the limits which the dull temper of the normal mind opposes to knowledge and thought and experience; and it had in seeking this point a boundless courage and yet a sure tread. Thus it carried each tangent of philosophic thought, each line of spiritual experience to its farthest point, and chose to look from that farthest point at all existence, so as to see what truth or power such a view could give it. It tried to know the whole of divine nature and to see too as high as it could beyond nature and into whatever there might be of supradivine. When It formulated a spiritual atheism, it followed that to its acme of possible vision. When, too, it indulged in materialistic atheism,-though it did that only with a side glance, as the freak of an insatiable intellectual curiosity,-yet it formulated it straight out, boldly and nakedly, without the least concession to idealism or ethicism.

Everywhere we find this tendency. The ideals of the Indian mind have included the height of self-assertion of the human spirit and its thirst of independence and mastery and possession and the height also of its self-abnegation, dependence and submission and self-giving. In life the ideal of opulent living and the ideal of poverty were carried to the extreme of regal splendour and the extreme of satisfied nudity. Its intuitions were sufficiently clear and courageous not to be blinded by its own most cherished ideas and fixed habits of life. If it was obliged to stereotype caste as the symbol of its social order, it never quite forgot, as the caste-spirit is apt to forget, that the human soul and the human mind are beyond caste. For it had seen in the lowest human being the Godhead, Narayana. It emphasized distinctions only to turn upon them and deny all distinctions. If all its political needs and circumstances compelled it at last to exaggerate the monarchical principal and declare the divinity of the king and to abolish its earlier republican city states and independent federations as too favourable to the centrifugal tendency, if therefore it could not develop democracy, yet it had the democratic idea, applied it in the village, in council and municipality, within the caste, was the first to assert a divinity in the people and could cry to the monarch at the height of his power, "O king, what art thou but the head servant of the demos ?" Its idea of the golden age was a free spiritual anarchism. Its spiritual extremism could not prevent it from fathoming through a long era the life of the senses and its enjoyments, and there too it sought the utmost richness of sensuous detail and the depths and intensities of sensuous experience. Yet it is notable that this pursuit of the most opposite extremes never resulted in disorder; and its most hedonistic period offers nothing that at all resembles the unbridled corruption which a similar tendency has more than once produced in Europe. For the Indian mind is not only spiritual and ethical, but intellectual and artistic, and both the rule of the intellect and the rhythm of beauty are hostile to the spirit of chaos. In every extreme the Indian spirit seeks for a law in that extreme and a rule, measure and structure in its application. Besides, this sounding of extremes is balanced by a still more ingrained characteristic, the synthetical tendency, so that having pushed each motive to its farthest possibility the Indian mind returns always towards some fusion of the knowledge it has gained and to a resulting harmony and balance in action and institution. Balance and rhythm which the Greeks arrived at by self-limitation, India arrived at by its sense of intellectual, ethical and aesthetic order and the synthetic impulse of its mind and life.

I have dwelt on these facts because they are apt to be ignored by those who look only at certain sides of the Indian mind and spirit which are most prominent in the last epochs. By insisting only upon these we get an inaccurate or incomplete idea of the past of India and of the integral meaning of its civilization and the spirit that animated it. The present is only a last deposit of the past at a time of ebb; it has no doubt also to be the starting-point of the future, but in this present all that was in India's past is still dormant, it is not destroyed; it is waiting there to assume new forms. The decline was the ebb-movement of a creative spirit which can only be understood by seeing it in the full tide of its greatness; the renascence is the return of the tide and it is the same spirit that is likely to animate it, although the forms it takes may be quite new. To judge therefore the possibilities of the renascence, the power that it may reveal and the scope that it may take, we must dismiss the idea that the tendency of metaphysical abstraction is the one note of the Indian spirit which dominates or inspires all its cadences. Its real key-note is the tendency of spiritual realization, not cast at all into any white monotone, but many-faceted, many-coloured, as supple in its adaptability as it is intense in its highest pitches. The note of spirituality is dominant, initial, constant, always recurrent; it is the support of all the rest. The first age of India's greatness was a spiritual age when they sought passionately for the truth of existence through the intuitive mind and through an inner experience and interpretation both of the psychic and the physical existence. The stamp put on her by that beginning she has never lost, but rather always enriched it with fresh spiritual experience and discovery at each step of the national life. Even in her hour of decline it was the one thing she could never lose.

But this spiritual tendency does not shoot upward only to the abstract, the hidden and the intangible; it casts its rays downward and outward to embrace the multiplicities of thought and the richness of life. Therefore the second long epoch of India's greatness was an age of the intellect, the ethical sense, the dynamic will in action enlightened to formulate and govern life in the luster of spiritual truth. After the age of the Spirit, the age of the Dharma; after the Veda and Upanishads, the heroic centuries of action and social formation, typal construction and thought and philosophy, when the outward forms of Indian life and culture were fixed in their large lines and even their later developments were being determined in the seed. The great classical age of Sanskrit culture was the flowering of this intellectuality into curiosity of detail in the refinements of scholarship, science, art, literature, politics, sociology, mundane life. We see at this time too the sounding not only of aesthetic, but of emotional and sensuous, even of vital and sensual experience. But the old spirituality reigned behind all this mental and all this vital activity, and its later period, the post-classical, saw a lifting up of the whole lower life and an impressing upon it of the values of the spirit. This was the sense of the Puranic and Tantric systems and the religions of Bhakti. Later Vaishnavism, the last fine flower of the Indian spirit, was in its essence the taking up of the aesthetic, emotional and sensuous being into the service for the spiritual. It completed the curve of the cycle.

The evening of decline which followed the completion of the curve was prepared by three movements of retrogression. First there is, comparatively, a sinking of the superabundant vital energy and a fading of the joy of life and the joy of creation. Even in the decline the energy is still something splendid and extraordinary and only for a very brief period sinks nearest to a complete torpor; but still a comparison with its past greatness will show that the decadence was marked and progressive. Secondly, there is a rapid cessation of the old free intellectual activity, a slumber of the scientific and the critical mind as well as the creative intuition; what remains becomes more and more a repetition of ill-understood fragments of past knowledge. There is a petrifaction of the mind and life in the relics of the forms which a great intellectual past had created. Old authority and rule become rigidly despotic and, as always then happens, lose their real sense and spirit. Finally, spirituality remains but burns no longer with the large and clear flame of knowledge of former times, but in intense jets and in a dispersed action which replaces the old magnificent synthesis and in which certain spiritual truths are emphasised to the neglect of others. This diminution amounts to a certain failure of the great endeavour which is the whole meaning of Indian culture, a falling short in the progress towards the perfect spiritualization of the mind and the life. The beginnings were superlative, the developments very great, but at a certain point where progress, adaptation, a new flowering should have come in, the old civilization stopped short, partly drew back, partly lost its way. The essential no doubt remained and still remains in the heart of the race and not only in its habits and memories, but in its action it was covered up in a great smoke of confusion. The causes internal and external we need not now discuss; but the fact is there. It was the cause of the momentary helplessness of the Indian mind in the face of new and unprecedented conditions.

It was at this moment that the European wave swept over India. The first effect of this entry of a new and quite opposite civilization was the destruction of much that had no longer the power to live, the deliquescence of much else, a tendency to the devitalisation of the rest. A new activity came in, but this was at first crudely and confusedly imitative of the foreign culture. It was a crucial moment and an ordeal of perilous severity; a less vigorous energy of life might well have foundered and perished under the double weight of the deadening of its old innate motives and a servile imitation of alien ideas and habits. History shows us how disastrous this situation can be to nations and civilizations. But fortunately the energy of life was there, sleeping only for a moment, not dead, and, given that energy, the evil carried within itself its own cure. For whatever temporary rotting and destruction this crude impact of European life and culture has caused, it gave three needed impulses; it rehabilitated life and awakened the desire of new creation; it put the reviving Indian spirit face to face with novel conditions and ideals and the urgent necessity of understanding, assimilating and conquering them. The national mind turned a new eye on its past culture, reawoke to its sense and import, but also, at the same time, saw it in relation to modern knowledge and ideas. Out of this awakening vision and impulse the Indian renaissance is arising, and that must determine its future tendency. The recovery of the old spiritual knowledge and experience in all its splendour, depth and fullness is its first, most essential work; the flowing of this spirituality into new forms of philosophy, literature, art, science and critical knowledge is the second; an original dealing with modern problems in the light of Indian spirit and the endeavour to formulate a greater synthesis of a spiritualised society is the third and most difficult. Its success on these three lines will be the measure of its help to the future of humanity.

The Spirit is a higher infinite of verities; life is a lower infinite of possibilities which seek to grow and find their own truth and fulfillment in the light of these verities. Our intellect, our will, our ethical and our aesthetic being are the reflectors and the mediators. The method of the West is to exaggerate life and to call down as much-or as little-as may be of the higher powers to stimulate and embellish life. But the method of India is, on the contrary, to discover the spirit within and the higher hidden intensities of the superior powers and to dominate life in one way or another so as to make it responsive to and expressive of the spirit and in that way increase the power of life. Its tendency with the intellect, will, ethical, aesthetic and emotional being is to sound indeed their normal mental possiblities, but also to upraise them towards the greater light and power of their own highest intuitions. The work of the renaissance in Indian must be to make this spirit, the higher view of life, this sense of deeper potentiality once more a creative, perhaps a dominant power in the world. But to that truth of itself it is as yet only vaguely awake; the mass of Indian action is still at the moment proceeding under the impress of the European motive and method and, because there is a spirit within us to which they are foreign, the action is poor in will, feeble in form and ineffective in results, for it does not come from the roots of our being. Only in a few directions is there some clear light of self-knowledge. It is when a greater light prevails and becomes general that we shall be able to speak, not only in prospect but in fact, of the renaissance of India.

The Fifteenth of August 1947

August 15th, 1947 is the birthday of free India. It marks for her the end of an old era, the beginning of a new age. But we can also make it by our life and acts as a free nation an important date in a new age opening for the whole world, for the political, social, cultural and spiritual future of humanity.

August 15th is my own birthday and it is naturally gratifying to me that it should have assumed this vast significance. I take this coincidence, not as a fortuitous accident, but as the sanction and seal of the Divine Force that guides my steps on the work with which I began life, the beginning of its full fruition. Indeed, on this day I can watch almost all the world-movements which I hoped to see fulfilled in my lifetime, though then they looked like impracticable dreams, arriving at fruition or on their way to achievement. In all these movements free India may well play a large part and take a leading position.

The first of these dreams was a revolutionary movement which would create a free and united India. India today is free but she has not achieved unity. At one moment it almost seemed as if in the very act of liberation she would fall back into the chaos of separate States which preceded the British conquest. But fortunately it now seems probable that this danger will be averted and a large and powerful, though not yet a complete union will be established. Also, the wisely drastic policy of the Constituent Assembly has made it probable that the problem of the depressed classes will be solved without schism or fissure. But the old communal division into Hindus and Muslims seems now to have hardened into a permanent political division of the country. It is to be hoped that this settled fact will not be accepted as settled for ever or as anything more than a temporary expedient. For if it lasts, India may be seriously weakened, even crippled: civil strife may remain always possible, possible even a new invasion and foreign conquest. India's internal development and prosperity may be impeded, her position among the nations weakened, her destiny impaired or even frustrated. This must not be; the partition must go. Let us hope that that may come about naturally, by an increasing recognition of the necessity not only of peace and concord but of common action, by the practice of common action and the creation of means for that purpose. In this way unity may finally come about under whatever form- the exact form may have a pragmatic but not a fundamental importance. But by whatever means, in whatever way, the division must go; unity must and will be achieved, for it is necessary for the greatness of India's future.

Another dream was for the resurgence and liberation of the peoples of Asia and her return to her great role in the progress of human civilization. Asia has arisen; large parts are now quite free or are at this moment being liberated: its other still subject or partly subject parts are moving through whatever struggles towards freedom. Only a little has to be done and that will be done today or tomorrow. There India has her part to play and has begun to play it with an energy and ability which already indicate the measure of her possibilities and the place she can take in the council of the nations.

The third dream was a world-union forming the outer basis of a fairer, brighter and nobler life for all mankind. That unification of the human world is under way; there is an imperfect initiation organized but struggling against tremendous difficulties. But the momentum is there and it must inevitably increase and conquer. Here too India has begun to play a prominent part and, if she can develop that larger statesmanship which is not limited by the present facts and immediate possibilities but looks into the future and brings it nearer, her presence may make all the difference between a slow and timid and a bold and swift development. A catastrophe may intervene and interrupt or destroy what is being done, but even the final result is sure. For unification is a necessity of Nature, an inevitable movement. Its necessity for the nations is also clear, for without it the freedom of the small nations may be at any moment in peril and the life even of the large and powerful nations insecure. The unification is therefore to the interests of all, and only human imbecility and stupid selfishness can prevent it; but these cannot stand for ever against the necessity of Nature and the Divine Will. But an outward basis is not enough; there must grow up an international spirit and outlook, international forms and institutions must appear perhaps such developments as dual or multilateral citizenship, willed interchange or voluntary fusion of cultures. Nationalism will have fulfilled itself and lost its militancy and should no longer find these things incompatible with self-preservation and the integrality of its outlook. A new spirit of oneness will take hold of the human race.

Another dream, the spiritual gift of India to the world has already begun. India's spirituality is entering Europe and America in an ever increasing measure. That movement will grow; amid the disasters of the time more and more eyes are turning towards her with hope and there is even an increasing resort not only to her teachings, but to her psychic and spiritual practice.

The final dream was a step in evolution which would raise man to a higher and larger consciousness and begin the solution of the problems which have perplexed and vexed him since he first began to think and to dream of individual perfection and a perfect society. This is still a personal hope and an idea, an ideal which has begun to take hold both in India and in the West on forward-looking minds. The difficulties in the way are more formidable than in any other field of endeavour, but difficulties were made to be overcome and if the Supreme Will is there, they will be overcome. Here too, if this evolution is to take place, since it must proceed through a growth of the spirit and the inner consciousness, the initiative can come from India and, although the scope must be universal, the central movement may be hers.

Such is the content which I put into this date of India's liberation; whether or how far this hope will be justified depends upon the new and free India.

(From *Renaissance in India,* Shri Aurobindo Ashram, Pondicherry, 1986, pp 1-20).

12

E.V. Ramaswami Periyar

Life and Times

E.V. Ramaswami Naicker, also known as Periyar, (1879-1973) was a rationalist, atheist, iconclast freedom-fighter, activist, and founder of *Self-Respect Movement*. Though born in an upper caste family, Periyar fought against untouchability, the rituals of Hinduism and the caste system, describing him a fool who had created god, a scoundrel who had spread his name, and a barbarian who would worship him. Periyar was born on September 17, 1879, in Erode, Tamil Nadu. The name Naicker denoted caste his identity. Periyar's father, a rich businessman, was Venkata Naicker, and his mother was Chinna Thayammal, alias Muthammal. Periyar had one elder brother named Krishnaswamy and two sisters named Kannamma and Ponnuthoy. He later came to be known as "Periyar" meaning 'respected one or 'elder' in Tamil.

At a young age, Periyar witnessed numerous incidents of racial, caste and gender discrimination. He married when he was 19, and had a daughter who lived for only 5 months. His first wife was Nagammai,died in the year 1933 He married for a second time on July, 1948. His second wife. Maniammai continued Periyar's social work even after his death in 1973.but still his thoughts and ideas were being spread by Dravida Kazhagam.

Periyar's parents were deeply religious and they frequency arranged religious discourses to be given at a temple or in other public places. While all the other members of the family listened to the discourses with great devotion, even in his early teens, Periyar displayed a keen rationalistic tendency and temperament and ridiculed the pundits who gave the talks, by pointing out the contradictions in their statements and also their incredible exaggerations. Referring to this early experience of his, Periyar wrote later in one of his autobiographical articles: "It gave me extraordinary pleasure to fling at the pundits their own contradictions and thus, perplex them. It also gave me the reputation among our neighbours of being a clever speaker. I believe that it was this experience which deprived me of faith in castes and communities, in religion, in puranas, in shastras and in god." It is an irony that the religious discourses, which were intended to kindle piety and religiosity in all listeners, produced the opposite effect on Periyar. As he grew up, he became convinced that some people used religion only as mask to deceive innocent people. That was why he took it as a mission in his life to warn people against superstitions and priests.

Periyar was known as the Voltaire of South India, particularly, in Tamil Nadu. Both were rationalists who aroused their people to realize that all men are equal and it is the birthright of every individual to enjoy liberty, equality and fraternity. Both opposed religion virulently because the so-called men of religion invented myths and superstitions to keep the gullible, innocent and ignorant people in darkness and to go on exploiting them. In one of his articles, speaking about the religious men. Voltaire had said, "They inspired you with false beliefs and made you fanatics so that they might be your masters. They made you superstitious, not that you might fear god but that you might fear them."

The revolution, which Periyar brought about, was a bloodless one and he had to spend more than fifty years of his life opening the eyes of people to their want of education and consequent backwardness, their faith in superstitions, the deception and exploitation to which they are subjected by cunning people and also on the need for them to develop self-respect and self-confidence. It is interesting to note the term 'self-respect' as used by Periyar, includes the three concepts-liberty, equality and moral faculties; all have the right to live in dignity. That is why that he wanted to put an end to all kinds of discrimination. There is, he believed, a need for promoting social justice and rational outlook among all.

Periyar propagated the principles of rationalism, self-respect, women's rights and eradication of caste. He opposed the exploitation and marginalization of the non-Brahmin indigenous Dravidian peoples of South India and the imposition of what he considered Indo-Aryan India. His work has greatly revolutionized Tamil society and has significantly removed caste-based discrimination. He is also responsible for bringing new changes to the Tamil alphabet. However, at the same time, Periyar is also held responsible for making controversial statements on the Tamil language, Dalits and Brahmins and for endorsing violence against Brahmins.

In 1929, Periyar announced the deletion of his caste title Naicker from his name at the First Provincial Self-Respect Conference of Chenggalpattu. He could speak three Dravidian languages: Kannada, Tamil and Telugu. His mother tongue was Kannada. Periyar attended school for five years after which he joined his father's trade at the age of 12. He used to listen to Tamil Vaishnavite gurus who gave discourses in his house enjoying his father's hospitality. At a young age. he began questioning the apparent contradictions in the Hindu mythological stories which he opined to be lies spread by the Indo-Aryan race. As Periyar grew, he felt that people used religion only as a mask to deceive innocent people and therefore took it as one of his duties in life to warn people against superstitions and priests.

In 1904, Periyar went on a pilgrimage to Kasi to worship in the revered Siva temple of Kashi Vishwanath. Though regarded as one of the holiest sites of Hinduism, he witnessed immoral activities, begging, and floating dead bodies. His frustrations extended to functional Hinduism in general when he experienced what he called Brahminic exploitation. However, one particular incident in Kasi had a profound impact on Periyar's ideology and future work. At worship site there were free meals offered to guests.

To Periyar's shock, he was refused meals at choultries which exclusively fed Brahmins. Due to extreme hunger, Periyar felt compelled to enter one of the choultries disguised as a Brahmin with a sacred thread on his bare chest, but was betrayed by his moustache. The gatekeeper at the temple concluded that Periyar was not a Brahmin as Brahmins were not permitted by the Hindu Shastras to have moustaches. He not only prevented Periyar's entry but also pushed him rudely to the street. As his hunger became intolerable, Periyar was forced to feed on leftovers from the streets. Around this time, he realized that the choultry which had refused him entry was built by a wealthy non-Brahmin from South India. This discriminatory attitude dealt a blow to Periyar's regard for Hinduism, for the events he had witnessed at Kasi were completely different from the picture of Kasi he had had in mind, as a holy place which welcomed all. Periyar was a theist till his visit to Kasi. But his views changed and he became an atheist.

Periyar joined the Indian National Congress in 1919 after quitting his business and resigning from public posts. He held the chairmanship of Erode Municipality and wholeheartedly undertook constructive programs spreading the use of Khadi, picketing toddy shops, boycotting shops selling foreign cloth, and eradicating untoucliability. In 1921, Periyar courted imprisonment for picketing toddy shops in Erode. When his wife as well as his sister joined the agitation, it gained momentum, and the administration was forced to come to a compromise. He was again arrested during the Non-Cooperation movement. In 1922, Periyar was elected the President of the Madras Presidency Congress Committee during the Tirupur session where he advocated strongly for reservation in government jobs and education. His attempts were defeated in the Congress party due to a strong presence of discrimination and indifference. He later quit the party on those grounds in 1925.

In Vaikom, a small town in Kerala state, there were strict laws of untouchability in and around the temple area. Dalits were not allowed into the close streets around and leading to the temple, let alone inside it. Anti-caste feelings were growing and in 1924 Vaikom was chosen as a suitable place for an organized Satyagraha, passive resistance campaign as practiced by Gandhi. Under his guidance a movement had already begun with the aim of giving all castes the right to enter the temples. Thus, agitations and demonstrations took place. On April 14, Periyar and his wife Nagamma arrived in Vaikom. They were met with arrest and imprisoned for participation. In spite of Gandhi's objection to non-Keralites and non-Hindus taking part, Periyar and his followers continued to give support to the movement till it was withdrawn. He received the title Vikkom Veeran, mostly given by his Tamil followers who participated in the Satyagraha. However, a considerable section of intellectuals feel that Periyar's participation in the Indian independence movement and his contribution in the Vaikom Satyagraha have been highly exaggerated. The way in which the Vaikom Satyagraha events have been recorded provides a clue to the image of the respective oraganizers. Furthermore, the editor of *Periyar's Thoughts* states that Brahmins purposely suppressed news about Periyar's participation. A leading Congress magazine *Young India* in its extensive reports on Vaikom never mentions Periyar.

Periyar and his followers campaigned constantly to influence and pressurize the government to take measures for removing social inequality even while other nationalist forerunners focused on the struggle for political independence. The Self-Respect Movement was described from the beginning, as dedicated to the goal of giving non-Brahmins a sense of pride based on their Dravidian past. In 1952. the *Periyar Self-Respect Movement Institution* was registered with a list of objectives of the institution — to allow people to live a life of freedom from slavery to anything against reason and self respect: to do away with needless customs, meaningless ceremonies, and blind superstitious beliefs in society; to put an end to the present social system in which caste, religion, community and traditional occupations based on the accident of birth, have chained the mass of the people and created "superior" and "inferior" classes and to give people equal rights; to completely eradicate untouchability and to establish a united society based on brother and sisterhood; to give equal rights to women; to prevent child marriages and marriages based on law favorable to one sect, to conduct and encourage love marriages, widow marriages, inter

— caste and inter-religious marriages and to have the marriages registered under the civil law; and to establish and maintain homes for orphans and widows and to run educational institutions.

Propagation of the philosophy of self respect became the full-time activity of Periyar since 1925. A Tamil weekly *Kudi Arasu* started in 1925. while the English journal *Revolt* started in 1928 carried on the propaganda among the English educated people. The Self-Respect Movement began to grow fast and received the sympathy of the heads of the Justice Party from the beginning. Conferences followed in succession throughout the Tamil districts of the former Madras Presidency. A training school in Self-Respect was opened at Erode, the home town of Periyar. The object was not just to introduce social reform but to bring about a social revolution to foster a new spirit and build a new society.

Between 1929 and 1935, under the strain of World Depression, political thinking worldwide underwent in chenge with the spread of international communism. The Indian political parties, movements and considerable sections of leadership were also affected by intercontinental ideologies. The Self-Respect Movement also came under the influence of the leftist philosophies and institutions. Periyar after establishing the Self-Respect Movement as an independent institution began to look for strengthening it politically and socially. And for this, he undertook a study of the history and politics of different countries combined with personal observation of the systems at work.

Periyar toured Malaysia for a month from December 1929 to January 1930 to propagate the self-respect philosophy. In December 1931 he undertook a tour of Europe, to personally acquaint himself—with their political systems, social movements, way of life, economic and social progress and administration of public bodies. He visited Egypt, Greece, Turkey, Russia, Germany, England, Spain, France and Portugal, staying in Russia for three months. On his return journey he halted at Ceylon and returned to India in November 1932.

The tour shaped the political ideology of Periyar to achieve the social concept of self-respect. The communist system obtained in

Russia appealed to him as appropriately suited to deal with the social ills of the country. Thus, on socio-economic issues Periyar was marxist, but he did not advocate for abolishing private ownership. Immediately after his return, Periyar in alliance with the enthusiastic communist, Singaravelu Chettiar, began to work out a socio-political scheme incorporating socialist and self-respect ideals. This marks a crucial stage of development in the Self-Respect Movement which got politicized and found its compatibility in Tamil Nadu. In 1937, when Rajagopalachari became the Chief Minister of Madras state, he introduced Hindi as a compulsory language of study in schools, igniting thereby a series of anti-Hindi agitations. Tamil nationalists, the Justice Party under A. D. Panneerselvam, and Periyar organized anti-Hindi protests in 1938 which ended with numerous arrests by the Rajaji government.

During the same year, the slogan "Tamil Nadu for Tamilians" was first raised by Periyar in protest against the introduction of Hindi in schools. He explained that the introduction of Hindi was a dangerous mechanism used for the infiltration of Aryans on Dravidian culture. He reasoned that the adoption of Hindi would make Tamils subordinate to Hindi-speaking North Indians. Periyar explained that Hindi would not only halt the progress of Tamilians but would completely destroy their culture and nullify the progressive ideas that had been successfully inculcated through Tamil in the recent decades. Cutting across party lines, South Indian politicians rallied together in their opposition to Hindi. There were recurrent anti-Hindi agitations in 1948, 1952 and 1965.

A political party known as the South Indian Libertarian Federation was founded in 1916. principally to oppose the economic and political power of the Brahmin groups. The party was later named the Justice Party, and its stated goal was to render social justice to non-Brahmin groups. In order to gain the support of the masses, non-Brahminpoliticians began propagating an ideology of equality among non-Brahmin groups. Brahminical priesthood and Sanskritic social class-value hierarchy were blamed for the existence of inequalities among non-Brahmin groups.

In 1937, when the government required that Hindi be taught in the school system, Periyar organized opposition through the Justice

Party to this policy. After 1 937, the Dravidian movement derived considerable support from the student community. In later years, opposition to Hindi played a big rote in the politics of Tamil Nadu. The fear of the Hindi language had its origin in the conflict between Brahmins and non-Brahmins. To the Tamil, acceptance of Hindi in the school system was a form of bondage. When the Justice Party weakened in the absence of mass support, Periyar took over the leadership of the party after being jailed for opposing Hindi in 1939. Under his tutelage the party prospered, but the party's conservative members, most of whom were rich and educated, withdrew from active participation. At a rally in 1944, Periyar, in his capacity as the leader of the Justice Party, declared that the party would henceforth by known as the Dravida Kazhagam or Dravidian Association.

In 1949, Periyar's chief lieutenant, Conjeevaram Natarajan Annadurai established a separate association called the Dravidu Muntra Kazhagam (DMK). This was due to differences between the two where Periyar advocated a separate independent Dravidian or Tamil state, Annadurai compromised with the Delhi government combined with claims of increased state independence. Periyar was convinced that individuals and movements that undertake the task of eradicating the social evils in the Indian sub-continent have to pursue the goal with devotion and dedication without deviating from the path and with uncompromising zeal. Thus, if they contest elections aiming to assume political power, they would lose vigor and sense of purpose. But amongst his followers, there were those who had a different view. They wanted to enter into politics and have a share in running the government. They were looking for an opportunity to part with Periyar. Thus, when Periyar got married to Maniammai on July 9, 1948, they quit the Dravidar Kazhagam stating that Periyar set a bad example by marrying a young woman in his old age - he was 70 and she 30. Those who parted company with Periyar joined the DMK.

In 1956, despite warnings from Tamil Nadu Congress , Periyar organized a procession to the Marina in order to burn pictures of the Hindu god, Rama. Periyar was subsequently arrested and confined to prison. The activities of Periyar continued when he went to Bangalore in 1958 to participate in the All India Official Language Conference. There he stressed the need to retain English as the Union Official Language instead of Hindi. Five years later, Periyar travelled to North India to advocate on the eradication of the caste system. Nearing Periyar's last years, an award was given to him by the UNESCO, and it was presented to him by the Union Education Minister. Triguna Sen in Chennai on June 27. 1970. The citation awarded by the UNESCO described Periyar as "the prophet of the new age, the Socrates of South East Asia, father of social reform movement and arch enemy of ignorance, superstitions, meaningless customs and base manners". In his last meeting at Thiagaraya Nagar, Chennai in 1973, Periyar gave a call for action to gain social equality and a dignified way of life. On December 24. 1973 Periyar passed away at the age of 94.

Social Reform or Social Revolution?

Social reform is a project in which I had much hope but have now lost it. The problem facing the nationalists, self-respectors, and socialists is, to my mind, not social reform, but really what may be called destructive work undertaken with courage and resolution. I may submit that I have come to this conclusion only after deep self-introspection and practical experience.

Let me illustrate my point. Let us suppose that there is a big pond considered holy, with an old and popular *purana* attached to it which says that even a drop of water from the pond taken into the mouth or smeared over the body would not only save the worst sinner from perdition, but would also take him to heaven. But if the condition of the water in the tank today is such as to cause indigestion if taken by the mouth or to cause itches and sores if smeared over the body, what should we do? First we should try to kill the poisonous bacteria in the pond by spreading insecticide on the surface of the water, and if the position does not improve we should next try to empty the tank and clean it. And if the water is still found to be poisonous, we should decide that the very springs are polluted. In the circumstances would you still have faith in the *purana* and the holiness attached to the pond and continue to use the water only, to invite disease and death, or choose to close the tank once and for all by filling it with mud and debris?

In the above illustration, social reform is like cleaning the water with insecticide or baling out the water to clean the tank. To close the pond is to destroy it. I am a destructionist only in this sense. I say this only because social reform has had its day in our hand. I do not refer to the modern types of reform, which are really not worth the name, as they are indulged in by some educated people and some plutocrats merely to hoodwink the innocent common man. They are not calculated to improve his lot. But yet the common man has been deceived by propaganda, with the result that his position is actually going from bad to worse.

The principal reason for this state of affairs is that the people who are really responsible for the degradation of the masses have come out as reformers for purely political reasons. But the reformers I have in mind are the great Siddas, Buddas, Thiruvalluvar, Ramanujar and the like, who were reputed to have attempted social reform, but yet failed miserably.

Social reform varie from country to country. In the West, proposals for social reform apply to the whole community in equal measure, but in our country, the measures seem to apply separately to each group or community, involving inequality both in application and in result. The most important item of social reform in our country refers to the inequality based on birth which in not to be seen anywhere else in the world. The next in importance are the beliefs and practices based on superstition, which are mostly allied to ideas about god, heaven and hell. Reform of these have been sought after great minds as said above like Buddha, Thiruvalluvar, Ramanujar, Siddas, etc. Yet it cannot be said that anything effective has been achieved at any time. What a little has been done by way of changing our people's habits and thoughts, is the result or reformation in the west, foisted on the country either for the self-interest of our western rulers or in the genuine desire for reform. It is impossible to say that any reform has been done by our reformers genuinely for the benefit of the massage. The obstruction posed by belief in god, religion, Vedas, Sastras, is the main reason for lack of any initiative or effort on the part of our reformers. However, the divisions in Indian society have benefited and still benefit certain castes, who have all along turned a deaf ear to all talk of reform.

The obstacles to reform have all been met by learned arguments and logic by great seers like Buddha, Kapilar, Thiruvalluvar, and Ramanujar, and it is difficult to say that greater things can either be said or done by any in future. The o9bstructionists who still happen to benefit by the divisions and superstitions in our society, are still active and flourishing. Yet it must be admitted that conditions in modern days are vastly different from those that obtained in ancient days. But the absence of any change in religious or superstitious beliefs even under modern conditions, is the principal block to all ideas of social reform.

It must be understood that god and religion are erected on the foundation of the superstitious beliefs of the people. Our daily life is regulated by superstition. As such it cannot be said that it is outside the pale of social reform to preach against blind faith and superstitious beliefs. On the other hand these are the targets for destructive attack in social reform. But as destructive tactics are ordinarily considered to be consistent with reform, it may be necessary to call the attempt reconstruction, meaning thereby that we destroy first and then reconstruct anew.

The engage in such reconstructive work, one must exhibit courage founded on conviction, as otherwise it will amount to suicide. It would be necessary for the iconoclast to work against serious and severe orthodox resistance which are the fruits of long tradition and selfish vested interests. Whatever are the causes of resistance they must be rooted out of existence. I am firmly of opinion that if anything of old, based on blind faith and superstition is sought to be retained or tolerated, the result will be the total failure of reform. I am not one of those who feel that social reformers must necessarily be restrained by moderation and patience. I know that this would be distasteful to may. But it must be recognized that none can excel the moderation, patience and tolerance of great seers like the Buddha, in whom I believe, these virtues were their weaknesses. People who are cautious about themselves and afraid of public opinion and heightened resistance, can never be effective reformers, and their panaceas can never bear fruit. Reformers ought strictly not to be bound down by any traditional rules. Instead they should be ready to sweep away everything before them.

How not our old reformers tried long enough to change the people by peaceful persuasion, kind sermons and cooperative approaches? What has happened to their great efforts? How long are we to repeat the same processes? It is possible that sermons from the lips of savants like Vivekananda and Gandhi would be quoted against me. I am certainly opposed to their views. We all know that people worship portraits of these savants and glibly quote from their sermons; but what is the condition of our society still, I ask! Value is ascribed to a thing not by what it looks like buy by what is obtained by it for posterity.

There are those who beseech that we should not in the name of reform destroy and end symbols and arts. But the fact is that what they regard as glorious in the ancient symbols, arts, and fineries, are to my mind the very things that contributed to the downfall of our people and the humiliation of our land. For instance, Ramanujar, firmly convinced of the validity or utility of the ancient symbols of Namam and Poonool, attempted to corner every pariah, palla and chakkili (cobbler) and invest him with these ancient symbols; and by that queer process he is supposed to have established equality among men. The result was the preservation of the symbols without an iota of change in the inequality of man. Inequality even amongst the wearers of these symbols not only persists, but their dislike of those not addicted to these symbols became more pronounced.

Our temples are the most sacred of our symbols. Almighty god is said to reside in them. They are essentially the places created to worship god. Yet what is the condition of these temples? What is the benefit derived from them by the people? Could any one gainsay the fact that the very evils to eradicate which the temples were created, are being freely perpetrated right in the presence of the mighty god? Have not brothels and drinking dens been compared to the temples? The position is similar in regard to the other arts of old.

On may ask what good have the Vedas, Sastras, Itihasas and Purana, containing the doings of god on earth and all ostensibly produced or revealed for the benefit of mankind achieved so far. What have the Ramayana, Mahabaratha, Sivapurana, Vishnupurana, Periapurana, etc. so much praised and propitiated by our Pandits and seers, done to the people? Do not these stories of gods contain incidents and characteristics worse than what we seen in the lowest strata of our society? Can anyone deny that these puranas have been more a hindrance than an aid to human progress? Yet do we not see the reformers still being resisted by the traditionalists by these ancient so-called divine, symbols and arts, and literature? It is not uncommon to find our pandits trot our obscure passages from these puranas in support of certain reformatory ideas. I believe these insertions are only to hoodwink the credulous people, as exceptions are said only to prove the rule. The miraculous incidents with which the puranas are replete, are, as you all know, beyond human comprehension and utterly devoid of reality and practicality, and therefore outside the range of repetition in the modern age.

Instances are related in puranas of a few pariahs being admitted into the temples, where the all-kind god is stated to have given them grace and outright salvation. If it is asked why such things never happen these days, the reply is that those pariahs were different from those we see now. If that is really so, where is the need to preserve these old arts and letters? Untouchability may be pardonable in view of human ignorance, yet we have stories to say that even god recognizes untouchability.

What are the things that require reform?

Of the things that cry out for reform the principal ones are, to my mind, god and religion, for the very simple reason that these are the two things that are invariably put in opposition to all reforms.

The less I say of god the better it would be. Talk on god may be likened to a dripping pot, which is full when it leaves the water surface but arrives empty at the top of the well. It is a matter for empty discussion and not for substantial results. However the best of prophets have said that god is something that cannot be seen or touched and is beyond human knowledge; and finally that it is something that exists only when believed in. There is really not much to argue about in such a definition of god.

Religion is another thing that does not give much help to understanding. As far as I can see, no religion appears to have given man peace or prosperity. Yet in the name of religion, war and propaganda have filled man's history to the brim. Every particular religionist is convinced that salvation is possible only though his own creed, that his prophet is the only son of god, and that whatever that prophet said is god's own work. There is also no denying the fact that there are numerous subdivisions or sects in each major religion. It is impossible to find out who is representing the truth, and whose threat of hell is to be feared most. Where is the need for so much competition to gain god's affection, I ask? Do these religious heads really feel so much as to strive to take men to god? If these questions are calmly given thought, the absurdity and uselessness of religion will be apparent.

Even as one adventurer seizes power to become king ostensibly for the benefit and good of his people, and later, forgetting his mission, oppresses the people and leads them on to wage war to conquer other people's lands, so do these religious heads begin to lead people apparently for their benefit, and later, as power increases, try to engulf all others in their particular creed as being the only one calculated to give all men salvation, whatever that may mean. Truth is therefore inconsistent with many religious and creeds and numerous agents of god on earth. Hence it is that it is difficult to identify religion with god, though each religion is supposed to be connected with god. If it were said that religion is meant to give a code of conduct to people in each region or country, and variable according to time and age, there might be some excuse for it. Instead of that it is said that the religious prescriptions are divine expressions not susceptible of any change whatsoever. Then it is nothing other than meaningless bigotry, fit only to be destroyed by all reformers. Social reform must go in step with man's change and experience.

Status of Men and Women

Women in general have been treated as sub-humans in society. Woman has been taken for granted as man's slave, even as it is said that cattle have been made to serve as food for the tiger or that rats have been made for the benefit of cats. If this was really god's law, our first duty would be rid the world of the god.

Chastity: The status to women all the world over is bad; more so in India. The rules of chastity imposed on them make one shudder. Chastity is help up as the sole criterion of their merit. Our puranas glory in a particular type of chastity, which covers implicit and slavish obedience to the husband or lord. If the husband says that cold rice is hot, the wife must simply throw it away. If the lord calls her while she is drawing water from the well, she must leave the pot in mind-air and the pot must also remain suspended in space till her lord sends her back. This means that if the pot drops back into the well, she is not chaste at all. What more is needed to emphasise woman's slavery and nothingness, I cannot say. Have our gods in the puranas treated their wives this way? We see them instead carrying them on their heads or tongues or thighs or shoulders. If women are slaves, their children can only be slave-bred herds. Where woman is a slave, there cannot spring a decent self respecting society. Woman's freedom and equality with man is therefore a desideratum for civilization, and this is what a reformer should strive for. In order to ensure freedom for women, all extreme ideas of chastity require to be abrogated. Chastity enforced under compulsion is really no chastity. Love and companionship should alone condition chastity. One standard for men and another for women is totally reprehensible and cannot survive under the principle of equality. It would be moon-shine to expect men to voluntarily great equality. It is the duty of women to strive for the goal. Government has also a responsibility in this regard. They can no longer take shelter under the plea of tradition and religion, any more than social reformers.

Turkey, and China has already given the necessary lead in this matter. It must be remembered that the eyes of Turkish women and the feet of Chinese women have been freed from fetters.

Widowhood: A few words in regard to widowhood in India may not be out of place here. It must be plain to you that what is against natural instincts has been for long imposed on the unfortunate widows. This imposition not only betrays man's cruelty to women, but his total lack of proportion as well. It is really strange that a land in which goddesses are worshipped, the rivers are named after women, and the male gods are depicted as giving honoured seats to their wives on their heads or thighs, women in actual daily life should be treated as worse than dolls.

There dose not appear to be any sense whatever in compulsory widowhood. One does not know who is actually benefited by this enforcement, unless it be that some sadhus and sannyasins felt the need for the existence of such a group of women. It cannot also be that the ancient Sate feared a disproportionate growth of women and the consequent difficulty of matrimony among girls. At any rate this is a state that should not be tolerated any longer. Widows should henceforward strive for their freedom, find husbands for themselves, and take lessons from many of the lower castes, in which widows do marry. Social reformers have a special responsibility in this matter.

Caste Differences: Caste did not arise by itself in human society. It is an institution that has been deliberately enforced under penal provision. The basis for caste is that the stronger grind down the weaker. Caste is a proof of the fact that our people are not really a· civilized people. Where is the need for caste divisions based on birth? There is nothing to prove that any man in any man in any caste is incapable of any human avocation or character or culture of intelligence. All men are born equal, and inequality taught and enforced in after life is contrary to nature itself.

All good people have wanted the caste system to end. Efforts this way have not been wanting down the ages. But yet we do not hope to witness any change through pious persuasion, searching of heart, or national need. The institution can be attacked onl\ :t government level through representation in all things in proportion to strength in population of each caste. Equality in the enjoyment of material goods will ultimately lead to equality in status and the automatic withering away of all ideas of high and low, on which foundation alone caste has been constructed.

Equality or representation in all things ensures absence of exploitation of the weak by the strong. This demand cannot be outside the range of social reformers. Some nationalists raise the objection that claims based on caste would only perpetuate caste. They patriotically plead for equality of treatment, knowing full well that it is the high-caste man who will benefit by equal treatment amongst unequally developed castes. There are, besides, religious and psychological inhibitions to restrain and pull back the lower castes and push forward and encourage the higher castes. It is for these reasons that representation on a population basis is the panacea, as a first step to ultimately eradicate caste.

Untouchability: A system which says that one man should not touch another man for rear of polluting himself, is horrid to contemplate. One wishes that a country in which such a system obtains should be destroyed by fire or earthquake or floods. How on earth it is possible to credit the mighty god with the attributes of mercy, grace and benevolence, when untouchability as an institution has persisted for ages, passes one's understanding. Would it not be desirable for the untouchables to free themselves by force or violence and perish in the attempt? Can5an institution has persisted for ages, passes one's understanding? Would it not be desirable for the untouchables to free themselves by force or violence and perish in the attempt? Can an institution has persisted for ages, passes one's understanding. Would it not be desirable for the untouchables to free themselves by force or violence and perish in the attempt? Can a country that harbors this system, really crave for political freedom, Swaraj, and a civilized life? There are people, I know, who have said that these injustices will go once political freedom is achieved. They forget that the horrid institution of untouchability was ruled by godlike kings like Rama and Harishchandra. The cause of untouchability is not political slavery. It is the Hindu religion, pure and simple. Social reformers have perforce to kill the demon of untouchability if necessary by killing the Hindu religion.

Education: Social reform necessarily covers the subject of education. According to me education should conform to nature general human character. The rest can only be magic.

What is practicable and natural to the world of men, should find a place in education. What is taught to-day is contrary to these fundamentals. What would serve the rulers, be they kings or priests by ensuring the unalloyed subservience of the people to the powers that be, is what is served to our children. The present education, further, is calculated to subserve the interests of the exploiting classes that live on other's labour. To be brief, I would say that worship of god, practice of religion, propitiation of the rulers, which are all calculated to keep people in mental salvery, should never enter the portals of education. Further, education should more particularly be diverted to women, the untouchables, and other backward classes; and denied altogether to those who credit themselves with divinity of intelligence through their birth itself. At least for some fifteen years, high caste pupils should be denied admission in all colleges and technical schools. An honest government, I feel, should do this unhesitatingly if it is intent on social equality and destruction of caste; and s0ocial reformers should oblige government to ac t in this way.

Superstition: That blind beliefs and superstitious practices should fall within the targets of social reformers, need hardly be restated, as it is already the general talk everywhere. Except for those who live by exploiting these beliefs and practices, there is no one else to gain by them. But for want of courage and resolution, the others are unable to change the position. God, religion, piety, Vedas are not the only things that encourage superstition. Beliefs about good days, vows, fasts, theerthas, sacred spots, and tributes to saints, etc. all help to spread superstition, which in addition make men waste their energy, wisdom, wealth, and time. Although endowed with natural resources, India is enslaved, poor and primitive only because of our people's blind faith in superstitious practices. Some of the countries of the world that were very backward have with in a few decades progressed in all arts and sciences, only because they struck at the root of the superstition that long enslaved their people's mind.

Our people dread to change even a small item of their senseless practices. God, religion, puranas and smritis stand opposed to them. The objection of "of "our ancestral ways" is the worst of all. Crores are wasted in these practices. There are temples in India whose annual incomes run into crores, and they are wasted on useless rituals and for the especial benefit and aggrandizement of a few exploiters. To betray the credulous people into these senseless practices and beliers, we have any number of puranas, agama sastras, legends of achariars, auspicious days and sacred places, ceremonies, etc. Even governments and foreigners are not free from the desire to exploit the people's credulity. Take the railways in India as an instance. None can say that their authorities have any faith in our sacred places, rituals, pilgrimages, etc. Yet it is interesting to see what the railways do." Do go for Thula Bath", "Vaikunta Ekadasi invites you", "Come to Dhanushkodi for Adi Amavasai," "Witness Karthikai Deepam at Thiruvannamalai," "Don't you go to kumbha Mela at Haridwar?" "Come for Mahamagham at Kumbakonam" are some of the posters that one finds at railway stations and in the newspapers. Pictures of beautiful women are also some times put in the posters to attract and deceive our people. They do not do all this to conduct people to heaven. You all know it is solely to make money I believe that the amount wasted by the people on this pilgrimages, rituals and talismans, would be more than what they pay to government for not doing this and that for the good of the people, do to seem to bother at all about the money that people otherwise squander. In fact it is easier for economists, politicians, and journalists to attack the government for their omissions and commissions, than to turn their eyes and ears to the superstitious practices on which fortunes are spent. Experts who flare up at government for the least interference with superstition are also not wanting in this country.

If the money and energy spent on superstitious beliefs had been diverted to popular education, should we have the lowest percentage literacy in this holy land of ours? The ultimate source of our illiteracy, poverty, and disease, is superstition.

Social reformers who preach on the platform, but do not follow their own teaching in practice are many. They seem to be stunned and deterred on facing facts. To keep up superstitious beliefs, the activities of the exploiters never cease. Almost every religious sect, like the Saivas, Vaisnavas, Siddhantis, etc. conduct conference and Kalakshepams on *Ramayana, Mahabharata*. Social reformers must steel their minds and reinforce their activities to face these tremendous hostile forces if never they are to succeed. To minimize the power and strength of the forces of superstition embedded in religion and god, is to court failure; and to grand omnipotence and permanence to superstition is to betray intellectual bankruptcy. The fact that a practice or belief has lasted for ages and that it has a literature behind it, is no criterion of its truth. The world is full of able efforts of great men and great people who have succeeded in breaking down old and hallowed practices and in changing the ways of men.

Since I have lost hope in social reform through constitutional persuasive methods, I feel that a totalitarian government pledged to rationalism and socialism will along be able to do something. A government pledged to eradicate caste, must be in a position to proscribe all books and literature that glorify caste, division, however ancient and sacred they may be. A public bonfire must be made of all those books that harbour superstition and caste. All those Sankaracharyas and Matathipadhis the still practice caste must be jailed or exiled. The wealth hoarded in the temples by way of jewels and utensils must be confiscated and spent for the education of the illiterate and for finding jobs for the unemployed. It is necessary to prepare the country for a government that can boldly attempt these reforms. It may be perhaps be necessary for many reformers to sacrifice their lives in the process. More than all, it is very necessary for reformers not to be afraid of being labeled atheists. The real fact is that all those who lose faith in the Brahmin priests, the *Vedas, Shastras, Itihasas* and *Puranas,* are called atheists. If the superstition and exploitation of the priests cannot be destroyed without one becoming an atheist, well, there is nothing wrong in becoming an atheist, Indeed I am convinced that social reformers, if they are to face the world effectively, must straightway declare themselves atheists. It is only then that the scare about atheism will dwindle and vanish. It must never be forgotten the priests and plutocrats will ever be enemies of socialism and therefore democracy and therefore of all reformers. It must also be remembered that the people who oppose one religion for another, put faith in one prophet as against another, and in consequence invite people to join their narrow fold, are all equally opposed to reform and enlightenment. It is necessary to warn people against such propaganda so that in their innocent credulity they may not be taken in by the false and misguided call for a change of faith. All religionists sail in the same sinister boat. A change of religion is no solution to man's ills. No religion is the solution.

A warming is essential in regard to those Brahmins and other orthodox people who easily seem to establish themselves as great reformers, merely because they have lately taken to meat eating, drinking, or eating in anybody's house. There are others who feel they contribute to social reform merely because they have made no distinction about caste in there marriages or in their concubines. It is wrong to regard these specimens as social reformers. At the same time let it not be made out that Brahmins alone are guilty of caste behaviour. It is found in all other castes, though perhaps not to that pronounced extent. I am aware of the criticism that while the non-Brahmins are bitter about the superiority complex of the Brahmins, they themselves for not grant equality to those below them in the infamous caste hierarchy. There is much truth in this criticism. My only reply is that the Brahmins have to take the greatest blame, because their forebears have been the authors of caste and it is they who have meticulously striven to preserve the system; and that if there were a change of heart in the Brahmins, the top of the ladder, reformation in all other rungs would be easier and smoother. I must repeat that representation in services and schools in proportion to population must be accorded to all castes irrespective of their old status in the hierarchy.

In conclusion, I may say that the ultimate object of social reform should be to each of social reform should be to teach good habits, extend knowledge, observe the principle of equality in all things, realize self-respect, and practice socialism and secularism in their true senses.

Caste and Hinduism

What am I? What do I preach?

First - I speak opposing the god-idea.

Second - I belittle the organized religions of the world.

Third - I denounce the Shatras, Puranas, and their gods, and all upon the people to burn and destroy them.

I have said all these and have gone further and broken the idols of Pillaiyar or Vinayaka and burnt pictures of Rama. If in spite of these words and acts of mine, there are thousands of people to throng to my meetings, it only indicates that self-respect and wisdom have dawned on the people.

What does the Dravidar Kazhagam movement stand for? It stands to do away with the wretched Hindu caste system that divides the people undemocratically into high and low. In doing so the Dravidar Kazhagam condemns the gods and sastras that support caste in one way or the other.

Even in 1958, long after independence, caste dominates the life of our people only to emphasis eth primitive back-wardness of the country. In no other country has caste or class divided the people into thousands of watertight compartments. It is strange people do not spend some time in thinking over these matters. The dearth of real selfless leaders is very great in this country. The few who profess to be public men in the name of nationalism or party politics are men who are not in the lest interested in the real problems of India. They are men who try to make a living out of the very things that make our country people backward. The advance towards social reform and national progress in other countries after their political independence towers far above what our leaders and government have attempted to do.

Is there any party in this country which categorically demands the abolition of caste, except us in the Dravidian movement? There may be people to congratulate or praise our movement in its fight against caste, but they are again men who would be scared to go before the people openly to preach against caste. Thus is why barbaric practices and superstitious beliefs still rule the lives of our credulous people. Communities that were once barbaric in the west when Indian were civilized have gone so much forward in their civilization as to leave the Indians far behind. The white men of Europe not long ago roamed the forests clothed in skins or leaves to gain a miserable livelihood. They fished in the rivers and hunted in the forest. Their sex life was full of incest. Not knowing the art of cooking, they ate vegetables raw like animals. What are they to-day? They have begun to challenge and complete with god in inventing and making great things. Electricity, Radio, Television, Telephone, Railways, Aeroplanes, etc., have all been invented by them. They have sent into space artificial moons and are now trying to make homes for themselves on the moon it self.

In what way are Indians lower than the Europeans? In very ancient times, Indians invented many things, gave free vent to their thinking and lived in tune with nature. But in later times, free thinking was muzzled through false beliefs in gods, region, caste and superstition. The rational attitude was arrested and wisdom got imprisoned in priest craft. Anybody who stood up against god and the sastras and puranas was immediately denounced as an atheist, anti Hindu or anti-social anarchist. Until the self-respect movement arose in the south there has been none so far to spread against the false gods and creeds.

As far as I am concerned I do not speak for or against the existence of god. I do not also ask people to simply accept my thesis without giving much thought themselves to the problems posed by me. Atheism is no easy situation for a man. Any fool can call himself a theist. It does not require a great intellectual to assert the existence of god. But courage and conviction are needed to make a man an agnostic or atheist. This is possible only for intelligent persons with power to reason out and convince themselves about their position. There is no possibility of blind belief in atheism.

I suppose that there are about a thousand millions of people in the world to-day who have lost faith in god. Believers are certainly greater in number. The Christian and Muslim believe in one god. That god has no name and shape and has no desire. Why don't we have one like that? Why should there be thousand of them for us? If one starts writing out their names, the pen would get dry but the names would not get exhausted. What is the origin of these gods? Ask any priest and he will start quoting silly Puranas. Had it not been for the rationalist urge of the modern days, it is not impossible that the milestones on the highways would have been converted into gods and dismay caused to the travelers! It does not take much time for a Hindu to stand a mortar stone in the house and convert it into a great god by smearing red and yellow powders on it. Have people really thought about these things?

Almost all fine-looking animals and birds have become our gods. Elephants, pigs, crows and snakes have not only become divine, but have also honoured human bodies with their heads, Why all these half-human and half-animal gods? Ant-hills invite the gift of milk from our women folk. The vulture flying high in the sky calls for the pious to beat their cheeks. The cow on the road is touched and worshipped by the passer-by. Our gods have from one to ten faces and their tummies sometimes cave in or bulge out. What are all these caricatures for? What do they do? Where is the need to exhibit god or ourselves? Why don't people think about these things?

We are told that out ancients made some animals and birds gods in order that people might respect them treat them well and kindly. The explanation is absurd on the face of it. Are cows, monkeys, does and rats ill-treated in countries where they are not worshipped? Indian cattle are the most famished in the world. Without trying to take care of them, the old cows and bullocks are let loose into the streets to starve and find a slow death. The bulls let loose in the streets as a religious and pious duty add to the misery of the street hawkers and pavement traders. The monkeys worshiped as god Rama's devoted bhakta and emissary cannot be killed in India. The criminals waste perpetrated by the monkey in home gardens in towns and cities is enormous. Nobody has bothered to measure the quantity of food products in the form of both vegetables and fruits that is daily wasted by monkey mischief. The fad about cow slaughter has only added to India's food problem and is an economic drain on the already bankrupt finances of India, which still imports even rice and wheat from America and other countries. But who cares?

More than two thousand years ago, Buddha tried to liberate the mind from the tentacles of the Hindu religion. He asked people to say the why, how and what of things. He called the Vedas so much humbug. He refused to acknowledge the authority of rishis and mahatmas for anything. He called upon the people to think for themselves in their own living languages and arrive at simple truths of life. What was the result? The people who preached rationalism were killed on the oiled pole, their women dishonoured and their houses burnt down. With the extermination of Buddhism failed to flourish in the land of the Buddha. It went into China and Japan, not to ruin them out to make them great. Who can excel the Japanese in their national character, in which discipline, clearness, honesty and hospitality are of the highest order?

After the Buddha, the great Thiruvalluvar was born in India, about the beginning of the Christian era. He preached what Buddha had taught. His inestimable *Tiukkural* was thrown into the waste paper basket, to shamelessly hug the Gita and Manu's code.

The Sankaracharyas of our modern times are being propitiated by the people, not knowing that they are really godless. The advaita preaches the oneness of all in god, and the Sankaracharya goes to the extent of identifying himself with god. Where then is god for him. The vibhuti drawn on his body, the worship of the female goddess as Shakti, and the wearing of the saffron cloth are all for deceiving the public and camouflaging his nihilism.

How can god have birth and death? Take all our gods. Rama was born in Navami. Subramanya was born in Shasti. Krishna says he was born in Astami. All these gods die, according to their Puranas. Is it not strange that we should still be worshipping these gods? Why should one spread food before him? Why should he be undressed, bathed, and dressed daily? Even the female gods are being undressed and bathed by the male priest! Neither the goddess nor her bhaktas are outraged by the obscenity!!

Why do the gods want wives? They are generally not satisfied with one partner. Sometimes they need concubines. Why should the god in Tirupathi want to go to a Muslim concubine by name Nachchiar? And all these gods are to be married every year. What happened to last year's marriage? When were they divorced?

Which court granted them divorce? Has all this fun about god made our people wiser, more united, and more clean?

The Christian, Muslim and Buddhist gods are declared to be embodiments of mercy, grace, and benevolence. Christian and Buddhist idolatry bespeaks these characteristics. Take our gods. Take our gods. One god will wear a spear, another a bow and arrow. The mace, dagger and shield adorn other gods. Why all these? The terrible chakra ever swirls about the finger of one god. To kill whom? If love and grace conquer men's hearts, why all these murderous weapons for the gods? Obviously our gods are able to conquer evil only by force, murder and war. And have they succeeded? We live in modern times, and true to it, is it not time that our gods are properly equipped with modern weapon? Should not the bow and arrow be replaced by the machine gun and the hand grenade? Should not Krishna ride a tank instead of the obsolete chariot? I want people to think and see the ridicule and shame still being put on god in this atomic age.

(From *Social Refrom or Social Revolution*? Dravidar Kazhagam Publication, Cheannai, 1998)

13

Manavendra Nath Roy

Life and Times

Manavendra Nath Roy (1886-1954) was perhaps the most fascinating radical among the Indian nationalists of his generation. But the story of his life shows that the political criterion is not the only criterion of judgment of nationalist thought. Other criteria sometimes have as much claim to application. The historian of ideas must, somehow, personally adjudicate between their often contrasting claims, and the picture he constructs is a result of the exact way in which he judges them. Roy's radicalism was surely powerful and sincere; but it carried, at a deeper level, what Sudipta Kaviraj says the 'guilt of his heteronomy', the tendency to see events through an overriding primacy of European history. Events do not remain simple events, they become allegories to the sacred events of another, more significant history. It is startling to find within this nationalist discourse such adoration of the idea of the primacy of Europe: to regard European history as the rule, and the rest of the world's history as the massive exception. This does not mean, of course, that what we generally know about M.N. Roy's thinking should be given up; rather this means that what we know should be read through this element too—to construct a picture that is surely more complex but perhaps also more realistic. This does not make Roy's thought less radical, but makes his radicalism more complex." In any case, this existence of heteronomy, within aspirations for independence, is not peculiar to Roy. It was true of a strand of nationalism. In some ways perhaps it was the common and general 'tragedy' of colonial history. Colonial thought is not able to escape this contradiction: its greatest autonomy is often marked secretly by a peculiar inscidious dependence. Even to break with the other, it needs the other. In Ashis Nandy's phrase, it has an "intimate enemy". One works to defeat and destroy the enemy who is very intimate, very close. He has become part of one's being and personality.

Manavendra Nath Roy was born on 6 February 1886 and died on 25 January 1954. He was born into a Bengali Brahmin family in a village outside Calcutta. His earlier name was Narendranath Bhattacharya. He was a revolutionary from his student days. In his early years he was influenced by Swami Vivekananda, Swami Ramtirtha and Swami Dayananda Saraswati. When Bengal had been undergoing the tremendous ferment of the Swadeshi period, Roy received his political vision and began his revolutionary activities. He was enthusiastic about the political ideas of Bipin Chandra Pal, Aurobindo Ghosh and Surendranath Banerjee. The oratorical skill of Pal and Banerjee moved him. He also worked in co-operation with the leaders and workers of the Yugantara group. He was fairly intimate with Jatin Mukherjee. He drew considerable inspiration from the life of sacrifice and sufferings of V.D. Savarkar. In 1910 Roy was sentenced to imprisonment in connection with the Howrah conspiracy case. He was arrested again in 1915 in connection with a political dacoity in Calcutta.

In 1915 Roy fled to Dutch Indies. He also went to Java, Philippines and to Korea and Manchuria. Later, he went to the USA where for some time he worked in collaboration with Lala Lajpat Rai. From the USA he went to Mexico. He was called by Lenin after the Bolshevik Revolution, to Russia. He reached Russia in the beginning of 1920 and became the adviser of the Bolshevik Party on colonial problems. But Roy had a difference of opinion with Lenin at the time of the Second Congress of the Communist International. Lenin held that during the finance-capitalist and imperialist phase of world economy, it was essential to achieve an integration between the bourgeois nationalistic struggles of the colonial world and the rising proletarian movements in the advanced countries of the West. But M.N. Roy was of the view that the bourgeoisie in the colonial countries may enter into a coalition with the imperialists for the joint exploitation of the suppressed strata. Roy prepared a different thesis where he tried to expose the anti-proletarian attitude of the Asian nationalist leaders. Lenin's view was based on the experiences of the Western countries where the bourgeoisie had been the spokesmen of a national democratic revolution. Roy agreed that imperialism is the highest stage of capitalism and hence the colonial struggle for liberation was a part of the international struggle against morjbund capitalism. But Roy felt that the situation, in the Oriental countries in the early twentieth century was not the same as in Europe in the eighteenth and nineteenth centuries. In such a situation the class structure of the leadership of the national freedom movement was bound to be different from that of the West. Lenin was generous enough to see the strength of Roy's standpoint. Roy stated his views in his India in Transition. Perhaps Roy's views were more realistic as they proceeded from his greater experience of the colonial countries. Even Lenin was impressed by Roy's analysis.

In 1922 M.N. Roy made a sociological study of contemporary India in his India in Transition. He differed from the three current explanations of India in Transition. The British imperialists of the school of Montague believed in the cult of slow progressive development of responsible government. The exponents of Indian liberalism and constitutionalism had faith in the motives and intuitions of the British statesmen and wanted to work out the reforms contemplated in the Government of India Act of 1919. Roy derided them as impotent constitutionalists serving the purpose of the bourgeoisie. The third was the group of extremists and nationalists. Roy ridiculed the confusion and the medievalist revivalism of this group with its antiquated religious ideology. He offered a fourth— the Marxist explanation of India in transition. He prophesied that the future Indian nation was going to be shaped by the 'inexorable evolution' of the progressive forces latent in Indian society. The Indian transition was a consequence of the movement of social forces which were struggling for the replacement of the old bankrupt decadent socio-economic structure.

Behind the political turmoil, Roy read the pangs of new social forces which were in contradiction to the exploitative tendencies of the hour. The secret of the inhuman misery of the rural population of India lay in the fact that capitalist economy had brought under its control almost the whole of agriculture production. Thus the Indian peasantry was subjected to the double exploitation of foreign as well as Indian capital. The existence of a huge amount of capital invested in land was forcing the rapid concentration of capital in the possessions of non-agrarian sections. The belated growth of the urban proletariat in India was a natural consequence of the retarded industrial development of the country. At the time of the British invasion, India could have passed from the stage of manufacture to machine production but India did not pass from the stage of mercantile capitalism to industrial capitalism. In India the struggle for national freedom was going side by side with the raging class struggle. He discussed in this book three basic social phenomena—the rise of the Indian bourgeoisie, the pauperization of the peasantry, and the impoverishment of the urban proletariat. The development of large-scale industry would determine the future of India. Industrial growth was bound to swell and strengthen the ranks of the labourers and hence the bourgeoisie of India would seek compromise and the Government of India. Necessarily the task of wining the liberation of India would have to be shouldered by the workers and peasants consciously organized and fighting on the grounds of class-struggle.

Towards the end of 1922, M.N. Roy published a book India's Problem and Its Solution. In this book, in a thoroughly Marxist vein, he criticized the medievalism and conservatism of the Gandhian social ideology. Using the favourite Marxist terminology he characterized the proceedings of the Ahmedabad Congress of 1921 as a betrayal by the bourgeois leadership of the revolutionary forces. He expressed dissatisfaction with the constructive programme of resolution adopted at Bardoli on 12 February 1922. He pleaded for the creation of revolutionary mass party which would ferment discontent against the existing political and economic system of the country and would intensify discontent in those places where it did exist. He advised mass strikes and demonstrations to develop the revolutionary determination of the masses. These mass strikes were to be led by the 'class conscious vanguard' pledged absolutely to the acceptance of the thesis of class struggle. In place of the civil disobedience which was the ideology of the Congress, Roy advised 'militant action of the masses'. A romantic concept of the nation based upon the adumbration of the remote idealism of a futurist Utopia could not canalize mass energy. What was needed was a clear and explicit statement of the objectives for which the people were to fight. He stated that the non-cooperation movement had been inspired by the ideology of lower middle classes and did not contain any revolutionary programme. He put great faith in the mass awakenings in India in the early twenties which were characterized in several quarters as 'hooliganism' and held 'imperious economic laws' to be responsible for the mass upheaval.

In 1923 M.N. Roy published *One Year of Non-Cooperation.* Here he paid tributes to the saintly personality of Mahatma Gandhi and compared him to Thomas Aquinas, Savonarola and Francis of Assissi. He acknowledged the efforts of Gandhi in mobilizing mass action from 1919 to 1922. He recognized four constructive contributions of Gandhism: (i) use of mass action for political purpose, (ii) consolidation of the Indian National Congress, (iii) the liberation of the national forces from governmental repression by the 'slogan of nonviolence', and (iv) the adoption of the techniques of non-cooperation, non-payment of taxes and civil disobedience.

But in this book Roy noted several shortcomings of Gandhism: (i) Gandhism lacked any economic programme to win mass support. (ii) It wanted to unite all sections of Indians—exploiters like the landlords and capitalists with the exploited peasants and workers. (iii) The incorporation of metaphysical propositions into political action was unfortunate because political dynamism was sacrificed at the altar of subjective considerations of conscience, (iv) The reactionary economics of charkha. (v) Roy also criticized the vacillation of Gandhism. He did not like Gadhiji's seeking interviews with the viceroy. Hence, he said that Gandhism was not revolutionism but 'week and watery' reformism.

In 1926 M.N. Roy wrote *The Future of Indian Politics* wherein he dealt with significance of a 'People's Party'. This book was written in the context of the general political slump in India prompted by the death, of C.R. Das, the virtual retirement of Gandhi from politics and his prime concern with constructive work, the disintegration of the Swaraj Party due to inner schisms generated by class contradictions and the slow progress of revolutionary forces. He wrote this book when the 1926 elections were only a few months ahead. The People's Party, envisaged by Roy, was to be a supplement and not a substitute for a proletariat party. The proletariat, Roy as a communist considered to be the vanguard of the national liberation forest but in the Indian situation there were other numerically large social classes which also had to be taken into consideration. Roy believed that the future of Indian politics would still be dominated by the interests of these classes-students, petty intellectuals, artisans, small traders and peasantry. The Indian revolutionaries had to concentrate upon the transformation of these classes into forces of national revolution in a democratic party. The 'People's Party' was to help in bringing this transformation. Roy argued that the Swaraj Party as a staunch defender of nationalism, should be shifted from the big landlords and the bourgeoisie to the masses. He did not put any hope in any Labour Party concerned with trade unionism and parliamentarianism and characterized the advocates of a Labour Party in India as representing economism. Hence the only alternative was to create a democratic party of the people binding together the petty bourgeoisie, the peasantry and the proletariat.

There was no open rupture as yet between Roy and the Bolsheviks. He was the head of the Oriental department of the Moscow Institute. He was even sent to China at the end of 1926 along with Borodin and Blucher. He had gone there as the representative of the Communist International and stayed there till the middle of 1927. He advised the Chinese communists to embark upon a plan of agrarian revolution in order to extend their social basis. But the Communist Party .of China did not act on this advice. This amounted, according to Roy, to a betrayal not only of the peasants but also of the proletariat. Roy regarded Sun-Yat-Sen, as an apostle of essentially reactionary pseudo-radicalism. In Sun-Yat-Sen, he found a marked hostility to individualism and a desire to create neo-Confucian state. Roy has some hard words for the Chinese Communist Party of those days (1926-1927) which due to its miscalculations was isolated from the urban democratic masses and thus was almost rootless in the industrial areas. In the late twenties there was a conflict between Roy and the communists. Roy was opposed to the monopolization of the leadership of the Third international by the Russian Communists who claimed to be masters both of Marxist theory and practice. The slogan of socialism in one country proclaimed by Stalin in 1924, prevented the possibility of the realization of international communism. Roy at the time of the Sixth World Congress of the Communist International, advocated the 'decolonization' theory. Decolonization signified the growing exhaustion of British imperialist finance and the partial transfer of its benefits to the Indian bourgeoisie. Roy propounded the changing character of imperialism. The decolonization thesis stressed the growing exhaustion of the exportable capital of the imperialist countries, necessitating a joint partnership with the native bourgeoisie. Roy prophesied that in the long run the depreciating value of imperialism would compel the foreign capitalists to part with power. The Sixth World Congress passed a resolution warning the Indian people against their possible betrayal by the counter-revolutionary Indian National Congress. Roy's criticism of Stalin's red sectarianism and extreme leftism led to the final break between Roy and the Communist International in 1928-29. When the Simon Commission was to visit India in 1927, M.N. Roy suggested that there should be a demand for a constituent assembly for India. Perhaps it was a premature demand. The orthodox communists criticized him for sponsoring this slogan of constituent assembly and they considered him to be a bourgeois nationalist democrat.

He came to India in disguise in 1930 and was put in jail for six years (1931-36) in connection with the Kanpur conspiracy case. Thus after fifteen years' exile and six years of prison life, in 1936 Roy was in a position to enter actively into Indian political life.

After his release in 1936, he intensified his campaign against Gandhism. He condemned Gandhism as a reactionary social philosophy teaching the impracticable concept of social harmony. Nonviolence, he regarded, as a mask for hiding the true nature of grim social exploitation. In the late thirties M.N. Roy headed an anti-communist Marxist group. He regarded the Gandhian Ahimsa as a subtle intellectual device for concealing the capitalist exploitation of the country. He criticized the bankruptcy of the Congress leadership and stated that under Gandhi's leadership the Congress was being turned into a spinners' association. Nonviolence, he said, arrested the revolutionary urge of the Indian masses.

In June 1939 Roy organized the League of Radical Congressmen. He contested the presidentship of the Indian National Congress in 1940 but was defeated by Abul Kalam Azad. After his defeat Roy left the Congress in September 1940. He organized his Radical Democratic Party in December 1940 and moved towards 'New Humanism'. He regarded the Second World War as neither an imperialist war nor a war between nations. The terrible conflict in which the great powers of the world were involved was really, according to Roy, an international civil war. The enemy was not a state but a rampant ideology.

During the Second World War (1940-45) Roy was a protagonist of twentieth century Jacobinism. According to him Jacobinism is historically the forerunner of Bolshevism, even when it is the creed of a bourgeois revolt. Roy explained his thesis of twentieth century Jacobinism as something midway between a bourgeois revolution and a proletarian revolution. There were two implications of the twentieth century Jacobinism, (i) The Indian revolution was to be led by a multi-class party and not solely by the proletarian minority, (ii) The immediate issue in India was not socialism or communism but a political bourgeois-democratic revolution. That would provide the transition to socialism.

Roy law argued that domination by the European colonial powers not only denied political sovereignty to the non-European societies but also deprived them of intellectual resources of self-expression. The story of colonialism unfolds at two levels: a political level and a level of culture. Nationalist ideology sought to break out of these political and cultural bondages of colonialism.

Thus, culture of colonialism is a 'world of tragic paradoxes'. It is a culture marked by a constantly renewed contradiction between its two fundamental characteristics from either of which it is unable to escape. These are the urge towards independence and the given ness of a heteronomous existence. Nowhere is this contradiction more explicit than in its political thought. Nationalist politics, except for minor aberrant trends, symbolize the urge for political emancipation; yet the concepts, categories or ideas which this politics employs to recognize and interpret its world, its acts, its history, and even the arguments it uses against the enemy are often taken from the colonizer. Almost all solutions which can be worked out within the historical confines of this language and experience are tragic in this sense.

Roy felt that applying Marxist theory to the colonies, had its own contradictions. Marxist theory assumed that politics depended on the nature of society and its class structure. But the primary difficulty arose because these colonial societies were structured quite differently from the European societies which had either undergone capitalist transformation, or were on the verge of it. As a result, there could be several ways of 'applying' Marxism to colonial societies especially in regard to two crucial tasks: (i) the analysis of classes in colonial society, and (ii) the political strategy which followed from this. Aalyzing the class structure of a society involved not a simple transfer of the class analysis Marx had made of nineteenth century European states, but the application of his method to a society that was structured in a very different way. It was not the concepts or the formulations that were to be common between the European analysis and the colonial analyses, but. {he method. But method might require the application of quite different categories.

On the eve of the Second Congress of the Co:nintern, Lenin invited Roy to prepare a draft thesis on the colonial question, besides Lenin's own as Lenin felt he was unfamiliar with the concrete political situation in the colonies. The perspective that Roy advanced in his draft theses was, however, in important respects different from Lenin's. Surely, Roy's thesis too applied the conceptual apparatus of Marxist political economy, but his judgments on political questions were vastly different. In 1920, in the aftermath "of the great failures of the European communist parties, there was considerable substance in Roy's view that a crisis of the world capitalist structure should be expected from the side of the colonies, not from the metropolitan centers.

Roy's picture of the political economy of colonial India was markedly similar to Marx's depiction of Germany in the mid-nineteenth century. He overestimated the strength of the proletariat both in economic terms and politically. Owing to both these reasons—the relative weakness of the bourgeoisie and the relative strength of the working class—bourgeois political groups like the Congress seemed predestined to compromise with feudal and imperialist interests. The political implications of this understanding of colonial economy were equally significant. This meant that the bourgeoisie, and of course its political organizations, were predestined to 'betray' the national movement, exactly as the German bourgeoisie of Marx's times did. Roy's political strategy was determined by these theoretical premises. He anticipated a continuous process of radicalizaiion in the national movement. Leading classes, like the bourgeoisie would assume leadership for some time. Every change in leadership would polarize the movement and give it a higher political content. Each of these would be transcended eventually by the movement's growing militancy. Leading groups would be terrified by popular initiative and restrain the struggle and be cast in the capacious 'dustbin of history.' Only the communists were capable of leading national movements to final victory.

Supplementary Thesis on Colonial Question

1. To determine the relation of the Communist International to the revolutionary movements in the countries dominated by capitalistic imperialism is one of the most important questions before the Second Congress of the Third International. The

history of the world revolution has come to a period when a proper understanding of this relation is indispensable; the great European war and its results have shown clearly that the masses of the non-European subjected countries and inseparable connected with the proletarian movement in Europe, as a consequence of the centralized world capitalism.

2. The fountainhead from which European capitalism draws its main strength is no longer to be found in the industrial countries of Europe, but in the colonial possessions and dependencies. Without the control of the extensive markets and vast fields of exploitation in the colonies, the capitalist powers of Europe cannot maintain their existence even for a short time. England, the stronghold of imperialism, has been suffering from overproduction since more than a century ago. But for the extensive colonial possessions acquired for selling her surplus product is and as a source of raw materials for her ever growing industries, the capitalist structure of England would have crushed under its own weight long ago. By enslaving the hundreds of millions of inhabitants of Asia and Africa, English imperialism succeeded so far in keeping the British proletariat under the domination of the bourgeoisie.

3. Superprofit gained in the colonies is the mainstay of modern capitalism and so long as it is not deprived of this source of Superprofit, it will not be easy for the European working class to overthrow the capitalist order. Thanks to the possibility of intensive and extensive exploitation of human labour and natural resources in the colonies, the capitalist nations of Europe are trying, not without success, to recuperate their present bankruptcy. By exploiting the masses in the colonies, European imperialism will be in a position to give concession after concession to the proletariat at home. It will not hesitate to go to the extent of sacrificing the entire surplus value in the home country so long as it continues in the position to gain its huge superprofits in the colonies.

4. Without the breaking up of the colonial empire, the overthrow of the capitalist system in Europe does not appear possible. Consequently, the Communist International must widen the

sphere of its activities. It must establish relations with those revolutionary forces that are working for a overthrow of imperialism in the countries subjected politically and economically.

5. Such relation of the Communist International with the revolutionary movement in the subject countries is not tantamount to their former's upholding the doctrine of nationalism. The Communist International is the concentrated will of the world revolutionary proletariat. Its mission is to organize the working class of the whole world for the overthrow of the capitalist order and the establishment of communism. The Third International is a fighting body which has outgrown the realm of pure doctrinarism.

   Dominated as it was by a group of politicians, permeated with bourgeois culture, the Second International failed to appreciate the importance of the colonial question. For them the world did not exist outside of Europe.

   They could not see the necessity of co-ordinating the revolutionary movement in Europe with those in the non-European countries. Instead of giving moral and material help to the revolutionary movements in the colonies, the members of the Second International themselves became imperialists.

6. Foreign imperialism imposed on the eastern peoples prevented them from developing socially and economically side by side with their fellows in Europe and America. Owing to the imperialistic policy of preventing industrial development of the colonies, a proletarian class in the strict sense of the term could not come into existence until recently. The indigenous craft industries were destroyed to make room for the products of the centralized industries in the imperialistic countries; consequently a big majority of the population was driven to the land to produce food grains and raw materials for export to foreign lands. On the other hand, there followed a rapid concentration of land, the proprietary right of which was vested in the state thus creating a huge landless peasantry. The great bulk of the population was kept in a state of illiteracy. As a result of this policy, the spirit of revolt latent in every subject

people found its expression only through the small, educated middle class.

The foreign domination has obstructed the free development of the social forces – therefore its overthrow is the first step towards the revolution in the colonies. So, to help overthrow the foreign rule in the colonies is not to endorse the nationalist aspirations of the native bourgeoisie but to open up the way to the smothered proletariat there.

7. The revolutionary movements in the colonies are essentially an economic struggle. The bourgeois democratic nationalist movements are limited to the small middle class which does not reflect the aspirations of the masses. Without the active support of the masses, the national freedom of the colonies will never be attained. But in many countries, especially in India, the masses are not with the bourgeois nationalist leaders – they are moving towards revolution independently of the bourgeois nationalist movement. There are to be found in the dependent countries two distinct movements which every day grow father and farther apart from each other. One is the bourgeois democratic nationalist movement, with a programme of political independence and the other is the mass action of the ignorant and poor peasants and workers. The former endeavour to control the latter and often succeed to a certain extent, but it would be a mistake to assume that the bourgeois nationalist movement expresses the sentiments and aspirations of the general population. For the overthrow of foreign imperialism, the first step towards revolution in the colonies, the cooperation of the bourgeois nationalist elements may be useful. But the Communist International must not find in them the media through which the revolutionary movement in the colonies should be helped. The mass movements in the colonies are growing independently of the nationalist movements. The masses distrust the political leaders who always lead them astray and prevent them from revolutionary action.

8. The real strength of the liberation movement in the colonies is no longer confined to the narrow circle of bourgeois democratic

nationalists. In most of the colonies there already exist organized socialist or communist parties, in close relation to the mass movement. The relation of the Communist International with the revolutionary movement in the colonies should the through the medium of these parties or groups, because they are the vanguard of the working class in their respective countries. They may not be very big today, but they reflect the desire of the masses and the masses will follow them to the revolution. The communist parties of the different imperialistic countries must work in conjunction with these proletarian parties of the colonies and through them give, all the moral and material support to the revolutionary movements in general.

9. The supposition that, owing to the economic and industrial backwardness, the peoples in the colonies are bound to go through the stage of bourgeois democracy is wrong. The events and conditions in many of the colonies do not corroborate such a supposition. It is true that the revolution in the colonies is not going to be a communist revolution in its first stages. But if from the beginning the lead of the revolution is in the hands of a communist vanguard, the revolutionary masses would not be led astray but would go straight ahead through the successive periods of development of revolutionary experience. Indeed, it would be very difficult in many of the oriental countries to solve the agrarian problem along pure communist principles. In its first stages, the revolution in the colonies must be carried on with a programme in which will be included many petty bourgeois reform clauses – for instance, division of land, etc. but from this it does not necessarily follow that the leadership of the revolution will have to be surrendered to the bourgeois democrats.

10. The bourgeois national democrats in the colonies strive for the establishment of a free national state, whereas the masses of workers and poor peasants are revolting, even though in many cases unconsciously, against the system which permits such brutal exploitation. Consequently, in the colonies, we have two contradictory forces; they cannot develop together. To support

the colonial bourgeois democratic movements would amount to helping the growth of the national spirit which will surely obstruct the awakening of class consciousness in the masses; whereas to encourage and support the revolutionary mass action through the medium of a communist party of the proletarians will bring the real revolutionary forces to action which will not only overthrow the foreign imperialism, but lead progressively to the development of Soviet power, thus preventing the rise of a native capitalism in place of the vanquished foreign capitalism, to further oppress and exploit the people.

11. To initiate at the early a stage as possible the class struggle in the colonies means to awaken the people to the danger of a transplanted European capitalism which, overthrown in Europe, may seek refuge in Asia, and to defeat such an eventuality before its beginning.

(From *M.N. Roy-Philocopher Revolutionary* (ed) Sibanarayan Ray, Ajanta Publications, Delhi, 1995. pp 45-49)

Politics without Power

The very term power-politics suggests that there might be other kinds of politics, that politics need not necessarily be associated with power. But it has come to be taken for granted so widely that few can conceive of the possibility of politics without power. In consequence, politics throughout the world has degenerated into a scramble for power. All realize the dangerous. Consequences of that practice, but doubt whether politics without power is possible.

In the modern world, politics has become associated with parties as the instruments of democratic politics. All politics is practised by parties. Political parties are organized with different programmes, and the system of one party replacing another in the government of a country has come to be considered as the essence of parliamentary democracy. But if democracy is government of the people and by the people, then the party system has led to the result of defeating the object of democratic politics. Because any party government is at best government for the people, the party system contradicts the former two and most essential terms in the definition of democracy. It cannot establish a government of the people and by the people. Today one party rules a country for the people and by the people. Today one party rules a country for the people, and tomorrow another does so also with the same pretention. These is little essential difference between this kind of democratic government and those of pre-democratic times. Indeed, there has never been any system of government which did not claim to rule for the welfare of the people. Absolute monarchies of the past and dictatorships of the present alike have claimed to be the custodians of popular welfare. If government for the people was democratic government, then benevolent despotism should be considered as the highest form of democracy. For these considerations, party governments of our time cannot claim to be essentially different from governments of the pre-democratic age. The only difference is that the people did not elect the kings, whereas today parties are placed in power by popular suffrage. In fact, in the olden days, even kingship was an elective office. But while education for democracy is universally neglected, elections are no guarantee for democracy.

At the close of the Middle Ages in Europe, the revolt against feudal absolutism was inspired by the doctrine that sovereignty belongs to the people. Democratic governments were born of that revolt. Largely from the ancient Stoic tradition, inherited by early Christianity, it was deduced that man was a moral entity and as such naturally sovereign. The belief in the sovereignty of the individual thus was the foundation of modern democratic theory. By way of corollary, it was believed that the people of a particular State, being composed of sovereign individuals, possessed a collective sovereignty. Therefore, it was maintained, a democratic government could alone be the instrument for a fair and just administration of public affairs, because it obtained authority from the sovereign people. That original conception of a democratic government was certainly progressive and liberating. A truly democratic government was to be a good government. But the government was an entity separate and remote from the people, and the gulf has increasingly widened as the functions of government became more complex and centralized in the hands of experts.

In course of time, democratic practice deviated more and more from the principles of democracy. That was not a deliberate fraud on the part of politicians; it resulted from the inability to solve the problem of practicing democracy in large modern States with numerous populations. In the eighteenth century, the advocates of democracy in Europe had in their mind the pattern of direct democracy of the City States of ancient Greece. But it was evident that the entire people of France could not possibly gather in one place and elect their government directly. The solution of the problem was found in the doctrine of representation government, of the delegation of power by the citizens. Thus, from its very birth modern democratic governments in reality came to be governments for the people. Between the government and the electorate there grew a series of intermediary institutions depriving the people of all possibility to control the governments which claimed to rule on their behalf and derived authority from the sovereignty of the people. Governments for the people in reality became rulers of the people. The sovereign was degraded to the position of the ruled. But sovereignty cannot be transferred, because it is an inalienable right. Therefore, a representative government represents only the party which controls it, and the membership even of the largest party is only a small fraction of the people. In other words representative party government ins rule of a minority.

The degeneration of democracy resulted from the inability to devise ways and means for the practice of direct democracy in modern States. To be real, democracy must be direct; government must be under the direct control of the people. Is that possible? That is the problem before the political thinkers of our time. Its solution is to raise political practice above the scramble for power carried on by parties in the name of democracy. In so far as democracy is not government of the people and by the people, it is not democracy. With the rise of the party system, the idea of popular sovereignty became a constitutional fiction. The party system resulted from the difficulty of practicing direct democracy in large modern States with numerous populations. And with the rise of the party system, politics became a scramble for power. So, the possibility of politics without power presupposes elimination of parties from the central position in democratic practice, as is bound to happen in an educated mature Democracy.

Those who identify democracy with the party system overlook the fact that political parties are relatively recent institutions. At the time of the French Revolution, there were no parties as they exist today. Neither the Jacobins nor the Girondists filled the role. In England, there were parties even in the seventeenth century; but they were not political parties as we know them today are a development only of the nineteenth century, when the doctrine of representative government replaced the earlier idea of democracy. Parliamentarism, based on the theory of the delegation of power to elected representatives, made of democracy a mere formality.

It is said that at the time of elections the people can exercise their sovereign right to choose men whom they trust. Given a sufficiently high standard of education on the part of the electorate, that might be the case, provided that parties did not interfere. It is so partially in England even today, because there parliamentarism developed before the rise of the party system. Not until late in the nineteenth century did political parties compete for the suffrage of the people; previously individual candidates who might be associated with this or that party, appealed to their respective constituencies, and the latter voted for individual candidates, not for impersonal party machines. The candidates could not entirely rely upon their party affiliation, but had to win the confidence of the electorate as individuals of proved moral integrity with a clean record of public service.

But under different circumstances, for instance under the system of proportional representation, the people are called upon to vote for this or that party not even knowing the men who would rule on their authority and in their behalf. Even where the system of proportional representation is not introduced, as for instance in Britain, impersonal party machines have eclipsed individual candidates; the choice is between parties. In this situation, practical considerations must prevail. A very good man may belong to a small party; there is little chance of its ever coming to power. Therefore, his chance of being elected is nil.

Under such circumstances, the sovereignty of the individual becomes meaningless; democracy demands that the sovereign individual must merge himself in a party, be a subservient part of an impersonal party machine. In an atmosphere of political backwardness and general ignorance, this system can be abused; people of questionable character can occupy positions of public trust by virtue of belonging to a particular party. A party gives priority and prominence to people not so much for their intellectual merit or moral integrity, but to those who can be of the greatest help for it to capture power. The result is that parties often serve the purpose of promoting the ambition of individuals either thirsting for power for the sake of power or for material gains.

But the people are nowhere in the picture of this scramble for power to which political practice has been debased by the party system. Until now, there has been no case of a party capturing power on behalf of the people, administering it actually under the control of the people. Consequently, under the parliamentary system, we have party dictatorships, and no democratic constitution creates a foolproof guarantee against the rise of such dictatorships. Any majority party can establish a dictatorial regime. The only guarantee is its moral sense. But an impersonal machine can have no sense of morality. Therefore, formal parliamentarism is no guarantee against dictatorship. That curious situation is created by the degeneration of democracy into party politics, into the scramble of parties for power. Contemporary history records cases of dictatorships established democratically in the formalist sense, dictatorships claiming the sanction of parliamentary support. A more than ninety percent majority of the German people voted for Hitler, and in many other countries dictatorial regimes were established constitutionally.

Because of all these defects of formal democracy, efforts have been made to make it more real. But no effort, however earnest and sincere, will bear fruit unless it is borne in mind that an educated electorate is the precondition for democracy, education not in the technical sense, but a sufficiently high general cultural level, so that the people can think for themselves, cannot be swayed by demagogic appeals to emotions, and therefore are capable of exercising their intelligent judgment. In a country where this precondition exists at least to some extent, democracy may have a chance; but even there it is destroyed by the party system, which thrives best in the atmosphere of cultural backwardness and popular ignorance.

Parties are organized according to certain political doctrines with the object of introducing specified social measures, revolutionary or otherwise, which would be good for the people. It is further believed that a party must be a office, that is to say, control the government of a country, in order to put its programme into practice. The immediate object of any political party, therefore, is to capture power, which need not necessarily involve acts of violence. Expressions like capture of power or seizure of power are used by revolutionary parties. But parties advocating constitutional methods or non-violence also want to be in office, which is only a less violent expression of the same purpose. That is how the parliamentary party system becomes a scramble for power. All brands of politics as practised today are party-politics. If party-politics is bad, politics itself is bad. It is easy to see how this system is bound to lead to demoralization.

A group of people may have very good ideas and be quite honest in their desire to do certain things for the people. But they are convinced that without power they can do nothing. Therefore, if they are serious about doing those things, they must do everything to come to power. All other parties are exactly in the same position. All try to get the greater number of votes; the usual method is to lure voters by promises. Caught in the whirlpool, even the most honest politician loses his sense of proportion and makes promises which he knows cannot be fulfilled. Thus democracy degenerates into demagogy.

Under these circumstances, associated with the party system, politicians cannot appeal to the intelligent judgment of the people.

The necessary predisposition for the people to be carried away by platform speeches and press campaigns is created by inflaming emotions and inciting passions. False or imaginary issues are raised to cloud the judgment of the people, to create mass hysteria. Whichever party possesses greater skill in election manoeuvres and the means to maintain the largest party machinery and organs of propaganda, has the greatest chance of winning elections and capturing power. In the hysterical atmosphere created by election campaigns, even otherwise intelligent citizens are swayed to vote in a way which they would not do if they were allowed to think rationally. Therefore, to confuse, deceive and mislead the sovereign people, is a necessity of the party system; the practice may vary in degrees, but is essentially the same everywhere. The practice being palpably immoral, and party politics having to rely on it to succeed, it can never be purified. There must be other forms of politics to decide any genuine issues and principles which parties represent.

Once it is assumed that nothing can be done for the good of the society without political power, the evils of the party system necessarily follow. The control of government being the precondition for going anything, everything must be done to gain power. The means become the end and the end is forgotten. It is remembered only to advance the questionable doctrine that it justifies the means. Politics is divorced from morality. If one is not interested in power, he is supposed to be not concerned with politics, indifferent to social problems.

Notwithstanding the fact that in some countries a considerable measure of social reform was carried out under the parliamentary system, the other side of the picture must not be overlooked. Diffusion of power is the essence of democracy, because concentration of power leads to tyranny and dictatorship, which may be hidden behind a façade of empty formalities. The electorate delegates its sovereign power to a party; only a few members of the party go to the Parliament; there they are subject to party discipline, are whipped into the party lobby. Fewer still actually compose the government and wield power. It is not inconceivable that only men of good faith and honest intention may come to the actual seats of power. But that means no more than that, at best, parliamentary democracy can be a benevolent despotism, which constitutionally restricts liberty and regiments economic life to establish a welfare state.

But for other reasons also the best of men are corrupted by the party system. The period of office is limited. As within a few years non can bring heaven on earth, the first concern of politicians in power is to have a second, a third and more terms in power. The most skilful and resourceful party may be perpetually in power. The approximation to that ideal of the party system is attained by winning the next elections; and to do so, greater demagogy is practised. Even if they have failed to do what they promised at the time of a previous election, party politicians must say that they have succeeded, prove black to be white. When the electorate cannot be deceived by all too obvious facts, the argument is that the time was too short to do much; therefore, some more time must be given. Any party which would honestly admit that they advocated a wrong programme, and appeal to the electorate for another chance to rectify its mistakes, would have no chance to win an election. To compete with demagogues in a system which puts a premium on dishonesty, a politician must come down to this level if he wants to succeed. Thus, practically nobody engaged in politics as it is practised today, can remain entirely untouched by its corrupt atmosphere. The "sea-green incorruptible" have always been affection; personalities are built up by propaganda. Robespierre was an upright man, stern, ascetic, completely dedicated to a cause, yet, this virtue turned out to be the pretext for abominable vices.

But politics is a social necessity. Society cannot do without a political organization, that is to say, there must be a State. Government must be carried on. The question, therefore, is whether a different practice of politics is possible. In other words, can politics be raised above the scramble for power? This question cannot be answered within the limits of the usual political discussion. A new politics presupposes a new social philosophy; and the problem of human nature is the basic problem of social philosophy. We shall have to go still further. If we want to free politics from its present evils, we must reexamine our philosophy of life. The old social and political philosophies, conservative, liberal, socialist or communist, are all frankly, or in effect, collectivist. In them, the individual does not count for anything. Some give him the freedom to vote occasionally, but prevent him to do so intelligently. Others declare that the individual becomes free by losing himself in the masses. Those of the first category, in spite of their formal profession of individualism, place institutions above men. But society is not an abstract thing. It is the sum total of the men and women composing it.

So long as individuals cannot judge and discriminate and decide what is right and wrong, there cannot be a good society. Disgust with power politics will produce no result unless it compels us to remember the fundamental principles of democracy, the sovereignty and dignity of the individual, in the light of modern scientific knowledge.

Power can be divorced from political associations and defined as the ability to do things. Thus conceived, it is precisely man's power which can make a better job of human society. But the usefulness of power is eclipsed and leads to abuses when it is concentrated to such an extent that the community as a whole becomes totally powerless. When that happens, the most powerful State may have the most powerless citizens. Power being associated with the function of the State, some political theoreticians of recent times have defined the State as an organ of coercion, an instrument created by a certain class or section of society with the purpose of exercising its domination over the rest. The corollary to this definition is that a just and fair social order is impossible so long as the State exists. Therefore, thinking out their thoughts consistently, these political theorists came to the conclusion that in an ideal society the State would wither away. The anarchist denial of the very necessity of the State is only an exaggerated version of what may be called the communist utopia.

(From *Politics, Power and Parties,* M.N. Roy, Ajanta Publications, Delhi, 1999. pp 65-78)

14

Jawaharlal Nehru

Life and Times

Jawaharlal Nehru (1889-1964) was one of the greatest figures of modern India, an outstanding statesman whose services to the cause of human freedom are unforgettable. As a fighter for freedom he was illustrious, as a maker of modern India his services were unparalleled. His life and work have had a profound influence on our psyche, social structure and intellectual development. It will be difficult to reconcile ourselves to the image of India without Nehru's creatively active and all pervasive leadership.

As a man Nehru combined a fine sensitivity of mind, a rare delicacy of feeling, with large and generous impulses. Though nurtured in a life of sheltered ease and comfort, he drew himself into the national struggle and became a great leader second only to Gandhi. To the weak and the frustrated his heart went out in profound sympathy. He was an author of distinction. His autobiography, which tells the story of his life and struggle without a touch of self-pity or moral superiority, is one of the most remarkable books of our time.

Nehru held the office of the prime minister of our country ever since the dawn of independence; and in the long years of his premiership tried to put our country on a progressive, scientific, democratic and secular foundation. His steadfast loyalty to certain fundamental principles of democracy, freedom socialism and secularism gave direction to our thought and life. He used the existing social and political institutions and breathed into them a new spirit, a new vitality.

Nehru by his series of public utterance educated our people to an appreciation of the values he had cherished. His fought for a high level of human life and burnt his ideals into the uderstanding of the common people. By his own powerful and vibrant voice, which we will not hear anymore, he created, moulded, insprired and kindled a whole generation of Indians to a loyalty to the first principles which he held so ear.

The story goes, in January 1889, Motilal Nehru, a twenty-seven-year-old lawyer from Allahabad, in UP, travelled to Rishilkesh, a town holy to Hindus, up in the foothills of the Himalayas on the banks of the sacred river the Ganga to seek the blssing of a yogi to have a child. Motilal was facing down by personal tragedy. Married as a teenager, in keeping with custom, he had soon been widowed, losing both his wife and his first-born son in childbirth. In due course he had married again, an exquisitely beautiful woman named Swarup Rani Kaul. She soon blessed him with another son—but the boy died in infancy. Motilal's own brother, Nandlal Nehru, then died at the age of forty two, leaving Motilal the care of his widow and seven children. The burden was one he was prepared to bear, but he desperately sought the compensatory joy of a son. It seemed destinyy would not smile on him. Motilal with his two young Brəhmin companions, visited a famous yogi renowned for the austerities to seek his blessings. As the story goes ten months later, at 1.30 p.m. on 14 November 1889, Motilal Nehru's wife Swarup Rani gave birth to a healthy baby boy. He was named Jawaharlal and he would grow up to be one of the most remarkable men of the twentieth century.

The young Jawaharlal Nehru's mind was shaped by two sets of parental influences that he never saw as contradictory-the traditional Hinduism of his mother and the other womenfolk of the Nehru household and the modernist, secular cosmopolitanism of his father.

The Nehrus were Kashmir pundits, scions of a community of Brahmins from the northernmost reaches of the subcontinent who had made new lives for themselves across northern and central India since at least the 1700s. Kashmiris had been largely converted to Islam in the sixteenth and seventeenth centuries, but Kashmir Muslims followed a syncretic version of the faith, imbued with the gentle mysticism of Sufi preachers, and co-existed in harmony with their Hindu neighbours. Though the pundits left Kashmir in significant numbers, they did so not as refugees fleeing muslim depredation, but as educated and professionally skilled migrants in quest of better opportunities. It was no accident, for instance, that Motilal 's chief household retainer was a Muslim , Munshi Mubarak Ali. Jawaharlal learned a great deal from him.

The family's original name was Kaul. Jawaharlal Nehru's ancestor, Raj Kaul, settled in Mughal Delhi in the eighteenth century and, perhaps because there were other Kauls of prominence in the city, assumed the hyphenated name of Kaul-Nehru, the sufix indicating the family's residence on the edge of a canal, or nehar. The Kaul-Nehrus moved to Agra in the mid-nineteenth century, where the compound form soon disappeared. It was simply as a Nehru that Motilal made his name at the Allahabad Bar.

Along with the name and the money that came with his success as a lawyer, Motilal acquired the trappings of a Victorian-gentleman of means, an elegant house 'Anand Bhavan', in a desirable residential area, with mostly British neighbours; a lancy carriage; a .stable of Arabian steeds; and a wardrobe full of English suits, many tailored in Savile Row. Jawaharlal grew up surrounded by every imaginable comfort. Not only did he have electricity and running water in the house but the family home was equipped with such unusual perquisites as a private swimming pool and a tennis court. Motilal ordered the latest toys for him from England, including the newly-invented tricycle and bicycle. Motilal himself owned Allahabad's first car, imported in 1904. Jawaharlal enjoyed lavish birthday parties, holidays in Kashmir, a plenitude of clothes.

Nehru embodied the Westernization in his early upbringing; he had two British governesses at home, and from 1901 to 1904 a private tutor, the Irish-French Ferdinand T. Brooks.

Motilal a free-thinking rationalist, saw in Western science and English reasoning, rather than in Hindu religion or ritual, the real hope of progress for India. Inevitably, when Jawaharlal was just fifteen, his father enrolled him at the prestigious British public school, Harrow. By an intriguing coincidence, some fifteen years earlier the school had educated young man called Winston Churchill, who was already embarking upon a prodigious career in British public life. 'India,' Winston Churchill once remarked, 'is not a country or a nation. It is merely a geographical expression.' But ironically, it was Churchill's view of India that would one day make Jawaharlal Nehru's 'invention ol India' necessary.

The radical streak in Jawaharlal Nehru began to show from the moment of his arrival in England. The news of the Japanese naval triumph over Russia at Tsushima in 1905 thrilled him with the realization that a great European power could be defeated by an Asian nation. A later visit to Ireland also revealed to Jawaharlal the force ol nationalist agitation, with the Sinn Fein movement and Irish calls for a boycott of British goods reinforcing his extremist sympathies. He also read widely, developing a great admiration for the works of George Bernard Shaw, and finding in the books of some British writers of the period, notably William Morris and Meredith Townsend, persuasive arguments against both capitalism and imperialism that seemed to predict the inevitable decline of the British Raj in India. In October 1907, Jawaharlal Nehru entered Trinity College, Cambridge, and graduated with a mediocre second class degree. Though in later years he was to be identified with the Fabian Socialism that had already begun to flourish in Cambridge intellectual circles, there is no evidence of his having had anything to do with the Fabian Society at the university.

On his return to India in 1912, he started practising Law at the United Province High Court. But gave it up as he found it very uninteresting. He had by this time developed a keen interest in Indian nationalism and the movement for its independence. For the first time he met Gandhiji at the Lucknow Session of Indian National Congress in 1916. His initial impression of Gandhiji was not positive. He appeared to be very distant and different and impolitical. However, his impression about Gandhiji changed for the better as he came in close contact with him. He realised that Gandhiji had mass appeal, and that his non-violent, non-cooperation movement was the best method of fighting for independence.

In quick succession Nehru assumed leadership positions not only in the Indian National Congress, but also in different other organisations and movements. Nehru's political career took a decisive turn in December 1929 when he was elected as the President of the Indian National Congress. He was then just forty. Under his presidentship the Congress adopted the famous Independence Resolution on the bank of the river Ravi at Lahore on 31st December 1929. He declared 26 January 1930 as the Independence Day—'it is the inalienable right of the Indian people as of any other people to have freedom and to enjoy the fruits of their toil and have the necessities of life.' A section of Congress was prepared to accept the 'Dominion Status' for India. But Nehru, opposing this demand, demanded 'Purna Swaraj' or complete independence for India.

At the call of Gandhiji the Civil Disobedience Movement started with the launching of the Dandi March on 12 March 1930. Nehru was arrested in April 1930 and kept in jail until January 1931. In February 1934 Nehru was arrested and put in Alipur Jail. But he was then conditionally released on the ground of the serious illness of his wife, Kamala Nehru. Kamala, only thirty-seven, died in Switzerland on 28 February 1936. To add to his emotional shock, his mother died a few years later.

For many years, his writing, quite literally, kept him from losing his mind. This was during his various imprisonments as an agitator for Indian freedom. His autobiography came out of prison. He did a work on history, *The Discovery of India*. Of all his prison writings, however, perhaps none is more remarkable than the collection of letters to his daughter Indira, later published under the title *Glimpses of World History*.

In 1936 Nehru was elected as the Congress President for the second time. He then placed more emphasis on socialism as the key to the solution of the problems of India as well as the world. In

1937 he was elected as the President of Indian National Congress for the third time. Under his leadership, the Congress participated in provincial assembly elections and secured majority in seven states. In 1938 he visited Spain, Britain and Czechoslovakia, and in 1939 he paid a visit to China. He returned to India after the outbreak of the Second World War in 1939. On his return to India, he was arrested in 1940. During his trial in the court, he told the English Judge, 'Though I am standing before you on my trial, it is the British Empire itself that is on its trial before the bar of the world.'

It was not easy for the Indian National Congress to decide upon its response to the Second World War. Nehru, very much critical of Fascism and Nazism, was not in favour of taking any steps which might hinder or undermine the war efforts of Allied Powers against the Axis Powers. Britain was a leading Allied Power. But it was also the colonial ruler of India. Nehru was ready to support Britain's war efforts if it clarified its policy towards India and other colonies after the war was over. But London was not prepared to do that. It just wanted to buy time by making vague statements. This annoyed and disappointed Gandhiji who spearheaded the individual satyagraha. Nehru was arrested and kept in jail till December 1941. At the AICC session in January 1942, Gandhiji declared Nehru as his successor.

Nehru was re-elected as the President of Congress in August 1946. On invitation by Lord Wavel, he headed the Interim Government in August 1946. This government stayed in power till the partition in August 1947. In August 1947, the British government partitioned India into India and Pakistan. Pakistan was created on the basis of Jinnah's 'Two Nation Theory.' Though the Congress strongly opposed the partition, it finally accepted it. While greeting India's independence, Nehru said: "Long years ago, we made a tryst with destiny and now time comes when we shall redeem our pledge, not wholly or in full measure, but substantially. At the stroke of the midnight hour, when the world sleeps, India will awake to life and freedom. A moment comes which comes but rarely in history, when we step out from the old to the new, when an age ends and when the soul of a nation, long suppressed, finds utterance."

As the first Prime Minister of independent India, he shouldered the responsibility of leading a poor and backward country with a large number of serious problems and challenges. In the aftermath of the partition, communal violence led to death of many. The government had to grapple with the demand for reorganisation of states mainly on the basis of language. From time to time caste conflicts threatened the social fabric. Poverty was huge, and inequality was deeply entrenched.

In addition to these internal problems, the new nation was dragged into a war as a result of invasion of Kashmir by Pakistan. After the accession of Jammu and Kashmir to India, the government of India sent its troops to Kashmir to counter Pakistani aggression. As a result of UN mediation, a ceasefire was enforced in early 1948, but by that time one third of the state had come under Pakistani occupation. Kashmir remained a serious security issue for the Nehru government. The Chinese aggression in 1962 was a severe blow to the Nehru government. It was considered a personal failure of Nehru who considered China a close friend. He did not live long to recover from this shock.

Nehru was now seventy-four years old. By 1964 the signs of mortality were impossible to ignore. He was visibly ailing; the puffy face, the sunken eyes, the shuffling gait were of a man in irreversible decline. His visits to Parliament were, in the words of a senior opposition member, those of "an old man, looking frail and fatigued with a marked stoop in his gait and slow, faltering steps, clutching the backrests of benches for support as he descended." He suffered a cerebral stroke at the annual Congress session in January at Bhubaneswar and missed most of it, but within days was back in New Delhi trying to manage his usual routine. Work was his lifeblood. Jawaharlal Nehru passed away in his sleep after a massive aortic rupture. On his bedside table were found, jotted down in his own hand, the immortal lines from Robert Frost's 'Stopping By Woods on a Snowy Evening'.

The nation was plunged into mourning; tributes poured in from around the world. An earthquake rocked the capital on the day of his death, a portentous omen to some. Cynics waited for the survivors to fight over the spoils; many predicted India's inevitable disintegration. But Jawaharlal had prepared his people well, instilling in them the habits of democracy, a respect for parliamentary procedure, and faith in the constitutional system. There were no succession squabbles. Lal Bahadur Shastri, a modest figure of unimpeachable integrity and considerable political and administrative acumen, was elected India's second Prime Minister. The country wept, and moved on.

Nationalism and Internationalism

My reaction to India thus was often an emotional one, conditioned and limited in many ways. It took the form of nationalism. In the case of many people the conditioning and limiting factors are absent. But nationalism was and is inevitable in the India of my day; it is a natural and healthy growth. For any subject country national freedom must be the first and dominant urge; for India, with her intense sense of individuality and a past heritage, it was doubly so.

Recent events all over the world have demonstrated that the notion that nationalism is fading away before the impact of internationalism and proletarian movements has little truth. It is still one of the most powerful urges that move a people, and round it cluster sentiments and traditions and a sense of common living and common purpose. While the intellectual strata of the middle classes were gradually moving away from nationalism, or so they thought, labour and proletarian movements, deliberately based on internationalism, were drifting towards nationalism. The coming of war swept everybody everywhere into the net of nationalism. This remarkable resurgence of nationalism, or rather a re-discovery of it and a new realization of its vital significance, has raised new problems and altered the form and shape of old problems. Old established traditions cannot be easily scrapped or dispensed with; in movement of crisis they rise and dominate the minds of men, and often, as we have seen a deliberate attempt is made to use those traditions to rouse a people to a high pitch of effort and sacrifice. Traditions have to be accepted to a large extent and adapted and transformed to meet new conditions and ways of thought, and at the same time new traditions have to be built up. The nationalist ideal is deep and strong; it is not a thing of the past with no future significance. But other ideals, more based on the ineluctable facts of today, have arisen, the international ideal and the proletarian ideal, and there must be some kind of fusion between these various ideals if we are to have a world equilibrium and a lessening of conflict. The abiding appeal of nationalism to he spirit of man has to be recognized and provided for, but its sway limited to a narrower sphere.

If nationalism is still so universal in its influence, even in countries powerfully affected by new ideas and international forces, how much more must it dominate the mind of India? Sometimes we are told that our nationalism is a sign of our backwardness and even our demand for independence indicates our narrow-mindedness. Those who tell us so seem to imagine that true internationalism would triumph if we agreed to remain as junior partners in the British Empire of Commonwealth of Nations. They do not appear to realize that this particular type of so-called internationalism is only an extension of a narrow British nationalism, which could not have appealed to us even if the logical consequences of Anglo-Indian history had not utterly rooted out its possibility from our minds. Nevertheless, India, for all her intense nationalistic fervour, has gone further than many nations in her acceptance of real internationalism and the co-ordination, and even to some extent the subordination of the independent nation state to a world organization.

The search for the sources of India's strength and for her deterioration and decay is long and intricate. Yet the recent causes of that decay are obvious enough. She fell behind in the march of technique, and Europe, which had long been backward in many matters, took the lead in technical progress. Behind this technical progress was the spirit of science and a bubling life and spirit which displayed itself in many activities and in adventurous voyages of discovery. New techniques gave military strength to the countries of Western Europe, and it was easy for them to spread out and dominate the East. Tat is the story not only of India, but of almost the whole of Asia.

Why this should have happened so is more difficult to unravel, for India was not lacking in mental alertness and technical skill in earlier times. One senses a progressive deterioration during centuries. The urge to life and endeavour becomes less, the creative spirit fades away and gives place to the imitative. Where triumphant and rebellious thought had tried to pierce the mysteries of nature and the universe, the wordy commentator comes with his glosses and long explanations. Magnificent art and sculpture give way to meticulous carving of intricate detail without nobility of conception or design. The vigour and richness of language, powerful yet simple, are followed by highly ornate and complex literary forms. The urge to adventure and the overflowing life which led to vast schemes of distant colonization and the transplantation of Indian culture in far lands: all these fade away and a narrow orthodoxy taboos even the crossing of the high seas. A rational spirit of inquiry, so evident in earlier times, which might well have led to the further growth of science, is replaced by irrationalism and a blind idolatry of the past. Indian life becomes a sluggish stream, living in the past, moving slowly through the accumulations of dead centuries. The heavy burden of the past crushes it and a kind of coma seizes it. It is not surprising that in this condition of mental stupor and physical weariness India should have deteriorated and remained rigid and immobile, while other parts of the world marched ahead.

Yet this is not a complete or wholly correct survey. If there had only been a long and unrelieved period of rigidity and stagnation, this might well have resulted in a complete break with the past, the death of an era, and the erection of something new on its ruins. There has not been such a break and there is a definite continuity. Also, from time to time, vivid periods of renascence have occurred, and some of them have been long and brilliant. Always there is visible an attempt to understand and adapt the new and harmonize it with the old, or at any rate with parts of the old which were considered worth preserving. Often that old retains an external form only, as a kind of symbol, and changes its inner content. But something vital and living continues, some urge driving the people in a direction not wholly realized, and always a desire for synthesis between the old and the new. It was this urge and desire that kept them going and enabled them to absorb new ideas while retaining much of the old. Whether there was such a thing as an Indian dream through the ages, vivid and full of life or sometimes reduced to the murmurings of troubled sleep. I do not know. Every people and every nation has some such belief or myth of national destiny and perhaps it is partly true in each case. Being an Indian I am myself influenced by this reality or myth about India, and I feel that anything that had the power to mould hundreds of generations, without a break, must have drawn its enduring vitality from some deep well of strength, and have had the capacity to renew that vitality from age to age.

Was there some such well of strength? And if so, did it dry up, or did it have hidden springs to replenish it? What of today? Are there any springs still functioning from which we can refresh and strengthen ourselves? We are an old race, or rather an odd mixture of many races, and our racial memories go back to the dawn of history. Have we had our day and are we now living in the late afternoon or evening of our existence, just carrying on after the manner of the aged, quiescent, devitalized, uncreative, desiring peace and sleep above all else?

No people, no races remain unchanged. Continually they are mixing with others and slowly changing; they may appear to die almost and then rise again as a new people or just a variation of the old. There may be a definite break between the old people and the new, or vital links of thought and ideals may join them.

History has numerous instances of old and well-established civilizations fading away or being ended suddenly, and vigorous new cultures taking their place. Is it some vital energy, some inner source of strength that gives life to a civilization or a people, without which all effort is ineffective, like the vain attempt of an aged person to play the part of a youth?

Among the peoples of the world today I have sensed this vital energy chiefly in three – Americans, Russians, and the Chinese; a queer combination! Americans, is spite of having their roots in the old world, are a new people, uninhibited and without the burdens and complexes of old races, and it is easy to understand their abounding vitality. So also are the Canadians, Australians, and New Zealanders, all of them largely cut off from the old world and facing life in all its newness.

Russians are not a new people, and yet there has been a complete break from the old, like that of death, and they have been reincarnated anew, in a manner for which there is no example in history. They have become youthful again with an energy and vitality that are amazing. They are searching for some of their old roots again, but for all practical purposes they are a new people, a new race and a new civilization.

The Russian example shows how a people can revitalize itself, become youthful again, if it is prepared to pay the price for it, and tap the springs of suppressed strength and energy among the masses. Perhaps this war, with all its horror and frightfulness, might result in the rejuvenation of other peoples also, such as survive from the holocaust.

The Chinese stand apart from all these. They are not a new race, nor have they gone through that shock of change, from top to bottom, which came to Russia. Undoubtedly, seven years of cruel was has changed them, as it must. How far this change is due to the war or to more abiding causes, or whether it is a mixture of the two, I do not know, but the vitality of the Chinese people astonishes me. I cannot imagine a people endowed with such bed-rock strength going under.

Something of that vitality which I saw in China I have sensed at times in the Indian people also. Not always, and anyway it is difficult for me to take an objective view. Perhaps my wishes distort my thinking. But always I was in search for this in my wanderings among the Indian people. If they had this vitality, then it was well with them and they would make good. If they lacked it completely, then our political efforts and shouting were all mark believe and would not carry us far. I was not interested in making some political arrangement which would enable our people to carry on more or less as before, only a little better. I felt they has vast stories of suppressed energy and ability, and I wanted to release these and make them fell young and vital again. India, constituted as she is, cannot play a secondary part in the world. She will either count for a great deal or not count at all. No middle position attracted me. Nor did I think any intermediate position feasible.

Behind the past quarter of a century's struggle for India's independence and all our conflicts with British authority, lay in my mind, and that of many others, the desire to revitalize India. We felt that through action and self-imposed suffering and sacrifice, through voluntarily facing risk and danger, through refusal to submit to what we considered evil and wrong, would we recharge the battery of India's spirit and waken her from her long slumber. Though we came into conflict continually with the British Government in India, our eyes were always turned towards our own people. Political advantage had value only in so far as it helped in that fundamental purpose of ours. Because of this governing motive, frequently we acted as no politician, moving in the narrow sphere of politics only, would have done, and foreign and Indian critics expressed surprise at the folly and intransigence of our way. Whether we were foolish or not, the historians of the future will judge. We aimed high and looked far. Probably we were often foolish, from the point of view of opportunist politics, but at no time did we forget that our main purpose was to raise the whole level of the Indian people, psychologically and spiritually and also, of course, politically and economically. It was the building up of that real inner strength of the people that we were after, knowing that the rest would inevitably follow. We had no wipe out some generations of shameful subservience and timid submission to an arrogant alien authority.

The Idea of India

Though books and old monuments and past cultural achievements helped to produce some understanding of India, they did not satisfy me or give me the answer I was looking for. Nor could they; for they dealt with a past age, and I wanted to know if there was any real connection between that past and the present. The present for me, and for many others like me, was an odd mixture of medievalism, appalling poverty and misery and a somewhat superficial modernism of the middle classes. I was not an admirer of my own class or kind, and yet inevitably I looked to it for leadership in the struggle for India's salvation; that middle class felt caged and circumscribed and wanted to grow and develop itself. Unable to do so within the framework of British rule, a spirit of revolt grew against this rule, and yet this spirit was not directed against the structure that crushed us. It sought to retain it and control it by displacing the British. These middle classes were too much the product of that structure to challenge it and seek to uproot it.

New forces arose that drove us to the masses in the villages, and for the first time, a new and different India rose up before the young intellectuals who had almost forgotten its existence or attached little importance to it. It was a disturbing sight, not only because of its stark misery and the magnitude of its problems, but because it began to upset some of our values and conclusions. So began for us the discovery of India as it was, and it produced both understanding and conflict within us. Our reactions varied and depended on our previous environment and experience. Some were already sufficiently acquainted with these village masses not to experience any new sensation; they took them for granted. But for me it was a real voyage of discovery, and, while I was always painfully conscious of the failings and weaknesses of my people, I found in India's country folk something, difficult to define, which attracted me. That something I had missed in our middle classes.

I do not idealise the conception of the masses and, as far as possible, I try to avoid thinking of them as a theoretical abstraction. The people of India are very real to me in their great variety and, in spite of their vast numbers, I try to think of them as individuals rather than as vague groups. Perhaps it was because I did not expect much from them that I was not disappointed; I found more than I had expected. It struck me that perhaps the reason for this, and for a certain stability and potential strength that they possessed, was the old Indian cultural tradition which was still retained by them in a small measure. Much had gone in the battering they had received during the past 200 years. Yet something remained that was worth while, and with it so much that was worthless and evil.

During the twenties my work was largely confined to my own province and I traveled extensively and intensively through the towns and villages of the forty-eight districts of the United Provinces of Agra and Oudh, that heart of Hindustan as it has so long been considered, the seat and centre of both ancient and medieval civilization, the melting pot of so many races and cultures, the area where the great revolt of 1857 blazed up and was later ruthlessly crushed. I grew to know the sturdy Jat of the northern and western districts, that typical son of the soil, brave and independent looking, relatively more prosperous; the Rajput peasant and petty landholder, still proud of his race and ancestry, even though he might have changed his faith and adopted Islam; the deft and skilful artisans and cottage workers, both Hindu and Moslem; the poorer peasantry and tenants in their vast numbers, especially in Oudh and the eastern districts, crushed and ground down by generations of oppression and poverty, hardly daring to hope that a change would come to better their lot, and yet hoping and full of faith.

During the thirties, in the intervals of my life out of prison, and especially during the election campaign of 1936-37, I traveled more extensively throughout India, in towns and cities and villages alike. Except for rural Bengal, which unhappily I have only rarely visited, I toured in every province and went deep into villages. I spoke of political and economic issues and judging from my speech I was full of politics and elections. But all this while, in a corner of my mind, lay something deeper and more vivid, and elections or the other excitements of the passing day meant little to it. Another and a major excitement had seized me, and I was again on a great voyage of discovery and the land of India and the people of India lay spread out before me. India with all her infinite charm and variety began to grow upon me more and more, and yet the more I saw of her, the more I realized how very difficult it was for me or for anyone else to grasp the ideas she had embodied. It was not her wide spaces that eluded me, or even her diversity, but some depth of soul which I could not fathom, though I had occasional and tantalizing glimpses of it. She was like some ancient palimpsest on which layer upon layer of thought and reverie had been inscribed, and yet no succeeding layer had completely hidden or erased what had been written previously. All of these existed in our conscious or subconscious selves, though we may not have been aware of them, and they had gone to build up the complex and mysterious personality of India. That sphinx like face with its elusive and sometimes mocking smile was to be seen throughout the length and breadth of the land. Though outwardly there was diversity and infinite variety among our people, everywhere there was that tremendous impress of oneness, which had held all of us together for ages past, whatever political fate or misfortune had befallen us. The unity of India was no longer merely an intellectual conception for me: it was an emotional experience which overpowered me. That essential unity had been so powerful that no political division, no disaster or catastrophe, had been able to overcome it.

It was absurd, of course, to think of India or any country as a kind of anthropomorphic entity. I did not do so. I was also fully aware of the diversities and divisions of Indian life, of classes, castes, religions, races, different degrees of cultural development. Yet I think that a country with a long cultural background and a common outlook on life develops a spirit that is peculiar to it and that is impressed on all its children, however much they may that is impressed on all its children, however much they may differ among themselves. Can anyone fail to see this in China, whether he meets an old-fashioned mandarin or a Communist who has apparently broken with the past? It was this spirit of India that I was after, not through idle curiosity, though I was curious enough, but because I felt that it might give me some key to the understanding of my country and people, some guidance to thought and action. Politics and elections were day to day affairs when we grew excited over trumpery matters. But if we were going to build the house of India's future, strong and secure and beautiful, we would have to dig deep for the foundations.

Often, as a wandered from meeting to meeting, I spoke to my audience of this India of ours, of Hindustan and of *Bharata*, the old Sanskrit name derived from the mythical founder of the race. I seldom did so in the cities, for there the audiences were more sophisticated and wanted stronger fare. But to the peasant, with his limited outlook, I spoke of this great country for whose freedom we were struggling, of how each part differed from the other and yet was India, of common problems of the peasants from north to south and east to west, of the *Swaraj* that could only be for all and every part and not for some. I told them of my journeying from the Khyber Pass in the far north-west to *Kanya Kumari* or Cape Comorian in the distant south, and how everywhere the peasants put me identical questions, for their troubles were the same – poverty, debt, vested interests, landlords, moneylenders, heavy rents and taxes, police harassment, and all these wrapped up in the structure that the foreign government had imposed upon us – and relief must also come for all. I tried to make them think of India as a whole, and even to some little extent of this wide world of which we were a part. I brought in the struggle in China, in Spain, in Abyssinia, in Central Europe, in Egypt and the countries of Western Asia. I told them of the wonderful changes in the Soviet Union and of the great progress made in America. The task was not easy; yet it was not so difficult as I had imagined, for our ancient epics and myths and legends, which they knew so well, had made them familiar with the conception of their country, and some there were always who had traveled far and wide to the great places of pilgrimage situated at the four corners of India. Or there were old soldiers who had served in foreign parts in World War I or other expeditions. Even my references to foreign countries were brought home to them by the consequences of the great depression of the 'thirties.

Sometimes as I reached a gathering, a great roar of welcome would greet me: *Bharat Mata ki Jai* – 'Victory to Mother India.' I would ask them unexpectedly what they meant by that cry, who was this *Bharat Mata,* Mother India, whose victory they wanted? My question would amuse them and surprise them, and then, not knowing exactly what to answer, they would look at each other and at me. I persisted in my questioning. At last a vigorous Jat, wedded to the soil from immemorial generations, would say that it was the *dharti,* the good earth of India, that they meant. What earth? Their particular village patch, or all the patches in the district or province, or in the whole of India? And so question and answer went on, till they would ask me impatiently to tell them all about it. I would endeavour to do so and explain that India was all this that they had thought, but it was much more. The mountains and the rivers of India, and the forests and the broad fields, which gave us food, were all dear to us, but what counted ultimately were the people of India, people like them and me, who were spread out all over this vast land. *Bharat Mata,* Mother India, was essentially these millions of people, and victory to her meant victory to these people. You are parts of this *Bharat Mata,* I told them, you are in a manner yourselves *Bharat Mata,* and as this idea slowly soaked into their brains, their eyes would light up as if they had made a great discovery.

The diversity of India is obvious; it lies on the surface and anybody can see it. It concerns itself with physical appearances as well as with certain mental habits and traits. There is little in common, to outward seeming, between the Pathan of the North-West and the Tamil in the far South. Their racial stocks are not the same, though there may be common strands running through them; they differ in face and figure, food and clothing, and, of course, language. In the North-Western Frontier Province there is already the breath of Central Asia, and many a custom there, as in Kashmir, reminds one of the countries on the other side of the Himalayas. Pathan popular dances are singularly like Russian Cossack dancing. Yet, with all these differences, there is no mistaking the impress of India on the Pathan, as this is obvious on the Tamil. This is not surprising, for these border lands, and indeed Afghanistan also, were united with India for thousands of years. The old Turkish and other races who inhabited Afghanistan and parts of Central Asia before the advent of Islam were largely Buddhists, and earlier still, during the period of the Epics, Hindus. The frontier area was one of the principal centres of old Indian culture and it abounds still with ruins of monuments and monasteries and, especially, of the great university of Taxila, which was at the height of its fame two thousand years ago, attracting students from all over India as well as different parts of Asia. Changes of religion made a difference, but could not change entirely the mental backgrounds which the people of those areas had developed.

The Pathan and the Tamil are two extreme examples; the others lie somewhere in between. All of them have their distinctive feature, all of them have still more the distinguishing mark of India. It is fascinating to find how the Bengalis, the Marathas, the Gujratis, the Tamils, the Andhras, the Oriyas, the Assamese, the Canarese, the Malayalis, the Sindhis, the Punjabis, and the Pathans, the Kashmiris, the Rajputs, and the great central block comprising the Hindustani – speaking people, have retained their peculiar characteristics for hundred of years, have still more or less the same virtues and failings of which old tradition or record tells us, and yet have been throughout these ages distinctively Indian, which the same national heritage and the same set of moral and mental qualities. There was something living and dynamic about this heritage which showed itself in ways of living and a philosophical attitude to life and its problems. Ancient India, like ancient China, was a world in itself, a culture and a civilization which gave shape to all things. Foreign influences poured in and often influenced that culture and were absorbed. Disruptive tendencies gave rise immediately to an attempt to find a synthesis. Some kind of a dream of unity has occupied the mind of India since the dawn of civilization. That unity was not conceived as something imposed from outside, a standardization of externals or even of beliefs. It was something deeper and, within its fold, the widest tolerance of belief and custom was practised and every variety acknowledged and even encouraged.

Differences, big or small, can always be noticed even within a national group, however closely bound together it may be. The essential unity of that group becomes apparent when it is compared to another national group, though often the differences between two adjoining groups fade out or intermingle near the frontiers, and modern developments are tending to produce a certain uniformity everywhere. In ancient and mediaeval times, the idea of the modern nation was non-existent, and feudal, religious, racial, or cultural bonds had more importance. Yet I think that at almost anytime in recorded history an Indian would have felt more or less at home in any part of India, and would have felt as a stranger and alien in any other country. He would certainly have felt less of a stranger in countries which had partly adopted his culture or religion. Those who professed a religion of non-Indian origin or, coming to India, settled down there, became distinctively Indian in the course of a few generations, such as Christians, Jews, Parsees, Moslems. Indians converts to some of these religions never ceased to be Indians on account of a change of their faith. They were looked upon in other countries as Indians and foreigners, even though there might have been a community of faith between them.

Today, when the conception of nationalism has developed much more, Indians in foreign countries inevitably form a national group and hang together for various purposes, in spite of their internal differences. An Indian Christian is looked upon as an Indian wherever he may go. An Indian Moslem is considered an Indian in Turkey or Arabia or Iran, or any other country where Islam is the dominant religion.

All of us, I suppose, have varying pictures of our native land and no two persons will think exactly alike. When I think of India, I think of many things: of broad fields dotted with innumerable small villages; of towns and cities I have visited; of the magic of the rainy season which pours life into the dry parched up land and converts it suddenly into a glistening expanse of beauty and greenery, of great rivers and flowing water; of the Khyber Pass in all its bleak surroundings; of the southern tip of India; of people, individually and in the mass; and, above all, of the Himalayas, snow-capped, or some mountain valley in Kashmir in the spring, covered with new flowers, and with a brook bubbling and gurgling through it. We make and preserve the pictures of our choice, and so I have chosen this mountain background rather than the more normal picture of a hot, subtropical country. Both pictures would be correct, for India stretches from the tropics right up to the temperate regions, from near the equator to the cold heart of Asia.

(From *The Discorery of India*, Jawaharlal Nehru, Oxford University Press, New Delhi, 2001. pp 52-61)

15

Bhimrao Ramji Ambedkar

Life and Times

Bhimrao Ramji Ambedkar (1891-1956) is an untouchable himself, who championed the cause of the Dalits and fought relentlessly throughout his life to ensure equality, social justice, self-respect and freedom for them. He stood for the social equality, economic emancipation and political freedom of the downtrodden millions—a task never undertaken by any high-caste Hindu leader with so much vigour and force.

Bhimrao Ramji Ambedkar is known as the leader of India's untouchables, the oppressed, deprived and dispossessed a is the 'modern Manu' for his work in piloting the Constitution of independent India through the Constituent Assembly, as well as, in Nehru's words, a symbol of revolt against all the oppressive features of Hindu society. He epitomised the relentless struggle of the Dalit masses for human rights, dignity and freedom. He founded three political parties: he served in the cabinets of both the British India and independent India; and he wrote and spoke extensively on political problems and the political process. Although Ambedkar's basic political beliefs in human equality, parliamentary democracy and legal redress for social wrongs were formed early in his life, his political philosophy in practical details was often shaped by the politics of social reform and by India';; special brand of minority politics.

Since Ambedkar's political thought and social action was also. formed in relationship to his own caste status and the Maharashtran world around him, ii is necessary to note the events of his life in those special contexts. Ambedkar was born at Mhow near Indore in the erstwhile Central Province in the British India. He was born to Ramji Sakpal and Bhimabai on 14th April, 1891. Ramji Skapal belonged to the Konkan region of the Bombay presidency. He belonged to the Mahar community, one of the leading untouchable communities considered robust, adaptable, intelligent and brave. The Mahars formed the backbone of the Maratha army and were the first to come in contact with the Europeans in India. They formed an important part of the Bombay Army of the East India Company.

Ramji Sakpal's father Maloji Sakpal also had army background. Ramji was the only son and Meera the only daughter. The family was greatly influenced by the Bhakti Movement and particularly Kabir. It was but natural that the Bhakti school had a number of devotees among the untouchables who found consolation in the human attributes like compassion, benevolence and devotion of God. The Bhakti movement was opposed to the caste system which was condemned by the Bhakti poets and sages like Kabir. The followers of Kabir argued that anybody who was devoted to God belonged to Him irrespective of caste and birth.

Ramji Sakpal was married to Bhimabai who belonged to the Murbadkar untouchable family. Her father and uncles also had army background and were followers of the Bhakti movement of Kabir. Like his father, Ramji also joined the British army. He had keen interest in reading and acquisition of knowledge. He utilised the facilities in the army School and attained proficiency in English. Later, he obtained a diploma in teaching from the Army School in Poona and became a teacher in the army school. For 14 years he served as Headmaster in an army school. Ramji Sakpal's 14th child Bhim was bom at Mhow Cantonment area where Ramji Sakpal was residing during his service as Headmaster in the army school.

Ramji Sakpal retired in 1893 when Ambedkar was just two years old. After retirement the family settled at Dapoli in the Konkan region of Bombay presidency. Ambedkar was admitted to primary school at Dapoli in 1896. He lost his mother in the same year. Later, Ramji shifted to Satara where he got a job. Ambedkar completed his primary education and began high school education at the Government High School.

Ambedkar had to face many humiliations and difficulties which every untouchable had to face those days. At school he was insulted frequently and not allowed to mingle with other students. Many a time he had to go without water as the untouchables had no right to drink water from the common source. Ambedkar and his brother were made to sit in a comer of the class on a piece of gunny bag which they carried to the school. The teachers were reluctant to touch their notebooks and even avoided putting questions to them, for fear of being polluted. The Sanskrit teacher refused to teach them Sanskrit. And Ambedkar was forced to take Persian as the second language in the high school. The conditions in the school and the locality were so oppressive that Ambedkar thought of taking up petty jobs in the railway station or in a Bombay mill. Once he thought of stealing money from his aunt's purse to go to Bombay and join as a factory worker. After several attempts he got hold of the purse and he found that it contained only an 'anna' which was not sufficient to go to Bombay. This experience was a turning point in his life and he decided to give up all truant habits, study hard, get through the examinations fast and earn a livelihood. Thus he became very diligent in his studies. Ambedkar's teacher entered in school record his surname as Ambedkar changing his old surname Sakpal.

Ambedkar concentrated on his studies inspite of the humiliations he was subjected to. In his childhood he got encouragement from his father who was a Bhakti devout and a strict disciplinarian concerned about the all round development of the children, spiritually, mentally and physically. His philosophical inclination towards Bhakti, humanism and social change enunciated by Mahatma Phule and others also had a clear impact on Ambedkar. Ramji had keen interest in the problems of the Mahars. When the Government banned their recruitment in the Army in 1892, he sought the help of Ranade in drafting the petition to change these orders. He had also taken up other problems with the Governor of Bombay.

The Satyashodak movement of reform begun by Jotirao Phule, a non-Brahman, was at a low ebb at the time of Ambedkar's birth but the movement inspired the Maharajas of Baroda and Kolhapur who helped Ambedkar get his extraordinary education. Although Ambedkar experienced discrimination, he was never locked into the village pattern of traditional work and status. He grew up in an atmosphere of changing aspirations and incipient organisation among his own caste-fellows, and in a caste which accounted for 10 per cent of the Marathi-speaking areas. And although the intellectual elite of that area spoke for the removal of the disabilities of the untouchables, they did not seriously promote any action. Apart from the educational efforts of non-Brahman reformers—Phule in the nineteenth century and V.R. Shinde in the early twentieth—the reformers left the leadership of any movement for change up to the untouchables themselves. The result of all these factors was to create an opportunity of unusual proportions for an untouchable of Ambedkar's intelligence and character.

Ambedkar's family had moved to Bombay in his youth to enable their brightest child to attend good and fairly open schools. After graduation from Elphinstone college in 1913, Ambedkar was sent by the Gaikwad of Baroda to Columbia University in New York, where he received a Ph.D. Chhatrapati Shahu Maharaj of Kolhapur provided Ambedkar financial support which enabled him to get a D.Sc. from University of London and to pass the Bar from Grey's Inn. Ambedkar returned from his two trips to America and Europe finally in 1923, one of the best educated men in the province of Bombay. The influence of these years seems to have been the development of pragmatism and self-confidence, faith in education and a deep belief in flexible parliamentary democracy. Curiously enough, any sort of doctrinnaire socialism left no mark on him, and he had no alliances with European political groups. He seems to have returned with the idea that India must evolve its own form of parliamentary democracy and its own cure for its problems of inequality.

Until 1935, Ambedkar's work took three direction: the most visibly successful was the awakening and organising of the untouchables— through newspapers of their own, social and cultural institutes, and widely attended conferences. Then he called 'Depressed Classes' conferences. He also participated in every opportunity to petition the British government for political representation for untouchables, and these opportunities were many; the Southborough Committee on Franchise, the Simon Commission to evaluate the reforms and the famous Round Table Conferences in London. Ambedkar also served in the Bombay Legislature to which his efforts had won token representation for the untouchables. The third direction his work took was that of encouraging education among the lower classes, first by exhortation and the founding of hostels so they would have a place to stay while attending school, and eventually by establishing a network of colleges under the People's Education Society.

These years of activity reveal some changes in Ambedkar's political ideology, but more striking are the constant patterns. He believed that only untouchables could lead untouchables. He never joined or supported any caste Hindu-led group, although he invited high caste Hindus to serve on his institutes and in his activities. He firmly believed in untouchable's self-improvement, and constantly wrote and spoke against practices which were associated with low caste behaviour with the corollary that the lower classes were capable of exemplary behaviour and self-respect. He was sure that honest and sufficient representation in governing bodies would enable the depressed classes to redress their grievances through legal means. There is also a pattern during these years of attempts to claim equality within Hinduism: three temple satyagrahas, none of them successful, none of them supported by Gandhi or the Indian National Congress; efforts to join the popular Ganapati festivals in Bombay; at least one public donning of the sacred thread of the three upper varnas; multi-caste dinners in which sympathetic caste Hindus, chiefly from marginal higher castes, joined with untouchables. It seems clear that Ambedkar never placed much trust in the ability of Hinduism to reform itself.

Two instances during the early years of Ambedkar's leadership seem to mark the turning points in his philosophy: the Mahad

Conferences of 1927 and the battle with Gandhi over the Communal Award that was the outcome of the Round Table conferences of 1930-32. During the first Mahad Conference, untouchables and some non-Brahmins met at a town south of Bombay. A sudden impulse to test the Resolution of the Bombay Legislative Assembly (which had declared all public places open to untouchables) led the conferees to the town pond to drink water. They were met with open violence and retreated from Mahad, only to return to a second Conference later in 1927. Here, in a historic gesture, the classic Hindu law book the *Manusmriti* which explicitly condoned the practice of untouchability, was burned in public. In spite of this highly publicised act, however, Ambekdar pursued the matter of the right to water in Mahad in the courts, not n the streets, winning a legal victory years later.

Mahad is seen as the real beginning of Ambedkar's leadership of the untouchables; the Round Table Conference is seen as a recognition by all of that leadership. Ambedkar attended all three Conferences during 1930-32 as one of the two untouchable delegates chosen by the British government. At the second Conference, he came into direct conflict with Gandhi. Ambedkar's public position was not at variance with Gandhi's before the conferences. In 1930, at a Depressed Classes Conference in Nagpur, he urged independence for India—the first untouchable leader to urge the British to leave. His position on political rights for untouchables, articulated most recently in testimony to the Simon Commission, urged joint electorates for both the Depressed Classes and the Muslims, but with adult suffrage and reserved seats, as well as some special attention to the education and employment of the Depressed, Classes in government positions. In the midst of the clamour in London of every other minority for separate electorate, Ambedkar changed his position to one demanding separate electorates for untouchables.

Gandhi opposed Ambedkar in London, but his most effective opposition came later in 1932, after the Communal Award of the British government granted separate electorates for the Depressed Classes. He fasted unto death in his cell in the Yeravda prison in Poona, protesting against separate electorates as a device which would separate the untouchables from the Hindu society forever. As Gandhi weakened, Ambedkar capitulated, but only when some Hindu leaders gathered to pledge their help in the removal of untouchability, and the agreement that the untouchables would have reserved seats in the elected bodies.

The mid-thirties, however, found Ambedkar in an obstinate mood. He cut off the seven years of temple entry satyagrahas with an announcement in 1935 that he 'would not die a Hindu', and called a conference in 1936 to discuss conversion. There is no reason to think that Ambedkar was not sincere in his personal rejection of Hinduism. Ambedkar's dramatic rejection of Hinduism took place at a conference of 10,000 Depressed Classes people meeting at a site not far from Nasik, the scene of a five years bitter battle over the right to enter the famous Kalaram temple there. The 1936 conference was well publicised, and Ambedkar began to receive requests to visit the Depressed Classes in the north and in Kerala. This announcement shocked the Gandhians and the Hindu leaders who had been pursuing their campaign of attempting to persuade temple committees to open their temples to the Depressed Classes. A pamphlet published by Ambedkar in 1936, *Annihilation of Caste* demanded the necessity to uproot the concept of the hereditary priesthood in order to make Hinduism more than a 'religion of rules'. It was as defiant a gesture as his own personal vow to leave Hinduism.

The religion he had been drawn to since boyhood, Buddhism, had no visible remnant left in India, and there was little understanding of it as a living religion, even among the elite. The choice was not at all clear, and Ambedkar simply moved along in the political world, shelving the religious aspects of the movement for two decades.

Ambedkar's first political party, the Independent Labour Party was born in great optimism to fight the election of 1937, the first elections in which the Scheduled Castes, were to have a specific number of designated seats according to their strength in numbers. The first announcement of the party came in August 1936. Two months after the conference called by Ambedkar declared that the Mahar caste was ready to leave Hinduism. The spirit of the two moves was much the same—independent, innovative, intolerant of paternalism, determined to build new structures outside the old ways, determined to make a mark on India.

The platform of that party reveals much of Ambedkar's political ideology—socialist, centrist, committed to industrialisation and to education, with specific remedies for specific economic problems. The platform paid no attention to religion, and indeed the securing of reserved seats for the untouchables was dependent upon their being in the Hindu fold. But the party was not to serve the needs of untouchables alone; its aim was 'mainly to advance the welfare of the labouring classes'.

This detailed account of Ambedkar's first political venture is necessary to point several factors. Most important, perhaps, is the fact that Ambedkar's electoral success was a small and lonely minority in a legislature dominated by a majority party. Second was the knowledge that in the areas in which untouchables' action had been highly public, the Congress untouchable would win the reserved seat over the untouchable allied with Ambedkar. The record of the Congress in the 1937-39 legislatures also led Ambedkar to distrust its economic and social platform.

Ambedkar's further political efforts had to deal with matters such as the impotence of minority, the unlikelihood of a 'trouble-making' untouchable being elected by a caste-Hindu constituency, and a Congress far less committed to socialism. He never found a solution to these problems. His attempts included the foundation of the Scheduled Castes Federation in 1942 and to press for separate electorates once again. The federation combined with socialists in some areas, but with such a lack of success that Ambedkar himself was defeated. Ambedkar wanted to unite all the dispossessed untouchables, scheduled tribes, the working men and the poor, with all those yearning for a better India. This party, like the first one, was the product of a time when Ambedkar's mind was turning to religion, and here the connection is much closer than that of the Independent Labourer Party with the rejection of Hinduism. The Buddhist conversion movement, xl in motion two months before Ambedkar's death in 1956, was to offer a new way for all those dissatisfied with Hinduism to participate in a religion that was truly Indian, but cleansed of inequality, the hereditary preiesthood the faults, as Ambekdar saw them, of Hinduism. "Ambedkar's political contributions, however, encompass more than the winning of political representation and establishing political parties. He was. as much, a statesman as a politician, and in 1942. Ambedkar was appointed Labour Member in the Viceroy's Executive Council, and he held the position until 1946. In this post, he was able to secure such benefits for Scheduled Castes as a Mahar battalion in the Indian army and overseas scholarship for untouchable boys, but his main work was in the field of labour arbitration law, the condition of industry, and such far-reaching projects as the Damodar Dam.

The years between 1942 and 1946 were also years in which Ambedkar was harshly critical of the Congress. Nevertheless, after he was elected to the Constituent Assembly in 1946, Ambedkar was named as the nominee for the cabinet post of Minister of Law. Shortly after independence was achieved on 15th August 1947, Ambedkar became a member of Nehru's first cabinet and Chairman of the Drafting Committee of the Constituent Assembly.

Ambedkar could not continue for long as the Law Minister in Nehru's Cabinet. He resigned in protest against the unceremonious burial of the Hindu Code Bill through which he sought to have a uniform civil code and equal property rights to women. Through his dauntless struggles against untouchability, Ambedkar realised that there is no solution to untouchability and casteism within the Hindu religious framework. After the long drawn out struggle for temple entry at Nashik, he declared at the Yeola Conference that he would not die as a Hindu. After resignation from Nehru's Cabinet in 1951, Ambedkar sought to arrive at a lasting fundamental solution to the problem of Indian humanity. He picked up the lost thread of India's struggle for salvation, humanity's urge for liberation and turned towards Buddhism.

From 1948 onwards, Ambedkar became personally more committed to Buddhism, visiting Buddhist countries and working on the Buddhism and his Dhamma. He appreciated the fact that morality, rather than God, occupies the central place in Buddhism.

Moreover, according to him, other religions concentrate on 'problems of the soul and of worship'. Ambedkar's governmental work, and the matter of the important benefits which to serve as 'compensatory discrimination' for the Scheduled Castes and which would be forfeited by conversion, delayed a call for mass conversion until 1956.

In a sense, the conversion to Buddhism was Ambedkar's ultimate answer to the question of how to eradicate the practice of untouchability. He could not test the efficacy of the conversion, however, since he died within two months of the great event at Nagpur in October 1956. He may have been misled into thinking that not only the untouchables but many from other castes would enter the Buddhist fold, since creative writers like Tagore, scholars like Dharmanand Kosambi and even Nehru himself had expressed admiration for Buddhism. Independent India's symbols of the lion pillar of Ashoka and the wheel of law were Buddhist; her neighbours were Buddhist and she was more aware of them as she took her place as a leader in Asia, but in any case. however hopeful Ambedkar was about it widespread turn to Buddhism he had created over forty years a set of principles, standards and goals relating to the removal of untouchability, and these must be considered perhaps more basic than conversion.

Ambedkar was married, according to the customs then in vogue, at the age of 14. His wife Ramabai was aged 9 years. His daughter Indu and three sons—Ramesh, Gangadhar and Rajratna died in their childhood. His eldest son Yaswant died a few years back. Ramai, a sober and dedicated companion died on May 27, 1935. Ambedkar married second time Dr. Miss Lakshmi Kabir, a Saraswat Brahmin on April 15, 1948. Ambedkar died on December 6, 1956.

The nation's highest decoration of Bharat Ratna was posthumously conferred on Ambedkar by the President R. Venkataraman on 14th April 1990. A life-size painting of Ambedkar was also installed in the Central Hall of the Parliament House on 11th April 1990.

The Indian academic landscape has disarticulated Babasaheb Ambedkar by studious theoretical silence. Even on the eve of his birth centenary, we do not have a complete corpus of his writings. Comparisons are odious, but we have organised corpus of texts of Mahatma Gandhi, Nehru, Rajendra Prasad and Sardar Patel. But Ambedkar's corpus has just begun to emerge and that too, at the initiative of the Government of Maharashtra. Rightly Upendra Baxi has remarked that if the market for knowledge also operated according to the. laws of supply and demand, we have to ruefully conclude that Ambedkar's construction of the Hindu society, nationalist movement, and resurgent post-colonial India are commodities for which there is no organised demand either from "epistemic entrepreneurs or cognitive consumers" in India.

This complete disregard by the academia of Ambedkar poses a critical question concerning the modes of production of knowledges through the formal educational and research systems in India. He has asked how is it that these knowledge systems have produced a near, "total annihilation of the very author of *Annihilation of Caste,* how is it that the most contemporary fighter of the Depressed Classes does not figure even as a representative of heretical thought, how is it that after four decades of reservations, emergent communities of research scholars belonging to the Depressed Classes have also felt inhibited in organising the discourse around Ambedkar's life and contribution. Even the subaltern studies have to pause after six volumes, to acknowledge Ambedkar. How do we characterise this lack or absence? Do we explain this by saying that Ambedkar does not deserve any theoretical labour? Or do we say that the lack betrays a collective conspiracy of silence on the part of Indian scholarship? These are the questions Upendra Baxi has asked.

In style of Foucault, Baxi asserts that the "communities of knowledge and communities of power" in India have united in their marginalisation of Ambedkar. Neither power nor knowledge have discovered in him a vision towards which India may move.

Increasingly involved in the discourse on transfer of power Ambedkar was drawn into the processes of constitution-making. So pre-eminent was his role that, in a deep irony, the man who made a bonfire of Manusmriti was hailed as a 'Modem Manu', but even this modern Manu was ultimately reduced to a backroom boy— when the Constitution he helped make and move for adoption was acclaimed by the Constituent Assembly, the incantation was 'Mahatma Gandhi ki jai'.

The process of co-optation of a radical Dalit leader was historically now complete. He was no longer relevant and useful, For full four years and fifty-six days, he remained as the Law Minister in Nehru's cabinet. One must read in full his statement released on 10 October 1954 on the eve of his resignation from the cabinet. This poignant statement reveals his own sense of humiliation at not being treated as an equal. Not merely did be feel misled and betrayed by Nehru on the moving of the Hindu Code Bill for parliamentary deliberations, he also articulated his anguish and anger at the neglect of the Scheduled Castes by the Government. The Nehru government did not merely betray the promises of urgent ameliorative action for the Atisudras. it also treated Ambedkar with historic nonchalance. He bitterly complained that he was given only the law portfolio—a portfolio of no administrative importance. He desired labour and planning portfolios or at least some association with planning, given his excellent economics background, and the prerogative of influencing allocation of resources for the betterment of the weaker sections.

These questions may be taken seriously in terms of a collective self-understanding of the making of a modern India. Our understanding of leading historic figures like Gandhi or Nehru is bound to remain incomplete, both in the sense of biography and history, in the absence of the grasp of their relations with Ambedkar. In postmodernist terms, Ambedkar was the 'Other' of the nationalist discourse which was being forged by Gandhiji and Nehru. The absence of such an understanding has flawed and fractured our grasp of the making of modern India.

The Annihilation of Caste

I

It is a pity that case even today has its defenders are many. It is defended on the ground that the caste system is but another name for division of labour and if division of labour is a necessary feature of every civilized society then it is argued that there is nothing wrong in the caste system. Now the first thing to be urged against this view is that caste system is not merely division of labour. *It is also division of labourers.* Civilized society undoubtedly needs divisions of labour. But in no civilized society is division of labour accompanied by this unnatural division of labourers into water-tight compartments. The caste system is not merely a division of labourers which is quite different from division of labour – it is an hierarchy in which the division of labourers are graded one above the other. In no other country is the division of labour accompanied by this gradation of labourers. There is also a third point of criticism against this view of the caste system. This division of labour is not spontaneous, it is not based on natural aptitudes. Social and individual efficiency requires us to develop the capacity of an individual to the point of competency to choose and to make his own career. This principle is violated in the caste system in so far as it involves an attempt to appoint tasks to individuals in advance, selected not on the basis of trained original capacities, but on that of the social status of the parents.

Looked at from another point of view this stratification of occupations which is the result of the caste system is positively pernicious. Industry is never static. It undergoes rapid and abrupt changes. With such changes an individual must be free to change his occupation. Without such freedom to adjust himself to changing circumstances it would be impossible for him to gain his livelihood. Now the caste system will not allow Hindus to take to occupations where they are wanted if they do not belong to them by heredity. If a Hindu is seen to starve rather than take to new occupations not assigned to his caste, the reason is to be found in the caste system. But not permitting readjustment of occupation, caste becomes a direct cause of much of the unemployment we see in the country. As a form of division of labour the caste system suffers from another serious defect. The division of labour brought about by the caste system is not a division based on choice. Individual sentiment, individual preference has no place in it. It is based on the dogma of predestination. Considerations of social efficiency would compel us to recognize that the greatest evil in the industrial system is not so much poverty and the suffering that it involves as the fact that so many persons have callings which make no appeal to those who are engaged in them. Such callings constantly provoke one to aversion, ill-will and the desire to evade. There are many occupations in India which on account of the fact that they are regarded as degraded by the Hindus provoke those who are engaged in them to aversion. There is a constant desire to evade and escape from such occupations which arises solely because of the blighting effect which they produce upon those who follow them owing to the slight and stigma cast upon them by the Hindu religion. What efficiency can there be in a system under which neither men's hearts nor their minds are in their work? As an economic organization caste is therefore a harmful institution, inasmuch as, it involves the subordination of man's natural powers and inclinations to the exigencies of social rules.

II

Some have dug a biological trench in defence of the caste system. It is said that the object of caste was to preserve purity of race and purity of blood. Now ethnologists are of opinion that men of pure race exist nowhere and that there has been mixture of all races in all parts of the world. Especially is this the case with the people of India. Mr. D. R. Bhandarkar in his paper on *Foreign Elements in the Hindu Population* has stated that:

"There is hardly a class, or Caste in India which has not a foreign strain in it. There is an admixture of alien blood not only among the warrior classes – the Rajputs and the Marathas – but also among the Brahmins who are under the happy delusion that they are free from all foreign elements."

The caste system cannot be said to have grown as a means of preventing the admixture of races or as a means of maintaining purity of blood. As a matter of caste system came into being long after the different races of India had commingled in blood and culture. To hold that distinctions of castes are really distinctions of race and to treat different castes as though they were so many different races is a gross perversion of facts. What racial affinity is there between the Brahmin of the Punjab and the Brahmin of Madras? What racial affinity is there between the untouchable of Bengal and the untouchable of Madras? What racial difference is there between the Brahmin of the Punjab and the Chamar of the Punjab? What racial difference is there between the Brahmin of Madras and the Pariah of Madras? The Brahmin of the Punjab is racially of the same stock as the Chamar of the Punjab and the Brahmin of Madras is of the same race as the Pariah of Madras.

The caste system does not demarcate racial division. The caste system is a social division of people of the same race. Assuming it, however, to be a case of racial divisions one may ask: What harm could there be if a mixture of races and of blood was permitted to take place in India by intermarriages between different castes? Men are no doubt divided from animals by so deep a distinction that science recognizes men and animals as two distinct species. But even scientists who believe in purity of races do not assert that the different races constitute different species of men. They are only varieties of one and the same species. As such they can interbreed and produce an offspring which is capable of breeding and which is not sterile. An immense lot of nonsense is talked about heredity and eugenics in defence of the caste system. Few would object to the caste system if it was in accord with the basic principle of eugenic because few can object to the improvement of the race by judicious mating. But one fails to understand how the caste system secures judicious mating.

Caste system is a negative thing. It merely prohibits persons belonging to different castes from intermarrying. It is not a positive method of selecting which two among a given caste should marry. If caste is eugenic in origin then the origin of sub-castes must also be eugenic. But can anyone seriously maintain that the origin of sub-caste is eugenic? I think it would be absurd to contend for such a proposition and for a very obvious reason. if caste means race then differences of sub-castes cannot mean differences of race because sub-castes become *exhypothesia* sub-divisions of one and the same race. Consequently the bar against intermarrying and interdining between sub-castes cannot before the purpose of maintaining purity of race or of blood. If sub-castes cannot be eugenic in origin there cannot be any substance in the contention that caste is eugenic in origin. Again if castes is eugenic in origin one can understand the bar against intermarriage. But what is the purpose of the interdict placed on interdining between castes and sub-castes alike? Inter dining cannot infect blood and therefore cannot be the cause either of the improvement or of deterioration of the race. This shows that caste had no scientific origin and that those who are attempting to give it an eugenic basis are trying to support by science what is grossly unscientific. Even today eugenics cannot become a practical possibility unless we have definite knowledge regarding the laws of heredity. Professor Bateson in his *Mendel's Principles of Heredity* says,

There is nothing in the descent of the higher mental qualities to suggest that they follow any single system of transmission. It is likely that both they and the more marked developments of physical powers result rather from the coincidence of numerous facts than from the possession of any one genetic element.

To argue that the caste system was eugenic in its conception is to attribute to the forefathers of present-day Hindu a knowledge of heredity which even the modern scientists do not possess. A tree should be judged by the fruits it yields. If caste is eugenic what sort of a race of men is should have produced? They are a race of pygmies and dwarfs stunted in stature and wanting in stamina. It is a nation nine-tenths of which is declared to be unfit for military service. This shows that the caste system does not embody the eugenics of modern scientists. It is a social system which embodies the arrogance and selfishness of a perverse section of the Hindu who were superior enough in social status to set it in fashion and who had authority to force it on their inferiors.

III

Caste does not result in economic efficiency, Caste cannot and has not improved the race. Caste has however done one thing. It has completely disorganized and demoralized the Hindus.

The first and foremost thing that must be recognized is that Hindu society is a myth. The name Hindu is itself a foreign name.

it was given by the Mohammedans to the natives for the purpose of distinguishing themselves. It does not occur in any Sanskrit work prior to the Mohammedan invasion. They did not feel the necessity of a common name because they had no conception of their having constituted a community. Hindus society as such does not exist. It is only a collection of castes. Each caste is conscious of its existence. Its survival is the be all and end all of its existence. Castes do not even form a federation. A caste has no feeling that it is affiliated to other castes except when there is a Hindu-Muslim riot. On all other occasions each caste endeavours to segregate itself and to distinguish itself from other castes. Each caste not only dines among itself and marries among itself but each caste prescribes its own distinctive dress. What other explanation can there be of the innumerable styles of dress worn by the men and women of India which so amuse the tourists? Indeed the ideal Hindu must be like a rat living in his own hole refusing to have any contact with others. There is an utter lack among the Hindus of what the sociologists call 'consciousness of kind'. There is no Hindu consciousness of kind.

In every Hindu the consciousness that exists is the consciousness of his caste. That is the reason why the Hindus cannot be said to form a society or a nation. There are however many Indians whose patriotism does not permit them to admit that Indians are not a nation, that they are only an amorphous mass of people they have insisted that underlying the apparent diversity there is a fundamental unity which marks the life of the Hindus in as much as there is a similarity of habits and customs, beliefs and thoughts which obtain all over the continent of India. Similarity in habits and customs, beliefs and thoughts there is. But one cannot accept the conclusion that therefore, the Hindus constitute a society. To do so is to misunderstand the essentials which go to make up a society. Men do not become a society by living in physical proximity any more than a man ceases to be a member of his society by living so many miles away from other men.

Secondly, similarity in habits and customs, beliefs and thoughts is not enough to constitute men into society. Things may be passed physically from one to another like bricks. In the same way habits and customs, beliefs and thoughts of one group may be taken over by another group and there may thus appear a similarity between the two. Culture spreads by diffusion and that is why one finds similarity between various primitive tribes in the matter of their habits and customs, beliefs and thoughts, although they do not live in proximity. But no one could say that because there was this similarity the primitive tribes constituted one society. This is because similarly in certain things is not enough to constitute a society. Men constitute a society because they have things which they possess in common. To have similar things is totally different from possessing things in common with one another is by being in communication with one another. This is merely another way of saying that society continues to exist by communication indeed in communication. To make it concrete, it is not enough if men act in a way which agrees with the acts of others. Parallel activity, even if similar, is not sufficient to bind men into a society. This is proved by the fact that the festivals observed by the different castes amongst the Hindus are the same. Yet these parallel performances of similar festivals by the different castes have not bound them into one integral whole. For that purpose what is necessary is for a man the share and participate in a common activity so that the same emotions are aroused in him that animate the others. Masking the individual a sharer or partner in the associated activity so that he feels its success as his success, its failure as his failure is the real thing that binds men and makes a society of them. The caste system prevents common activity and by preventing common activity it has prevented the Hindus from becoming a society with a unified life and a consciousness of its own being.

IV

The Hindus often complain of the isolation and exclusiveness of a gang or a clique and blame them for anti-social spirit. But they conveniently, forget that this anti-social spirit is the worst feature of their own caste system. One caste enjoys singing a hymn of hate against another castes as much as the Germans did in singing their hymn of hate against the English during the last war. The literature of the Hindus is full of caste genealogies in which an attempt is made to give a noble origin to one caste and on ignoble origin to other castes. The *Sahyadrikhand* is a notorious instance of this class of literature. This anti-social spirit is not confined to caste alone. It has gone deeper and has poisoned the mutual relations of the sub-castes as well. In my province the Golak Brahmins, Deorukha Brahmins, Karada Brahmins, Palshe Brahmins and Chitpavan Brahmins, all claim to be sub-divisions of the Brahmin caste. But the anti-social spirit that prevails between them is quite as marked and quite as virulent as the anti-social spirit that prevails between them and other non-Brahmin castes. There is nothing strange in this. An anti-social spirit is found wherever one group has 'interests of its own' which shut it out from full interaction with other groups, so that its prevailing purpose is protection of what it has got. This anti-social spirit, this spirit of protecting its own interests is as much a marked feature of the different castes in their isolation from one another as it is of nations in their isolation. The Brahmin's primary concern is to protect 'his interest' against those of the non-Brahmins and the Non-Brahmins's primary concern is to protect their interests against those of the Brahmins. The Hindus, therefore, are not merely an assortment of castes but they are so many warring groups each living for itself and for its selfish ideal. There is another feature of caste which is deplorable. The ancestors of the present-day English fought on one side or the other in the wars of the Roses and the Cromwellian War. But the descendents of those who fought on the one side do not bear any animosity – any grudge against the descendents of those who fought on the other side. The feud is forgotten. But the present-day non-Brahmins cannot forgive Shivaji. The present-day Kayasthas will not forgive the present-day Brahmins for the infamy cast upon their forefathers by the to the caste system. The existence of caste and caste consciousness has served to keep the memory of past feuds between castes green and has prevented solidarity.

V

The recent discussion about the excluded and partially included areas has served to draw attention to the position of what are called the aboriginal tribes in India. They number about 13 millions if not more. Apart from the questions whether their exclusion from the new Constitution is proper or improper, the fact still remains that these aborigines have remained in their primitive uncivilized state in a land which boasts of a civilization thousands of years old. Not only are they not civilized but some of them follow pursuits which have led to their being classified as criminals. Thirteen million people living in the midst of civilization are still in a savage state and are leading the life of hereditary criminals! But the Hindus have never felt ashamed of it. This is a phenomenon which in my view is quite unparalleled. What is the cause of this shameful state of affairs? Why has no attempt been made to civilize these aborigines and to lead them to take to a more honourable way of making a living? The Hindus will probably seek to account for this savage state of the aborigines by attributing to them congenital stupidity. They will probably not admit that the aborigines have remained savages because they had made no effort to civilize them, to give them medical aid, to reform them, to make them good citizens. But supposing a Hindu wished to do what the Christian missionary is doing for these aborigines, could he have done it? I submit not. Civilizing the aborigines means adopting them as your own, living in their midst, and cultivating fellow-feeling, in short loving them. How is it possible for a Hindu to do this? His whole life is one anxious effort to preserve his caste. Caste is his precious possession which he must save at any cost. He cannot consent to lose it by establishing contact with the aborigines, the remnants of the hateful anaryas of the *Vedic* days. Not that a Hindu could not be taught the sense of duty can enable him to overcome his duty to preserve his caste. Caste is, therefore, the real explanation as to why the Hindus has let the savage remain a savage in the midst of his civilization without blushing or without felling any sense of remorse or repentance. The Hindus has not realized that these aborigines are a source of potential danger. If these savages remain savages they may not do any harm to the Hindu. But if they are reclaimed by non-Hindus and converted to their faiths they will swell the ranks of the enemies of the Hindus. If this happens the Hindus will have to thank himself and his caste system.

VI

Not only has the Hindu made no effort for the humanitarian cause of civilizing the savages but the higher – caste Hindus have deliberately prevented the lower castes who are within the pale of Hinduism from rising to the cultural level of the higher castes. I will give two instances, one of the Sonars and the other of the Pathare Prabhus. Both are communities quite well-known in Maharashtra. Like the rest of the communities desiring to raise their status these two communities were at one time endeavouring to adopt some of the ways and habits of the Brahmins. The Sonars were styling themselves Daivadnya Brahmins and were wearing their 'dhotis' with folds on the using the word *namaskar* for salutation. Both, the folded way of wearing the 'dhoti' and the *namaskar* were special to the Brahmins. The Brahmins did not like this imitation and this attempt by Sonars to pass off as Brahmins. Under the authority of the Peshwas the Brahmins successfully put down this attempt on the part of the Sonars to adopt the ways of the Brahmins. They even got the President of the Councils of the East India Company's settlement in Bombay to issue a prohibitory order against the Sonars residing in Bombay.

At one time the Pathare Prabhus had widow remarriage as a custom of their caste. This custom of widow remarriage was later on looked upon as a mark of social inferiority by some members of the caste especially because it was contrary to the custom prevalent among the Brahmins. With the object of raising the status of their community some Pathare Prabhus sought to stop this practice of widow remarriage that was prevalent in their caste. The community was divided into two camps, one for and the other against the innovation. The Peshwas took side of those in favour of widow remarriage and thus virtually prohibited the Pathare Prabhu from following the ways of the Brahmins. The Hindu criticize the Mohammedans for having spread their religion by the use of the sword. They also ridicule Christianity on the score of the inquisition. But really speaking who is better and more worthy of our respect – the Mohammedans and Christians who attempted to thrust down the throats of unwilling persons what they regarded as necessary for their salvation or the Hindu who would not spread the light, who would endeavour to kept others in darkness, who would not consent to share his intellectual and social inheritance with those who are ready and willing to make it a part of their own make-up? I have no hesitation in saying that if the Mohammedan has been cruel, the Hindu has been mean and meanness is worse than cruelty.

VII

Whether the Hindu religion was or was not a missionary religion has been a controversial issue. Some hold the view that it was never a missionary religion. Others hold that it was. That the Hindu religion was once a missionary religion must be admitted. It could not have spread over the face of India, if it was not a missionary religion. That today it is not a missionary religion is also a fact which must be accepted. The question therefore is not whether or not the Hindu religion was a missionary religion. The real question is why did the Hindu religion cease to be a missionary religion? My answer is this : Hindu religion ceased to be a missionary religion when the caste system grew up among the Hindus. Caste is inconsistent with conversion. Inculcation of beliefs and dogmas is not the only problem that is involved in conversion. To find a place for the convert in the social life of the community is another and a much more important problem that arises in connection with conversion. That problem is where to place the convert, in what caste? It is a problem which must baffle every Hindu wishing to make aliens converts to his religion. Unlike the club the membership of a caste is not open to all the sundry. The law of caste confines its membership to person born in the caste. Castes are autonomous and there is no authority anywhere to compel a caste to admit a newcomer to its social life. Hindu society being a collection of castes and each caste being a closer corporation there is no place for a convert. Thus it is the caste which has prevented the Hindus from expanding and from absorbing other religious communities. So long as caste remains, Hindu religion cannot be made a missionary religion and *Shudhi* will be both a folly and a futility.

VIII

The reason which has made *Shudhi* impossible for Hindus is also responsible for making *Sanghatan* impossible. The idea underlying *Sanghatan* is to remove from the mind of the Hindu that timidity and cowardice which so painfully mark him off from the Mohammedan and the Sikh and which have led him to adopt the low ways of treachery and cunning for protecting himself. The question naturally arises: From where does the Sikh or the Mohammedan derive his strength which makes him brave and fearless? I am sure it is not due to relative superiority of physical strength, diet or drill. It is due to the strength arising out of the feeling that all Sikhs will come to the rescue of a Sikh when he is in danger and that all Mohammedans will rush to save a Muslim if he is attacked. The Hindu can derive no such strength. He cannot feel assured that his fellows will come to his help. Being one and fated to be alone he remains powerless, develops timidity and cowardice and in a fight surrenders or runs away. The Sikh as well as the Muslim stands fearless and gives battle because he knows that though one he will not be alone. The presence of this belief in the one helps him to hold out and the absence of it in the other makes him to give way. If you pursue this matter further and ask what is it that enables the Sikh and the Mohammedan to feel so assured and why is the Hindu filled with such despair in the matter of help and assistance you will find that the reasons for this difference lie in the difference in their associated mode of living. The associated mode of life practised by the Sikh as and the Mohammendans produces fellow-feeling. The associated mode of life of the Hindus makes them *Bhais.*

Among Hindus there is not such cement explain why a Sikh says and feels that one Sikh, or one Khalsa is equal to *Sava Lakh* men. This explains why one Mohammedan is equal to a crowed of Hindus. This difference is undoubtedly a difference due to caste. So long as caste remains, there will be no *Sanghatan* and so long as there is no *Sanghatan* the Hindu will remain weak and meek. The Hindus claim to be a very tolerant people. In my opinion this is a mistake. On many occasions they can be intolerant and if on some occasions they are tolerant that is because they are too weak to oppose or too indifferent to oppose. This difference of the Hindus has become so much a part of their nature that a Hindu will quite meekly tolerate an insult as well as a wrong. You see amongst them, to use the words of Morris:

The great reading down the little, the strong beating down the weak, cruel men fearing not, kind men daring not and wise men caring not.

With the Hindu Gods all forbearing, it is not difficult to imagine the pitiable condition of the wronged and the oppressed among the Hindus. Indifferentism is the worst kind of disease that can infect a people. Why is the Hindu so indifferent? In my opinion this indifferentism is the result of the caste system which has made *Sanghatan* and cooperation even for a good cause impossible.

IX

The assertion by the individual of his own opinions and beliefs, his own independence and interest as over against group standards, group authority and group interests is the beginning of all reform. But whether the reform will continue depends upon what scope the group affords for such individual assertion if the group is tolerant and fair minded in dealing with such individuals they will continue to assert and in the end succeed in converting their fellows. On the other hand if the group is intolerant and does not bother about the means it adopts to stifle such individuals they will perish and the reform will die out. Now a caste has an unquestioned right to excommunicate any man who is guilty of breaking the rules of the caste and when it is realized that excommunication involves a complete censer of social intercourse it will be agreed that as a form of punishment there is really little to choose between excommunication and death. No wonder individual Hindus have not had the courage to assert their independence by breaking the barriers of caste. It is true that man cannot get on which his fellows. But it is also true that he cannot do without them. He would like to have the society of his fellows on his terms. If he cannot get it on his terms then he will be ready to have it on any terms even amounting to complete surrender. This is because he cannot do without society. A caste is ever ready to take advantage of the helplessness of a man and insist upon complete conformity to its code in letter and in spirit. A caste can easily organize itself into a conspiracy to make the life of a reformer a hell and if a conspiracy is a crime I do not understand why such a nefarious act as an attempt to excommunicate a person for daring at act contrary to the rules of caste should not be made an offence punishable in law. But as it is, even law gives each caste an autonomy to regulate its membership and punish dissenters with excommunication. Caste in the hands of the orthodox has been a powerful weapon for persecuting the reformer and for killing all reform.

X

The effect of caste on the ethics of the Hindus is simply deplorable. Caste has killed pubic spirit. Caste has destroyed the sense of public charity. Caste has made public opinion impossible a Hindu's public is his caste. His responsibility is only to his caste. His loyalty is restricted only to his caste. Virtue has become caste ridden and morality has become caste-bound. There is no sympathy to the deserving. There is no appreciation of the meritorious. There is no charity to the needy. Suffering as such calls for no response. There is charity but it begins with the caste and end with the caste. There is sympathy but not for men of other caste. Would a Hindu acknowledge and follow the leadership of a great and good man? The case of a Mahatma apart, the answer must be that he will follow a leader it he is a man of his caste. A Brahmin will follow a leader only if he is a Brahmin, a Kayastha if he is a Kayastha and so on. The capacity to appreciate merits in a man apart form his caste does not exist in a Hindu. There is appreciation of virtue but only when the man is a fellow caste-man. The whole morality is as bad as tribal morality. My caste-man, right or wrong; my caste-man, good or bad. It is not a case of standing by virtue and not standing by vice. It is a case of standing or not standing by the caste. Have not Hindus committed treason against their country in the interests of their caste?

XI

I would not be surprised if some of you have grown weary listening to this tiresome tale of the sad effects which caste has produced. There is nothing new in it. I will therefore turn to the constructive side of the problem. What is your ideal society if you do not want caste is a question that is bound to be asked of you. If you ask me, my ideal would be a society based on *Liberty, Equality and Fraternity.* And why not? What objection can there be to fraternity? I cannot imagine any. An ideal society should be mobile, should be full of channels for conveying a change taking place in one part to other parts. In an ideal society there should be varied and free points of contract with other modes of association. In other words there must be social endosmosis. This is fraternity, which is only another name for democracy. Democracy is not merely a form of government. It is primarily a mode of associated living, of conjoint communicated experience. It is essentially an attitude of respect and reverence towards fellowmen. Any objection to liberty? Few object to liberty in the sense of a right to free movement, in the sense of a right to life and limb. There is no objection to liberty in the sense of a right to property, tools and materials as being necessary for earning a living to keep the body in due state of health. Why not allow liberty to benefit by an effective and competent use of a person's powers? The supporters of caste who would allow liberty in the sense of a right to life, limb and property, would not readily consent to liberty in this sense, inasmuch as it involves liberty to choose one's profession. But to object to this kind of liberty is to perpetuate slavery. For slavery does not merely mean a legalized form of subjection. It means a state of society in which some men are forced to accept from others the purposes which control their conduct. This condition obtains even where there is no slavery in the legal sense. It is found where, as in the caste system, some persons are compelled to carry on certain prescribed callings which are not of their choice. Any objection to equality? This has obviously been the most contentious part of the slogan of the French Revolution.

The objection to equality may be sound and one may have to admit that all men are not equal. But what of that? Equality may be a fiction but nonetheless one must accept it as the governing principle. A man's power is dependent upon (1) physical heredity, (2) social inheritance or endowment in the form of parental care, education, accumulation of scientific knowledge, everything which enables him to be more efficient than the savage, and finally, (3) on his own efforts. In all these three respects men are undoubtedly unequal. But the question is, shall be treat them as unequal because they are unequal? This is a question which the opponents of equality must answer. From the standpoint of the individualist it may be just to treat men unequally so far as their efforts are unequal. It may be desirable to give as much incentive as possible to the full development of everyone's powers. But what would happen if men were treated unequally as they are, in the first two respects? It is obvious that those individuals in whose favour there is also birth, education, family name, business connections and inherited wealth would be selected in the race. But selection under such circumstances would not be a selection of the able. It would be the selection of the privileged. The reason therefore, which forces that in the third respect we should treat men unequally demands that in the first two respects we should treat men as equally as possible. On the other hand it can be urged that it is good for the social body to get the most out of its members, it can get most out of them only by making them equal as far as possible at the very start of the race. That is one reason why we cannot escape equality. But there is another reason why we must accept equality. A statesman is concerned with vast numbers of people. He has neither the time nor the knowledge to draw fine distinctions and to treat each equitably *i.e.* according to need or according to capacity. However desirable or reasonable an equitable treatment of men may be, humanity is not capable of assortment and classification. The statesman, therefore, must follow some rough and ready rule and that rough and ready rule is to treat all men alike not because they are alike but because classification and assortment is impossible. The doctrine of equality is glaringly fallacious but taking all in all it is the only way a statesman can proceed in politics which is a severely practical affair and which demands a severely practical test.

XII

But there is a set of reformers who hold out a different ideal. They go by the name of the Arya Samajists and their ideal of social organization is what is called Chaturvarnya or the division of society into four classes instead of the four thousand castes that we have in India. To make it more attractive and disarm opposition the protagonists of Chaturvarnya take great care to point out that their Chaturvarnya is based not on birth but on *guna* (worth). At the outset, I must confess that notwithstanding the worth-basis of this Chaturvarnya, it is an ideal to which I cannot reconcile myself. In the first place, if under the Chaturvarnya of the Arya Samajists an individual is to take his place in the Hindus society according to his worth I do not understand by the Arya Samajists insist upon labeling men as Brahmin, Kshatriya, Vaishya and Shudra. A learned man would be honoured without his being labeled a Brahmin. A soldier would be respected without his being designated a Kshatriya. If European society honours its soldiers and its servants without giving them permanent labels, why should Hindu society find it difficult to do so is a question, which Arya Samajists have not cared to consider? There is another objection to the continuance of these labels. All reform consists in a change in the notions, sentiment and mental attitudes of the people towards men and things. It is common experience that certain names become associated with certain notions and sentiments, which determine a person's attitude towards men and things. The names Brahmin, Kshatriya, Vaishya and Shudra, are names which are associated with a definite and fixed notion in the mind of every Hindu. That notion is that of a hierarchy based on birth. So long as these names continue, Hindus will continue to think of the Brahmin, Kshatriya, Vaishya and Shudra as hierarchical divisions of high and low, based on birth, and act accordingly. The Hindus must be made to unlearn all this but how can this happen if the old labels remain and continue to recall to his mind old notions. If new notions are to be inculcated in the minds of people it is necessary to give them new names. To continue the old name is to make the reform futile. To allow this Chaturvarnya, based on worth to be designated by such stinking labels of Brahmin, Kshatriya, Vaishya, Shudra, indicative of social divisions based on birth, is a snare.

XIII

To me this Chaturvarnya with its old labels is utterly repellent and my whole being rebels against it. But I do not wish to rest my objection to Chaturvarnya on mere grounds of sentiments. There are more solid grounds on which I rely for my opposition to it. A close examination of this ideal has convinced me that as a system of social organization, Chaturvarnya is impracticable, harmful and has turned out to be a miserable failure. From a practical point of view, the system of Chaturvarnya raises several difficulties which its protagonists do not seem to have taken into account. The principle underlying caste is fundamentally different from the principle underlying *Varna*. Not only are they fundamentally different but they are also fundamentally opposed. The former is based on worth. How are you going to compel people who have acquired a higher status based on birth without reference to their worth to vacate that status? How are you going to compel people to recognize the status due to a man in accordance with his worth, who is occupying a lower status based on his birth? For this you must first break up the caste system, in order to be able to establish the *Varna* system. How are you going to reduce the four thousand caste, based on birth, to the four *Varnas,* based on worth? This is the first difficulty which the protagonists of the Chaturvarnya must grapple with. There is a second difficulty which the protagonists of Chaturvarnya must grapple with, if they whish to make the establishment of Chaturvarnya a success.

Chaturvarnya presupposes that you can classify people into four definite classes. Is this possible? In this possible? In this respect, the ideal of Chaturvarnya has, as you will see, a close affinity to the Platonic ideal. To Plato, men fell by nature into three classes. In some individuals, he believed mere appetites dominated. He assigned them to the labouring and trading classes. Others revealed to him that over and above appetites, they have a courageous disposition. He classed them as defenders in war and guardians of internal peace. Others showed a capacity to grasp the universal reason underlying things. He made them the law-givers of the people. The criticism to which Plato's *Republic* is subject, is also the criticism which must apply to the system of Chaturvarnya, in so far as it proceeds upon the possibility of an accurate classification of men into four distinct classes. The chief criticism against Plato is that his idea of lumping of individuals into a few sharply marked-off classes is a very superficial view of man and his powers. Plato had no perception of the uniqueness of every individual, of his incommensurability with others, of each individual forming a class of his own. He had no recognition of the infinite diversity of active tendencies and combination of tendencies of which an individual is capable. To him, there were types of faculties or powers in the individual constitution. All this is demonstrably wrong. Modern science has shown that lumping together of individuals into a few sharply marked-off classes is a superficial view of man not worthy of serious consideration. Consequently the utilization of the qualities of individuals in incompatible with their stratification by classes, since the qualities of individuals are so variable. Chaturvarnya must fail for the very reason for which Plato's Republic must fail, namely that it is not possible to pigeon men into holes, according as he belongs to one class or the other. That it is impossible to accurately classify people into four definite classes is proved by the fact that the original four classes have now become four thousand castes.

There is a third difficulty in the way of the establishment of the system of Chaturvarnya. How are you going to maintain the system of Chaturvarnya, supposing it was established. One important requirement for the successful working of Chaturvarnya is the maintenance of the penal system which could maintain it by its sanction. The system of Chaturvarnya must perpetually face the problem of the transgressor. Unless there is a penalty attached to the act of transgression, men will not keep to their respective classes. The whole system will break down, being contrary to human nature. Chaturvarnya cannot subsist by its own inherent goodness. It must be enforced by law. That, without penal sanction the ideal of Chaturvarnya cannot be realized is proved by the story in the Ramayana of Rama killing Shambuka. Some people seem to blame Rama because he wantonly and without reason killed Shambuka. But to blame Rama for killing Shambuka is to misunderstand the whole situation. Ram Raj was a Raj based on Chaturvarnya. As a king, Rama was bound to maintain Chaturvarnya. It was his duty therefore to kill Shambuka, the Shudra, who had transgressed his class and wanted to be a Brahmin. This is the reason why Rama killed Shambuka. But this also shows that penal sanction is necessary for the maintenance of Chaturvarnya. Not only penal sanction is necessary, but penalty of death is necessary. That is why Rama did not inflict on Shambuka a lesser punishment. That is why Manu-Smriti prescribes such heavy sentences as cutting off the tongue or pouring of molten lead in the ears of the Shudra, who recites or hears the *Veda*. The supporters of Chaturvarnya must give an assurance that they could successfully classify men and they could induce modern society in the twentieth century to reforge the penal sanctions of *Manu-Smriti*.

This protagonists of *Chaturvarnya* do not seem to have considered what is to happen to women in their system. Are they also to be divided into four classes, Brahmin, Kshatriya, Vaishya and Shudra? Or are they to be allowed to take the status of their husbands. If the status of the woman is to be the consequence of marriage what becomes of the underlying principle of Chaturvarnya, namely, that the status of a person should be based upon the worth of that person? If t5hey are to be classified according to their worth is their classification to be national or real? If it is to be nominal then it is useless and then the protagonists of Chaturvarnya must admit that their system does not apply to women. If it is real, are the protagonists of Chaturvarnya prepared to follow the logical consequences of applying it to women? They must be prepared to have women priests and women soldiers. Hindus society has grown accustomed to women teachers and women barristers. It may grow accustomed to women brewers and women butchers. But he would be a bold person, who would say that is will allow women priests and women soldiers. But that will be the logical outcome of applying Chaturvarnya to women. Given these difficulties, I think no one except a congenital idiot could hope and believe in a successful regeneration of the Chaturvarnya.

XIV

Assuming that Chaturvarnya is practicable, I contend that it is the most vicious system. That the Brahmins should cultivate knowledge, that the Kshatriya should bear arms, that the Vaishya should trade and that the Shudra should serve sounds as though it was a system of division of labour. Whether the theory was intended to sate that the Shudra need not or that whether it was intended to lay down that he must not, is an interesting question. The defenders of Chaturvarnya give it the first meaning. They say, why should the Shudra need trouble to acquire wealth, when the three *Varnas* are there to support him? Why need the Shudra bother to take to education when there is the Brahmin to whom he can go when the occasion for reading or writing arises? Why need the *Shudra* worry to arm himself because there is the Kshatriya to protect him? The theory of Chaturvarnya, understood in this sense, may be said to look upon the Shudra as the ward and the three *Varnas* as his guardians. Thus interpreted it is a simple, elevating and alluring theory. Assuming this to be the correct view of the underlying conception of Chaturvarnya, it seems to me that the system is neither fool-proof nor knave-proof. What is to happen, if the Brahmins, Vaishyas and Kshatriyas fail to pursue knowledge, to engage in economic enterprise and to be efficient soldiers which are their respective functions? Contrary-wise, suppose that they discharge their functions but flout their duty to the *Shudra* or to one another, what is to happen to the *Shudra* if the three classes refuse to support him or fair terms or combine to keep him down? Who is to safeguard the interests of the *Shudra* or for the matter of that of the Vaishya and Kshatriya when the person, who is trying to take advantage of his ignorance is the Brahmin? Who is to defend the liberty of the *Shudra* and for the matter of that, of the Brahmin and the Vaishya when the person who is robbing him of it is the Kshatriya? Inter-dependence of one class on another class is inevitable. Even dependence of one class upon another may sometimes become allowable. But why make one person depend upon another in the matter of his vital needs? Education everyone must have. Means of defence everyone must have. These are the paramount requirements of every man for his self preservation. How can the fact that his neighbour is educated and armed help a man who is uneducated and disarmed. The whole theory is absurd.

These are the questions, which the defenders of Chaturvarnya do not seem to be troubled about. But they are very pertinent questions. Assuming their conception of Chaturvarnya that the relationship between the different classes is that of ward and guardian is the real conception underlying Chaturvarnya, it must be admitted that it makes no provision to safeguard the interests of the ward from the misdeeds of the guardian. Whether the relationship of guardian and ward was the real underlying conception, on which Chaturvarnya was based, there is not doubt that in practice the relation was that of master and servants. The three classes, Brahmins, Kshtriyas and Vaishyas although not very happy in their mutual relationship managed to work by compromise. The Brahmin flattered the Kshatriya and both let the Vaishya live in order to be able to live upon him. But the three agreed to beat down the Shudra. He was not allowed to acquire wealth lest he should be independent of the three *Varnas.* He was prohibited from acquiring knowledge lest he should keep a steady vigil regarding his interests. He was prohibited from bearing arms lest he should have the means to rebel against their authority. That this is how the *Shudras* were treated by the Tryavarnikas is evidenced by the Laws of Manu. There is no code of laws more infamous regarding social rights than the Laws of Manu. Any instance from anywhere of social injustice must pale before it. Why have the mass of people tolerated the social evils to which they have been subjected? There have been social revolutions in other countries of the world. Why have there not been social revolutions in India is a question which has incessantly troubled me. There is only one answer, which I can give and it is that the lower classes of Hindus have been completely, disabled for direct action on account of this wretched system of Chaturvarnya. They could not bear arms and without arms they could not rebel. They were all ploughmen or rather condemned to be ploughmen and they never were allowed to convert their ploughshare into swords. They had no bayonets and therefore everyone who chose could and did sit upon them. On account of the Chaturvarnya, they could receive no education. They could not think out or know the way to their salvation. They were condemned to be lowly and not knowing the way of escape and not having the means of escape, they became reconciled to eternal servitude, which they accepted as their inescapable fate.

It is true that even in Europe the strong have not shrunk from exploitation, may the spoliation of the weak. But in Europe, the strong have never contrived to make the weak helpless against exploitation so shamelessly as was the case in India among the Hindus. Social was has been raging between the strong and the weak for more violently in Europe than it has ever been in India. Yet, the weak in Europe has had in his freedom of military service his *physical weapon,* in suffering his *political weapon* and in education his *moral weapon*. These three weapons for emancipation were never withheld by the strong from the weak in Europe. All these weapons were, however, denied to the masses in India by Chaturvarnya. There cannot be a more degrading system of social organization than the Chaturvarnya. It is the system which deadens, paralyses and cripples the people from helpful activity. This is no exaggeration. History bears ample evidence. There is only one period in Indian history which is a period of freedom, greatness and glory. That is the period of the Maurya Empire. At all other times the country suffered from defeat and darkness. But the Maurya period was a period when Chaturvarnya was completely annihilated, when the Shudras, who constituted the mass of the people, came into their own and became the rulers of the country. The period of defeat and darkness is the period when Chaturvarnya flourished to the damnation of the greater part of the people of the country.

(From *The Essential Writings of B.R. Ambedkar* (ed) Valerian Rodrigues, Oxford University Press, New Delhi, 2009. pp 263-284)

Challenges of Democracy

I

In taking the side of the Congress as an organization 'fighting for freedom,' the foreigner does not stop to make a distinction between the freedom of a country and the freedom of the people in the country. In not stopping to make this distinction, the foreigner, it must be said, far from understanding the matter, is allowing himself to be misled, if not deceived. For words such as society, nation and country are just amorphous, if not ambiguous, terms. There is no gainsaying that 'Nation', though one word means many classes. Philosophically it may be possible to consider a nation as a unit but sociologically it cannot but be regarded as consisting of many classes and the freedom of the nation if it is to be a reality must vouchsafe the freedom of the different classes comprised in it, particularly those who are treated as the servile classes. Consequently, it is foolish to take solace in the fact that because the Congress is fighting for the freedom of India, it is, therefore, fighting for the freedom of the people of India and of the lowest of the low.

The question whether the Congress is fighting for freedom has very little importance as compared to the question for whose freedom is the Congress fighting. This is a pertinent and necessary inquiry and it would be wrong for any lover of freedom to support the Congress without pursuing the matter and finding out what the truth is. But the foreigner who takes the side of the Congress does not care even to raise such a question? Why is the foreigner so indifferent to so important a question? So far as I am able to judge, the reason for such indifference is to be found in the wrong notions of self-government and democracy which are prevalent in the West and which form the stock-in-trade of the foreigner who takes interest in Indian politics.

It is propounded by Western writers on politics that all that is necessary for the realization of self-government is the existence among a people of what Grote called constitutional morality. By constitutional morality is meant Habits of paramount reverence for the form of the constitution, enforcing obedience to the authorities acting under and within those forms yet combined with the habit of open speech, of action subject only to definite legal control, and unrestrained censure of those very authorities as to all their public acts—combined, too, with a perfect confidence in the bosom of every citizen, admits the bitterness of party contest, that the forms of constitution will be not less sacred in the eyes of his opponents than in his own.

If in a populace these habits are present, then according to Western writers on politics, self-government can be a reality and nothing further need be considered. Similarly, Western writers on democracy believe that what is necessary for the realization of the ideal of democracy, namely, government by the people, of the people and for the people, is the establishment of universal adult suffrage. Other means have been suggested such as recall, plebiscite and short parliaments and in some countries they have been brought into operation. But in a majority of countries nothing more than adult suffrage is deemed to be necessary.

I have no hesitation in saying that both these notions are fallacious and grossly misleading. If democracy and self-government have failed everywhere, it is largely due to these wrong notions. Habits of constitutional morality may be essential for the maintenance of a constitutional form of government. But the maintenance of a constitutional form of government is not the same thing as self-government by the people. Similarly, it may be granted that adult suffrage can produce government of the people in the logical sense of the phrase, i.e. in contrast to the government of a king. But it cannot by itself be said to bring about a democratic government, in the sense of government by the people and for the people.

These views of Western writers on politics regarding democracy and self-government are erroneous for very many reasons. In the first place, they omit to take into account the incontrovertible fact that in every country there is a governing class grown up by force of historical circumstances, which is destined to rule, which does rule and to whom adult suffrage and constitutional morality are no bar against reaching places of power and authority and to whom the servile classes, by reason of the fact that they regard the members of the governing classes as their natural' leaders, volunteer to elect as rulers.

Secondly, they fail to realize that the existence of a governing class is inconsistent with democracy and self-government and that given the fact that where the governing class retains its power to govern, it is wrong to say that democracy and self-government exist unless democracy and self-government are regarded as mere matters of form.

Thirdly, they do not seem to be aware that self-government and democracy become real not when a Constitution based on adult suffrage' conies into existence but when the governing class loses its: power to capture the power to govern.

Fourthly, they seem to overlook the fact that while in some countries the servile classes may succeed in ousting the governing class from the seat of authority with nothing more than adult suffrage, in other countries the governing class may be so well entrenched that the servile classes will need other safeguards besides adult suffrage achieve the same end.

Lastly, they seem to pay no heed to fact that given the existence of the governing class what matters most in the consideration of any scheme of democracy and self government is the social outlook and social philosophy of the governing class, for so long as the governing class retains its means to capture the power to govern, the freedom and the well-being of the servile classes must depend upon the social outlook, the social conscience of the governing class and its philosophy of life.

The recognition of the existence of a governing class as fundamental and a crucial fact confronting democracy and government is the only safe and realistic approach to those wish for democracy and self-government to come into their our it is a fatal blunder to omit to take account of it in coming to conclusion as to whether in a free country freedom will be the privilege of the governing class only or it will be the possession of all. In my view, therefore, what the foreigner who chooses to side with the Congress should ask is not whether the Congress is fighting for freedom. He should ask: For whose freedom is the Congress fighting? Is it fighting for the freedom of the governing class in India or is it fighting for the freedom of the people of India? If he finds that the Congress is fighting for the freedom of the governing class, he should ask Congressmen: Is the governing class in India fit to govern? This is the least he can do before siding with the Congress.

What are the answers which Congressmen have to give to these questions? I do not know. But I can give what I think are the only true answers to these questions.

II

To start with it is well to know who constitute the governing class in India. The governing class in India consists principally of the Brahmins. It is strange that the present-day Brahmins repudiate the .allegation that they belong to the governing class though at one time they described themselves as *Bhudevas* (God on Earth). What can this *volte face* be due to? Is it due to a guilty conscience born out of the realization that they have committed criminal breach of the trust imposed upon the intellectual sections in every community by the sacred law of humanity not to serve the interest their own class but to safeguard the interest of all and therefore dare not stand before the bar of the world? Or is it due to their sense of modesty? It is unnecessary to stop to speculate as to which is the truth.

That the Brahmins are a governing class is hardly open to question. There are two tests one could apply. First is the sentiment of the people and the second is the control of administration. I am sure there cannot be better and more decisive tests than these two. As to the first, there cannot be any doubt. Taking the attitude of the people, the person of the Brahmin is sacred. In ancient times, he could not be hanged no matter what offence he committed. As a sacred person he had immunities and privileges which were denied to the servile class. He was, entitled to first fruits. In Malabar, where the Sambandham marriage prevails, the servile classes such as the Nairs regard it an honour to have their females kept as mistresses by Brahmins. Even kings invited Brahmins to deflower their queens of *prima noctis*. There was a time when no person of the servile class could take his food without drinking the water in which the toes of the Brahmins were washed.

Under the British Government and by reason of its equalitarian jurisprudence these rights, immunities and privileges of the Brahmins have ceased to exist. Nonetheless the advantages they gave still remain and the Brahmin is still pre-eminent and sacred in the eyes of the servile classes and is still addressed by them as 'Swami' which means 'Lord.'

Whether the Brahmins claim themselves to be members of the governing class or not, the facts that they control the administration and that their supremacy is accepted by the servile classes, are enough to establish the point. History shows that the Brahmin has always had other classes as his allies to whom he was ready to accord the status of governing class provided they were prepared to work with him subordinate co-operation. In ancient and medieval times he made such an alliance with the Kshatriyas or the warrior class and the two ruled the masses, indeed ground them down, the Brahmin with his pen and the Kshatriya with his sword. At present, the Brahmin has made an alliance with the Vaishya class called Banias. The shifting of this alliance from Kshatriya to Bania is natural. In these days of commerce money is more important than sword. That is one reason for this change in party alignment. The second reason is the need for money to run the political machine. Money can come only from the Bania. It is the Bania who is financing the Congress largely because Mr Gandhi is a Bania and also because he has realized that money invested in politics gives large dividends. Those who have any doubts in the matter might do well to read what Mr Gandhi told Mr Louis Fisher on 6 June 1942. Reports Fisher :

'I said I had several questions to ask him about the Congress Party. Very highly placed Britishers, I recalled, had told me that Congress was in the hands of big business and that Gandhi was supported by the Bombay millowners who gave him as much money as he wanted. 'What truth is there in these assertions,' I asked.

'Unfortunately, they are true,' he declared simply, 'Congress hasn't enough money to conduct its work. We thought in the beginning to collect four annas (about eight cents) from each member per year and operate on that. But it hasn't worked.'

'What proportion of the Congress budget,' I asked, 'is covered by rich Indians?'

'Practically all of it', he stated. 'In this ashram, for instance, we could live much more poorly than we do and spend less money. But we do not and the money comes from our rich friends.'

For this reason, it is impossible for the Brahmin to exclude the Bania from the position of a governing class. In fact, he has established not merely a working but a cordial alliance with the Bania. The result is that the governing class in India today is a Brahmin-Bania instead of the Brahmin-Kshatriya combine as it used to be. The existence of the governing class does not cover the whole story. What is significant is that the members of the governing class in India are quite conscious of the fact that they do belong to the governing class and that they alone are destined to rule. The late Mr Tilak could never forget that he was a Brahmin and belonged to the governing class. The same is reported to be the case about Pandit Jawaharlal Nehru and his sister Mrs Vijaya Laxmi Pandit.

Nor is Mr Vallabhbhai Patel free from the feeling that he belongs to the governing class. Mr Tilak is held out as the father of the Swaraj movement. Pandit Nehru and Mr Vallabhbhai Patel are the leading members of the Congress High Command. Not only are they conscious of the fact that they belong to the governing class but some of them hold that the servile classes are a contemptible people, who must remain servile and who must never aspire to rule. Indeed, they have felt no shame and no remorse in giving public expression to such views. In 1918, when the Non-Brahmins and the Backward Classes had started an agitation for separate representation in the Legislature, Mr Tilak in a public meeting held in Sholapur said he did not understand why the oil pressers, tobacco shopkeepers, washermen, etc.—that was his description of the Non-Brahmms and the Backward Classes—should want to go into the Legislature. In his opinion, their business was to obey the laws and not to aspire for power to make laws. In 1942, Lord Linlithgow invited 52 important Indians representing different sections of the people to discuss what steps could be taken to make the Central Government more popular with a view to enlist the sympathy and co-operation of .all Indians in war effort. Among those that were invited were members belonging to the Scheduled Castes. Mr Vallabhbbai Patel could not bear the idea that the Viceroy should have invited such a crowd of mean men. Soon after the event, Mr Vallabhbhai Patel made a speech in Ahmedabad and said:

The Viceroy sent for the leaders of the Hindu Mahasabha, he sent for the leaders of the Muslim League and he sent for Ghanchis (oil pressers), Mochis (cobblers) and the rest.

Although Mr Vallabhbhai Patel in his malicious and stinging words referred only to Ghanchis and Mochis, his speech is indicative of the general contempt in which the governing class and the members of the Congress High Command hold the servile classes of this country. Further illustrations of this attitude of the governing class and the Congress High Command can be found from incidents that have taken place in the election campaigns. They are so relevant and so revealing that a special mention must be made of them.

III

What is TO be the fate of the servile classes of India under this governing class?

The Congress promises to do wonders for the servile classes— the Congress speaks of masses, it ought really to speak of them as the servile classes held in bondage by the governing classes— when Swaraj comes. It says that it would like to make revolutionary changes but it has no power to make them and it must wait for Swaraj. It is this glib talk which .goes to deceive the gullible foreigner. Leaving aside the boast and bluster which lie behind the statement, one may ask what really can happen if 'India does become a sovereign and an independent state? One thing is certain. The governing class will not disappear by the magic wand of Swaraj. It will remain as it is and having been freed from the incubus of British imperialism will acquire greater strength and vigour. It will capture power as the governing classes in every country do. In short, Swaraj will not be government by the people but it will be a government run by the governing class and in the absence of government by the people, government for the people will be what the governing class will choose to make of it.

What will the governing class do when India becomes a sovereign and independent state? Some hope that they will undertake reform of tenancy laws, enlarge factory legislation, extend primary education, introduce prohibition and train people to ply charkha, construct roads and canals, improve currency, regulate weights and measures, open dispensaries and undertake other measures to ameliorate the condition of the servile classes. No one from the servile class can be very enthusiastic about such a programme. In the first place, there is nothing very great in it. In the world of today, no governing class can omit to undertake reforms which are necessary to maintain society in a civilized state.

Personally, I have grave doubts about the governing class in India coming forward to carry out even such a modest programme of social amelioration. Most people forget that what leads the Congress today to mouth such a programme is the desire to show that the Congress is better than the British bureaucracy. But once the bureaucracy is liquidated, will there be the same incentive to better the lot of the masses? I entertain very grave doubts on the point. Apart from this, is social amelioration the be-all and end-all of Swaraj? Speaking for the servile classes, I have no doubt that what they expect to happen in a sovereign and free India is a complete destruction of Brahminism as a philosophy of life and as a social order. If I may say so, the servile classes do not care for social amelioration. The want and poverty which has been their lot is nothing to them as compared to the insult and indignity which they have to bear as a result of the vicious social order. Not bread but honour, is what they want. The question therefore is: Will the governing classes in India having captured the machinery of the State, undertake a programme for the reform of the social order as distinguished from a programme of social amelioration?

The statement by Congressmen that Congress can do wonders if only India was a sovereign and an independent State, supposing that it is an honest aspiration and not mere propaganda, proceeds on the assumption that for a man to do what he wants, nothing more is necessary than power. Such a belief is not only pitiable but is really a dangerous illusion. Those who are inclined to cherish such an illusion forget that there are serious limitations on sovereignty, no matter how absolute it is. None has described these limitations in more telling language than Dicey. In his *Law of the Constitution*, he says:

> The actual exercise of authority by any sovereign whatever, and notably by Parliament, is bounded or controlled by two limitations. Of these the one is an external, the other is an internal limitation.
>
> The external limit to the real power of a sovereign consists in the possibility or certainty that his subjects or a large number of them will disobey or resist his laws.

This limitation exists even under the most despotic monarchies. A Roman Emperor, or a French King during the middle of the eighteenth century, was (as is the Russian Czar at the present day) in strictness a 'sovereign' in the legal sense of that term. He had absolute legislative authority. Any law made by him was binding, and there was no power in the empire or kingdom which could annul such law.... But it would be an error to suppose that the most absolute ruler who ever existed could in reality make or change every law at his pleasure.

The authority, that is to say, even of a despot, depends upon the readiness of his subjects or of some portion of his subjects to obey his behests and this readiness to obey must always be in reality limited. This is shown by the most notorious facts of history. None of the early Caesars could at their pleasure have subvened the worship of fundamental institutions of the Roman world. The Sultan could not abolish Mahommedanism. Louis the Fourteenth at the height of his power could revoke the Edict of Nantes, but he would have found it impossible to establish the supremacy of Protestantism, and for the same reason which prevented James the Second from establishing the supremacy of Roman Catholicism. What is true of the power of a despot or of the authority of a constituent assembly is specially true of the sovereignty of Parliament; it is limited on every side by the possibility of popular resistance. Parliament might legally establish an Episcopal Church in Scotland; Parliament might legally tax the Colonies; Parliament might without any breach of law change the succession to the throne or abolish the monarchy; but everyone knows that in the present state of the world the British Parliament will do none of these things. In each case widespread resistance would result from legislation which, though legally valid, is in fact beyond the stretch of parliamentary power.

The internal limit to the exercise of sovereignty arises from the nature of the sovereign power itself. Even a despot exercises his powers in accordance with his character, which is itself moulded by the circumstances under which he lives, including under that head the moral feelings of the time and the society to which he belongs. The Sultan could not if he would, change the religion of the Mahommedan world, but if he could do so

> it is in the very highest degree improbable that the head of Mahommedanism should wish to overthrow the religion of Mahomet; the internal check on the exercise of the Sultan's power is at least as strong as the external limitation. People sometimes ask the idle question why the Pope does not introduce this or that reform? The true answer is that a revolutionist is not the kind of man who becomes a Pope, and that the man who becomes a Pope has no wish to be a revolutionist.

None can gainsay the truth of what Dicey has said. What the governing class may do depends not so much upon the degree of its sovereignty as upon what Dicey calls the external and internal limitations in sovereignty. Of these two, if the failure to do good arises out of the external limitations, nobody need blame the governing class. The fear of external limitations blocking progress need not cause much apprehension. For it is the internal limitations of the governing class that have a greater determining force than the external limitations. Progress depends more upon internal limitations of the governing class than upon external limitations. What are the factors which determine these internal limitations? The internal limitations are born out of the outlook, traditions, vested interests and the social philosophy of the governing class. The purpose of this discussion is to warn the foreigner that before believing what the Congress proposes to do for the servile classes, he should make it a point to ask: What is the outlook of the governing, class? What are its traditions? What is its social philosophy?

To take the Brahmins first. Historically they have been the most inveterate enemy of the servile classes (Shudras and the Untouchables) who together constitute about 80 per cent of the total Hindu population. If the common man belonging to the servile classes in India is today so fallen, so degraded, so devoid of hope and ambition, it is entirely due to the Brahmins and their philosophy. The cardinal principles of this philosophy of Brahmariism are five: (1) graded inequality between the different classes; (2) complete disarmament of the Shudras and the Untouchables; (3) complete prohibition of the education of the Shudras and the Untouchables; (4) ban on the Shudras and the Untouchables occupying places of power and authority; (5) ban on the Shudras and the Untouchables acquiring property. (6) complete subjugation and suppression of women. Inequality is the official doctrine of Brahminism and the suppression of the lower classes aspiring to equality has been looked upon by them and carried out by them without remorse as their bounden duty. There are countries where education did not spread beyond a few. But India is the only country where the intellectual class, namely, the Brahmins not only made education their monopoly but declared acquisition of education by the lower classes, a crime punishable by cutting off of the tongue or by the pouring of molten lead in the ear of the offender. The Congress politicians complain that the British are ruling India by a wholesale disarmament of the people of India. But they forget that disarmament of the Shudras and the Untouchables was the rule of law promulgated by the Brahmins. Indeed, so strongly did the Brahmins believe in the disarmament of the Shudras and the Untouchables that when they revised the law to enable the Brahmins to arm themselves for the protection of their own privileges, they maintained the ban on the Shudras and the Untouchables as it was without lessening its rigour. If the large majority of people of India appear today to be thoroughly emasculated, spiritless, with no manliness, it is the result of the Brahminic policy of wholesale disarmament to which they have been subjected for the untold ages.

There is no social evil and no social wrong to which the Brahmin does not give his support. Man's inhumanity to man, such as the feeling of caste, untouchability, unapproachability and unseeability is a religion to him. It would, however, be a mistake to suppose that only the wrongs of man are a religion to him. For the Brahmin has given his support to the worst wrongs that women have suffered from in any part of the world. Widows were burnt alive as *sattees*. The Brahmin gave his fullest support to *Sattee*, the burning alive of a widow. Widows were not allowed to remarry. The Brahmin upheld the doctrine. Girls were required to be married before 8 and the husband had the right to consummate the marriage at any time thereafter, whether she had reached puberty or not did not matter. The Brahmin gave the doctrine his strongest support.

The record of the Brahmins as law-givers for the Shudras, for the Untouchables and for women is the blackest as compared with the record of the intellectual classes in other parts of the world. For no intellectual class has prostituted its intelligence to invent a philosophy to keep his uneducated countrymen in a perpetual state of ignorance and poverty as the Brahmins have done in India. Every Brahmin today believes in this philosophy of Brahminism propounded by his forefathers. He is an alien element in the Hindu Society. The Brahmin vis-a-vis Shudras and the Untouchables is as foreign as the German is to the French, as the Jew is to the Gentile or as the White is to the Negro. There is a real gulf between him and the lower classes of Shudras and Untouchables. He is not only alien to them but he is also hostile to them. In relationship with them, there is no room for conscience and there is no call for justice.

The Bania is the worst parasitic class known to history. In him the vice of money-making is unredeemed by culture or conscience. He is like an undertaker who prospers when there is an epidemic. The only difference between the undertaker and the Bania is that the undertaker does not create an epidemic while the Bania does. He does not use his money for production. He uses it to create poverty and more poverty by lending money for unproductive purposes. He lives on interest and as he is told by his religion that money lending is the occupation prescribed to him by Manu, he looks upon it as both right and righteous. With the help and assistance of the Brahmin judge who is ready to decree his suits, he is able to carry on his trade. Interest, interest on interest, he adds on and on and thereby draws families perpetually into his net. Pay him as much as a debtor may, he is always in debt. With no conscience, there is no fraud, and no chicanery that he will not commit. His grip over the nation is complete. The whole of poor, starving, illiterate India is mortgaged to the Bania.

To sum up, the Brahmin enslaves the mind and the Bania enslaves the body. Between them, they divide the spoils which belong to the governing classes. Can anyone who realizes what the outlook, tradition and social philosophy of the governing class in India is, believe that under the Congress regime, a sovereign and independent India will be different from the India we have today?

(From *Dr. Babasaheb Ambedkar's Writings and Speeches*, published by Education Department, Government of Maharastra, Mumbai Vol-9, 1990, pp 201-217).

16

Jaya Prakash Narayan

Life and Times

Socialism both evolutionary and revolutionary cast a spell on the colonial India particularly after the Bolshevik Revolution of 1917. Broadly speaking, Indian socialism derived its principles and programmes from three sources- Marxism, British socialism and Gandhism, though the three influenced different socialist thinkers in different measure, and many of them reinterpreted and reformulated the ideas and doctrines of their mentors. For example, Narendra Dev and Jaya Prakash Narayan (JP) were among the greatest of the Indian Marxists but they had their independent interpretation of marxism, while Lohia whose socialist ideas had a distinctly Gandhian stamp was at best a 'non-conformist' Gandhian. Moreover, there were thinkers like Dr. Sampoornanand and later on JP who conceived life in broader and deeper perspective, rather in Vedantic terms, and could never accept a social order wedded to material and economic objectives alone as it did not ensure man's lasting good. Dr. Gyan Chand, the eminent economist is right in holding that socialism in India was at first distrusted because of its imputed materialist philosophy and it could become a force to reckon with only after it adapted itself to the deep currents of national life and urges of its inmost spirit.

Jaya Prakash Narayan (1902-1979) occupies a unique place in the history of Indian socialism. Born in 1902 in a middle class family in Bihar, his political life began in 1921 while he was still a college student at Patna. Gandhi's stirring call to countrymen to cease to cooperate with the British government in every sphere led young JP to leave studies and participate in the non-cooperation movement. This cost him his scholarship he had been receiving in the college. In 1922 he went to USA for higher studies and earned for his maintenance through various petty works. He spent about seven years in America and studied at the universities of California, Iowa, Wisconsin and Ohio. There he came into the contact with the Marxian ideology and some east European intellectuals. The Marxist ideologue M. N. Roy also influenced him. As he later said, " in the company of Jewish and European- born fellow students, I drank deep at the fountain of Marxism..............we left nothing unread of Marxism that was available." After his return to India in 1929, Nehru who was the congress president, decided to use his services in organizing the Labour Research Department of the Indian National Congress. He was one of the founders of Congress Socialist Party in 1934 and displayed remarkable genius in popularizing the party and its programme.

JP was a valiant fighter for the national freedom. He was one of the heroes of Quit India Movement of 1942. During the movement, he was imprisoned but he miraculously escaped from the Hazaribagh Central Jail ' to stem the ebb-tide of the August struggle.' He along with Lohia and others engaged in the underground activities and led the national struggle while most of the Congress leaders were in jail. Throughout the colonial period, JP often advocated the use of arms and clearly stated that he was no believer in Gandhian non-violence. He was subsequently arrested. After his release in 1946, he opposed the acceptance of Cabinet Mission Plan because he and the Congress Socialist Party thought in terms of mass revolution against the British government.

As India was inching towards freedom, a subtle yet perceptible transformation was taking place in the thinking of JP. He was losing faith in the efficacy and sufficiency of external, institutional changes, particularly of changes brought about through political power. Gandhian emphasis on the moral regeneration as the key to just and peaceful social order now greatly appealed to him. In

1954, he resigned from the national executive of P.S.P. and later snapped all relation with party politics. The key to India's reconstruction, he found in Sarvodaya and along with Vinoba Bhave he dedicated himself to the task of bringing about a social order based on Sarvodaya principles.

His major involvement in the national politics of post-independent India was to come in 1974 when he spearheaded a mass-movement against the government of Mrs. Indira Gandhi which, he said, epitomized moral decadence of the ruling class of India. His heroic struggle led to the crushing defeat of Mrs. Gandhi in the general election of 1977 and coming to power of the Janata government. However, sordid happenings in the party and government greatly saddened him and he came face to face with the bitter truth that ' total revolution' was a lofty ideal beyond the capacity of petty politicians. He passed away in 1979. His main writings are-*Why Socialism?*, *From Socialism to Sarvodaya*, *A Plea for the Reconstruction of Indian Polity*.

JP was a thinker whose ideas kept on evolving not out of expediency but out of conviction. In his early phase, he was a staunch marxist, but later on realizing the limitations and futility of insurrectionary methods of social change, he turned to democratic-socialism. However with collectivist creeds getting deformed for one reason or other, he turned to the philosophy of Sarvodaya and found it distinctly superior to existing social philosophies and systems. Thus his ideological journey can be divided in three broad phases-(i) the Marxist phase between 1929-1946 (ii) The social-democratic phase between 1946-1954 and (iii) the Sarvodaya phase since then.

When JP returned to India from U.S.A. in 1929, his conversion to Marxism had been completed. The Marxian science of revolution appealed him more than Gandhian technique of civil disobedience as far as India's freedom was concerned. Besides, Marxism provided another beacon of light- equality and brotherhood to him. He found in socialism an economic doctrine which through state or social ownership of the means of production was capable of eradicating concentration of wealth in fewer and fewer hands. He favoured socialization of key industries and elimination of the class of princes, landlords and capitalists.

As a marxist, he had unflinching faith in the theory of dialectical materialism. He agreed with the marxian proposition that man and his institutions are the reflection of the material forces and "social division is an organic process of society.................its primary source lay in the manner in which men earned their livelihood." Socialism, he said, is 'and inquiry into the causes of economic inequality, into the origin of exploitation'. He called Marx an 'environmentalist' because it was the social and economic environment that moulded the individual and his institutions.

In his book *Why Socialism?* published in 1934, JP praised the economic and social reconstruction of Russia under 'world leader' Stalin, and said that Russian society was 'as free from exploitation as any society of idyllic fancy'. He defended the use of violence as necessary for creating a new social order. He said that Russia was a symbol of steady economic progress in the midst of capitalist paralysis and contradictions. He pleaded for the cooperative and collective farming because present individualistic organization of agriculture was wasteful. JP ridiculed the Gandhian theory of trusteeship and went on to characterize Gandhism as being "a serious bog of timid economic analysis, good intentions and ineffective moralizing." He also felt that ancient Indian social philosophy of Varnas and Ashramas could not offer any insight into or solution for the complex problems of modern industrial society.

The policies of C.P.I. and the happenings in Soviet Russia during Stalin's rule indicated the process of alienation of JP from Marxism-Leninism. He could not digest C.P.I.'s denunciation of national movement as bourgeoisie. The fact that Indian communists were meekly following the policy of Third International under Stalin greatly shocked him. The misdeeds of Stalinist regime accelerated this process and led him to re-examine the Marxist theory. In the earlier years, he had concluded that C.P.I. and Soviet Russia were misapplying Marxian principles to India in particular and world in general. But now he became sure that these things are not aberrations but part and parcel of Marxism-Leninism. Marxism regards any means as good provided they serve the ends of social revolution. Thus as a philosophy of action, it is amoral. The evil ends that had resulted from the evil means in Russia revolted him from 'the revolutionary ethics' of Marxism and led him to ponder whether good ends could ever be achieved by the bad means. Moreover the unabashed concentration of power would result, as it did in Russia, not only in the denial of freedom but also of justice and equality.

Having broken with Marxism-Leninism, JP like Lohia and other socialists started thinking in terms of democratic-socialism. In his writings such as 'Democratic Socialism-the Ideal and the Method' and ' The Ideological problems of Socialism', he talked about a democratic road to socialism citing Marx's famous speech at Hague in which he had admitted the possibility of peaceful transition to socialism in favourable circumstances. As a democratic-socialist, he advocated the following;

State should be guided by the ethical values. State should be decentralized. Both economic structures and ownership should be dispersed. Peaceful democratic methods which include mass-action of a non-violent character must be used to achieve the goal of socialist society. Man must learn to restrict and control his material needs. Without self-control, there can be no equality and freedom.

But democratic-socialism proved to be small consolation to the quest of Jaya Prakash Narayan. His quest for a total philosophy could not have been satisfied by various one-sided ideologies. He was finally face to face with the fundamental issue of materialism *vs* spiritualism; and in this respect, the Gandhian world-view was a valuable guide to him. He observed in one of his writings- "For many years I have worshipped at the shrine of goddess of Dialectical Materialism, which seemed to me intellectually more satisfying than any other philosophy. But while the main quest of philosophy remains unsatisfied, it has become patent to me that materialism of any sort robs man of the means to become truly human. In a material civilization, man has no rational incentive to be good. It may be that in the kingdom of dialectical materialism, fear makes men conform and the party takes the place of God. But when God himself turns vicious, to be vicious becomes a universal code". In course of his ideological journey from Marxism to Sarvodaya he was becoming convinced that materialism offered no basis or incentive to be good without which a just social order was inconceivable. If man is merely a combination of matter and energy fortuitously brought into existence and destined to dissolve into the infinite ocean of matter, and if there is no God, no cosmic order, no cycle of birth and death, the individuals may well ask, 'why should they be good?' Thus JP made a clean breast of materialist philosophy of Marx and asserted that spiritual regeneration of man was the only lasting basis of good society.

JP's conversion to Sarvodaya naturally changed his views regarding the role and significance of state, and this was reflected in his booklets 'A plea for the Reconstruction of Indian Polity' and 'the Swaraj for the People'. He was now arguing for establishing a social order in which the powers and functions of modern state were dispersed into the smaller units of 'communitarian centres' such as the village panchayats. In smaller units, there would be greater scope for individual initiative and participation. He said, "Ancient Indian thought and tradition, social nature of man, social science, ethical and spiritual goals of civilization, the demand of democracy that the citizens should participate in the ordering and running of his life, the need of saving man from alienation from himself and from the fate of robotism, the requirement that state and other institutions of society be reduced to a human scale, the ideal above all that man should become the centre of civilization- all these point in the same direction to a communitarian or communal way of life, communitarian ethics and education, commnitarian social, economic and political organization."

JP advocated the founding of a society on the basis of 'self-governing, self-sufficient, agro-industrial, urbo-rural local communities.' He calls it 'peoples' socialism' in as much as he wants to create and develop forms of socialist living through the voluntary endeavour of the people rather than by the use of the power of state. He observed "Socialist philosophy need not be opposed to communitarianism. But in that case, socialism will have to be less interested in institutions and more in man. The old faith that state ownership of the means of production, distribution and exchange plus planning will bring about socialism has been falsified ....But a new faith has not been created to take the place of old. For this, the socialists will have to go to pre-marxian socialist idealists, the philosophical anarchists, to Tolstoy, Ruskin and Morris, to Gandhi and Vinoba." However the devaluation of power did not necessarily mean weak centre, it only meant that centre had only as much of it as required to discharge its proper functions. To quote him "The centre authority, so long as it exists, would be like a danger chain in a railway train. Passengers do not always have their attention fixed on this chain, but they make use of it in times of danger."

Sarvodaya so often criticized as a Utopian ideal, a pipe-dream was for JP a panacea for modern industrial society. He had come to see through the perils and pitfalls of scientific ideologies of various hues. He like Plato came to conclusion that unless first principles were rightly laid down, a just and humane social order would remain a far cry. In the philosophy of Sarvodaya, he discerned the first principles of such an order.

The followig extract 'From Socialism to Sarvodaya' describes the ideological evolution of JP from a staunch marxist to an ardent follower of Gandhism and Sarvodaya. This metamorphosis had its genesis in his disenchantment with modern socialism and realization of the hollowness of the materialist world-view.

From Socialism to Sarvodaya

Thus far I traveled together with my colleagues in happy comradeship, the memory of which will sweeten the remaining part of my life. But some years back my journey took a turning where we parted company. That parting began with what has come to be grandiloquently known as *jeevandan,* but which was no more than a decision on my part to withdraw from party-and-power politics and to devote the rest of my life to the *bhoodan* and *sarvodaya* movement.

The same old beacon-lights of freedom, equality and brotherhood that had guided the course of my life and brought me to democratic socialism, drew me onwards around this turning of the road. My regret is that I did not reach this point in my life's journey while Gandhiji was still in our midst. However, some years back it became clear to me that socialism as we understand it today cannot take mankind to the sublime goals of freedom, equality, brotherhood and peace. Socialism, no doubt, gives promise to bring mankind closer to those goals than any other competing social philosophy. But I am persuaded that unless socialism is transformed into *sarvodaya,* those goals would remain beyond its reach; and just as we had to taste the ashes of independence, so future generations may have to taste the ashes of socialism.

Materialism and Goodness

My final break with Marxism, though not with politics, had come during the three weeks' fast at Poona. It was then that a long process of questioning started by the Russian purges came to an end and it became clear that materialism as a philosophical outlook could not provide any basis for ethical conduct and any incentive for goodness.

If man and his consciousness and the society and culture which he has built up are mere manifestations of matter-howsoever dialectically active-I can see no reason why in such a society, anyonc should try to be good, that is, be generous, kind, unselfish. Why sould then one feel sympathy with those who are weak, poor or sick? What is matter will dissolve into matter after death. So, what incentive can there be for moral behaviour? Lust for power or wealth, or desire to win the acclaim of the people, or the regard of one's peers, may be incentives to action. But such incentives can have no concern with valuations of right or wrong. Ethical ideas have no doubt a history and a social origin, but when the individual begins to question his inherited standards of conduct and asks himself why he should act ethically, materialism offers him no answer. A person may have grown up with the ideals of social service, sacrifice, freedom, equality and the rest. But if he begins later to ask himself why he should subscribe to those ideals at all and put himself to trouble and loss on their account the philosophy of materialism, dialectical or otherwise, would not be able to give him any satisfactory answer. I am not suggesting that among philosophical materialists there have not been examples of great sacrifice for noble causes. What I am suggesting is that their action was not consistent with their philosophy.

A way out of this difficulty may be the assumption that human being is an automation, that his behaviour is wholly conditioned and that he has no choice of action and no freedom of will. On this assumption, of course, Marx and Lenin could not help work and suffer for the exploited peoples of the earth. But I doubt whether even the most bigoted Marxist would be prepared to reduce man to such a mechanical entity. Indeed, the whole Marxian theory of revolutionary leadership is based on the assumption of free will.

A great debate has raged in philosophy whether matter came first or consciousness. The point is that no matter which came first, there are today modes of existence that may be described as matter and consciousness. The mistake Marxism made was to assume that consciousness (whatever its origin) could be understood in the same manner as matter. It did not realize that the laws of matter cannot be applied to the realm of consciousness. The study of matter, is an objective exploration, whereas that of consciousness is subjective realization. The study of matter, the objective exploration, science in short, is necessarily amoral. The Marxists (and the materialists generally), having reduced consciousness to a behaviour of matter, naturally knocked the bottom out of ethics. They talk a good deal no doubt of revolutionary ethics, but that is nothing more than the crassest application of the theory that the end justifies the means. Once and individual persuades himself, sincerely or otherwise, that he is on the side of the revolution (or the Party of the People) he is free to commit any infamy whatsoever.

Not only the Marxists and materialists, but also those who differ from them in philosophy attempt to understand consciousness by the methods of science. Mental science also, therefore, provides no basis for moral behaviour. Nor is it ever possible for science to understand consciousness which can only be subjectively experienced. Subjective experience is by its very nature incapable of being expressed in material categories. Therefore, all the mystics and *yogis* who had experience of subjective reality, or absolute consciousness, have been unable to express it in any language. As Roger Godel has said : "The philosopher *thinks* his philosophy; the sage *lives* his wisdom."

Modern science has reached a point where the dualism of matter and consciousness becomes too tenuous to be real. Says Godel in his essay on *The Contemporary Science and the Liberative Experience of Yoga:* "But now suddenly-around a bend of quantum mechanics-exploration of the objective field brings the theorist of the physical sciences to a most disquieting position; before him appears an ambiguous universe where the observer and the phenomenon observed are inextricably commingled. So close is their confrontation that each is reflected in the other powerless to separate or to fuse.

"In this realm of indetermination, all the symbols and formulas familiar to our experience of things vanish. Notions of energy and of matter require so profound a transformation as to lose their original meaning; energy condenses into matter, matter dematerialises into radiation. The waves associated with propagation of light quanta need no substratum in ordeer to propagate in space-time; they undulate neither in a fluid nor in a solid, nor yet in gas. Only the unreal thread of analogy links them to the image of a wage rippling the surface of water. They are in fact waves of probability, waves of consciousness which our thought projects afar : curvilinear variation of an abstract function."

Science cannot resolve this dualism completely, because in objective study the seer and the seen must remain different, no matter how "inextricably commingled." It is only in the ultimate spiritual experience that this dualism is shed and the seer and seen become one.

The root of morality lies in the endeavour of man to realize this unity of existence, or to put it differently, to realize his Self. For one who has experienced this unity, the practice of morality becomes as natural and effortless as the drawing of breath.

To some all this might appear to be irrelevant to the political and economic struggle. In all humility, I would demur. All actions, personal or public, political, economic or other should have an integration and the centre of this integration must be a philosophy of life.

Limitation of Wants and Socialism

This leads me at once to an aspect of the task of social and economic reconstruction that both socialists and communists have neglected. Socialism and communism both lay great emphasis on material prosperity, on evergrowing production and on an ever-rising standard of living. It cannot be denied that the material wants of man must be reasonably fulfilled. And when it is realized that socialists and communists are always the advocates of the poor and downtrodden, their emphasis on material progress and happiness can be appreciated. It is also true that in poor and backward countries like India it is the main task of social reconstruction to raise quite considerably the people's standard of living. But it would not do here or elsewhere to apotheosise material happiness and encourage an outlook on life that feeds an insatiable hunger for material goods. There can be no peace in the minds and hearts of men, nor peace amongst men, if this hunger gnaws at them continuously. That would necessarily set up an uncontrolled competition between individuals, groups and nations. Everyone would be trying to outdo his neighbour and every nation not only to catch up with other nations but to leave them all behind. In such a restless society violence and war would be endemic. All values of life would be subordinated to this overmastering desire for more. Religion, art, philosophy, science would have to serve that one aim of life : to have more and still more. Equality, freedom, brotherhood would all be in danger of being submerged in a universal flood of materialism. There would be no poise in human life, no real satisfaction because the possession of more would only whet the appetite for still more.

I am aware that there have been and are quite a number of socialists who have been aware of the danger of a purely materialistic view of life, but nevertheless the main concern of socialism has been and is with the material aspects of life. The socialist or labour parties and the trade unions do not educate the people about a balanced or whole view of life. If the socialist movement became conscious of the issue I am raising, its whole attitude towards science, industrialization and social organization and international relations would be revolutionized.

Disciplining of the bodily appetites is essential for a moral life and growth of the human personality and the blossoming of all human qualities and values. This is true particularly of socialist values. The socialist way of life is a way of sharing together the good things that common endeavour may make available. The more willingly this sharing is practiced the less tension and coercion in society and the more of socialism. I believe that unless members of society learn to keep their wants under control, willing sharing of things may be difficult, if not impossible, and society would be bound to split into two division : (1) comprising of those who are trying to discipline others and (2) comprising of all the rest. Such a division of of society always leaves the question open : who would discipline the discipliners, rule the ruler? The examples of the communist countries and the experience of socialist governments show that the answer to this perennial question is extremely difficult. The only solution seems to be to restrict as much as possible the ned and area of disciplining from above by ensuring that every member of society practises self-discipline and the values of socialism, and among other things, willingly shares and cooperates with his fellowmen.

Rajniti and Lokniti or Party and Non-Party Politics

This brings me to the very heart of the problem of *sarvodaya* and socialism, party and power politics and non-party and non-power politics or *rajniti* and what Vinoba has simply called *lokniti.*

I decided to withdraw from party-and–power politics not because of disgust or sense of any personal frustration, but because it became clear to me that politics could not deliver the goods, the goods being the same old goals of equality, freedom, brotherhood, peace.

But was there an alternative to politics? Could society be changed and reconstructed in any other manner than through the agency of the state? Politics is but a science of the state.

There was an alternative. Mahatma Gandhi had placed it before us. But, I must admit, it was not clear to me at that time.

Gandhiji has shown us an alternative to armed conflict in the course of our struggle for freedom. And we had followed him-not so much out of conviction as because his prescription had worked. Nothing succeed like success-as the saying goes-and Ganghiji's satyagraha campaigns were topping success in that they stirred up the people and roused them to action as nothing had done before. All competing programmes and ideologies had to accept defeat and take a back seat.

Gandhiji's Lok Sevak Sangh

But Gandhiji had not time to give a practical demonstration of his non-violent technique fro changing and reconstructing society. No doubt, he had spoken and written much about it, but before he was able to put it into practice he was cruelly snatched away from our midst. Looking back, it seems clear now that he had already begun to lay the foundations of his future course of action. But the significance of what he was doing was entirely lost upon me, as perhaps upon many others. The significance of the fact, for instance, that after having led the freedom movement to a brilliant success, he did not take power himself to use it for remaking the country in accordance to his ideals, had completely escaped me. Likewise, when he proposed that the Congress should withdraw from the field of politics and turn itself into what he called a *Lok Sevak Sangh*, the import again of that extraordinary proposal was lost upon me. Nor had the country a chance to consider that proposal dispassionately, because the grief and anxiety into which it was plunged were too overpowering for clear thought. Besides, all eyes were turned to those who, in the absence of the ship's captain, were expected to steer her to safety. And from them not a word came about the Master's "last will and testament." On top of it all, when it was seen that every one of Gandhiji's political colleagues had taken to the traditional path of politics it could not even be suspected that there was in Gandhi-ism an alternative to the method of party and power.

Gandhiji and Party Politics

A question might be raised here why it should ever be suspected that Gandhiji, who had devoted his whole life to politics, should have at all thought in terms of an alternative to it. In my humble opinion Gandhiji never had anything to do with politics in the sense I am considering here. The movement for freedom that Gandhiji led was "political" in the sense that its goal was the national independence of India; it was not "politics" in the sense that it was a struggle for Power for any particular party. If its aim was power, it was power for the entire Indian people, including those who separated to form Pakistan and for all the paries that existed, or were to be formed in the future in both Indias. Gandhiji was not a party leader fighting for the freedom of his country : nay, he was a world leader of humanity working to free his fellow-men from bondage. The Indian freedom movement was a people's movement *par excellence.* It was not *rajniti* (politics of the state) but *lokniti* (politics of the people).

The Party System

Be that as it may, the questions raised by politics kept humming in my head, leaving me dissatisfied and urging me to seek an alternative. The party system with the corroding and corrupting struggle for power inherent in it, disturbed me more and more. I saw how parties backed by finance, organization and the means of propaganda could impose themselves on the people; how people's rule became in effect party rule; how party rule in turn became the rule of a caucus or coterie; how democracy was reduced to mere casting of votes; how even this right of vote was restricted severely by the system of powerful parties setting up their candidates from whom alone, for all practical purposes, the voters had to make their choice; how even this limited choice was made unreal by the fact that the issues posed before the electorate were by and large incomprehensible to it.

The party system as I saw it was emasculating the people. It did not function so as to develop their strength and initiative, nor to help them establish their self-rule and to manage their affairs themselves. All that the parties were concerned with was to capture power for themselves so as to rule *over* the people, not doubt, with their consent! The party system, so it appeared to me, was seeking to reduce the people to the position of sheep whose only function of sovereignty would be to choose periodically the shepherds who would look after their welfare! This to me did not spell freedom-the freedom, the *swaraj,* for which I had fought and for which the people of this country had fought.

Decentralization of Power from Below

Democratic socialists had no doubt talked vaguely of decetralisation of power, of the four-pillar state and of other similar concepts. But in practice I found that their entire concern was, as it still is, with the capture of power. They seem to believe that even decentralization of power was possible only after the present centres of power had been conquered, so that decentralization and de-institutionalisation could then be legislated into being. They do not see the absurdity of this procedure. Decentralisation cannot be effected by handing down power from above to people who have been politically emasculated and whose capacity for self-rule has been thwarted, if not destroyed, by the party sytem and concentration of power at the top. Today village panchayats are being established according to laws made in the Vidhan Sabhas. These are not true panchayats, not what Gandhiji understood by *gram raj.* In Gandhijis's pregnant words the panchayat "can function only under a law of its own making." This capacity to self-regulate the life of the community must be created and not bestowed form above in the name of decentralization. The process must be stared from the bottom. A programme of self-rule and self-management must be placed before the people, and by a constructive, non-partisan approach they must be helped to translate it into practice. It is clear now that it was in order to undertake such a programme on a nation-wide scale that Gandhiji was thinking of converting the Congress into a non-partisan *Lok Sevak Sangh.* It is exactly this task that Vinobaji has undertaken. Naturally, he did not have the lead in the race that Gandhiji would have had, but it is remarkable that in the brief span of six years he has succeeded in creating a movement of social revolution and reconstruction from below as well as a new band of *lok sevakas* to assist in the process.

Cooperative Politics

As a way out of the faults and failures of the party system, I toyed for some time with the idea of a cooperative, rather than a competitive, system of parties. I realized, however, that in the first place, there was no climate for such a political experiment, and in the second place, the experiment could not succeed within the given framework of struggle for power and the system of parliamentary democracy, except for limited purposes and limited periods. I still believe, however, that given the psychological climate for it, such a political experiment might yet be made. But for that the frame of reference will have to be changed from parliamentary democracy to something different. Be that as it may, my disenchantment with the party system kept on urging me to seek a better substitute for it. Gandhiji's non-partisan constructive approach towards people's self-rule seemed to offer one hopeful line of exploration.

The Place of the State

As questioning about politics were not confined to the party system alone, fundamental questions arose in my mind as to the lace and role of the state in human society, particularly in relation to the goals of social life that had fixed themselves before me. Perhaps my schooling in Marxism, with its ideals of a stateless society, made these questions more pointed and troublesome. Though I had given up the basic postulates of Marxism, because they did not promise to lead me to my goals, I continued to feel strongly that human freedom could be fully and wholly realized only in a stateless society. I was, and am, not sure if the state would ever wither away completely. But I am sure that it is one of the noblest goals of social endeavour to ensure that the power and functions and spheres of the state are reduced as far as possible. I became at this time, and still am, an ardent believer, like Gandhiji, in the maxim that that government was the best that governed the least. The test of human evolution for me became man's ability to live in amity, justice and cooperation with his fellowmen without outward restraints of any kind. That is why I have considered the human and social problem to be at bottom a moral problem.

With this conception of the role and place of the state in society at the back of my mind, I viewed with very deep apprehension the march of the state to greater and greater glory. Democratic socialists, communists, as well as welfarists (not to speak of the fascists), are all statists. They all hope to bring about their own variety of the millennium by first mastering and then adding to the powers and functions of the state.

The bourgeois state had monopoly of political power. The socialist state threatens to add to that the monopoly of economic power. Such a great concentration of power would require equal, if not greater power, to control and keep it in check. There would be no such power at hand in a socialist society. Paper constitutions could hardly be expected to guarantee freedom and sovereignty to the citizen. The economic and political bureaucracy would be so strong and in occupation of such vantage points that the liberties and rights of the people, as well as their bread, would be entirely at its mercy.

I am aware that democratic socialists are conscious of these dangers and are trying to devise "checks and balances." The independent trade unions are supposed to be a great bulwark of freedom, though it is recognized that the great trade unions are themselves becoming more and more ridden with bureaucracy. Plans for industrial democracy and public accountability for state enterprises have been drawn up. Consumers associations and cooperatives of all kinds are rightly supposed to function as balancing and restraining factors. Even decentralization of authority and functions has figured of late in socialist thinking. But after all is said and done the democratic socialist state remains a Leviathan that will sit heavily on the freedoms of the people.

People's Socialism vs. State Socialism

The only remedy for this that I could think of took me farther away from politics and towards sarvodaya. The remedy obviously is, as I have said above in the context of internal and external discipline, to make it possible for the people to do without the state as far as practicable and to run their affairs themselves directly. Speaking as a socialist, I would put it thus : the remedy is to create and develop forms of socialist living through the voluntary endeavour of the people rather than seek to establish socialism by the use of the power of the state. In other words, the remedy is to establish people's socialism rather than state.socialism. Sarvodaya is people's socialism. Whether every socialist agrees or not with sarvodaya, he should agree that the more of people's or voluntary socialism and the less of state-enforced socialism, the fuller and more real the socialism. Unfortunately, there are very few socialists who are giving much attention to people's socialism. Speaking of British socialists, Mr. Jack Bailey, the British Cooperative leader says : "In Britain the concentration of most socialists upon the capture and use of state power has tended to blind them to the validity of non-state forms of socialism." (Quoted by Harold Campbell in *Socialist Commentary*, July, 1957). What is true of Britain is true of all the world. It should be obvious that in order to develop non-state forms of socialism, it should be unnecessary for any one to function as a party or to engage in a struggle for the capture of power. Both power and party havae no relevance in this context. What is needed rather is a band of selfless workers prepared to live and move in the midst of the people and help them to reorganize their lives on a self-reliant and self-governing basis. One cannot help being reminded here of Gandhiji's *Lok Sevak Sangh* again.

The Community of the Future

The question now arises, what will be the form of that society in which it will be possible for the people to run their affairs directly and evelop all those values of life that characterize a socialist society : cooperation, self-discipline, sense of responsibility? This is a question to which socialists have paid the least attention so far. Human society has so grown that we have the complex industrial civilizations of today, with great human forests that are called cities, with economic and social relationships that are utterly impersonal and non-life giving, with modes of work that are irksome and bereft of joy and opportunities of creativity and that have the sole criterion of productivity and efficiency to recommend them. Science has shrunk the whole world into a neighborhood, but man has created a civilization that has turned even neighbours into strangers. Such a complex and top heavy society cannot but be heaven for bureaucrats, managers, technocrats, statists. Such a society cannot be a home for brothers to live together as brothers. Socialists, in the name of science, production, efficiency, standard of living and other hallowed shibboleths have accepted this whole Frankenstein of a society-lock, stock and barrel-and hope, by adding public ownership to it, to make it socialist. I submit that in such a society the very breath of socialism would be hard to draw. Self-government, self-management, mutual cooperation and sharing, equality, freedom, brotherhood-all could be practiced and developed far better if man lived in small communities. This is beginning to be realized by forward-looking thinkers even in the West.

Further, man is a product both of nature and culture. So, for his balanced growth it is necessary that a harmonious blend between the two is effected. This blending, in spite of parks and green avenues, is not possible in such centres of modern civilization as London, Paris, New York, Moscow. As a result, modern men's development is warped and one-sided. A harmonious blending of nature and culture is possible only in comparatively smaller communities. Let me quote Aldous Huxley from his *Science, Liberty and Peace* : "Now it seems pretty obvious that man's psychological, to say nothing of his spiritual, needs cannot be fulfilled unless, first, he has a fair measure of personal independence and personal responsibility within and toward a self-government group, unless, secondly, his work possesses a certain aesthetic value and human significance, and unless, in the third place, he is related to his natural environment in some organic, rooted and symbiotic way."

It was for these reasons that Gandhiji insisted that the Indian village and village self-government (*gram-raj*) were the foundations for his picture of society-the society of equal and free beings living as brothers in peace.

Science and Small Production

Living in small communities and producing mostly for self or local consumption of small machines may be regarded by some as setting the hand of science backwards. Science and centralized large-scale production and large conglomerations of human habitations are thought to go necessarily together. Nothing could be more absurd. Science is of two kinds : (a) pure science and (b) applied science. I would call pure science alone science and the other technology. Now, the application of science does not depend upon science itself but upon the character of society. Large-scale, bit machine production was profitable to the money makers, so technology took the course of that particular type of production. The money makers were the dominant class in society and their will had to be done. Governments also-irrespective of ideologies-preferred centralized, big-scale production because that was necessary for war making (or defence, if you please), and -no less important-because it also concentrated great economic, and, therefore, political power in their hands. Thus governments and profiteers combined to create the Frankenstein of modern society. Poor science had no say in the matter. Rather, had the scientists their way, many of them, I believe, would be happy to smash many of the engines of production and destruction that their discoveries had helped to create. But suppose society had pursued not the aims of power, profit and war, but of peace, goodwill, cooperation, freedom and brotherhood, science could have been equally applied to evolve the suitable technology. If that were to happen, it would be not regression of science, but progression in a creative rather than destructive direction. It should be pointed out that atomic energy has made more possible than ever before the dispersal of production and the development of small technology that is technology appropriate to production in small units and by small-sized machinery. Let me quote Huxley again :

"My own view, which is essentially that of the decentralists, is that, so long as the results of pure science are applied for the purpose of making our system of mass producing and mass distributing industry more expensively elaborate and more highly specialized, there can be nothing but ever greater centralization of power in ever fewer hands. And the corollary of this centralization of economic and political power is progressive loss by the masses of their civil liberties, their personal independence and their opportunities for self-government. But here we must note that there is nothing in the results of disinterested scientific research which makes it inevitable that they should be applied for the benefit of centralized finance, industry and government. If inventors and technicians so chose, they could just as well apply the results of pure science for the purpose of increasing the economic self-sufficiency and consequently the political independence of small owners, working either on their own or in cooperative groups, concerned not with mass distribution, but with subsistence and the supply of a local market. The Sabbath was made for man, not man for the sabbath : and the same is true of applied science."

Small Communities and the Great Society

I am not suggesting that the whole picture of this new society is clear to any one or that all its problems have been thought out and resolved. How, for instance, would these small self-reliant, self-governing communities be related together is a major question that immediaterly springs to the mind. There is, of course, Gandhiji's grand conception before us:

"In this structure, composed of innumerable villages, there will be ever widening, never ascending circles. Life will not be a pyramid with the apex sustained by the bottom. But it will be an oceanic circle whose centre will be the individual, always ready to perish for the village, the latter ready to perish for the circle of villages, till at last the whole becomes one life composed of individuals, never aggressive in their arrogance, but ever humble, sharing the majesty of the oceanic circle of which they are integral units."

Gandhiji's words give us direction, but much thought and experience will be necessary before the picture becomes more clear. However, one warning must be sounded. While it is undoubted that life in small communities, permitting and promoting personal relationships will be more suited to the realization of *sarvodaya* ideals, it should not be imagined that small communities ties by virtue merely of their size, will necessarily be sarvodaya communities. Had that been so, we would have encountered *sarvodaya* in every village of India today. The outward forms of living have relevance only when the inward forms are given. Men must understand and accept the sarvodaya view of life before they can proceed to investigate in what environment and social framework they could live that life best.

The fear is often expressed if self-reliant and self-governing communities will hold together and the unity and integrity of the nation will abide. In a sarvodaya world society the present nation states hve no place. The sarvodaya view is a world view, and individual standing at the cetre of Gandhiji's oceanic circle is a world citizen. But let us leave for the present the world picture of *sarvodaya.* There is no reason to suppose why self-governing small communities will be hostile to one another or isolationist or selfish in their inter-relationship. If the internal life of a community is laid on sound foundations, its external life cannot but be equally sound.

(From *From Socialism to Sarvoday,* Sarvaseva Sangh, Rajghat, Varanasi, 1998. pp 27-47)

17

Rammanohar Lohia

Life and Times

Among the founders of the organised socialist movement in India Rammanohar Lohia (1910-1967) occupies a massive position. He was not only one of the youngest among the leaders who formed the Congress Socialist Party but he was well-educated and intellectually very sharp. He was admired and respected in the socialist movement till the end of his life.

While Acharya Narendra Dev had only admirers and students inside and outside the socialist movement, Lohia had a band of fanatic followers, most of whom had surrendered there brains to him. They always stood by him and obeyed him without raising any doubts about the wisdom of his orders. Acharya Narendra Dev was a firm believer in marxism but it did not interfere with his belief in human re-birth. Lohia was opposed to marxism and was anti-communist.

Throughout the post-independence period Lohia remained an important leader in Indian politics and the influence of his ideas increased after mid-1960s and they continue to remain substantial even more today three decades after his death. His ideas touched no only the political sphere, but also very many other areas from man-woman relationship to the language question. Most of his followers even today maintain that Lohia was only next to

Mahatma Gandhi in giving expression to the suffering of common people and had Gandhi lived longer, he would have made Lohia rather than Nehru as his political heir. They believe that Lohia had come closer to Gandhi during his last days and it is asserted that the later had started realizing his mistake in nominating Nehru as his successor who was supposed to talk his language after his death. We do not, however, have any solid evidence to give credence to his belief.

There is no dispute that Lohia's was dynamic and remarkable personality. He was born on 23 March 1910 at Akbarpur in the district of Faizabad, UP in a trading family. His father and uncles dealt in clothes and iron and also had substantial landed property. His forefathers migrated to Mirzapur from Rajasthan during the 18th or 19th century, traded in iron and clothes and became very prosperous. Perhaps his great grandparents came to Akbarpur to set up business. His grandfather Sheonarayan was attracted towards national movement and got interested in Congress. It is said that his family played host to Jawaharlal Nehru in 1921, when he visited Akbarpur. Eleven-year old Lohia saw Nehru for the first time. Lohia's father Hiralal was an active Congress worker and participated in its activities including Satyagrahas. He also suffered imprisonment.

Lohia's mother came from a Marwari family of Chanpatia, West Champaran. Her family too was nationalist and had been sympathetic to Gandhi's Satyagraha in Champaran. Lohia was not fortunate enough to get the loving care and affection of his mother for long, as she passed away when Lohia was still an infant. His grandmother brought him up as his father did not re-marry.

Lohia was educated at the Tondon Pathshala up to class IV at Akbarpur. After a brief stint at the local Bisweshwarmath High School, he shifted to Bombay where his father had set up his business. He was a good student and excelled himself at examinations. He passed his matriculation examination from the Marwari school in 1925 in the first division. During his stay at Bombay he was exposed to national movement. He witnessed the massive strike by Bombay workers and people in August 1920 to mourn to death of Lokmanya Bal Gangadhar Tilak. He also witnessed encouraging responses to Gandhi's first non-cooperation movement. He himself left the school for a year in response to the call by Gandhi. He accompanied his father to Gandhiji and was deeply influenced by him. Incidentally, he had also accompanied his father to Ahmedabad Congress in 1918.

In 1925 he went to Varanasi and got himself enrolled for the intermediate course in arts at the Banaras Hindu University. Because of his involvement with national movement, he developed some kind of disinterest in his studies and as a result he could pass the intermediate examination only in third division. But this was more than compensate by his study of books on Indian culture and religions. He read books on classical Sanskrit literature. It may not be out of place to mention that he was attracted towards Nehru after reading his speeches and about his activities.

Shortly after, he arrived in Berlin and enrolled himself in the university. He remained there for four years, obtaining a doctorate after completing his master's degree. The topic of his doctoral thesis was 'Economics of Salt Satyagraha.' The choice of the topic indicated his nationalistic inclinations. It is a different matter that his dissertation in a far off land on a topic about which sufficient information and material were not available, nor were the implications of Gandhi's salt Satyagraha amply clear, could be little of value. It was an open secret that the decision to award him a doctorate was influenced by the attitude of German academics toward Indian freedom movement as a part of their country's relationship at the time with Britain in the wake of the defeat of Germany in the first world war and the aftermath of the Treaty of Versailles.

Throughout 1946 and the first half of 1947 socialists remained divided on most of the important issues like the participation in the Constituent Assembly, joining the interim government and the Cabinet Mission Plan. The decisions taken by the national executive of the CSP were accepted reluctantly by many leaders. The party gradually realized its impotence in stopping the proposed partition of the country. It was reflected in the last paragraph of what the national executive of the Socialist Party came out with after its June 1947 meeting.

Each act of surrender, perhaps not of much important by itself but of great effect as a link in the chain, and the refusal of the congress leadership to prepare a position and hold on to it have brought us to this fateful situation. The socialist part must also record its own failure and that of the wider revolutionary movement in working out an alternative and positive policy When the matter came up before the AICC meeting at Delhi on June 1947, Lohia on behalf of the Socialist Party, opposed it, but on the advice of Gandhiji, softened his stand and his party abstained from voting. At the Congress Working Committee meeting, Lohia was the strong opponent of the idea of country's partition. He told the CWC not to be panicky at the communal riots, because they were not going to last long. They would subside after some time when better sense prevailed. He pointed out that in the American civil war passions rose so high that 3 to 4 lakh people lost their lives in fratricide, but when passions cooled, the situation became normal. In India, Hindus and Muslims might kill one another in most brutal fashion, but they had to live together, because they had been living together for centuries.

The assassination of Mahatma Gandhi terribly shocked Lohia, because he had been under the impression that he was moving closer to him and regarded himself as the truest disciple of the Mahatma. Perhaps he was under the impression that the Gandhi would giving him the place which he had already given to Nehru. His bitterness was reflected when he was approached by JP and Kamala Devi Chattopadhyay to sign a joint statement condemning the RSS and other Hindu communal elements for spreading hatred and creating the situation leading to the assassination of Gandhiji and charging only Sardar Patel the then home minister with his failure to protect his life, Lohia wanted the name of the then prime minister Nehru also to be included as one of the persons responsible for failure to protect Gandhi's life. He insisted that they should demand Nehru's resignation from prime ministership and became very bitter when the other two signatories failed to underline Nehru's responsibility at the press conference. When a campaign ran against the Hindu forces and organizations, Lohia kept himself aloof.

In March 1948 Socialists met at Nasik and decided on leaving the Congress and constituting themselves in a separate and parallel political party. This decision was rejection of the old socialist proposal that the party should be allowed to remain in the Congress and not joint the government, but they must have full freedom to criticize the Congress and the government. The Congress High command did not accept this proposal, because in February 1948 it had altered its constitution to debar from its membership anybody who is a member of any political party which had a separate membership, constitution and programme. This made the position of socialists extremely difficult. If they wonted to remain in the Congress, they had no alternative but to dissolve their party, or if they wanted to have their separate and distinct identity, they had to leave the Congress. They chose the latter.

He along with certain other socialist leaders, finally left the Congress in 1948. In 1952 they merged with the Kisan Mazdoor Praja Party and formed the Praja Socialist Party. However, he resigned the Secretaryship of the party as a protest against the refusal of P.T. Pillai, Chief Minister of Travancore-Cochin, to quit office on the issue of police firing on language agitators in 1954. He formed the Socialist Party at Hyderabad and himself became chairman and editor of its journal, *Mankind*, in 1956. He was elected to the Lok Sabha in 1963. In 1964, the Socialist Party merged with the Praja Socialist Party, which then came to be known as Samyukta Socialist Party. However, strong difference continued on account of insistence of the followers of Ram Manohar Lohia on Hindi as the national language, the rights of untouchables and the principle of no compromise with either the Congress or the Communists. As a member of the Parliament, Lohia contributed a lot, to the cause of women and the downtrodden.

Lohia died on 12 October 1967. He left behind no property or any bank balance. He was not only a politician but also a philosopher having his own thinking, a social reformer pressing to the end the caste system and social discrimination and to improve the lot of women and backward communities; an economist, suggesting a number of steps for the economic progress of an underdeveloped country. In Madhu Limaye's words, Lohia was an original thinker, a unique leader and a rebel. He played an important part in the making of modern India. But he was not an ivory tower philosopher. He was essentially a man of action. The works of Lohia included the *Wheel of History, Aspects of Socialist Policy, Will to Power and Other Writings, Towards the Destruction of Castes and Classes, Marx, Gandhi and Socialism, The Culprits of the Division of Bharat, Power Determination.*

Materialist Interpretation of History

According to the view of history held by Karl Marx, man has traveled through various periods. Although he may not have purposely risen in ascent and this rise may not have been uninterrupted, there has been some force in history to cause a gradual climbing of man from earlier primitive or backward stages to the modern stage. How this happened has been very clearly enunciated and no one can accuse Marx of being ambiguous about it. Man has passed principally through the capitalist period. The first period may be left our of account, as it belongs to pre history. Through all these periods, there has been a motion of history, a law of history, deriving from developing styles of production. Through all the various modes and styles of production have clashed the forces of production on the one hand and the relations of production on the other, various tools and manner in which they are used on the one hand and property relationships on the other. These two phrases, forces of production and relations of production, are the significant core of Marx's teachings on history. The clash between them leads to class struggle. Marx says that all human history hitherto has been the history of class struggle.

This struggle has streaked through all of man's history and has taken various shapes. Class struggle in the feudal period is different from class struggle in the capitalist period, but that there are different classes in these various periods is not questioned and that a struggle takes place between them is also undisputed. The struggle is aimed to liberate the agencies and forces of production, which are thrust down on account of a particular type of ownership enforced by the prevailing civilization. Feudalism enforces an ownership of landed proprietors and does not permit production to grow beyond a point and the appropriate class of that period rises up to disrupt that order.

Similarly, in the capitalist period, the laws of property and its returns do not permit the full use of methods of industrialization, of the application of science to industry and agriculture. The forces of production stay imprisoned until the working class is sufficiently strong and organized to disrupt the property relationship and release them. This has little to do with the mind of man and its designs. It takes place automatically in society. Man has got to will it because there are forces which compel him to do so. All development of history is placed inside the mode of production with its mutually warring factors, the forces of production and the relations of production.

Whether the history of man in all the world and not alone in Europe could be compressed into those three or for periods is open to serious doubt. Facts will have to be distorted in order to prove that there was an aristocracy of a slave period in India. Facts will again have to be disorted in order to prove that there was a feudal civilization obtaining evenly over a demarcated period throughout the world, no matter that wide margins in years are permitted to verying climes.

A part from such violence to facts as will necessarily have to be undertaken in order to divide the history of mankind into these three or four congenial periods, the system of history which Karl Marx outlined may be examined experimentally with prophesied but actual developments. The system of class struggle diagnoses that capitalism produces its own grave digger. While it grows and magnifies, capitalism gives rise to concentration of capital on the one hand and socialization of labour on the other, to big capitalists owning and commanding larger and yet larger sectors of economy and the huge proletariat which gets organized not only because it wills so but more so because concentrated capital starts bigger factories and throws thousands of persons together to work in the same place. At the same time, exploitation of labour increases and its impoverishment is an inevitable consequence. This concentration of capital and socialization of labour and its increasing impoverishment go on side by side until labour is so sufficiently socialized as to strangle the capitalist hold over economy until the capitalist – worker relationship is destroyed, a communist or socialist order is established, and science is liberated in order to admit of its full application to industry and agriculture. Does it bear a close scrutiny successfully?

There undoubtedly has been concentration of capital, but what of socialization of labour and increasing poverty among the proletariat? What about the iron law of civilization which Marx enunciated that class struggle would so take place that the great masters of the capitalist world would be fore-runners and pioneers of the socialist world? If passages from Marx or Engels may be cited to prove that they admitted on one or two occasions the possibility of a revolution in Russia, most of the time they prophesied revolutions in Germany and England, and these passages anywhere are of little meaning. Such efforts are scholastic, for it would be possible to cull many kinds of stray passages from writings so voluminous. And anyway, China never was on Marx's agenda of communist revolutions. The search for stray passages has therefore stopped, and, inevitably also, the theoretical debate on the Marxian law of civilizations. The point is as to what law was laid down for development of mankind from the capitalist to the socialist period. Whether stray predictions have been right or wrong may be left unconsidered, the law in all its exactness is available to us and must be reviewed. The law says that class struggle will assume critical proportions in advanced capitalist countries will become so organized as to overthrow capitalism and usher in a communist or socialist civilization.

A neo-Marxist may well suggest that socialization of labour has taken place in advanced countries of capitalism while pauperization has occurred in retarded countries of Asia and Afriça. Marx himself had foreseen combined developments of these two factors. He thought that such a combined development would cause disruption of the capitalist order. A neo-Marxist might say that the disruption has been somewhat arrested because masses of people have been pauperized in India, China, Malaya, Burma, Africa and the like whereas the mass of the working class in U.K., Germany the US and similar countries have got into larger factories and have indeed got socialized but with better wages. On account of this split-up between socialization of labour in Western Europe and elsewhere and increasing poverty among the moss in India and elsewhere, the law has not operated as it was enunciated. The law then goes overboard. Should it be shown that with the pauperization of the mass of the people in colonies and erstwhile colonies, a revolution is likely to occur in these other areas, the whole edifice crumbles. It will no longer be possible to suggest that, with a change in property relationship, forces of production are automatically released so as to achieve plenty in the world. Revolutions will according to this view take place precisely in areas where forces of production have not gone much beyond the feudal stage or have even declined. Consequently, the new civilization will start with a halter round its neck.

But the materialist interpretation of history enables the new civilization to start in areas where capitalism is advanced so that, with socialist relations of property, use could be made of factories machinery and scientific agriculture of developed capitalism in order to provide the world with plenty. With such a view, one could have thought of a golden age that was just around the corner. If relationships of production alone had been throttling the progress of mankind, class struggle would end them and achieve a society which could organize itself collectively on the basis of socialist production and make the fullest use of all available machinery and agriculture. But this rosy picture of a golden age around the corner was drawn with false tints, for ruling lands of the existing civilization were expected to become the forerunners and pioneers of the succeeding civilization. There perhaps lies the clue to how this law got formulated. Every person is fond of maintaining the accomplishment of his age and land and Western Europe has undoubtedly achieved much. Its civilization has indicated unending progress at least in some directions, mightier and greater than any which mankind was able to achieve in any earlier period or clime. And none should blame the European mind for wanting to cling to this particular period of history or to outline a stupendous doctrine so that Europe may stay eternally on this pinnacle and may also achieve the imperishable glory of remaking the rest of the world in its own image.

In comparing the Marxist view of history with the Hegelian, either appears so utterly contradictory of the other. In their approaches and formulations, they may be set one against the other for, Marx found the motive of history in the mode of production whereas Hegel sees that motive in the spirit of man. But the essential result of either is similar. Hegel discovers history to be freedom broadening from primitive society in gradual stages to the Prussian state, which he thought was the greatest pinnacle of human achievement. He named this gradual ascent as freedom of one to freedom of some then on to freedom of many and finally freedom for all. One would find a close family resemblance between this freedom of one going on to freedom of all and the development of human history from the primitive communist period over feudal aristocracy and bourgeois democracy to the full social democracy of communism. According to Hegel, this freedom of all was embodied in the spirit of man, and the political society in which the Absolute had made itself manifest was the concrete Absolute of the Prussian state. According to Marx, the Hegelian Absolute had manifested itself in the concrete absolutes of England, Germany, and perhaps to some extent, France; for, they were the advanced capitalist countries of Europe, where the inevitable motive of class struggle, which is the Marxist spirit of history would cause the overthrow of capitalism and usher in a new socialist civilization

The leaders of existing civilisation are not fated to be forerunners of the succeeding civilisation. It has not happened in history but that need not be the only proof. It seems inherently to be impossible form in any civilisation, certain modes of production, certain styles of thought, some definite processes are firmly set. However much man may see that such modes of production and thought are no longer able to cope with the situation as it has developed, he is unable to change them because they are so firmly set. His whole edifice is centered round them or built over them and, however much human intelligence may be credited with the power to revise, and change, it seems to be a great strain on reason to imagine that a people, which has been the head of a particular type of civilization and got set in its ways, would again be elastic enough to throw overboard these ways and take up new ways better able to cope with another situation.

That is not to say that class-struggle has not obtained in human affairs. There has been struggle among classes throughout history and the time has now come to understand how it has actually operated. With an emotional like or dislike and the patriot's desire to preserve in his own country or age what has been achieved, a student of history may not concern himself. What has been the form and process of this class struggle should be objectively studied. That there has been internal inequality all through the ages and that this has been expressed in various classes who struggle with one another in an undisputed fact. Internal struggle of the classes has indeed gone alongside of the external struggle among nations. No time need be waster to prove the validity of these two struggles, Arnold Toynbee makes a continuing mention of two factors, the internal struggle and external struggle, and believes that a civilization disrupts of stagnates under the two pressures of the internal and the external struggle, the struggle inside a nation among the classes, and the struggle among the nations. Marx did not pay sufficient attention to the distinction between the internal proletariat and the external proletariat. If he had, he would have credited socialization or increasing poverty to the external proletariat.

The most fruitful examination of a system is that of its internal logic. Materialist interpretation of history is raised on the internal logic of maturing forces of production clashing with rigid relations of production. In fact, this logic is utterly self-contained, sure and consistent within itself. While Europeans may have rejected it after an experimental examination, a type of Asian mind it still infatuated with the doctrine's self-movement of society like the egg moving on to the chicken. Society moves itself and the materialist interpretation holds the key to this movement. The key consists of the clash between maturing forces and rigid relations, between the expropriated and the owners. The key is intoxicatingly simple and it seems to reveal so well the secret of the universe. But what is the dark chamber it throws light into? It only reveals that history is no history, that any given movement of the peaks and perhaps also the dips of history must always have been so in the past and ever continue like that in the future. At the present moment, a certain situation of matured forces has placed Europe and America on the peak of current history and the rest of the world at its bottom. The Marxist law should not take arbitrary refuge behind every explosion and revolution that took place consequent upon the clash between force and relations, the present moment of the power of Europe and America must always have existed and shall be ever lasting in accordance with the self-movement of the total mode of production.

While considering the general law of materialist interpretation, catastrophies may be excluded from purview. If they are to be more than an exception, the general rule goes. The general rule lays down that the self-movement of capitalist society will enable its most advanced regions of West Europe and America to herald the communist society; on the same reasoning applied backwards, these regions must have been the leaders of feudal and earlier societies. If the key is usable forwards in history, it should equally usable backwards. In fact, in the passage of man through the class-struggles and the self-movement of aristocracy, feudalism and capitalism, there should have been no history of the rise and decline of nations as we know it. Furthermore, any given moment for instance, the moment when India or Egypt were on the pinnacle of history, should have been everlasting both before and after according to the materialist interpretation of history. The world should have in all history known an unchanging visage, with a starred smile fixed on one side and a frozen tear pocking the other. That the European intellect, inspite of its severe hostility, has not submitted the Marxian logic of history to such an internal examination is full of significant meaning. The effort of Marx was, after all, a colossal construction of the mind to keep the smile on the visage of Europe ever dancing. It was a peerless attempt of the European spirit. What European mind would be able or want to drag up by its roots this highly spiritual effort at Europe's everlasting glory? Like most other modern doctrines emanating from Europe, the materialist interpretation of history is also a doctrine in the service of the status quo, at least that part of the status quo which means European glory. This examination of the internal logic of dialectical materialism as applied to history reveals it to be as spiritual as it is undialectical, and altogether unhistorical.

(From *Wheels of History*, Rammanohar Lohia, Samata Vidyalaya Nyas, Hyderabad, 1986. pp 14-20)

Class and Caste

Some may be inclined to think that caste is a specifically Indian phenomenon. In the sense that caste has endured an unbelievably long time, that it has acquired some very sharp features, it is a unique Indian institution. But as an institution in which different classes of population have found their proper place and do not dispute much with one another, it is universal. Classification by birth or its recognition by religion is not a necessary quality of caste. What distinguishes caste from class is immobility that has crept into class relationship, the immobility of an individual to get into a higher caste and of a whole caste to move up in status or income. Class is mobile caste. Caste is immobile class. Every society or civilisation has known this movement from class to caste and vice-versa. This movement is at the root of almost all internal happenings. It is almost always inspired by the demand for justice and equality but the initial demands have hitherto always been corrupted.

In ancient Rome, patricians and plebians were almost always engaged in a class struggle. Whenever Rome grew in strength and economic power, the struggle was permitted comparatively free play and classes could struggle to move up. Whenever this struggle became unbearable to the existence of society and outside pressures grew, the demand for a stable and intelligent order was made in the name of justice and equality. The Roman experience of movement from class to caste and caste to class went through various phases. Caste at one time was used as an instrument for creating the power and wealth of Roman citizen to achieve equality in society. Caste later became an instrument to prevent internal disruption and protect what had been achieved. At the very end, justice could no longer be contained in any achievable order of castes and disruption followed. All these movements from class to caste and the reverse took place alongside of the Roman effort to achieve efficiency in a limited direction. It may not be forgotten that the Roman latifundia can stand comparison with the most extensive corporation farms of the present day. These latifundia also withered away under their own weight and outside pressures.

India seems to have known two definite movements against caste. The earlier movement appears to have started over 2,600 years ago and continued for nearly five centuries. The literature of the time shows it to have been a movement of criticism and reform. It did cause a certain loosening of castes and a general stirring within the society occurred. Gautam Buddha had at one time to shut his monastic order to indebted persons and to those of the lower caste without the consent of their employers. The shift away from caste was also accompanied by a growth in political strength and economic prosperity. Different Kingdoms of the country tended to get united however loosely so that internecine wars were ended and trade prospered. Artisans multiplied, agriculture improved and the national income grew. One major invasion from Europe of those days was repelled before it could draw near and India sent our religious and cultural missions to distant land. The extraction of political tribute and rule over others was not in her blood, but she must have trade far and wide and manufactured for such trade. A certain rationality in thinking and general interest and awareness went alongside. Undoubtedly, this movement against caste and for class was accomplined by a growth of partial efficiency in the society as a whole.

Four hundred years had to intervene before the creative energies of Indian society awoke blossomed into a second movement against caste. The literature of the period shows it to have been a movement of outright condemnation. Caste was denounced on every ground and from all angles. In actual practice, however, there was not such a complete break and much the same partial efficiency of society and general movement of class as in the earlier period was repeated, although in a more developed form, the intervening period between these two class movements and the phase that seems now to have run out are the counterpart movements of caste. The earlier period seems to have been some what mild and unsettled by comparison, for the social scriptures of the time compromise a great deal and seek to achieve caste through a permission, however unwilling and hedged, to move up and down in habits of food and marriage. Indian society of the time was somewhat weak against foreign invasions, although it had not yet lost its capacity to repel and to absorb. The later movement towards caste has lasted a much longer time of over 1200 years. The rigidity of caste patterns is more or less complete in this period. Through a stupendous distinction between absolute truth and worldly truth, Shankaracharya laid down a philosophical basis for reconciling great flights of spirituality with a social order of perfidious dimensions. Foreign invasions and increasing poverty beset Indian society of this period and a total anaemia seizes hold of it. No purpose would be served by blaming this anaemia on the caste system or Shankaracharya's magnificent error.

The source of either evil lies in the attainment of maximum efficiency in a limited direction beyond which Indian society could not go and had inevitably therefore to fall prey to other societies seeking efficiency in a different direction. In a certain measure, caste and the mind that went with it acted as a protecting shield for the hibernating society. That the shield could be forged was as much of a marvel as was the dirt that it covered. It would be idle to speculate whether India would not have done better by disrupting without caste and Shankaracharya than by stagnating with them. The phase anyhow seems to be over. With Mahatma Gandhi has begun a general stirring of Indian castes up and down and a search for efficiency of the society as a whole. But it must not be forgotten that numerous humanist sets of a devotional or philosophical foundation; unbelievably generous in scope, have been his forerunners.

A philosophy of history may well seek to discover a rhythm in these alternations of class and caste and the time – span over which the successions endure. Historical material it yet sketchy for such refinements of what must for a long time stay as a broadly stated theory of India's movement between caste and class. How the specific system of caste known alone to India arose is itself a subject for much speculation. It did indeed achieve an adjustment as miraculous for its enduring acceptability as for the inevitable sloth that spread over the society. The adjustment appears still more miraculous when note is taken of the widely differing pigments and cephalic indexes that were adjusted; the most egalitarian civilisation known to man has so far shied away from such an attempt, But it took place largely on the religious and spiritual levels and the social level suffered increasing mal-adjustment in the recent most period of caste. Not only has injustice multiplied, but the identification of certain casts with tribal and facial characteristics, that has tended to sharpen in the phase of general inefficiency and poverty, has made the abolition of castes stubbornly difficult.

The integration attempted in India's caste system was however of such matchless dimension that no factor of race, language, religion colour or form could ever intimidate. In this breath-taking drama of human adjustment played out within India's frontiers may well lie the source of her famed tolerance as also her emotionally satisfying self-concern and distaste of imperialism. While this saga of India's movement back and forth between class and caste may reveal many gleams of a diamond, the outstanding glitter must not be missed. Internal caste and external decline go together, whatever may be the time-lag between the two. Increasing efficiency of society as a whole in invariably accompanied by internal stirring of various classes up and down.

The American social scene is often misunderstood and observes, native and foreign, question the existence of a class system in America. Such a misunderstanding arises from the confusion of class with caste. The older social groups of Europe have never quite been able to leave the taint of caste. Even in times of great mobility of classes moving up, democratic behaviour and intermarriage have not been easy or natural in Europe. There has been such fast moving up of the individual and the class in America and the attendant democratic relationships right up to eating and marrying habits that the existence of classes is somewhat obscured to those who confuse them with caste. Aside from such marginal groups as the Boston Brahmins and, indeed, the almost tribal distinction between the Negro and the White, caste does not exist in America. But classes do. These differ, one from another, in their income, power and status and, what is more, they struggle to move up both in status and income.

As long as such as internal movement for the removal of inequality continues in a society, class-structure and the attendant class struggle exist. That this class struggle has been able to win victories of the escalator clause and annual increments and aspires to achieve a guaranteed annual wage irrespective of employment is indeed a tribute to the country's trade unionism but more so to the expensive capacity of American economy. Someday, however technical efficiency will reach its maximum and a deadlock will be reached.

Aside from outside pressures of other societies reaching efficiency in their own directions, internal class movement will then become unbearable. The American people will, like every other people be placed before the choice between disruption and caste and even if they should succeed in attaining a system of castes, their relegation will only be a matter of time. Already, union meetings are singularly like caste meetings and the solidarity aroused is not that of the working-class as a whole but of workers in a particular craft or industry. The solidarity is not yet natural and has to be bolstered up with songs and other devices of a jarring character. This solidarity appears today to be an aggressive weapon for mobility but it should not take much time to change it into a protective shield. American social thinking, like its Europe counterpart, has already thrown up such vague and caste laden concepts as 'areas of agreement', 'exclusion of agreed areas from reach of politics', 'cooperative and employee society', 'functional status' and the like. They can come in handy at the appropriate time. Meanwhile it must be recognized that the youth and vitality and also the aggression of American economy is matched well with the youth and vitality and also the aggression with which America's classes have moved away from caste and cleaned themselves almost wholly of its taint.

Modern European history has romped over the surface of the earth with the majesty of power and it has equally been a swing away from the castes of around 700 years ago. The self bound to his master has been replaced by the freed peasant or the hired labourer on farms. Guilds of artisans with their caste rules of apprenticeship and admission were steadily broken down and have been replaced by the industrial factory with its labourers moving up and down the scale. To the professional classes, talent has gone from the whole population through a system of free education or scholarships. As a consequence of democracy, political power has somewhat drained from its earlier receptacles to parties of the common man, trade unions and the like. In the realms of the mind, science has continually wrested secrets from nature but has also as often disclosed to view darkness where there was supposed to be light. Rationality has become the base for the larger part of systematic thinking and the European man has achieved a special dignity unknown to earlier periods. But Europe has now ceased to straddle across the earth; the majesty of its power is at any rate bowed. Technological advance is reaching a deadlock and preparations for war are making too heavy a demand to permit rising standards of living. The struggle among classes becoming unbearable or futile. Men hanker after the stability of justice rather than risk disruption attained in place of desired equality. The larger part of Europe wants to fix social design, sanctified by reason or religion in which every man will find his status and fixed income, where there will be no dispute nor quarrel.

Recent most Europe has given birth to two such movements, the Hitler movement in Germany and the communist movement in Russia. These two movements have ordinarily been understood to be antagonistic of each other. They have indeed been so. But I venture to think that both these movements are similarly motivated in regard to the internal oscillation between class and caste. When the struggle amongst classes in Germany became insupportable and strikes kept on mounting, when relationships among armed forces, industry, the free professions, students, workers, and farmers became so strained that it was not possible to run the economy or government smoothly, the national socialist movement came along to achieve a system of caste in which classes seemed to be coordinated in a new and intelligent scheme, or at any rate a scheme which appeared to be intelligent to Germans of that time. An essential criterion is that this scheme must appear to be intelligent to the people of its time and that classes struggling for supremacy must accept it intellectually in order to cease their struggle. When this struggle amongst classes in Germany became unbearable and German society was threatened with internal disruption, the national socialist movement essayed to fix up the different classes into castes with their proportionate and fixed incomes and well-defined status. It showed them that their various orders were so coordinated as to yield a meaning and purpose of life no matter that this purpose had no enduring or religious quality and was narrowly national. It was essentially a caste movement. Class struggle in Europe has probably developed in such a fashion and has taken place inside a complex of civilisation, internally egalitarian and externally imperialist, that the achievement of caste is no longer possible. At any rate, Germany tried it and failed.

That the Russian effort is also a caste effort may be difficult of acceptance by persons superficially influenced by communist theory. They may think that it is an effort to destroy classes. That is largely a matter of how one examines the evidence coming out of Russia. The national socialist may well have pointed out that he kind of socialist integration attempt in his society and the corporate system that he was trying to introduce into Germany also did away with classes. Were not industrialists fixed in their income? They could not command more than 5 or 6 percent of their profit. They were curtailed in their powers and status. If it is a question of what men say about their own system, Russian Communism is indeed based upon the destruction of classes. But if we have studied human history, the suspicion should not be so lightly cast aside that whenever a society has found the struggle amongst classes insupportable it has tried to fix itself up in a system of caste. That these castes have been fixed at various levels is also undisputed. In India the caste fixed highest in her ancient integration was perhaps amongst the lowest paid or at any rate not as well paid as the second and third castes? There have been integrations known to mankind where the highest caste in status was not necessarily the richest. These fixations have taken place at various levels.

Status and income have often got disjoined and, if one is to think of the communist slogan "to every body according to his needs and from everybody according to his capacity", such adages abound in the writings of India's ancient sages and Marx after all was a modern sage. Whether this formula ever got worked out in the Indian caste system is more than I can say. It is sought to be worked out in the communist system although, for the time being, they say they have scarified it in favour of another which gives to everyone according to his labour. No matter what formula is enunciated, the fact remains that, inside Russia, various groups of toilers have got fixed up in their status and their incomes. It is not possible for them to struggle for changes in adjustment. What changes in adjustment may occur will occur from top. Furthermore, no such changes in adjustment will be possible after a time except such as may flow out of increases in the total income and do not cause disproportion. It may well be that the communist system puts an end to the struggle amongst classes, not so as to abolish all classes, but to create new caste whose status and income are fixed. If these two movements of recent European history, the Hitler and the communist movement, are an effort of the tormented and harried soul of Europe to end internal disharmony by achieving the harmony of caste, none should be surprised. It is a warning to those who have been infatuated and rightly so with the magical charm of abolition of classes that they should not make the mistake of creating castes over again in their effort to aboliah classes.

The Russian endeavour at caste is somewhat different from that of Germany. The German effort to achieve caste arose out of the need to protect a highly developed economy against an unbearable class struggle. It may also have been an answer to the need of German economy for outside substance. The Russian system of castes has probably arisen out of the need to create a highly industrial economy from an agriculture one, which may not have been possible in the climate of sharp class struggle. It may not be forgotten that Russia has a very low density of population compared to her lands and resources and the possibilities of creation are therefore enormous. Whether this slight difference between protective caste and creative caste is significant enough to help Russia change later into a system of classes can be anybody's guess, even assuming that she succeeds in developing he economy and outside pressures do not cancel her efforts. Furthermore, communist Russia is also exhibiting among other obnoxious features of caste the particularly odious characteristic of untouchability. If India's untouchables number nearly twenty percent of the population, those of Russia inside correction and concentration camps have ranged between 5 and 10 percent.

The Russian untouchability is not the result of assimilation of totally foreign elements, as may have been the case in India. Whatever may have been its cause, it serves the pitilessly grand design of using human labour at cheapest costs for economic reconstruction. That the Russian system is more glaringly cruel than the Indian is largerly deceptive, for time and religion may have rubbed off its sharper edges in India and, by making caste acceptable even to those who suffer, driven its cruelty underground into a pervasive but concealed virus.

An Indian should be perfectly familiar with the phenomenon of class solidifying into caste. It has shown itself throughout the ages and is showing itself in Europe right now. Whether the European soul would be able to evolve yet another system of cases is another matter. Its efforts may fail. A civilisation based on a permanent technological revolution may find it exceedingly difficult to accustom its people to a stable hierarchy of life. Even if declining efficiency and technological deadlock should incline European society to caste, the long tradition of egalitarian struggles would prove too stubborn to break. But the weakening capacity to wage war could incline either way, to seek remedy either in the effort towards caste or in heightened struggles for equality among classes. Then, the European civilisation would be relegated, would disrupt or be overpowered by another more powerful. When the internal struggle becomes unbearable, the trend to caste begins and none should ever confuse the phenomenon of achievement of castes with that of the abolition of classes. I am as keen about the abolition of classes as anybody can be, but I am fearful that under the cover of abolition of classes, castes have ever been created. All human history hitherto has been an internal movement between castes and classes, between classes solidifying into castes and castes loosening into classes.

Those who wish to abolish all classes and castes in society must get hold of this motive of human history and, after grasping it, devise such endevours as may put an end to both. History by itself will not do so. There is no automatic motion. India has so long stayed in a state of torpor and stagnation arising out of caste that her new found vitality is loosening her castes into classes and the struggle for removal in internal inequality has began. Whether any faulty thinking such as the bodily taking over of European thought, capitalist or communist, will arrest the process of loosening of castes into classes is more than I can say. Such European thought, capitalist or communist, if swallowed wholesale without any internal examination of how it arose and under what conditions, may well attack the emerging vitality in India of our age at the source. A caste structure may emerge in which the political party, the managerial class, the professional class are all fixed in their superior places and the rest of the populace is divided up into the hierarchical group of a lower order.

(From *Wheels of History*, Rammanohar Lohia, Samata Vidyalaya Nyas, Hyderabad, 1986. pp 24-33)

18

Subhas Chandra Bose

Life and Times

Subhas Chandra Bose (1887- ?) was born on 23 January 1887 at Oriya Bazar, Cuttack in Orissa. His father, Janakinath Bose, was a leading advocate at Cuttack bar. His mother, Prabhabati Bose, was a pious lady. Bose started his education in an English medium school. But he did not like it. He then took admission in the Ravenshaw Collegiate School at Cuttack. In the High School examination he stood second. For college education, Bose shifted to Calcutta. First he studied in the Presidency College. Prof Oaten of that college was assaulted for his derogatory comments on Indian nationalism and culture. Accused of being involved in that assault, Bose was asked to beg apology. When he refused to do that, he was' expelled from the college. However, with the effort of his family members and relations, he took admission in the Scottish Church College, Calcutta. Having passed BA (Hons.) in Philosophy in First Class, he went to England and succeeded in the ICS examination securing 4th position. But, being unhappy with the nature of the service, he resigned from Civil Service on 12 April 1921.

Bose met Gandhiji for the first time in July 1921 at Bombay. He was not impressed by Gandhiji. In his opinion, Gandhiji's 'vision' was beautiful, but he was propounding a 'vague philosophy.' Bose, on the other hand, was attracted to the Bengali leader, C.R. Das who, Bose thought, was much more practical than Gandhiji. The Swaraj Party, formed by C.R. Das after his conflict with Gandhiji, impressed Bose. He found this party to be more radical.

In 1927 C.R. Das passed away. But in the same year Bose and Nehru came close to each other to lead the Left Group within the Indian National Congress. In the Madras Session of Congress, they piloted a resolution on 'complete independence' which was passed. But this political collaboration between these two leaders did not last long. In 1929, with Gandhiji's support, Nehru was elected as the President of Congress. After this Nehru remained faithful to Gandhiji even though Nehru might have reservation about some aspects of the Gandhian struggle for independence. As a result of this, Nehru and Bose gradually drifted away from each other. While Nehru emerged as the most articulate spokesman of the Congress dominated by Gandhiji, Bose emerged as a bitter critic of Gandhiji.

Though alienated from Gandhiji, Bose did not quit Congress. On his own strength, he continued to agitate against the British and he seldom lost his influence over the masses. He was elected as the President of the All India Trade Union Congress, which was then the labour wing of Indian National Congress. He was also elected as the Mayor of Calcutta Corporation, from time to time he subjected Gandhiji to trenchant criticism. Having criticised the Gandhi-Irwin Pact and the suspension of the Civil Disobedience Movement by Gandhiji, Bose said, 'Gandhiji is an old, useless piece of furniture. He had done good service in\his time, but is an obstacle now.' Bose also criticised the participation of Congress in the Round Table Conference held at London. He said that it was a waste of time. In his view, no real change in history has ever been achieved by discussions. 'The only alternative is war,' he said.

Feeling uncomfortable with the growing influence of Leftists in Congress, Gandhiji thought of winning over Bose to his side. Accordingly, he got Bose elected as the Congress President in 1938 at its Haripura Session. But Bose continued to irritate Gandhiji by criticising Charkha, advocating industrialisation and asking people to get ready to launch an armed struggle against the British. This made Gandhiji oppose Bose when the latter sought re-election as the President of Congress. Dr Pattabhi Sitaramayya, as Gandhiji's candidate, contested Bose, but Bose defeated him on 21 January 1939 by 1580-1377 votes. This was considered a personal defeat for Gandhiji who apparently Because of this Gandhiji did not cooperate with Bose.

Though he was the President of Congress, Bose, due to ill-health, was not able to attend its Tripuri Session held in March 1939. In that session a resolution was adopted directing the President to nominate the Working Committee in accordance with the wishes of Gandhiji. Bose took it as an affront. He was provoked to write, 'Gandhi wing will not follow the lead of the writer (Subhas) and that... the writer would not agree to be a puppet President,' Against this background, Bose formed a new organisation called Forward Bloc. He wanted it to function within Indian National Congress as the Congress Socialist Party did. In March 1940, the Congress met at Ramgarh. At that time the Forward Bloc also organised a huge demonstration there under the banner. All India anti-compromise conference.' Gandhiji took it as a challenge to his leadership and the result was the expulsion of Bose from Congress. To add to the problems of Bose he was arrested on 2 July 1940.

The conflict between Gandhiji and Bose was not only ideological; it gradually became personal. Bose's ascendancy in Congress seemed to threaten Gandhiji's control over it. It has been alleged that Gandhiji saw to it that Bose left Congress. By non-cooperation, he did not allow Bose to function effectively as the President of Congress. Michael Edwards has observed, 'Gandhi now turned the technique of non-cooperation, not against the British, but against Congress's own President.' Similarly, Brecher has pointed out, 'of all the participants only Gandhi had a clear and consistent object to oust Bose.'

In the jail, Bose declared fast unto death. As his condition deteriorated, he was placed under house arrest. However, he was able to slip dranatirally out of his house on 17 January 1941 and reached Berlin via Peshwar and Kabul.

During his stay in Berlin, Bose tried to persuade the German leader to help him to liberate India from the British rule. The Second

World War had already started and Germany and Britain were then fighting against each other. Hitler and his colleagues showed sympathy for Bose's cause, but did not agree to make a declaration in support of India's independence. This attitude of Hitler and his colleagues disappointed Bose, but he was able to set up Azad Hind Radio in December 1941.

Having failed to get solid support from Germany and Italy, Bose flew to Japan seeking its help. The Japanese leaders agreed to declare their support for India's independence. A joint strategy to attack the British soldiers in India was finalised, However, Bose insisted that the first to set foot on India's soil would be the soldiers of INA and not the Japanese soldiers. He himself took over the command of INA. In his memorable nagretic address to the soldiers of INA on 5 July 1943, Subhas said:

"Comrades, my soldiers, Let your battle cry be to Delhi to Delhi. How many of us will individually survive in war of freedom I don't know. But I do know this, we shall ultimately win and our task will not end until our surviving heroes hold victory parade on another graveyard of the British Empire the Lal Kila or Red Fortress of ancient Delhi... Today is the proudest day of my life. For an enslaved people, there can be no greater pride, no bigger honour than to be the first soldier in the army of liberation. I assure you that I shall be with you in darkness and sunshine, in sorrow and joy, in suffering and in victory. For the present, I can offer you nothing except hunger, thirst, privation, forced marches and death. But if you follow in life and death, as I am confident you will, I shall lead you to victory and freedom. May God bless our army."

Subhas Chandra Bose was an ardent nationalist. He made supreme sacrifice for the nation. He asked his countrymen to dedicate themselves to their nation, and make sacrifices for liberating India from the colonial rule. "Give me blood, I will give you freedom", he thundered. He was influenced apparently by Vivekananda who said, 'there was no realisation without renunciation, and for political freedom, it was essential to undergo highest suffering.'

Bose's nationalism had religious and cultural roots. Being influenced by Ramakrishna, Vivekananda, Aurobindo, Tilak and

Bankimchandra, he took great pride in India's glorious cultural heritage and spiritualism. His nationalism was also, to some extent, shaped by the revolutionary roles of Mazzini and Garibaldi in the unification of Italy, and heroic leadership of George Washington in the American struggle for independence. Though he was influenced by them, he did not imitate them blindly. While India's lumirous past became his main source of inspiration his own vision guided him in his fight for its independence.

Described as the 'stormy petrel of Indian politics,' Bose was in favour of using sword against the British who had conquered India by using sword. Having belittled the Gandhian method of non-violence as 'outdated,' he urged his countrymen to be ready to make the supreme sacrifice at the altar of the motherland. Though the Congress deserted him, he has remained in the hearts of millions of Indians. Bose's dream to liberate India from British colonial rule was shattered by two incidents. Japan, which had agreed to help in this task, was forced to surrender after Hiroshima and Nagasaki were destroyed by American nuclear bombing on 6 August and 9 August 1945 respectively. In a mysterious circumstance, his plane flying from Singapore to Japan met an accident on 18 August 1945 at Taihoku in Farmosa. On 21 August 1945 his cremation took place at Taipeh. For so many years his death has remained a mystery.

Determined to make India free from the British rule, Bose sought the help of Axis Powers, namely, Germany, Italy and Japan. But he was not prepared to compromise India's honour and prestige. He suggested that through a tripartite agreement Germany and Italy had to make a declaration about India's independence. As Hitler did not agree to this suggestion, Bose left Germany and came to Japan in search of help to make India free. Bose was emphatic that India would gain independence with the shedding of Indian blood only.

Bose decided to take the help of Axis Powers for India's independence for two reasons. First, the time was importantly opportune. Britain, India's colonial ruler, was involved in a fierce war against the Axis Powers. Bose saw this as a golden opportunity for India to fight for its independence. Secondly, he felt that India was not strong enough to defeat Britain. Therefore, it had to take the help of other countries to defeat Britain. That is why he 'resolved to take the plunge.'

As a nationalist, Bose was vigorous and forceful, but he was not expansionist. He hated imperialism. He supported the freedom struggles of the subject nations of the world. He was cosmopolitan. He believed in the synthesis of the idealism of the East and the practical competence of the West. He envisioned a world of free nations respecting one another's independence and territorial integrity. He wanted these nations to be bound by the tie of mutual love, amity and cooperation. His ideal world was also to be free from racial discrimination.

A Democratic Manifesto

Friends, I thank you from the bottom of my heart for the high honour you have done me by requesting me to preside over the deliberations of the Sixth Session of the Maharashtra Provincial Conference. You are probably aware that I did not at first venture to accept the kind invitation, but by referring to the old relations between Bengal and Maharashtra some of my friends touched a most tender chord in my heart. The appeal then proved to be irresistible and every other consideration had to stand aside.

Before I proceed to place before you my view with regard to our present policy and programme, I would like to raise some fundamental problems and attempt to answer them. It is sometimes urged by foreigners that the new awakening in India is entirely an exotic product inspired by alien ideals and methods. This is by no means true.

I do not for one moment dispute the fact that the impact of the West has helped to rouse us from intellectual and moral torpor. But that impact has restored self-consciousness to our people, and the movement that has resulted there from and which we witness today is a genuine Swadeshi movement. India has long passed through the traditional period of blind imitation—of reflex action, if you put it in psychological language. She has now recovered her own soul and is busy reconstructing her national movement along national lines and in the light of national ideals.

I agree with Sir Flinders Petrie that civilizations, like individuals grow and die in a cycle fashion and that each civilization has certain span of life vouchsafed to it. I also agree with him that, under certain conditions, it is possible for a particular civilization to be reborn after it has spent itself. When this rebirth is to take place, the vital impetus, the elan vital, comes not from without but from within. In this manner has Indian civilization been reborn over and over again at the end of each cycle, and that is why India in spite of her hoary antiquity is still young and fresh.

The charge has often been levelled against us that since democracy is an Occidental institution, India, by accepting democratic or semi-democratic institutions, is being Westernized. Some European writers—Lord Ronaldshay for instance—go so far as to say that democracy is unsuited to the Oriental temperament and political advancement in India should not, therefore, be made in that direction. Ignorance and effrontery could not go further. Democracy is by no means a Western institution it is a human institution. Wherever man has attempted to evolve political institutions, he has hit upon this wonderful institution of democracy. The past history of India is replete with instances of democratic institutions. Mr. K. P. Jayaswal in his wonderful book, *Hindu Polity*, has dealt with this matter at great length and has given a list of 81 republics in ancient India.

The Indian languages are also rich in terminology required in connection with political institutions of an advanced type. Democratic institutions still exist in certain parts of India. Among the Khasis of Assam, for instance, it is still the custom to elect the ruling chief by a vote of the whole clan; and this custom has been handed down from time immemorial. The principle of democracy was also applied in India in the government of villages and towns. The other day while visiting the Varendra Research Society Museum at Rajshahi in North Bengal, I was shown a very interesting copper-plate inscription in which it was stated that civic administration in the good old days was vested in a committee of five, including the Nagar Sreshthi (i.e., our modern Mayor). With regard to village self-government, it is not necessary to remind an Indian audience about the village Panchayats—democratic institutions handed down to us from days of yore. Not only democratic but other socio-political doctrines of an advanced character were not unknown to India in the past. Communism, for instance, is not a Western institution. Among the Khasis of Assam, to whom I have referred, private property as an institution does not exist in theory even today. The clan as a whole owns the entire land. I am sure that similar instances can still be found in other parts of India and also in the past history of bur country,

I think it necessary at this stage to warn my countrymen, and my young friends in particular, about the attack that is being made on nationalism from more than one quarter. From the point of view of cultural internationalism, nationalism is sometimes assailed as narrow, selfish and aggressive. It is also regarded as a hindrance to the promotion of internationalism in the domain of culture. My reply to the charge is that Indian nationalism is neither narrow, nor selfish, nor aggressive. It is inspired by the highest ideals of the human race, viz., Satyam (the true), Shivam (the good), Sundaram (the beautiful). Nationalism in India has instilled into us truthfulness, honesty, manliness and the spirit of service and sacrifice. What is more, it has roused the creative faculties which for centuries had been lying dormant in our people and, as a result, we are experiencing a renaissance in the domain of India art.

Another attack is being made on nationalism from the point of view of international labour or international Communism. This attack is not only ill-advised but unconsciously serves the interests of our alien rulers. It would be clear to the man in the street that before we can endeavour to reconstruct Indian society on a new basis, whether socialistic or otherwise, we should first secure the right to shape our own destiny. As long as India lies prostrate at the feet of Britain, that right will be denied to us. It is, therefore, the paramount duty not only of nationalists but anti-nationalistic Communists to bring about the political emancipation of India as early as possible. I have already hinted that I plead for a coalition between labour and nationalism (I am using 'labour' here in a wider sense to include the peasants as well). It has to be admitted that though we have passed resolutions from the Congress platform time and again regarding the desirability of organising labour, much has not been achieved in that direction.

If we view the programme of the Congress during the last few years we shall find that only in our Khadi programme have we been able to offer to our masses something which means bread and butter to them. Khadi, I am glad to say, has brought food to thousands and thousands of hungry mouths all over India. Given money and organization there is plenty of scope for pushing on Khadi. There are lakhs and lakhs of poor Indians living on the verge of starvation to whom Khadi can offer a means of subsistence, But the appeal of Khadi cannot be universal. We find from bitter experience in some parts of Bengal that as soon as the masses are a little better off, their Charkhas lie idle and that the peasant who gets a better return from paddy or jute cultivation refuses to cultivate cotton.

Except when Congressmen have joined the Kisan movement, as in the U.P. or have taken up the question of jute cultivation, as in Bengal, or have undertaken a campaign for nonpayment of taxes in order to resist illegal taxation or oppressive legislation, as in Gujarat, we have seldom been able to make a direct appeal to the economic interests of the masses. And until this is done—human-nature being what it is—how can we expect the masses to join the freedom movement?

There is another reason why I consider it imperative that the Congress should be more alive to the interests of the masses. Mass consciousness has been roused in India, thanks to the extensive and intensive propaganda undertaken during the non-cooperation movement; and the mass movement cannot possibly be checked now. The only question is along what lines this mass consciousness should manifest itself. If the Congress neglects the masses it is inevitable that a sectional—and if I may say so, anti-national movement will come into existence and class war among our people will appear even before we have achieved our political emancipation. It would be disastrous in the highest degree if we were to launch class war while we are all bed-fellows in slavery, in order that we may afford amusement to the common enemy. I regret to say that there is at present a tendency among some Indian labourites to belittle the Congress and to condemn the Congress programme. This recrimination should cease and the organised forces of labour and of the Congress should join hands for furthering the economic interests of the masses and promoting the cause of India's political emancipation. Friends, you will pardon me if for one moment I ask you to lift your eyes from the realities of the present and attempt to scan the future that looms before us. It is desirable that we should search our hearts in order to find out what it is that we are running after, so that we and our succeeding generations may grow up in the light of the ideal and shape our course of action accordingly.

Speaking for myself, I stand for an independent Federal Republic. That is the ultimate goal which I have before me. India must fulfil her own destiny and cannot be content with colonial self-government or Dominion Home Rule. Why must we remain within the British Empire ? India is rich in resources, human and material. She has outgrown the infancy which foreigners have been thrusting upon her, and can not only take care of herself but can function as an independent unit. India is not Canada or Australia or South Africa. Indians are an Oriental People, a coloured race, and there is nothing common between India and Great Britain from which we may be led to think that Dominion Home Rule within the British Empire is a desirable consummation for India. Rather, India stands to lose by remaining within the Empire. Having been under British domination so long, it may be difficult for Indians to get rid of the inferiority complex in their relations with England. It may also be difficult to resist British exploitation so long as we remain an integral part of the British Empire.

The usual argument that India without the help of Britain cannot defend herself is puerile. It is the Indian army—much more than the British army—which is defending India today. If India is strong enough to fight the battles of England outside her borders—in Tibet, China, Mesopotamia, Persia, Egypt and Flanders—she is certainly strong enough to defend herself from foreign aggression. Moreover, once India is able to free herself, the balance of power in the world will save India, as it has saved China. And if the League of Nations becomes a living organization with some sanction behind it, invasion and aggression will be a thing of the past.

While striving to attain liberty we have to note all its implications. You cannot free one half of your soul and keep the other half in bondage. You cannot introduce a light into a room and expect at the same time that some portion of it will remain dark. You cannot establish political democracy and endeavour at the same time to resist the democratization of the society. No, my friends, let us not become a queer mixture of political democrats and social conservatives. Political institutions grow out of the social life of the people and are shaped by their social ideas and ideals. If we want to make India really great we must build up a political democracy on the pedestal of a democratic society. Privileges based on birth, caste or creed should go, and equal opportunities should be thrown open to all irrespective of caste, creed or religion. The status of women should also be raised and women should be trained to take a larger and a more intelligent interest in public affairs.

While I do not condemn any patch-up work that may be necessary for healing communal sores, I would urge the necessity of discovering a deeper remedy for our communal troubles. It is necessary for the different religious groups to be acquainted with the traditions, ideals and history of one another because cultural intimacy will pave the way towards communal peace and harmony. I venture to think that the fundamental basis of political unity between different communities lies in cultural rapprochement. As things stand today, the different communities inhabiting India are too exclusive.

In order to facilitate cultural rapprochement a dose of secular and scientific training is necessary. Fanaticism is the greatest thorn in the path of cultural intimacy, and there is no better remedy for fanaticism than secular and scientific education. This sort of education is useful in another way, in that it helps to rouse our economic consciousness. The dawn of economic consciousness spells the death of fanaticism. There is much more in common between a Hindu peasant and a Muslim peasant than between a Muslim peasant and a Muslim Zamindar. The masses have only got to be educated wherein their economic interests be, and once they understand it, they will no longer consent to be pawns in communal feuds. By working from the cultural, educational and economic side, we can gradually undermine fanaticism and thereby render possible the growth of healthy nationalism in this country. One of the most hopeful signs of the time is the awakening among the youth of this country. The movement has spread from one end of the country to the other end, as far as I am aware and has attracted not only young men but young women as well. The youth of this age have become self-conscious ; they have been inspired by an ideal and are anxious to follow the call of their inner nature and fulfil their destiny. The movement is the spontaneous self-expression of the national soul, and on the course of this movement depends the nation's future. Our duty, therefore, is not to attempt to crush this new-born spirit but to lend it our support and guidance.

Friends, I would implore you to assist in the awakening of youth and in the organization of the youth movement. Self-conscious youth will not only act, but will also dream; will not only destroy, but will also build. It will succeed where even you may fail; it will create for you a new India—and a free India—out of the failures, trials and experience of the past. And, believe me, if we are to rid India once for all of the canker of communalism and fanaticism, we have to begin work among our youth.

There is another aspect of our movement which has been somewhat neglected in this country—the women's movement. It is impossible for one-half of the nation to win liberty without the active sympathy and support of the other half. In all countries—and even in the Labour Party in England—women's organizations have rendered invaluable service. There are various non-political organization among women in different parts of the country, but I venture to think that there is room for a countrywide political organization among them. It should be the primary object of this organization, which will be run by women alone, to carry on political propaganda among their sex and to help the work of the Indian National Congress.

Our benign rulers and our self-appointed advisers are in the habit of lecturing day after day on our unfitness for Swaraj. Some say that we must have more education before we can hope to be free; others maintain that social reform should precede political reform; still others urge that without industrial development India cannot be fit for Swaraj. None of these statements is true. Indeed it would be far more true to say that without political freedom— i.e., without the power to shape our own destiny—we cannot have either compulsory free education or social reform or industrial advancement. If you demand education for your people as Shri Gokhale did long ago, the plea is put forward by Government that there is no money. If you introduce social legislation for the advancement of your countrymen, you find Miss Mayo's cousins on this side of the Atlantic arrayed against you and on the side of your social die-hards. When you are working yourself to death in order to bring about the economic and industrial regeneration of India you find to your infinite regret and surprise that your Imperial Banks, your Railways and your Stores Departments are least inclined to help your national enterprises. You pass resolutions in your Municipalities and in your Councils in favour of Prohibition and you find that the Government meets you with a stonewall of indifference or hostility. I have no doubt in my own mind that Swaraj and Swaraj alone is the sovereign remedy for all our ills. And the only criterion of our fitness for Swaraj is the will to be free.

How to rouse the national will within the shortest possible period is, then, the problem before us: our policies and programmes have to be drawn up with a view to this end. The Congress policy since 1921 has been a dual policy of destruction and obstruction; of opposition and consolidation. We feel that the bureaucracy has entrenched itself in this country by erecting a network of organizations and institutions and by appointing a hierarchy of officials to run them. These are the seats of bureaucratic power and through them the bureaucracy has a grip on the very heart of the people. We have to storm these citadels of power and for that purpose we have to set up parallel institutions. These parallel organizations are our Congress offices. As our power and influence increase through the organization of Congress Committees, we shall be able to capture the bureaucratic seals of power. We know from personal experience that in districts where Congress Committees are well organized, the capture of local bodies has been possible without any difficulty. The Congress offices are, therefore, the forts where we have to entrench ourselves and whence we have to stir out every day in order to raid the bureaucratic citadels. Congress Committees are our army, and no plan of campaign however skilfully devised, can succeed unless we have a strong, efficient and disciplined army at our command.

Friends, you will remember that when, after the Gaya Congress of 1922, there was a tendency among a large section of our countrymen to concentrate wholly on the constructive programme to the exclusion of everything else, Deshbandhu Das pointed out in the manifesto of the Swaraj Party that it was absolutely necessary to keep up a spirit of resistance to the bureaucracy. He firmly believed that without an atmosphere of opposition it was not possible to push on the constructive programme or achieve success in any other direction. But this basic principle we often seem to forget. "Non-cooperation is barren"—"opposition has failed"—"obstruction is fruitless"—these are catchwords which mislead the unwary public. The most tragic element in our character is that we do not look ahead; we are easily upset by failures. We lack the dogged tenacity of John Bull, and unlike him, we cannot therefore fight a longlasting game.

I have often been asked how the end will come, how the bureaucracy will ultimately be forced to accede to our terms. I have no misgivings in this matter for I have already had a foretaste of what will come. The movement will reach its climax in a sort of general strike or country-wide hartal coupled with a boycott of British goods. Along with the strike or hartal to bring about which labour and the National Congress will heartily co-operate, there will be some form of civil disobedience because the bureaucracy is not likely to sit idle while a strike is going on. It is also possible that there may be non-payment of taxes in some form or other, but this is not essential. When the crisis is reached the average Britisher at home will feel that to starve India politically means economic starvation for him. And the bureaucracy in India will find that it is impossible to carry on the administration in the face of a country-wide non-cooperation movement. The jails will be full as in 1921, and there will be general demoralization within the ranks of the bureaucracy, who will no logner be able to count upon the loyalty and devotion of their servants and employees. There will be a paralysis of the administration and possibly of foreign trade and commerce. The bureaucracy will consider the situation as chaotic but, from the point of view of the people, the country will be organized, disciplined and determined. The bureaucracy will then be forced to yield to the demands of the people's representatives, for saving themselves from unnecessary trouble and anxiety and for restoring their trade with India.

Our immediate task is among other things to make the boycott of the Simon Commission complete and effective. We, Congressmen, have never accepted the pernicious preamble of the Government of India Act, 1919. This Act has been forced down our throats but we have never owed willing allegiance to it; in fact we have tried our level best to non-cooperate with it. We take our stand on the sacred and inviolable rights of men, and the principle of self-determination. We maintain that it is for India to frame her own constitution according to her needs, and it is for Britain to accept it in to. This procedure has been followed not only in the case of countries that have won back their independence but in the case of the self-governing dominions within the British Empire including the Irish Free State.

The counterpart of this boycott, in fact its positive aspect, is the framing of a national constitution. The All Parties' Conference has taken this matter in hand and all lovers of India should wish the Conference complete success. The Secretary of State for India has in a fit of pompous pride challenged India to produce an agreed constitution. If there is a spark of honour and self-respect left in us, we should take up the gauntlet and give a fitting reply by producing a constitution.

(Presidential address at the Maharashtra Provincial Conference, Poona, 3 May, 1928. From *Netaji's Collected Works*, Vol. 5, Netaji Research Bureau, Calcutta, 1985, pp 242-252)

Index